The Drummer's Bible

How to Play Every Drum Style from Afro-Cuban to Zydeco

(Second Edition)

by

Mick Berry & Jason Gianni

See Sharp Press ◆ Tucson, Arizona ◆ 2012

For information contact See Sharp Press, P.O. Box 1731, Tucson, AZ 85702.
Web site: www.seesharppress.com.

Berry, Mick.
The drummer's bible : how to play every drum style from Afro-Cuban to Zydeco / by Mick Berry and Jason Gianni. – Tucson, Ariz. : See Sharp Press, 2004.
211 p. : ill., music ; 28 cm. + 2 sound discs (digital : 4 3/4 in.)
Includes approximately 500 musical examples, organized by style, with historical information preceding the drumming groves.
Includes bibliographical references.
ISBN 978-1-937276-19-5

1. Drum – Methods – Self-instruction. 2. Drum set – Studies and exercises (Rock) 3. Musical meter and rhythm. 4. Zydeco music. 5. Latin jazz. I. Title. II. Gianni, Jason.

786.9193 MT662.8

First Printing (original edition)—December 2003
Second Printing (second edition—ninth total printing)—January 2014

The drum examples on the accompanying compact discs were played by both Mick Berry and Jason Gianni. Audio voiceovers were spoken by Mick Berry. The tracks were recorded, mixed, and mastered at Trakworx Studios in South San Francisco, California in June 2003 by Justin Weis.

Cover design by Kay Sather. Interior design by Chaz Bufe.

To contact the authors, go to their web site: http://www.drummersbible.com

Jason Gianni would like to dedicate this book to
Gladys Shoenfeld.

The world was lucky enough to experience her
kind soul for 92 incredible years.
Now, heaven can benefit from it for
eternity. I miss her every day.

Mick Berry dedicates this book to
Charlotte Behre, Patricia Behre,
and Leah Behre-Miskimen

CONTENTS

Appendixes

Quick Reference

When you need to find a groove in a hurry!

CD Tracks

CD 1 Track Order

African

1.	**Rai**/Traditional Maghreb	(example)
2.	**World Beat**	(example)
3.	World Beat	(variation 2)
4.	**Soukous**	(example)
5.	Soukous	(variation 3)
6.	**Bikutsi**	(example)
7.	Bikutsi	(variation 1)
8.	Bikutsi	(variation 2)

Afro-Cuban

9.	**3-2** Son Clave	
10.	3-2 Rumba Clave	
11.	**2-3** Son Clave	
12.	2-3 Rumba Clave	
13.	**6/8** Clave (both notations)	
14.	6/8 Bell Pattern	(example)
15.	6/8 Drumset Grooves	(example)
16.	6/8 Drumset Grooves	(variation 1)
17.	6/8 Drumset Grooves	(variation 2)
18.	6/8 Drumset Grooves	(variation 3)
19.	6/8 Drumset Grooves	(variation 4)
20.	**Cascara** (3-2 son)	(example 1)
21.	Cascara (3-2 rumba)	(example 2)
22.	Cascara (2-3 son)	(example 1)
23.	Cascara (2-3 rumba)	(example 2)
24.	**Guaganco**	(example)
25.	**Mambo**	(example)
26.	Mambo	(variation 1)
27.	Mambo	(variation 2)
28.	**Cha Cha**	(example)
29.	Cha Cha	(variation 1)
30.	Cha Cha	(variation 2)
31.	**Mozambique**	(example)
32.	Mozambique	(variation 1)
33.	Mozambique	(variation 2)
34.	**Songo**	(example)
35.	Songo	(variation 2)
36.	Songo (Traditional)	(example 1)
37.	Songo (Traditional)	(example 2)
38.	**Bomba**	(example)
39.	**Merengue**	(example)
40.	**Beguine**	(example 1)
41.	Beguine	(example 2)
42.	**Bolero**	(example)
43.	**Conga**	(example)
44.	Conga	(variation 2)
45.	**Cumbia**	(example)
46.	**Danzon**	(example)
47.	**Palito**	(example)
48.	Palito	(variation 2)
49.	**Pilon**	(example)
50.	**Plena**	(example)

Blues

51.	**Shuffle**	(example)
52.	Shuffle	(variation 3)
53.	**Chicago Shuffle**	(example)
54.	Chicago Shuffle	(variation 2)
55.	**Backdoor Shuffle**	(example)
56.	Backdoor Shuffle	(variation)
57.	**12/8 Blues Pattern**	(example)
58.	12/8 Blues Pattern	(variation 1)
59.	12/8 Blues Pattern	(variation 2)
60.	**Blues Rock**	(variation 4)
61.	Blues Rock	(variation 5)
62.	**Purdie Shuffle**	(example)
63.	Purdie Shuffle	(half-time variation)
64.	**Blues Rumba**	(example)
65.	Blues Rumba	(variation)

Brazilian

66.	**Samba**	(example)
67.	Samba	(variation 1)
68.	Samba (Cruzado)	(variation 3)
69.	Samba (Reggae)	(variation 4)
70.	**Batukada** Floor Tom	(example A)
71.	Batukada Floor Tom	(example B)
72.	Batukada for Drum Set	(example)
73.	Batukada for Drum Set	(variation 1)
74.	Batukada for Drum Set	(variation 2)
75.	**Baiao**	(example)
76.	Baiao	(variation 2)
77.	**Bossa Nova**	(example)
78.	Bossa Nova	(variation 2)

Cajun / Zydeco

79.	**Cajun Two Step**	(example)
80.	**Cajun Waltz**	(example)
81.	**Zydeco Two Step**	(example)
82.	**Zydeco Shuffle**	(example)
83.	**Zydeco Waltz**	(example)
84.	**Zydeco Train Beat**	
85.	**Cajun Zydeco**	(example)

Caribbean

86. **Calypso** (example)
87. **Soca** (example)
88. Soca (variation 1)
89. **Ska** (example)
90. Ska (variation 1)
91. Ska (variation 3)
92. **Reggae** (example)
93. Reggae (variation 1)

CD 2 Track Order

Country

1. **Bluegrass** (example)
2. **Western Swing** (example)
3. **Two Beat** (example)
4. Two Beat (variation)
5. **Country Shuffle** (variation 2)
6. **Western** (example)
7. **Train Beat** (example)
8. **Country Waltz** (example)
9. Country Waltz (variation 2)
10. **Country Ballad** (variation 3)

Disco

11. Example
12. Variation 2

Drum and Bass / Jungle

13. Example
14. Variation 1
15. Variation 2
16. Variation 5

Flamenco

17. Example

Funk

18. **New Orleans Funk** (example)
19. New Orleans Funk (variation 3)
20. **Displaced Funk** (example)
21. Displaced Funk (variation 1)
22. Displaced Funk (variation 2)
23. **Linear Funk** (example)
24. Linear Funk (example 1A)
25. Linear Funk (example 1B)
26. Linear Funk (example 1C)
27. **Ghost Note Funk** (example)
28. **Funk Rock** (example)

(Heavy) Metal

29. Example
30. Variation 1
31. Variation 2 ("Blast Beat")
32. **Double Bass** (example)
33. Double Bass (variation 4)

Hip Hop / Rap

34. **Standard Hip Hop** (example 1)
35. **Slower Feel** (example 2)
36. **Half-Time Feel** (example 3)

Jazz

37. **New Orleans Second Line** (example)
38. New Orleans Second Line (variation 5)
39. **Dixieland** (example)
40. Dixieland (**Charleston**) (variation)
41. Dixieland (song ending)
42. **Big Band** (example)
43. Big Band Summary
44. **Small Band** **(independence figures)** (example 1)
45. Small Band **(independence figures)** (example 2)
46. Small Band **(independence figures)** (example 3)
47. Small Band Summary
48. **Jazz Waltz** (example)
49. Jazz Waltz (variation 1)
50. **Jazz Brushes** (example)
51. Jazz Brushes (variation 1)

Klezmer

52. **Bulgar** (examples 1 & 2)
53. **Freylakhs**
54. **Hora**
55. **Khosidl**
56. **Terkisher**

Latin Rock

57. Example 1
58. Example 2
59. Example 3

March

60. Example

Middle Eastern

61. Example 1
62. Example 2

Odd Time

Polka

Punk

Rock n' Roll

Surf

Techno

Wedding Dances

Polyrhythms

GLOSSARY

Abakwa (Abaqua/Abakua): One of several 6/8 Afro-Cuban rhythmic patterns for drum set.

Abanico: A timbale figure with a rim shot on beat 3 and roll on beat 4 (to beat 1 of the following measure). It is used as a transitional figure in Afro-Cuban styles, most often in Cha Cha.

Afro-Cuban 6/8: A triple-based rhythm sometimes written and felt in 4/4 which contains its own clave rhythm and bell pattern.

Avante Garde: A Jazz style from the late 1950s characterized by technically advanced musicianship, an obscured form and pulse, and complex chordal structures and melodies.

Back Beat: An informal term to describe a strong snare drum stroke/note, usually falling on beats 2 & 4 of a 4/4 measure.

Baqueteo: The musical figure played by the timbale player, primarily in the Afro-Cuban Danzon style.

Bateria: A percussion section/ensemble.

Bembe: 1. A 6/8 style of Afro-Cuban music for which the 6/8 back beat drum set pattern is particularly appropriate.

Blast Beat: A loud, rapid-fire, incessant Heavy Metal groove consisting of alternating 16th notes played between the snare drum and bass drum (with the ride hand usually doubling the bass drum notes).

Bombo: 1. The accent which falls on the + of beat 2 on the "3" side of an Afro-Cuban clave rhythm (son or rumba); 2. The large drum (bass drum) used in folkloric Afro-Cuban styles.

Bonguero: A bongo drum player.

Cascara: A rhythmic pattern used in Afro-Cuban music, copying a pattern called Palito.

Charleston: 1. A Ragtime-Jazz dance popularized in the United States during the 1920s. 2. A one-measure syncopated swung rhythm emphasizing beat 1 and the + of beat 2.

Clave: 1. A two-measure rhythmic pattern (son or rumba) serving as the foundation of most Afro-Cuban rhythms. The patterns are broken up to a "3" side (3 notes in one measure) and a "2" side (two notes in one measure) which can be started from either side (e.g. 3-2 or 2-3). 2. The percussion instrument which originally played the clave rhythm(s) in Afro-Cuban music. (For specific rhythms and description of the instrument and playing method, see Clave in the Afro-Cuban chapter.)

Columbia (Rumba): One of three styles of Afro-Cuban rumba often distinguished by its 6/8 feel. The others are Rumba Guaguanco and Rumba Yambu.

Comparsa: 1. The musical group which plays the Conga rhythm during Carnaval in Cuba; the instrumentation, mostly percussion, often includes horns, primarily trumpet. 2. A shortened term for "Conga de Comparsa."

Conguero: A conga drum player.

Contredanse/Contradanza: A European folk dance that evolved into the Cuban Danzon.

Displaced: Normally used in the terms "displaced note" or "displaced rhythm," this refers to stressing notes in places other than the standard 2 & 4 back beat, downbeats, or other common beats.

Four on the Floor: An informal term that describes the playing of all four quarter notes by the bass drum in a 4/4 meter.

Ghost Note: Any note that is played very lightly, usually on the snare drum. When written in musical notation, it is usually indicated by a parenthesis surrounding the note.

Guaguanco (Rumba): In addition to a style of drumming, one of the three types of Cuban rumba. The others are Rumba Columbia and Rumba Yambu.

Head: An informal term for the defining melody of a song played in a small band Jazz format.

In The Crack: Playing a rhythmic feel in between "swung" and "straight" time. Due to its unorthodox execution, it is virtually impossible to notate and consequently is best learned through listening and practicing rather than reading.

Independence: Playing contrasting and/or complimentary rhythms with different limbs simultaneously.

Jazz Form: The melody, chord progression, and structure of an entire song in a small band format.

Jure: A style of music invented by African-American laborers in the early 1900s which mixed singing, praying, hand clapping and dancing. Jure, along with La La, stands as the predecessor of modern day Cajun/Zydeco music.

La La: An early 20th century style of music combining Jure songs with Cajun music and culture, eventually resulting in Cajun/Zydeco.

Linear: A term which describes notes that occur one after another in a "line" of music with no notes being played simultaneously (that is, no limbs striking at the same time).

Loop: A repeating musical pattern (usually drum or rhythmic) originally programmed electronically that may be replicated by a live drummer.

Marakatu: 1. Coronation ceremonies and celebrations of the Brazilian-based slave kings and queens under Portuguese rule. 2. The tradition from which most modern-day Brazilian music, festivals, dance and culture developed.

Mersey Beat: A drum beat originally developed in Liverpool, England and made popular by Cliff Richards and the Shadows, played extensively by American Surf and Early Rock n' Roll drummers. (See the Surf chapter for its pattern.)

Montuno: 1. The repetitive, syncopated musical figure ordinarily played on a piano in an Afro-Cuban musical setting. 2. The section of an Afro-Cuban arrangement that supports improvisation.

Orchestration: 1. The distribution of individual notes on selected surfaces of the drum set (or other musical instruments). 2. The specific arrangement of notes on a musical score for an orchestra or ensemble.

Palito: 1. The Afro-Cuban rhythm played on the gua gua (hollowed out bamboo) which later became recognized as the Cascara pattern. 2. The sticks used to play the rhythm.

Partido Alto: 1. One of the most popular Samba styles in Brazil. 2. A rhythmic pattern played in the Samba and Bossa Nova. Traditionally, the pattern is played on agogo bells, cuica, pandeiro and/or tamborim. On drum set, it's often played on the snare drum.

Paseo: The first section (or introduction) to the traditional form of Afro-Cuban Danzon.

Polyrhythm: The combination of two contrasting rhythmic pulses simultaneously. There are two main types of polyrhythms: rhythms which carry "over the bar" and rhythms that exist "within the bar."

Ponche: An accent in Afro-Cuban music which emphasizes beat 4 of a 4/4 measure, usually used as a transitional figure.

Remix: A re-recording of a previously arranged song usually involving the substitution or addition of electronic instrumentation.

Rumba: 1. A traditional form of Afro-Cuban music which developed into three primary forms: Columbia, Guaguanco and Yambu. 2. A standard form of North American dance music loosely based on the original Cuban style of the same name.

Rumba Clave: One of two Afro-Cuban clave patterns (along with the son clave). The distinguishing characteristic is the placement of the third note on the "3" side being played on the + of beat 4. The pattern appears most often in the more modern Afro-Cuban genres (e.g. Songo, Mozambique).

Salsa: 1. A broad term which refers to the large spectrum of most Afro-Cuban musical styles, especially those primarily played for dance.

Saudi: An up-tempo, syncopated rhythm established in the Persian Gulf/Arabian peninsula area associated with a Middle Eastern style and dance known as Khaleegi.

Sayyidii: A medium tempo, syncopated rhythm from Egypt and the Persian Gulf/Arabian peninsula, also a member of a larger family of Middle Eastern rhythms known as Maqsuum.

Second Line: 1. Parade-style ensembles and music from the late 19th/early 20th centuries in New Orleans inspired by ex-slaves and their descendants. Second Line was the predecessor of Dixieland and led to all modern-day Jazz styles. 2. "Second Line" was a description for the various musicians and dancers who followed the "First Line" of the hearse and mourners in a funeral procession.

Shuffle: A swung pattern characterized by playing the first and third notes of every triplet grouping on every beat in a measure.

Son Clave: One of two Afro-Cuban clave patterns (along with the rumba clave). The distinguishing characteristic is the placement of the third note on the "3" side being played directly on beat 4. The pattern appears most often in the more traditional Afro-Cuban genres (e.g., Mambo, Cha Cha).

Subdividing: A method for reducing a pulse or rhythmic pattern into smaller components than those originally written or counted, for example counting a 4/4 measure as 8th or 16th notes.

Syncopation: Emphasizing a note (or group of notes) which is not part of the primary rhythmic pulse through the use of accents, note groupings or rests.

Tejanos: People of Mexican heritage born in Texas. Their culture blended European Waltzes and Polkas with the folk music traditions of Spain and Mexico to create a sub-genre of Country music known as Tex-Mex.

Timbolero: A Timbale player.

Time: 1. The internal pulse and feel of a drummer. 2. An informal term to describe a consistent drumming pattern, often the common ride cymbal and hi-hat (foot) pattern played in a Jazz setting.

Trading Fours: A four bar "call and response" exchange, in other words the "trading off" of solos between musicians. "Trading off" can also involve exchanges of any number of (generally even, e.g., two, four or eight) measures.

Train Beat: A rhythmic pattern used in Country, Bluegrass, Rockabilly, and Cajun/Zydeco music characterized by consistent 16th notes on a snare drum with accents on upbeats, simulating the sound of a train. (The Rockabilly Train Beat is swung in contrast with the other varieties of the beat.)

Trap Set: Short for "contraption," the original name for the drum set. The trap set initially contained more percussive devices utilized for sound effects such as woodblocks, cowbells, whistles and bird calls along with smaller, trashier-sounding cymbals and various drums.

Tumbao: 1. The rhythmic pattern primarily played by the bass in Afro-Cuban styles and usually doubled or enhanced (through accents) with the bass drum when a drum set is present. 2. A standard, repetitive conga pattern played predominantly on the high drum called the Quinto.

Two Step: A double time, up tempo (Polka-like) pattern for the drum set.

Walking Bass Line: A moving, generally prolonged, scale-like pattern of quarter notes (in a meter with a quarter-note pulse) played by the bassist.

Yambu (Rumba): One of three styles of Afro-Cuban rumba besides Rumba Columbia and Rumba Guaguanco. 2. An Afro-Cuban dance featuring the female dancer.

Yoruba: A Nigerian tribe/people that originated the 6/8 clave pattern.

INTRODUCTION

When I started playing the drums, during the 1960s, there weren't many books available on the different styles of drumming, or at least not many that I can remember. My "bible" at the time was *Modern Techniques for the Progressive Drummer,* written by the renowned English drum teacher, Max Abrams, to whom I was going for lessons, with the help of London's underground train service.

There were some books with descriptions of how to play certain dance rhythms, but there was really nothing of any depth. It was a question of listening to other drummers in order to find out how to play a certain groove.

In any case, I never had much patience with drum books, I learned mostly by listening to records, and I still find it hard to look at a drum book for any length of time. And now I am asked to write an intro to *The Drummer's Bible* and have been sent the draft of 181 pages plus two CDs containing almost 200 audio examples!

The first thing that strikes me is that this is really an encyclopedia, not a book that has to be read from cover to cover—a sigh of relief! The second thing that strikes me is that there is a brief history written about each style—now you have my attention! Thirdly, each rhythm is explained and written out in notation form, and you can also listen to each example (the CDs)! Things are looking up.

In fact I am learning some rhythms I knew nothing about, as well as their history and application, and I can check out the authors' performance of them, too. I think *The Drummers Bible* has just found a place in my home.

The amount of research that Mick Berry and Jason Gianni have done to write this book must have been absolutely colossal, and I can only equate it to being the Encyclopedia Galactica of drumming.

—Simon Phillips

PREFACE

The Drummer's Bible: How to Play Every Drum Style from Afro-Cuban to Zydeco is the culmination of a three-year project to create an in-depth and accurate guide for playing every genre of music a modern drum set player may even occasionally encounter. To this end, we've supplied nearly 400 drumming grooves and their appropriate fills. As well, uniquely among drumming guides, we've provided a history of the development of every style to promote appreciation and understanding and, in all likelihood, better playing—the better you understand a style, the more likely you are to play it accurately.

For the past three years we have eaten, slept, breathed and drummed this book. Our research began with brainstorming which familiar styles to cover, but it quickly blossomed into a historic and musical journey through countless genres of music we never imagined we would encounter. The researching and writing of this book took fully two-and-a-half years. Then, after completing our work to the best of our ability, we contacted drummers and other musicians expert in particular styles to check our work and improve upon it (see Acknowledgments). Their generous responses exceeded our expectations. And some of those kind enough to help us are even responsible for creating a particular genre of drumming.

The chapters are arranged in alphabetical order in a manner similar to that of an encyclopedia, which makes it easy to find information on any style in which you're interested. While some of the chapters cover only one style, others are "umbrella" chapters covering as many as 17 distinct styles (the Afro-Cuban chapter). There is at least one musical example (but generally more) showing an accurate way to play every style covered. Following the example(s) are variations expanding the groove choices. Though some grooves are challenging, all are presented clearly so that learning them is as easy as possible.

In addition to the grooves and style-development histories, this book has several other features:

1) NOTES: The notes within chapters provide detailed explanations of performance characteristics of the grooves and/or provide tips on limb independence, orchestration, syncopation, and/or producing additional drumming variations.

2) SPECIAL CHAPTERS: Following the 28 alphabetized chapters covering drumming styles, we've included two chapters directly related to performing the styles:

A. FILLS: While they're clearly secondary to drum grooves, fills are the other primary component in modern drumming. Thus we've included a large chapter on fills. We've also included a guide to which fills are appropriate to which styles.

B. POLYRHYTHMS: Though not a style in themselves, polyrhythms can be used in virtually all styles.

3) APPENDIXES: There are four appendixes. In addition to a bibliography and a large suggested listening section, we've included the following appendixes important to a well-rounded drummer:

A. TUNING: The drum set has undergone massive changes in the years since it first appeared. In order to accurately execute a style, it's necessary to tune a set in a manner appropriate to the style. This appendix describes four primary tunings for the drum set, and indicates which tuning is appropriate to every style covered in this book.

B. RUDIMENTS: Just as with polyrhythms, rudiments are not a style. However, they can be quite useful in developing drumming facility. Rudiments are as important to drummers as scales are to players of pitched instruments. We've reproduced the 40 standard rudiments here thanks to the Percussive Arts Society.

4) QUICK REFERENCE: Immediately following the table of contents and CD track listing, we've included an alphabetized listing of grooves that will allow you to find the groove for any style in the book almost instantly.

5) ACCOMPANYING CDs: The two CDs in the back of the book contain 192 grooves — virtually every main example and generally at least one or two variations for every style. In the book itself, the relevant CD track is listed next to every recorded groove. And, importantly, the grooves were recorded with the appropriate tuning for every genre. Therefore, the sounds you hear on the CD are an indication of the sounds you should strive for when playing any particular style.

Finally, we'd like to mention the importance of taking instructional drum lessons. Though this book is a well-arranged guide, it is important to find a good teacher to help you maximize your understanding of the content within these pages, and to accurately perform the styles covered here.

We hope that *The Drummer's Bible* proves useful to every drummer, from beginner to advanced professional. We hope that students of the drum set acquire as much stylistic versatility as possible through using this manual. In addition, we hope drum instructors will enjoy using it when teaching new generations of drum set players, and that professional drummers will find it useful in performance situations.

As well, composers and players of other instruments can utilize this book to improve their understanding of a drummer's role in particular styles, or when writing charts. (We can't tell you how many times we've had to play charts with drum style indicated only by the nonspecific term, "Latin.")

Finally, we hope that you, the learning and developing drummer, will find that this book expands your ability and passion for drumming, just as creating it and sharing the knowledge in it has inspired our love of drumming and our passion for it.

—Mick Berry
—Jason Gianni

PREFACE
TO THE SECOND EDITION

When we started work on the first edition of *The Drummer's Bible* in 2000, our naive and overly ambitious intention was to create the most well-rounded book on drum styles ever written. Had we known that the project would consume our lives—endless hours of work over the next three years—it's quite possible we would never have agreed to take it on. However, after at least ten hours per week of individual research, frequent phone meetings with our editor (Chaz Bufe), the reading of each chapter (and subsequent advice) by expert drummers in the individual styles, and the organization of several years of work, we finally completed the project (with a little help from our publisher breathing down our necks saying, "Enough! Wrap it up!").

In late 2003, *The Drummer's Bible* appeared, and we were proud of it. And we were exhausted. Though we were extremely pleased with the result, we also realized that it hadn't been possible to include everything in it that was conceivably useful in a style guide, and that we'd inevitably learn more about the individual styles in coming years. We also knew that due to the nature of *The Drummer's Bible* we'd eventually have to revise and update the contents. After we'd gathered enough information (and sales warranted it—over the last nine years, the book went through eight printings and sold nearly 20,000 copies), our publisher gave us the green light to update the book.

We did that over the past year, and are pleased with the result. We believe that this new, much expanded second edition of *The Drummer's Bible* is also a much improved edition—that it's more complete and more accurate than the first edition.

Since the moment we completed the first edition, we've had ample time to look at the book with a critical eye. Over the years, we became increasingly aware that we needed to beef up some of the chapters with additional grooves and updated or revised stylistic information. And we've learned a lot since publication of the first edition. We trust that it shows. After bouncing ideas back and forth, quadruple-checking our previous work, and sharing the new edits and additions with drumming friends and other reknowned musicians, we can now once again stand back and savor the best moment in the production of any book: the moment when you hold the first finished copy in your hands.

The first edition contained nearly 400 grooves. This new second edition contains closer to 500. We've added new grooves to over half of the chapters and have added new historical and stylistic information to most of them. We've also added styles to several chapters, and have considerably expanded the Bibliography and the Discography appendixes. We've also added a new, useful appendix, "The Most Commonly Played Grooves."

Our goal was to make the second edition of *The Drummer's Bible* even more complete and more useful than the original edition. We believe that we've done so. We hope that you'll agree.

We thank all of you for your kind comments about the first edition, and for your inspiration, guidance, and willingness to help us and other members of the drumming community.

—Mick Berry
—Jason Gianni

Acknowledgments

There are more people to thank than drumming strokes in this book. Of the many notable drummers and other musicians who gave generously of their time and expertise, the following deserve special thanks:

Walfredo Reyes, Sr. (Afro-Cuban), Simon Phillips, Rebeca Mauleon, pianist, composer, and educator (Afro-Cuban, Brazlian, Flamenco), Brian Fullen, Nashville session musician, clinician and educator (Country), Johnny Rabb (Drum n' Bass, Techno), Mike Clark of the Headhunters (Funk), John Vidacovich (Jazz, Funk, Cajun/Zydeco), Kevin Mummey of the San Francisco Klezmer Society (Klezmer), Stuart Brotman of Brave Old World (Klezmer), Steve Hambright (the whole damned book—he's a madman!), and a very special thanks to House of Love Productions.

These people also gave generously of their time and expertise:

Dave Weckl, Louie Bellson, Joel Rosenblatt, Ciara Lavers, David Garibaldi (Funk), Alan Hall (Jazz), Chris Miller (African), Eric "Ricky" McKinnie of the Blind Boys of Alabama (Gospel), Paul van Wageningen (Afro-Cuban, Brazilian, Carribean), Kevin Hayes of the Robert Cray Band (Blues), Graham Lear, formerly of Santana and Gino Vanelli (Latin Rock), Roger Kennedy, drummer for Cajun fiddler Amanda Shaw (Cajun/Zydeco), the ubiquitous Billy Lee Lewis (Rock n' Roll), Jeff Straw (Drum n' Bass, Techno) Martyn Jones of the Mermen (Surf), Carlos Aceituno of Fogo Na Ropa, (Brazilian), Robert Wallace of Rhythm and Expression (Brazilian), Kelly Fasman (Disco, Polka, March, Wedding Dances), Simone White (Acid Jazz), Sam Adatto of Sam Adatto's Drum Shop on 9th St. in SF (Punk and Heavy Metal), Jeff Senn (Middle Eastern), Michael Hyatt (Country), Jeff Raphael of the Nuns (Punk), Johnny Strike (Punk), Jimmie Crucefix (Punk), and bassist Steve Strom (Odd Time and Progressive Rock).

Several teachers have been instrumental in our personal development as drummers throughout the years. These special individuals include: James Black, Johnny Vidacovich, Paul van Wageningen, Walfredo Reyes Sr., Harvey Price, Tom Palmer, Dan Armstrong, Glenn Weber, Tony Schmaus, Dom Famularo, Kim Plainfield, Pete Zeldman, Mike Clark, Clayton Cameron, and the rest of the staff at the New York City Drummer's Collective.

Mick Berry sends thanks to Jason Gianni (without question, one of the hardest working people in show business), Chaz Bufe, for his support and encouragement over the years, and my immediate family: Charlotte Behre, Debbie Behre, Patricia Behre, and Leah Behre Miskimen. The following close friends continue to provide inspiration and comfort through the tougher times, and even greater happiness during the easier days: Ann Brewer, Rose Anne Raphael, Chris Meehan, Paul Lyons, Michael Edelstein, Scott St. Romain, Lawrence P. Beron, John Boyle, and Phil Alexander. Plus a special thanks to all of my students, in particular those who have been studying with me for many years: Alex Szotak, Amanda Albini, Ben Drogin, Kip Bassil, Robin Tuscher, Clay Mills, Ashley Metcalphe, Kai Barshak, Jason Carpenter, Mario Aparicio, James Landis and Sarah Monty.

Jason Gianni gives thanks to my partner-in-crime Mick Berry, our editor Chaz Bufe, Tony, Anthony, John and all the other staff at The Drummers Collective in NYC, Bob Berenson, Adam Budofsky, Billy Amendola and all the other folks at *Modern Drummer*, Andrew Shreve and Tim Shahady at Paiste, Bruce Jacoby and Matt Connors at Remo, Ben Davies and Joe Testa at Vic Firth, Greg Crane and John Whittman at Yamaha, Music Orange Studios, Dyna Mendoza, Phil Sollar and Marty Ruiz at Drum World in San Mateo, all at Haight Ashbury Music in San Francisco, Steve LaPorta, Justin Weis at Trakworx studios in South San Francisco, Ronni, Rick, Doug and Treva Levine, and Josh and Harper Aaron. Most importantly, thanks to Dale, Richard and Lisa Gianni Aaron for their unconditional support and love, and to Jody and Anabella Gianni for giving me my one and only reason to live every day to its fullest.

1 ACID JAZZ

ACID JAZZ draws on many musical styles—Funk (mainly 1970s Funk), Soul, R&B, Hip Hop, Afro-Cuban, Brazilian, and Jazz—and it has no standard beat(s). It originated in the late 1980s, primarily in England, but achieved greater popularity in the United States, especially in San Francisco and New York City. Acid Jazz precursors include jam bands such as The Grateful Dead, Parliament/Funkadelic, and Phish.

Prominent Acid Jazz bands include Alphabet Soup (drummer Jay Lane), the Mo'Fessionals (Loring Jones), Galactic (Stanton Moore), Brand New Heavies (Jan Kindaid), Groove Collective (Genji Siraisi), and Digable Planets (Gary Dann).

Acid Jazz has also found a large following in Japan. Japanese Acid Jazz groups include Mondo Grosso (Yasuo Sano), Gota and Simply Red (Gota Yashiki), and United Future Organization (Genta Egawa). There are also prominent Acid Jazz groups in Poland and Russia: Skalpel (Czeslaw Bartkowski) and Moscow Grooves Institute (mostly drum samples).

Instrumental music is as important as the lyrics in Acid Jazz, and the style is characterized by danceable grooves and lengthy, repetitive compositions. A typical Acid Jazz ensemble blends horns, a full rhythm section (often with percussion in addition to a drum set), a vocalist (singing and rapping), and even a DJ, employing sampling.

The role of a drum set player in Acid Jazz is to maintain a solid rhythmic foundation with a characteristic relaxed groove. This is achieved by playing specific patterns (usually Hip Hop or Funk, but often Swing/Jazz, Fusion, or Afro-Cuban) with a strong sense of time. A small set-up is common (hi-hat, snare, bass drum, cymbal), but some drummers use a larger kit depending on instrumentation and musical influences. Acid Jazz players strive for a consistent sound, often imitating that of a drum machine.

Acid Jazz tempo range varies according to the style being played (see individual styles below). The following grooves are practical for this genre.

EXAMPLE 1 (Hip Hop/Rap—CD 2, Track 34)

This is a common Hip Hop/Rap groove (for more variations see Hip Hop chapter), and is perhaps the most popular groove in Acid Jazz. **The tempo range is quarter note = 60–120 bpm.**

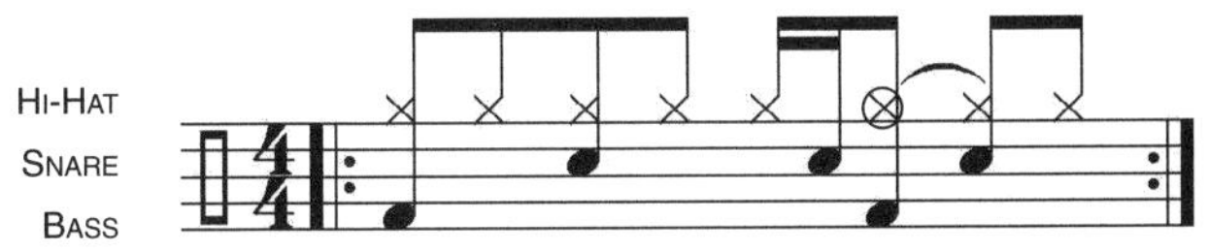

(Circled hi-hat note is played open)

Example 2 (Standard Rock—CD 2, Track 80)

This is the "Standard Rock Beat" (for more variations see Standard Rock in the Rock n' Roll chapter). The downbeat eighth notes are often accented louder than the off beats. **The most common tempo range is quarter note = 110–120 bpm.**

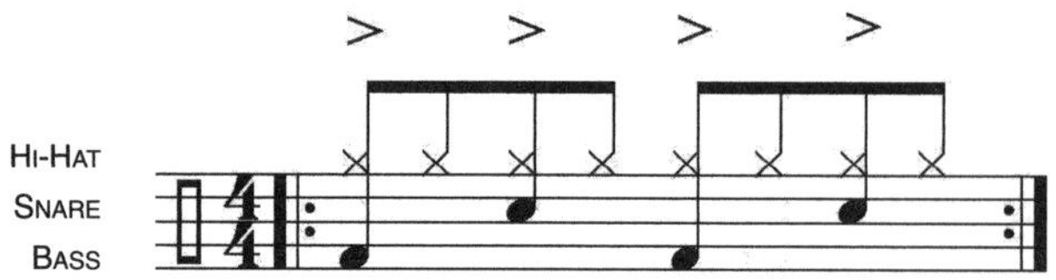

Example 3 (Swing—CD 2, Track 42)

This is the standard ride time Swing pattern (for more variations see Big Band in the Jazz chapter). Take note of the accents placed on beats 2 & 4 on the ride cymbal. These accents double with the hi-hat foot pattern, defining a strong "pocket" and a relaxed groove. **The wide tempo range for a standard time pattern is quarter note = 60–255 bpm (and even beyond).**

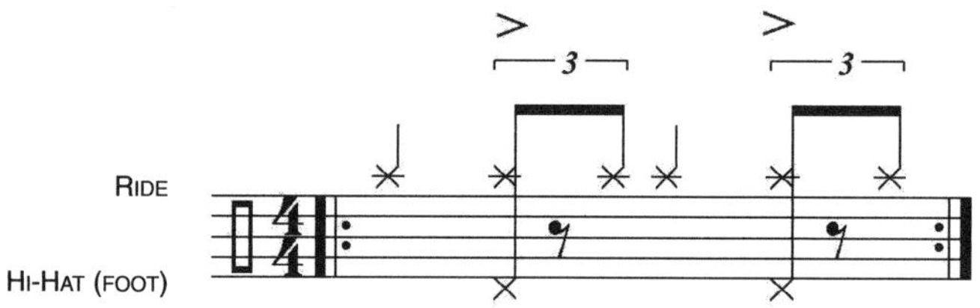

Example 4 (Bossa Nova—CD 1, Track 77)

This variation is the Bossa Nova rhythm (for more variations see Bossa Nova in the Brazilian chapter). Note that the snare hand plays the familiar "Brazilian Clave" rhythm as a rim click. **The style is counted and felt in 4/4 and usually played at a tempo of quarter note = 100–168 bpm.**

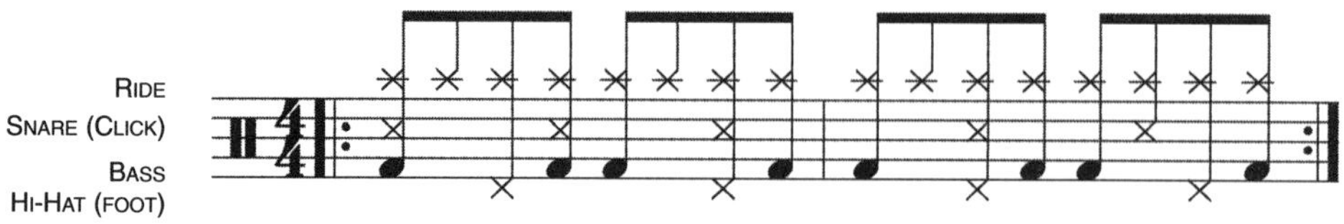

EXAMPLE 5 (Mambo—CD 1, Track 25)

This is the Mambo, a two-measure, up-tempo pattern. (For more variations, see the Afro-Cuban chapter.) Note the accents played on the mouth/edge of the cowbell or the ride cymbal bell. **The Mambo is usually played around quarter note = 180–220 bpm.**

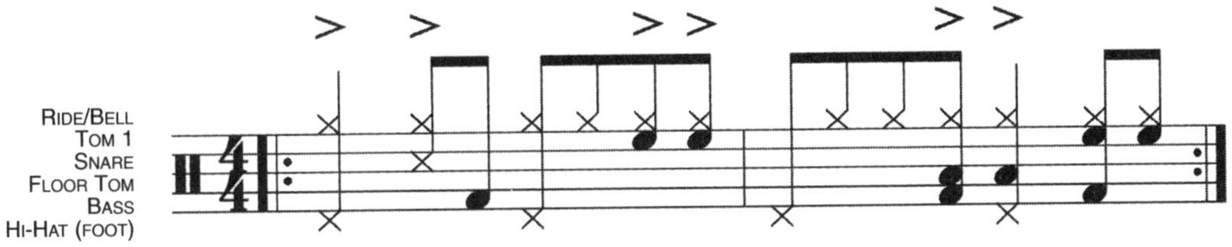

EXAMPLE 6 (Displaced Funk—CD 2, Track 21)

This is the Displaced Funk pattern (for more variations, see the Funk Chapter). Here, "Displaced" refers to the placement of the first snare drum note, which would normally be played on beat 2. In this groove it's played on the + of beat 2. **The tempo is quarter note = 100–138 bpm.**

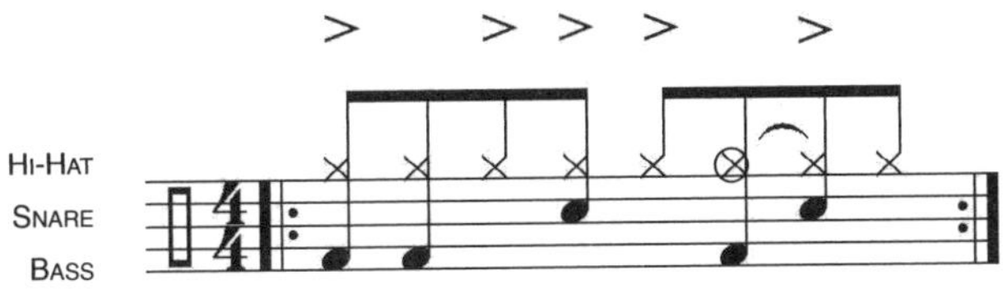

(Circled hi-hat note is played open)

2 AFRICAN (CONTEMPORARY)

WHILE AFRICAN MUSIC dates back to prehistoric times, the primary concern of the drum set player is contemporary African music. Since Africa has one-fifth the land mass and population of the planet, and literally hundreds of cultures, musical styles number in the thousands. Though a drummer may encounter other contemporary African styles (Nanigo, Zoblazo, Mapouka, Mbalax and Makossa are a few examples), the styles presented in this chapter are the most common types a drum set player may need to play.

Contemporary Sub-Saharan African music began with the sounds and rhythms of Afro-Cuban music in the 1920s and 1930s. At about that time, African composers began to create early versions of African Pop and Jazz. In the 1940s, Greek-run record labels helped promote the new music developing in the Congo-Zaire region of Western Africa. With the introduction of radio throughout Africa after World War II, and later through television broadcasts, contemporary African music achieved mass popularity across the continent. As Western instruments (most importantly the electric guitar) became cheaper through mass production, African musicians began to use them. This enabled composers to easily incorporate new developments in Western music (e.g., Rock n' Roll, Reggae) into African musical culture. Today, contemporary African music has achieved popularity on a global scale, influencing many other genres while continuing to develop in its own directions.

(Because of its musical characteristics—vocals in Arabic, use of quarter tones, very different rhythmic patterns—Northern African music has more in common with Middle Eastern music than with other African styles, and is covered in the Middle East chapter.)

WORLD BEAT

World Beat is associated with various African styles including Juju, Afrobeat, Afropop, and Highlife. These styles originated in the early 20th century in Ghana and Nigeria and eventually reached their peak in Africa toward the middle of the century. This music blends African tribal songs with popular music from the West. It originally incorporated the sounds from Big Band horn sections and later adopted grooves from the Caribbean as well as Rock and Soul music. A resurgence of World Beat in the last two decades has created a global following attracted to the music's celebratory and joyful nature. Important World Beat musicians include Fela Kuti (drummer Tony Allen), King Sunny Ade (Rasaki Alodokun), Chief Udoh Essiet (Nicolas "Ringo" Avom), Rex Lawson, and Prince Nico Mbarga (a drummer himself).

As this form of contemporary African music adopted styles from North America and the Caribbean, it's helpful to be thoroughly versed in playing Reggae, Ska, Soca, and Rock. Much as in other styles of dance music, the role of the drummer is to maintain a steady beat and strong time. In addition, relatively soft dynamics are an integral characteristic of World Beat, as the drum set functions primarily as a background instrument. **The tempo is quarter note = 100–138 bpm.**

EXAMPLE (CD 1, Track 2)

This features a rhythm similar to Soca (see Soca in the Caribbean chapter) rhythm on the snare drum.

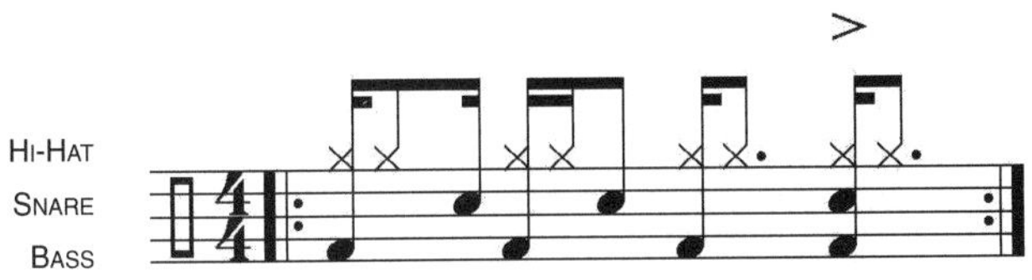

VARIATION 1

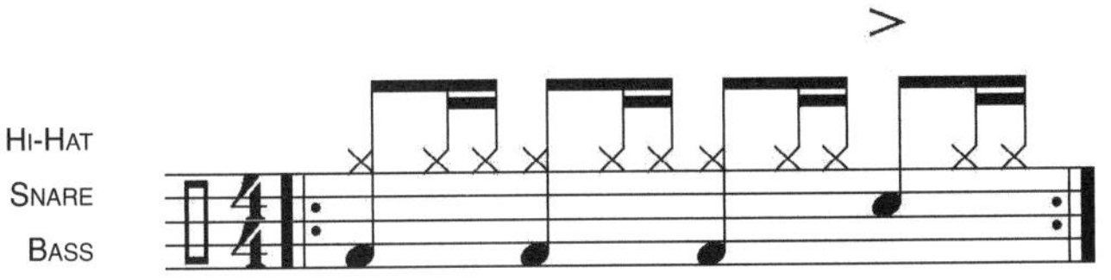

VARIATION 2 (CD 1, Track 3)

Notice the snare drum ghost notes and the accent on beat 4, as compared with variation 1.

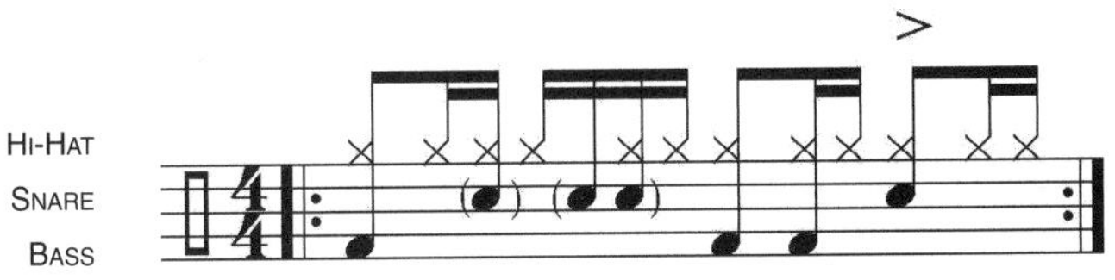

SOUKOUS

Soukous* is a type of dance music that emerged in the Congo/Zaire region in the early 1960s. Soukous (French for "to shake") is regarded by some as the most prevalent style of contemporary African music, with popularity that extends into Europe and North America. The roots of this style go back to the post-World War II era when radio stations in the Congo/Zaire region played Cuban Rumba music. African musicians used this sound to create what was originally called "African Jazz." Prominent Soukous bands and musicians include Zaiko Langa Langa, Franco, and Tabu Ley.

As Soukous is primarily dance music, the role of the drummer is to maintain a strong, unwavering pulse. Soukous grooves usually have a 16th-note feel and generally feature quarter notes on the bass drum (a "four on the floor" pattern).

Recent developments include a fast version (roughly 112–132 bpm) known as Soukous Ndombolo, which often uses a straight-up Soca beat. (See Caribbean chapter.) Performers include Dany Engogo, Mibilia Bel, and the groups Extra Musica and Wenge Musica.

As in Rock, the tempo range is relatively narrow at quarter note = 92–132 bpm.

EXAMPLE (CD 1, Track 4)

This features a march-like snare drum pattern.

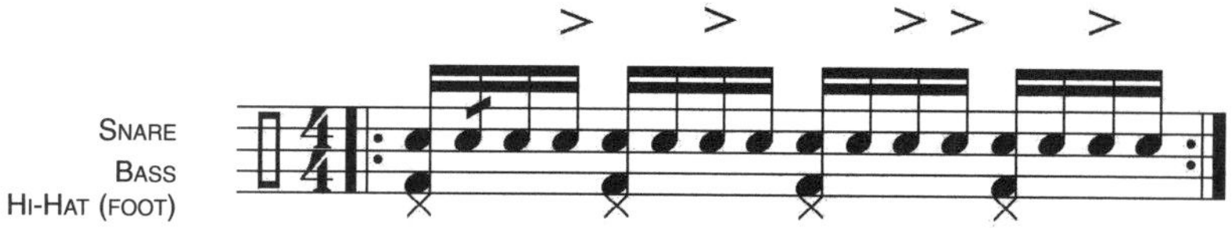

VARIATION 1

This features a Soca-like pattern (see Soca in the Caribbean chapter) with a prominent rim click on the snare drum.

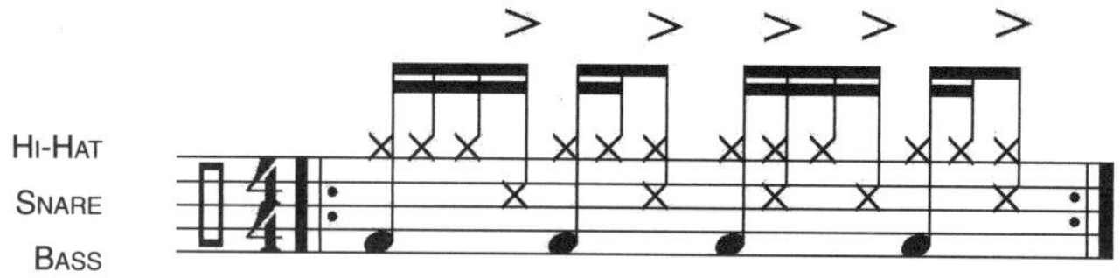

VARIATION 2

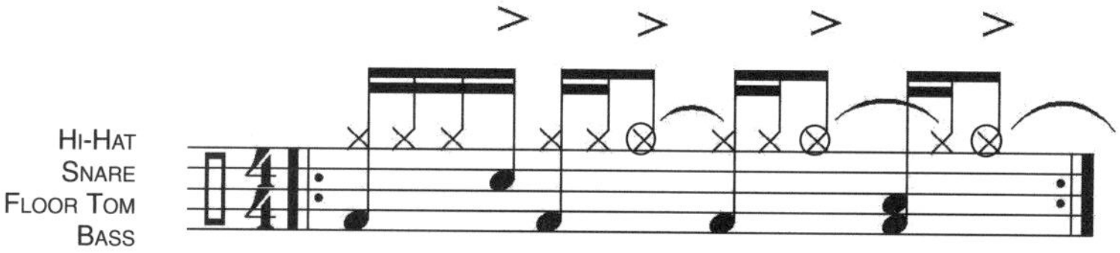

(Circled hi-hat notes are played open)

VARIATION 3 (CD 1, Track 5)

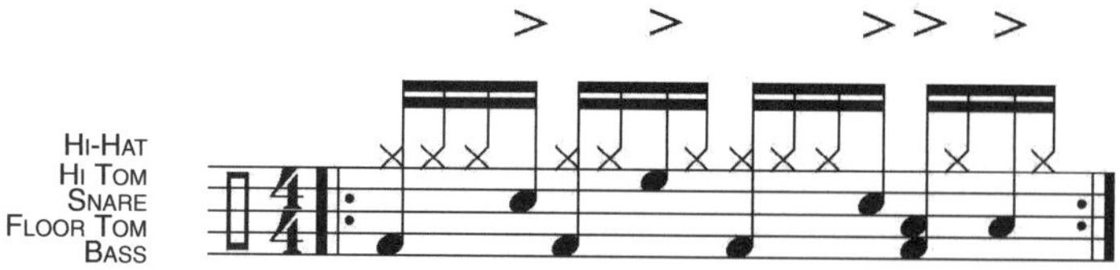

NOTE: Any combination of accents or open hi-hat notes can be played against the constant bass drum pattern in this style. Endless variations incorporating other drums also exist. Alternate bass drum patterns are possible as well, though they are not used as frequently as the other types of variations.

---

* For a thorough treatment of this style, refer to *Contemporary African Drumset Styles, Book 1: Soukous,* by Chris Miller.

Variation 4 (CD 1, Track 87)

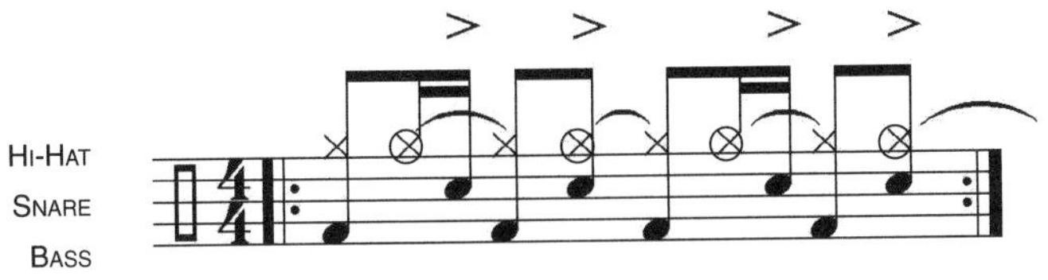

(Circled hi-hat notes are played open)

This is a standard Soca beat. (See Caribbean chapter).

Bikutsi

Bikutsi* developed in the Beti culture in Cameroon. The origin of the word stems from "Bi" (more than one), "Kut" (to strike) and "Si" (the ground), translating to "strike the ground repeatedly." Whereas Soukous began as an "African Jazz" interpretation of Afro-Cuban music, Bikutsi is a contemporary development of internal African musical ideas. Bikutsi attained popularity in Western Africa by the middle of the 20th century, but only achieved wide exposure in the mid-1980s through music videos. Following that, elements of Bikutsi began to appear in the music of popular Western composers, notably Paul Simon's 1990 recording, "Rhythm of the Saints." Individuals and groups responsible for Bikutsi's success include journalist/promoter Jean-Marie Ahanda, Theodore Epeme ("Zanzibar"), Les Tetes Brulees, and Patou Bass, whose music incorporates elements of Zouk (a West Indian music) and reggae.

Much like Soukous, Bikutsi is primarily dance music, mandating the drummer's role as timekeeper. Though occasionally played in 9/8, Bikutsi music usually has quick 6/8 feels (written below in 4/4) and usually contains a steady "four on the floor" bass drum pattern, which allows opportunities for improvisation around the consistent pulse. **The tempo is generally quarter note = 116–168 bpm.**

Example (CD 1, Track 6)

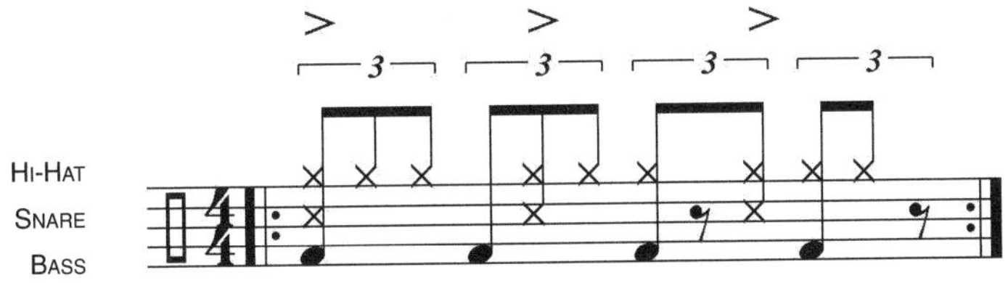

Variation 1 (CD 1, Track 7)

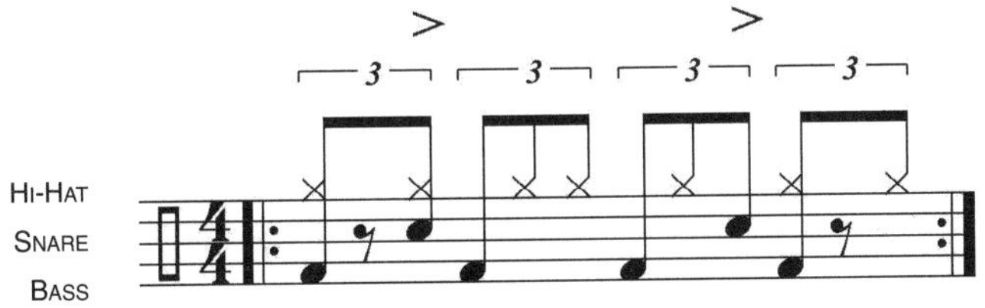

* For a thorough presentation on this style, refer to *Contemporary African Drumset Styles, Book 2: Bikutsi,* by Chris Miller.

VARIATION 2 (CD 1, Track 8)

This variation is played with syncopated accents on the snare drum.

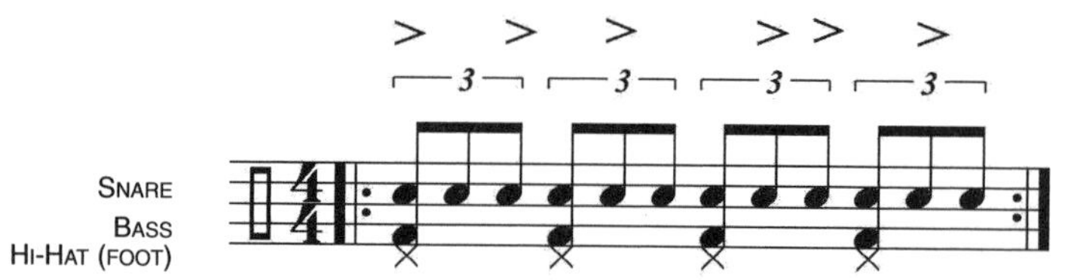

VARIATION 3

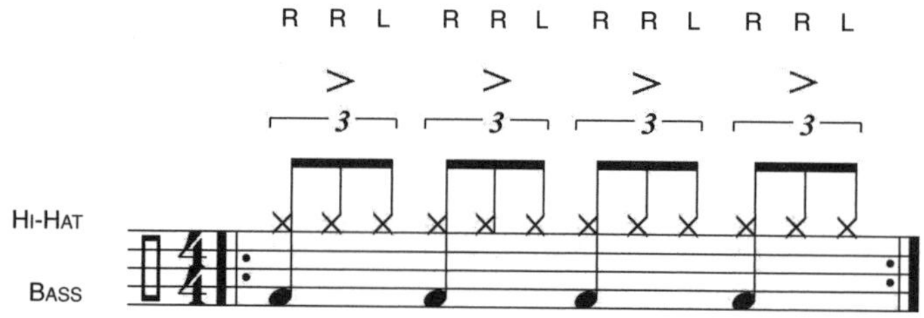

NOTE: Improvisation in this style usually centers around ride hand patterns playing over the constant bass drum pulse. Other surfaces besides a closed hi-hat (ride cymbal, cowbell, drum rim, etc.) can be used for the ride hand patterns; in such cases, the hi-hat foot usually doubles the bass drum quarter notes.

3 AFRO-CUBAN

WITHIN 50 YEARS AFTER COLUMBUS discovered the New World, the Spaniards instituted slavery in Cuba. Most of the slave trade was concentrated in the western part of the island, causing Afro-Cuban music to develop mostly in Matanzas, Havana Province, and the city of Havana, as the slaves' rich rhythmic and musical heritage gradually became integrated with the music of the Spanish colonizers. The Spanish permitted their slaves to worship through music and dance (in the Catholic religion), which led to the merging of the two cultures in both secular and religious aspects, establishing the foundation of Afro-Cuban music. What has survived is primarily a combination of the Spanish and West African cultures: Congolese, Yoruba and Dahomean (with their Cuban names Bantu, Lucumi' and Arara', respectively).

The styles presented here developed individually, so it's important to recognize the uniqueness of each style and its appropriate application in Afro-Cuban music. It's even more important to recognize and understand the differences between Afro-Cuban music (commonly referred to as "Salsa") and Brazilian music, because they're often lumped together under the vague term, "Latin Music." The information in the Afro-Cuban and Brazilian chapters will clarify the differences between these very different styles.

As a result of the extensive number of styles in the Afro-Cuban genre, this chapter is divided into two sections: More Frequently Played Styles and Less Frequently Played Styles. In addition, two non-Cuban styles have been included in More Frequently Played Styles—Bomba and Merengue. Though they're not of Cuban origin, it's necessary to know them when performing in most Afro-Cuban ensembles because of their widespread popularity. Similarly, there are other styles of non-Afro-Cuban origin included in the Less Frequently Played Styles section that are also played in the Afro-Cuban genre.

When playing Afro-Cuban music without other percussionists, the drummer takes the place of the traditional percussion section. That section usually consists of a Conga player (conguero), a timbale player (timbalero), and a bongo bell player (bonguero); hand-percussion instruments such as guiro, claves, and maracas are also often included. An understanding of the rhythms played on these instruments allows one drummer to assume the role of many percussionists.

The drum set is a modern addition to the Afro-Cuban percussion section. When other percussionists are present, the drum set rhythms are often stripped down or replaced by alternate rhythms to avoid duplicating the parts of other percussionists. When playing alone, the drum set player will assume the responsibility for all the percussion parts, increasing the demand for a high level of limb independence on the drum kit. This chapter not only provides the specific patterns to play, but also includes examples of how to apply the patterns when accompanied by other percussionists.

For additional information on this genre, perhaps the most comprehensive drum set book is *Afro-Cuban Rhythms for Drumset*, by Frank Malabe and Bob Weiner. For further info on Afro-Cuban and Salsa history, development, and the roles of other instruments, refer to *The Salsa Guidebook for Piano and Ensemble*, by Rebeca Mauleon. (We would like to give special thanks to Rebeca Mauleon for her generous help with this chapter.) The music of pioneer drummers/percussionists such as Tito Puente, Orestes Vilato, Walfredo Reyes Sr., Ignacio Berroa, Jose "Changuito" Quintana and modern-day drummers/percussionists such as Horacio Hernandez, Robby Ameen, Alex Acuña, Pete Escovedo (and family—including Sheila E.), Jimmy Branly, Calixto Oviedo, Antonio Sanches, Paul van Wageningen and Walfredo Reyes Jr. will provide a good introduction to the sounds of Afro-Cuban music and drumming.

CLAVE RHYTHMS

The most important feature in almost all Afro-Cuban music is the clave rhythm. ("Clave"is Spanish for "key," as in a piano or other musical instrument key; there's a separate word for the key to a lock ["llave"].) Therefore, the styles presented in this chapter include a specification of the order and type of clave: 3–2 or 2–3 son clave, 3–2 or 2–3 rumba clave, and 6/8 clave.

A repetitive two-measure pattern, the clave* has become a universal rhythm whose influence extends beyond Cuba to North American Jazz and even Rock n' Roll (e.g., the familiar "Bo Diddley beat"). Although "clave" generally refers to the rhythms found in Cuba (African in origin), a variation of the clave rhythm is found in Brazilian music as well. However, Brazilian music and rhythms are not built around the clave to the extent that Afro-Cuban music is.

The two most popular Cuban clave rhythms in 4/4 are the son clave and rumba clave. Both are two-measure patterns that contain three notes in one measure and two notes in the other. The order of the measures may begin with either the "3" side or the "2" side, hence the terms "3-2 clave" and "2-3 clave."

The sole difference between son clave and rumba clave is the placement of the last note of the "3" side of both rhythms. In son clave, the last note of the "3" side is on beat 4, while in rumba clave the last note of the "3" side is on the + of 4. Keeping in mind the difference between son and rumba clave and the order of 3-2 or 2-3 clave rhythms, there are only four possible combinations: 3-2 son, 3-2 rumba, 2-3 son and 2-3 rumba.

Knowledge of all the grooves in this chapter, the piano montuno (the familiar Salsa piano ostinato/rhythm), melody, experience of other ensemble musicians, listening skills, and even a possible indication on sheet music determine the specific clave rhythm of a song. The main consideration is that all musicians playing the song agree on the order of the clave (2-3 or 3-2) and the type of clave (son or rumba). Even in Cuba musicians often disagree on whether a song contains a 2-3 or 3-2 clave rhythm. However, it is extremely important that all musicians ultimately agree on what type of clave to play so that the rhythms throughout the ensemble will not clash. The examples below cover all four combinations of the two most popular clave rhythms in 4/4 as well as the 6/8 clave pattern.

3–2 Son Clave (CD 1, Track 9)

3–2 Rumba Clave (CD 1, Track 10)

2–3 Son Clave (CD 1, Track 11)

* In addition to the name of the rhythm, claves are also an instrument—two round, hand-held, machined-smooth pieces of hardwood typically about seven inches long and an inch wide (commonly made out of rosewood, though sometimes mahogany, and in northwest Mexico occasionally ironwood) that are struck together to create a loud, sharp sound.

Claves are often played incorrectly, with those playing them wrapping their hands all the way around them and holding them tightly. This greatly muffles the sound when the claves are struck together, reducing both sharpness and intensity, resulting in a medium-volume "clank" rather than the sharp, loud "crack" that one obtains by holding/playing claves correctly—cupping them loosely in the hands, with as much of the surface unobstructed as possible; when held correctly, the player's hand should go no more than about halfway around a clave, with the bottom clave resting in the cup of the hand rather than being held firmly.

2–3 Rumba Clave (CD 1, Track 12)

6/8 Clave Pattern (CD 1, Track 13)

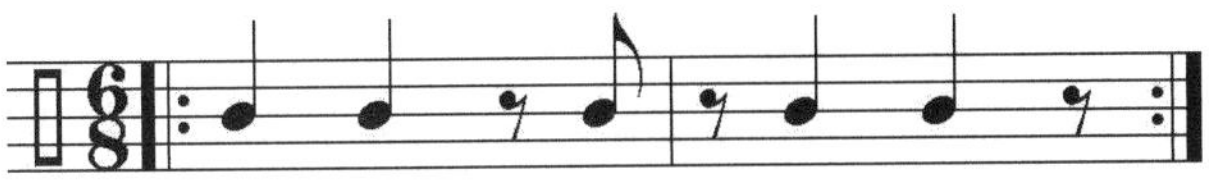

More Frequently Played Styles

Afro-Cuban 6/8

The two-part 6/8 clave pattern, from which the Cuban clave rhythms would emerge, developed in Africa, notably in the Nigerian Yoruba tribe. Unlike the son and the rumba clave, which are based on a duple feel, the 6/8 rhythm is based on a triple feel. Notice that the drum set patterns below have been written in 4/4 time in triplet groupings. Although the same patterns can be written in 6/8, transcribing these grooves to a 4/4 time signature helps establish the relationship and characteristics of Cuban clave and 6/8 clave.

In Cuba, two of the most common names for 6/8 styles are "Bembe" and "Abakwa" (also spelled "Abakua"). Bembes were religious celebrations which included music and dance, while Abakwas were exclusive organizations formed in Cuba by slaves descending from the Calibar area of western Africa. Both influences had a profound effect on the development of Afro-Cuban music. It is now quite common to hear 6/8 rhythmic styles interchanged with authentic Cuban styles (such as Mambo, Guaguanco, Songo, etc.). So, it is highly useful to develop the ability to flow from one feel to the other.

The Afro-Cuban 6/8 pattern for drum set replicates a signature melody of the conga drums along with the conventional 6/8 bell pattern. The main bell pattern itself is based around the 6/8 clave rhythm (containing two additional notes which are usually played more softly). The pulse is most commonly felt on each downbeat (played by the hi-hat foot). However, the same pattern may produce a different feel by changing the pulse to six beats within the pattern (see variation 4 of the 6/8 drum set patterns below). Although the 6/8 bell and drum set patterns are written as one-measure 4/4 patterns, the Afro-Cuban 6/8 does contain two "sides" similar to the son and rumba clave (i.e., 3-2 versus 2-3). It's good to develop the ability to start from the third beat of the 4/4 measure, creating a reversed order of the 6/8 pattern. **All 6/8 patterns below (clave, bell and drum set) start around quarter note = 100 bpm.**

Afro-Cuban 6/8 Clave Pattern

Example (CD 1, Track 13)

This is the Afro-Cuban 6/8 clave pattern written in 6/8. This transcription displays the two sides of the 6/8 clave. The 6/8 clave is most commonly played in a 3–2 order, as seen here and in the following examples.

Example (Time Signature Variant) (CD 1, Track 13)

This is the Afro-Cuban 6/8 clave pattern written in 4/4. Notice how the same pattern is now one measure long. Although the sides of the clave are not separated by a bar line, the pattern still retains both sides which relate to the son and rumba clave patterns.

Afro-Cuban 6/8 Cowbell Patterns

Example (CD 1, Track 14)

This is the 6/8 drum set cowbell pattern written in 4/4. This is the most commonly used bell pattern in Afro-Cuban 6/8 styles. It is exactly the same as the 6/8 clave pattern with the addition of two notes (usually played more lightly than the others). Please note that the cowbell notes can also be played on the ride cymbal bell or other surfaces.

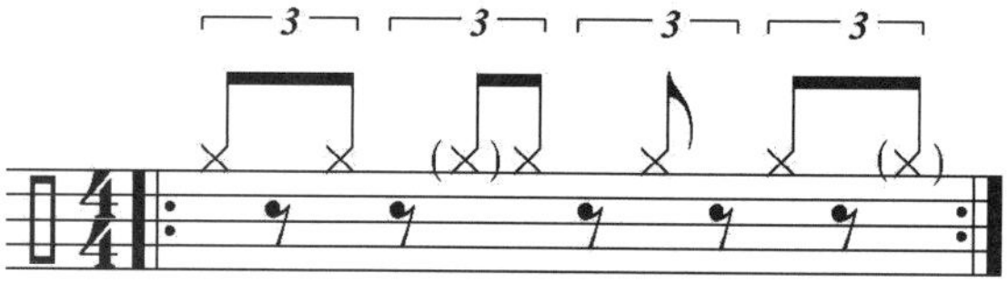

Variation 1

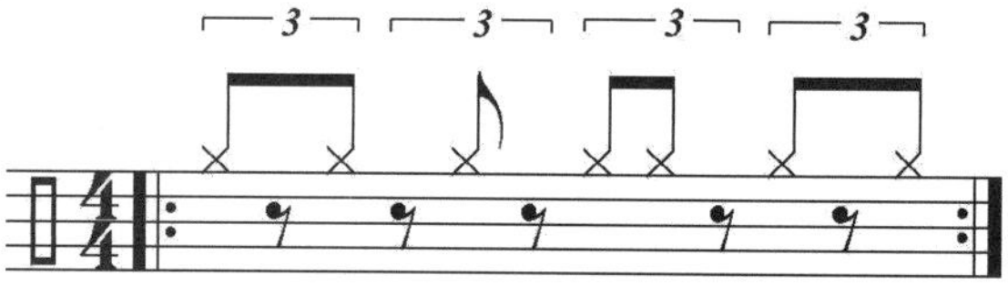

Variation 2

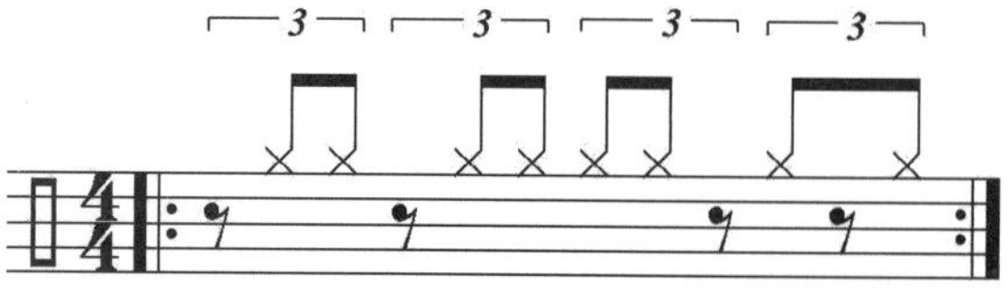

NOTE: The drum set patterns below utilize only the 6/8 bell pattern from the main example. The two variations above can be played with the same grooves but have not been included with grooves since they are played much less frequently and do not directly accent the 6/8 clave rhythm.

Afro-Cuban 6/8 Patterns for Drum Set

Example (CD 1, Track 15)

This is the most commonly played 6/8 drum set pattern, often called "Bembe." The ride hand plays the 6/8 bell pattern on the cowbell or ride cymbal bell, the bass drum plays beat 1 and the last triplet of beat 4, the snare hand plays the 6/8 conga melody between a snare rim click and the low and high toms, while the hi-hat foot plays quarter notes on each of the four downbeats. **Tempo is quarter note = 92–120 bpm.**

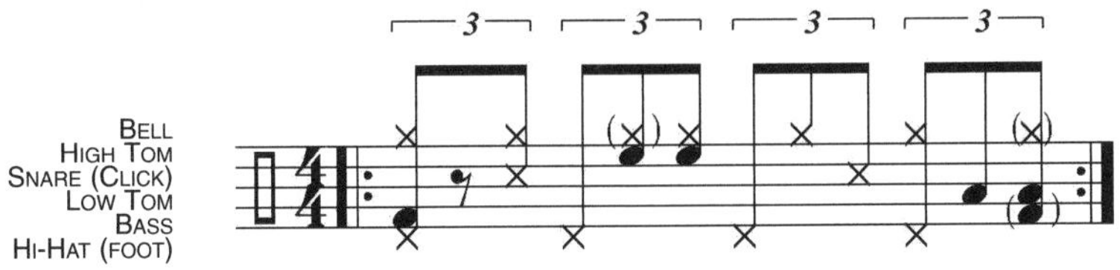

Variation 1 (CD 1, Track 16)

This pattern is often referred to as the 6/8 "back beat" rhythm for drum set, or the "Bembe Funk" rhythm, due to the accent on beat 3 of the snare. The ride hand plays the same 6/8 drum set bell pattern as above, while the snare hand fills in ghost notes between the notes of the ride hand and accents beat 3. The bass drum plays beat 1 of the measure while the hi-hat foot continues to play all four downbeats.

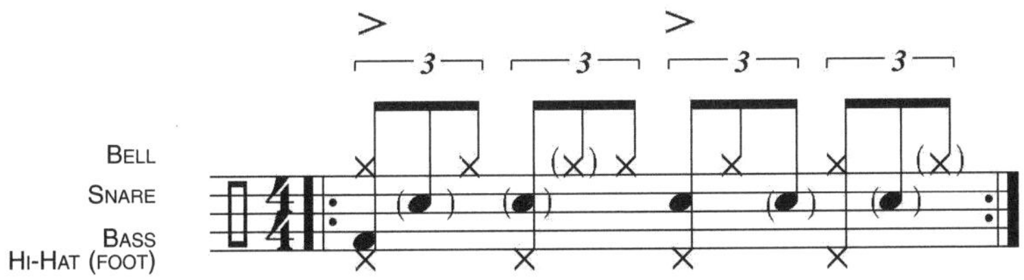

NOTE: For the purpose of variety, more bass drum notes may be added to the pattern by doubling any existing note(s) of the ride hand. Keep in mind to use extra bass drum notes sparingly.

Variation 2 (CD 1, Track 17)

This pattern is a traditional "Abakwa." The ride hand plays the 6/8 drum set bell pattern while the snare hand plays a simple 6/8 conga rhythm.

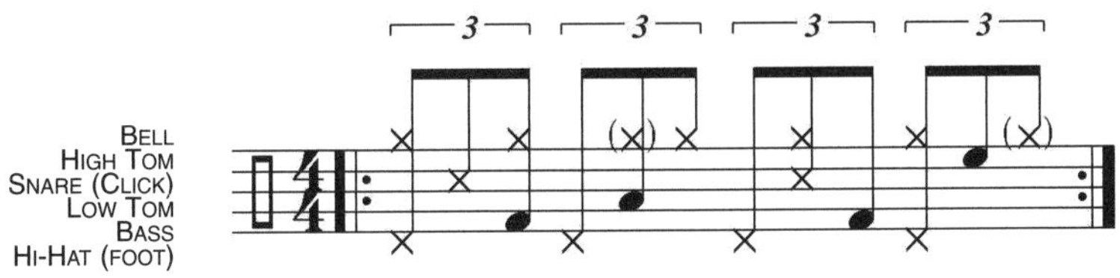

VARIATION 3 (CD 1, Track 18)

This is a more challenging "Abakwa." The ride hand plays the 6/8 drum set bell pattern while the snare hand plays a variation of the conga rhythm from the main example.

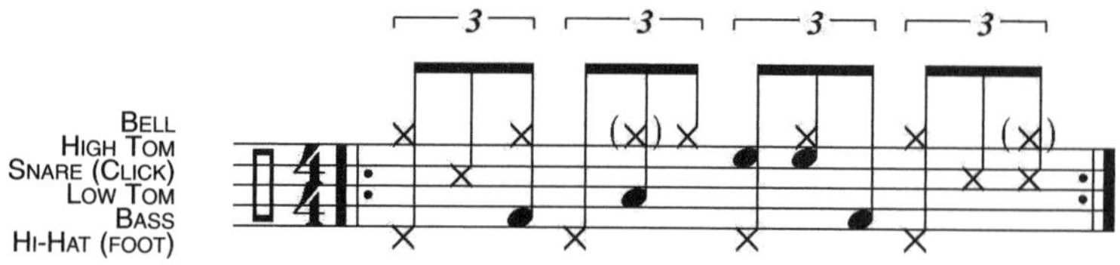

VARIATION 4 (CD 1, Track 19)

All of the above patterns can be played with various rhythms on the hi-hat foot (3 beats per measure or 6 beats per measure). This is the main example, now with 6 beats per measure on the hi-hat foot.

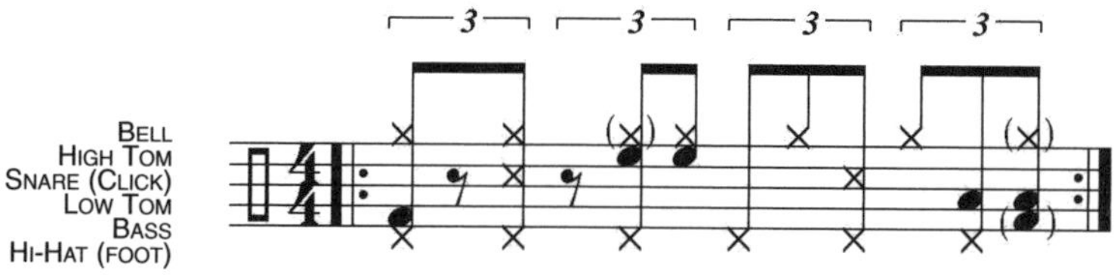

CASCARA

Unlike Mambo, Cha Cha, and other types of Afro-Cuban music, Cascara is not a musical style but a rhythmic pattern copied from another pattern called "palito" ("little stick"). The word Cascara means "shell," which indicates where the pattern is played: on the shell of the timbales. During the early part of the 20th century, the instrumentation of Son music expanded to include timbales (fairly wide but shallow single-headed drums). The use of this instrument led to the introduction of the Palito/Cascara pattern in Afro-Cuban ensembles.

When adapted for drum set, the Cascara rhythm is commonly played with the ride hand on either a closed hi-hat, the shell and/or rim of a floor tom, or a cowbell or ride cymbal bell. The snare hand plays a rim click or a wood block, while the bass drum plays a Tumbao pattern. The Cascara is a two-measure pattern which complements specific sides of the clave. Though it may be played as a 3-2 or a 2-3 clave (rumba or son), the position of the clave remains consistent with the notes of the Cascara pattern. This pattern is played in a wide range of tempos, depending on the style of music. The Cascara pattern can be used as a substitute for other patterns or styles (such as Mambo, Guaguanco, etc.) so as not to duplicate the parts of other percussionists and can be effective when playing during the softer sections of an arrangement. Note that the Cascara rhythm will be found in several of the patterns in this chapter.

The Cascara pattern may be substituted for any groove as long as it coincides with the clave pattern of that groove or the song itself (e.g., a Guaguanco should continue to have a rumba clave feel when it features a Cascara, a Mambo a son clave, etc.) And when playing the Cascara rhythm on a surface other than the closed hi-hat, the hi-hat foot may play beats 1 & 3 or 2 & 4 of both measures. **The tempo range for a Cascara depends on the style of music and covers a wide range at quarter note = 126–250 bpm.**

Cascara with 3-2 Clave

Example 1 (CD 1, Track 20)

The Cascara pattern is played on a closed hi-hat (or floor tom shell), a 3-2 son clave is played in the snare hand as a rim click, and the bass drum plays a constant Tumbao pattern.

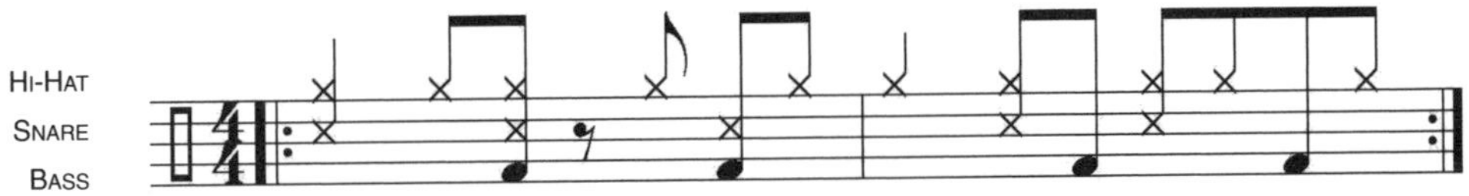

Example 2 (CD 1, Track 21)

This is the same as example 1 with a 3-2 rumba clave played by the snare hand.

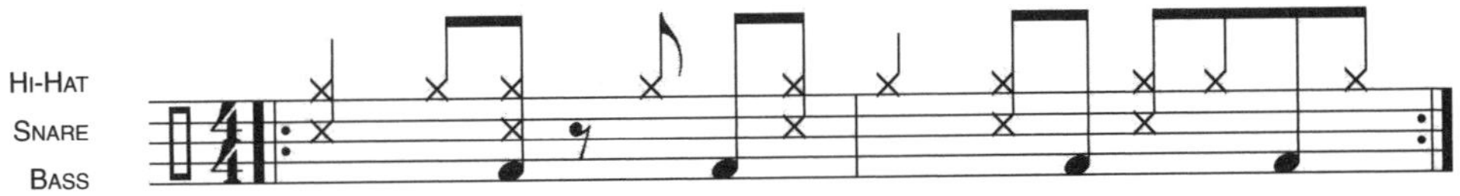

Cascara with 2-3 Clave

Example 1 (CD 1, Track 22)

The Cascara pattern is played on a closed hi-hat (or floor tom shell), a 2-3 son clave is played in the snare hand as a rim click, and the bass drum plays a constant Tumbao pattern.

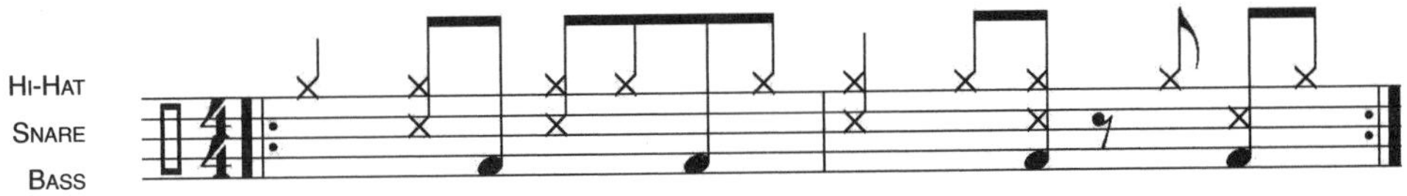

Example 2 (CD 1, Track 23)

The Cascara pattern is played on a closed hi-hat (or floor tom shell), a 2-3 rumba clave is played in the snare hand as a rim click, and the bass drum plays a constant Tumbao pattern.

NOTE: To play a more authentic Cuban pattern, limit the amount of bass drum notes to either just the Bombo note (the + of beat 2 on the "3" side of the clave) or the + of beat 2 in both measures.

Guaguanco

Guaguanco is the most popular form of Afro-Cuban Rumba. (Other Rumba styles are the Yambu and the Columbia.) A folkloric and intimate dance style, Rumba's roots can be traced back to Africa as well as southern Spain ("Rumba Flamenca"). During the early part of the 20th century, Guaguanco emerged as the most prevalent form of Rumba due to its fast, energetic, and passionate character.

A distinguishing sound of the Guaguanco is the conga pattern (the pattern that would be played on the congas in an ensemble without a drum set). As in other drum set patterns, the conga melody is played with the snare hand. The ride hand plays the Cascara pattern while the bass drum emphasizes the Bombo note (+ of beat 2 on the "3" side of the clave). The hi-hat foot can either play beats 2 & 4 or beats 1 & 3 in both measures. For advanced playing, the hi-hat foot may play the rumba clave pattern simultaneously. (It's a good idea to include a separate pedal to strike a wood block or cowbell mounted on a Gajate bracket).

The Guaguanco is a two-measure, up-tempo pattern based on a 3-2 rumba clave and is usually started on the "3" side of the clave. **Quarter note = 180–220 bpm.**

Example (CD 1, Track 24)

The standard Guaguanco for drum set is played with the Cascara rhythm on the ride hand (once again, played on the shell/rim of the floor tom, ride bell, or cowbell), the bass drum plays the Bombo note, the snare hand plays the conga pattern, and the hi-hat foot plays beats 1 & 3 in both measures.

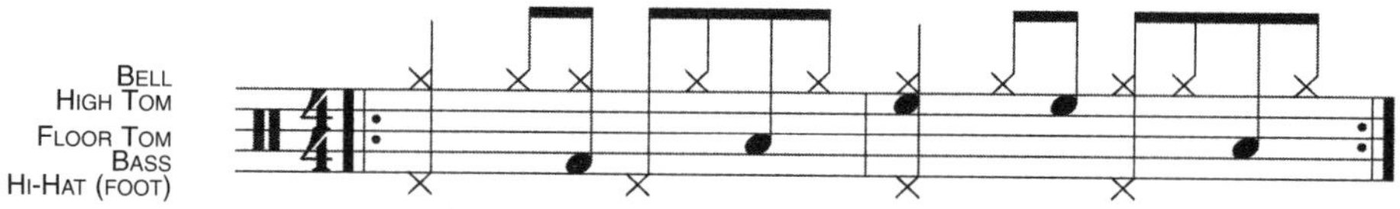

Variation

This is the same as the above example, except that the ride hand plays a variation of the bell pattern.

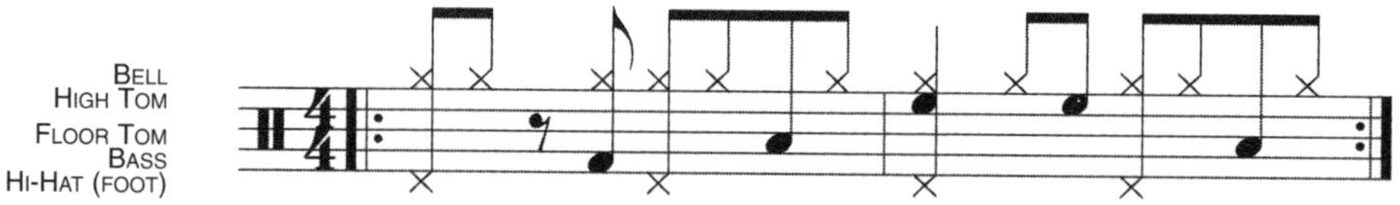

NOTE: One can substitute a Cascara for drum set pattern for either of the above Guaguanco patterns.

Mambo

The Mambo—instrumentation, improvisation, and musical voicings of American Swing fused with Cuban son rhythms—is arguably the most prominent and recognizable style in Afro-Cuban music. Although based on a dance that developed in the early 1940s in Havana, its name comes from an instrument originally used in Bantu rituals. It first appeared as an "open section" of the Danzon in the late 1930s, featuring improvisation by both dancers and musicians; but as a result of its popularity, the Mambo section started being played and recognized as its own style of music. It reached New York City by the late 1940s and attained its greatest popularity by the mid-1950s. Today, Mambo's influence is found in virtually all

Salsa music. While Cuban artists such as Israel "Cachao" Lopez, Arsenio Rodriguez, and Orestes Lopez created the Mambo, musicians such as Tito Puente and Dizzy Gillespie (in songs such as "Manteca" [translation: "Lard"]) did much to develop it.

The drum set player faces quite a challenge when performing an authentic Mambo, due to the demand for limb independence. The ride hand covers the common Mambo bell pattern (originally played by either a timbale player or a Bongo bell player), while the snare hand replicates the signature pattern from the congas. The bass drum supports the Tumbao pattern played by the bassist, sometimes in unison, other times broken up. The hi-hat foot can either play beats 2 & 4 or beats 1 & 3 in both measures. For advanced playing, much as when incorporating the clave into the Guaguanco, the hi-hat foot may play the son clave pattern simultaneously.

The Mambo is a two-measure, up-tempo pattern based on a 2-3 son clave; it can be started on either the "2" or "3" side of the clave. **Quarter note = 180–220 bpm.**

EXAMPLE (CD 1, Track 25)

Here the signature Mambo bell pattern is played by the ride hand on either a cowbell or a ride cymbal bell. Note the accents, which are played on the edge of the cowbell or the ride cymbal bell, but don't accent the notes too loudly. The conga pattern is played by the snare hand. (Notice the combination of rim click and tom notes.)

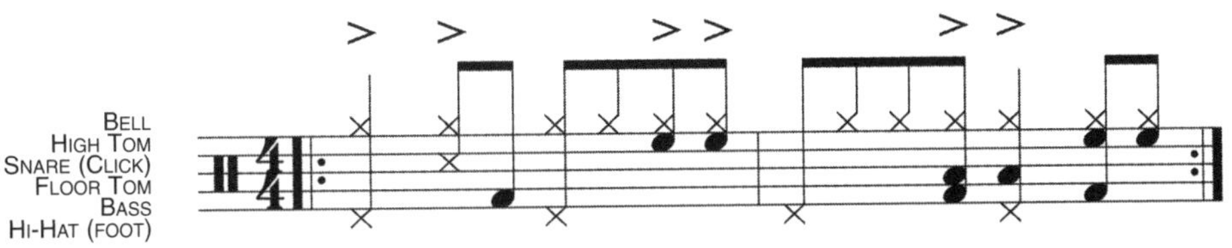

VARIATION 1 (CD 1, Track 26)

This is the same as the above example but includes the ride hand playing the Cascara pattern on either the shell/rim of the floor tom or the ride cymbal bell.

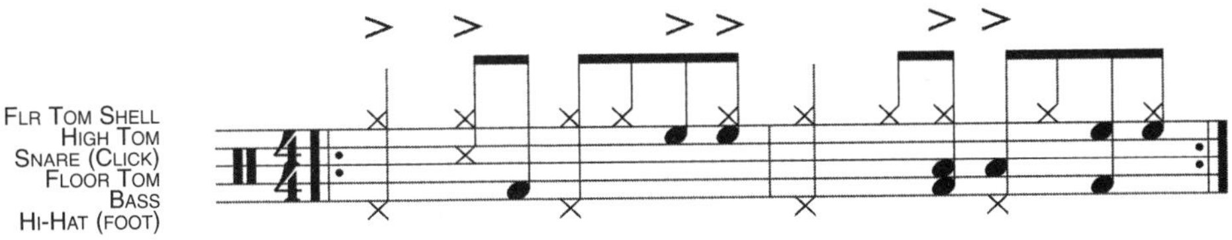

VARIATION 2 (CD 1, Track 27)

This is the same as the above example, but with the ride hand playing the Bongo bell pattern on either the cowbell (edge and body of the bell), or the ride cymbal bell.

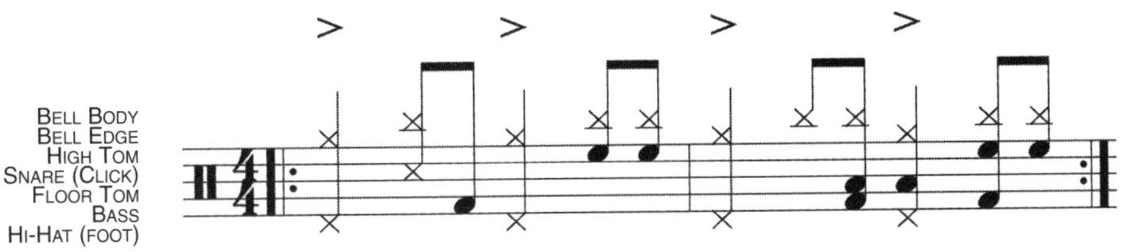

NOTE: The hi-hat foot may also play a 2-3 son clave pattern or an optional 2 & 4 pattern in all of the above.

Cha Cha

Cha Cha is the North American term for the Afro-Cuban/Salsa dance known as the "Cha cha cha," which refers to the sound of the "3 note rhythm" in the dance step. The style was developed by musicians and dancers desiring a slowed-down (half-time) version of a Mambo, taking it back to its roots in Danzon. Enrique Jorrin is credited with inventing and naming the Cha Cha in 1951. Its popularity reached a peak during that decade in dance clubs throughout Cuba and the United States. One of the most widely recognized Cha Chas in Latin and American pop music is "Oye Como Va" ("Listen How It Goes," written by Tito Puente, further popularized by Carlos Santana).

As in other Afro-Cuban styles, the drum set player takes on the roles of several percussionists at once. The defining sound of the style is the repetitive quarter notes on the Cha Cha bell (sometimes referred to as the "Cha bell"—usually played by the ride hand). In addition, a conga pattern (played between the snare and the high tom), and the bass drum pattern complimenting the bass player, help distinguish this style. **Cha Cha is generally played at a medium tempo starting around quarter note = 100–120 bpm.**

Example (CD 1, Track 28)

This features a constant quarter-note pulse (with the ride hand) on either a Cha Cha bell or the ride cymbal bell, a repetitive conga pattern in the snare hand (snare drum and high tom), and a supporting bass drum rhythm on the + of beat 2 and on beat 3. The hi-hat commonly doubles the quarter notes of the bell pattern, though it may simply play 2 & 4 to offset the bell pattern.

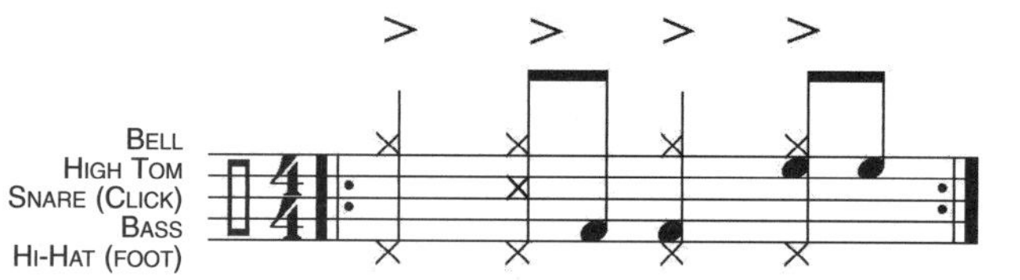

NOTE: The hi-hat foot can embellish the above example in several ways: playing the hi-hat on beats 1 and 3 or 2 & 4 of both measures. A more complex but effective pattern is to approximate the sound of a guiro, opening the hi-hat on beats 1 & 3 and closing it on beat 2, the + of 2, beat 4 and the + of 4.

Variation 1 (CD 1, Track 29)

This is a simplified version of a Cha Cha, most usable when playing with a conga player.

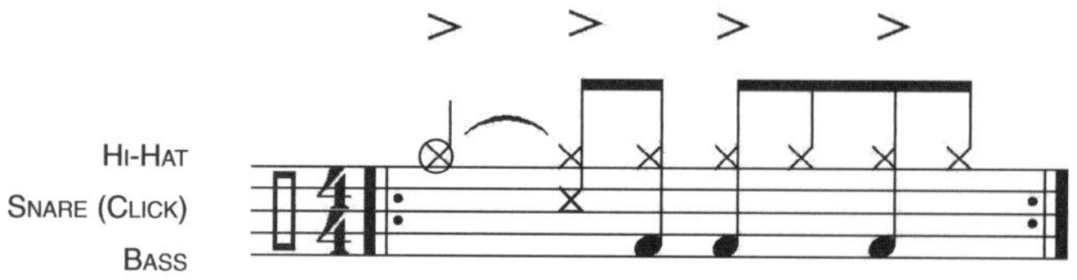

(Circled hi-hat note is played open)

Variation 2 (CD 1, Track 30)

This variation includes snare drum rim clicks on all quarter notes, replicating the sound of a cowbell.

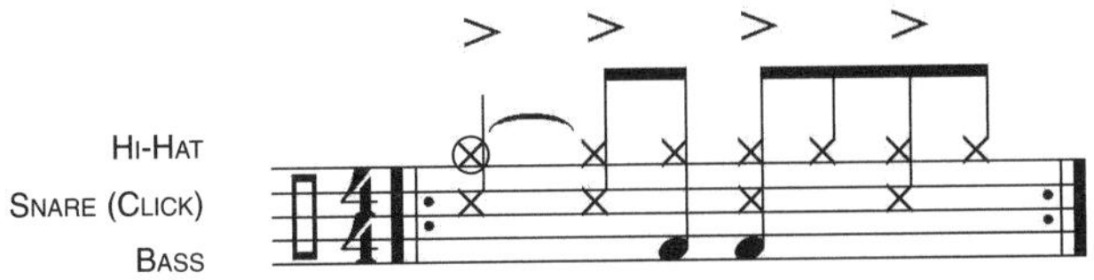

(Circled hi-hat note is played open)

NOTE: A fill that is frequently used at the beginning or at transitions in a Cha Cha is called an "Abanico." It involves a rim shot on the + of beat 2, a 5-stroke roll or a series of four 16th notes on beat 4, and a rimshot on beat 1 of the following measure. It can be played on the high timbale or the snare drum.

Mozambique

Mozambique, one of the more modern Afro-Cuban styles, can be traced to a single individual, Pedro Izquierdo ("Pello el Afroka'n"). Following the Cuban revolution of 1959, Izquierdo created a musical style combining many Afro-Cuban and African rhythms: Abakwa, Yoruba, Congo, Carabali, and Jiribilla. The original style employed a large percussion ensemble. According to Izquierdo, "The Mozambique is played with 12 conga drums . . . [played by] five conga drummers . . . two bass drums, three bells, a frying pan, four trumpets, and three trombones."

The Mozambique became popular immediately after its Cuban television debut in July 1963. Pianist Eddie Palmieri is credited as being the first to develop it in the U.S. After hearing a Cuban Mozambique played on the radio, Palmieri and drummer Manny Oquendo created the North American (specifically, New York City) version of the style. Other artists to explore the Mozambique include Issac Delgado, Carlos Santana, and finally Paul Simon with the song "Late in the Evening" (1980), played by the innovative drummer, Steve Gadd.

The Mozambique for drum set is as follows: The ride hand plays a bell pattern (slightly different from the Cascara rhythm) known as the "Mozambique bell pattern." The snare hand replicates the conga pattern, while the hi-hat foot and bass drum typically play simple rhythms. The "Steve Gadd" variation (variation 1), which is a fusion of an Afro-Cuban style and contemporary pop music, follows the main example. The original Cuban Mozambique is shown in variation 2. It differs to a notable degree from the Mozambique that emerged in North American music. *All three Mozambique patterns are based on a 2-3 rumba clave rhythm,* and, for more advanced playing, can also employ the hi-hat foot rumba clave simultaneously. **The groove is a two-measure, up-tempo pattern usually around quarter note = 200–220 bpm.**

Example (CD 1, Track 31)

The Mozambique for drum set pattern is played with the "Mozambique Bell pattern" in the ride hand on either the rim or shell of the floor tom or a cowbell or ride bell. The snare hand plays accents derived from the conga pattern on the snare, high tom, and floor tom.

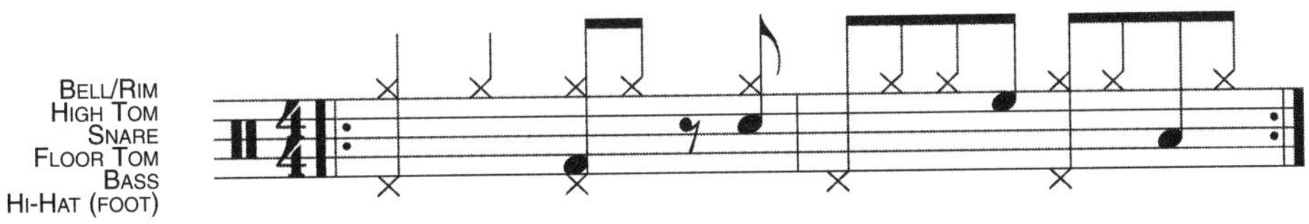

VARIATION 1 (CD 1, Track 32)

This is the "Steve Gadd" version of the Mozambique. The ride hand continues to play the "Mozambique Bell pattern" on the rim or shell of the floor tom or a cowbell or ride bell, the snare hand plays a Bomba rhythm on the toms (see Bomba section below), while the feet play in unison on beats 1 & 3 of both measures.

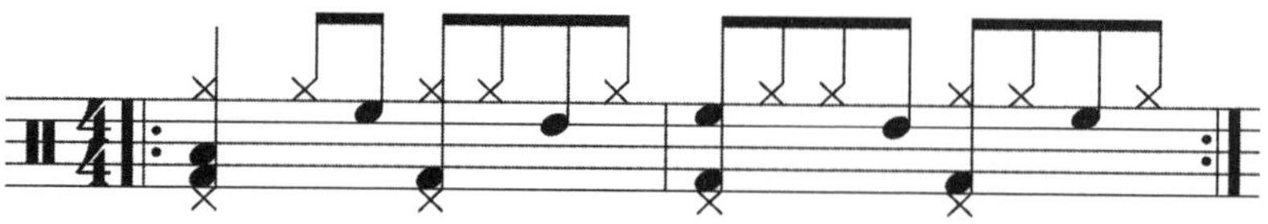

VARIATION 2 (CD 1, Track 33)

In the original Cuban Mozambique, the ride hand plays a bell pattern built around the rumba clave on the rim or shell of the floor tom or a cowbell or ride bell, and the snare hand plays a 2-3 rumba clave on a wood block or a rim click.

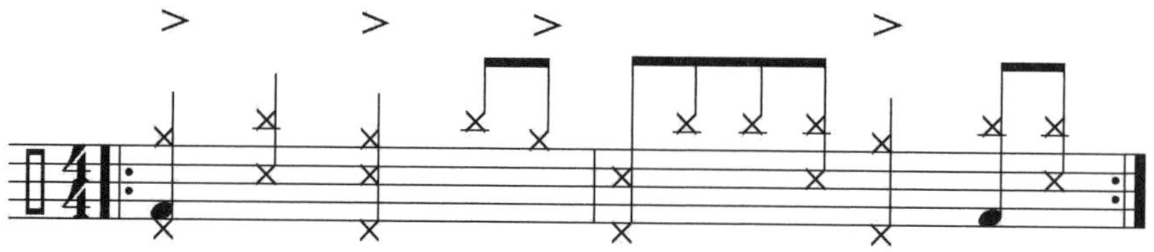

SONGO

Just as Jazz from the United States influenced the Mambo and Cha Cha, Funk and Soul inspired the Songo, which combines Cuban rhythms with Funk, Rock, Jazz, Fusion, and musical styles from the Caribbean and Brazil. Though influenced by Blas Egues (brother of Richard Egues, flautist with Orquesta Arago'n), Songo is primarily attributed to band leader Juan Formell (who is credited with naming Songo), pianist Cesar "Pupy" Pedrosa, and drummer/percussionist Jose Luis Quintana ("Changuito") from the group Los Van Van, which has been Cuba's most popular musical group for over 40 years.

As a result of its modern origin, Songo was the first Afro-Cuban musical style directly conceived from a drum set rhythm with the percussion instrumentation added later; and due to its role in Songo, the popularity of the drum set has increased in modern-day Afro-Cuban ensembles. Songo is a strong influence in the playing of modern drummers such as Dave Weckl, Joel Rosenblatt, Robbie Ameen, Horatio "El Negro" Hernandez, Ignacio Berroa, and numerous others.

Songo rhythms draw from all Afro-Cuban musical styles. The ride hand plays a steady pulse, the bass drum plays a tumbao rhythm in both measures, and the snare hand fills in syncopated notes around the other limbs to create a "linear" pattern (see Linear Funk in Funk chapter). (Take note of the accents in the snare hand which help establish the overall sound and feel of Songo.) Although Songo is its own style, Songo grooves can be used in other Afro-Cuban styles when the drummer is accompanied by other percussionists. As well, improvisation is common in Songo.

The primary Songo example is based on a 2-3 rumba clave rhythm. In more advanced playing, a hi-hat foot rumba clave can be added. However, it is important to note that the hi-hat foot clave tends to interrupt the overall feel if the initial groove is not clearly established. **The Songo groove is a two-measure, up-tempo pattern usually around quarter note = 180–220 bpm.**

Example (Nontraditional Songo) (CD 1, Track 34)

This is a standard Songo pattern for drum set with the snare hand creating a "linear" effect around the tumbao pattern on the bass drum and the ride hand pattern.

Variation 1

This is a variation in the bass drum tumbao pattern (only the + of beat 2 is played in both measures).

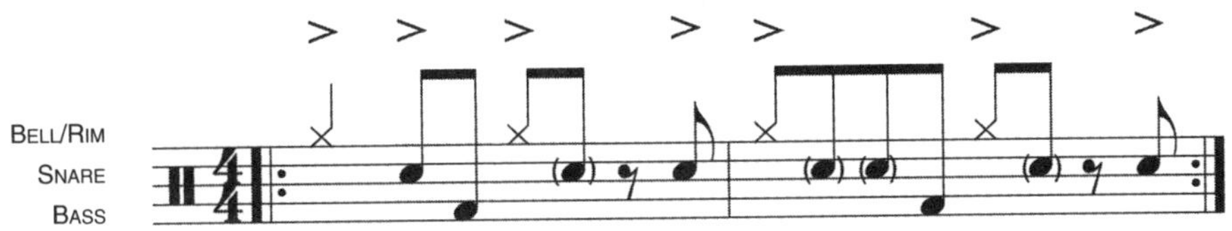

Variation 2 (CD 1, Track 35)

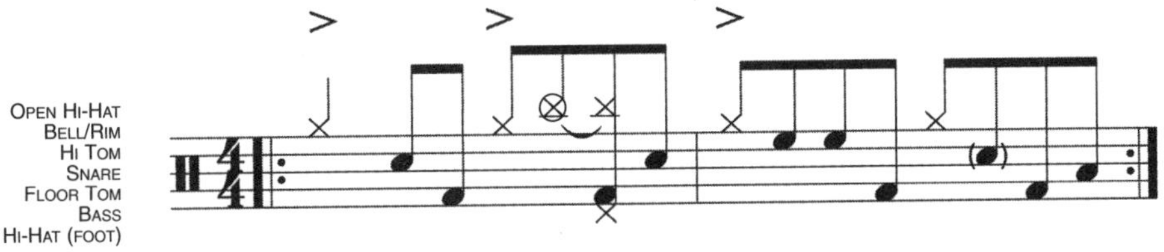

Example 1 (Traditional Songo) (CD 1, Track 36)

This is identical to the above example, with the addition of a bongo bell pattern played by the ride hand.

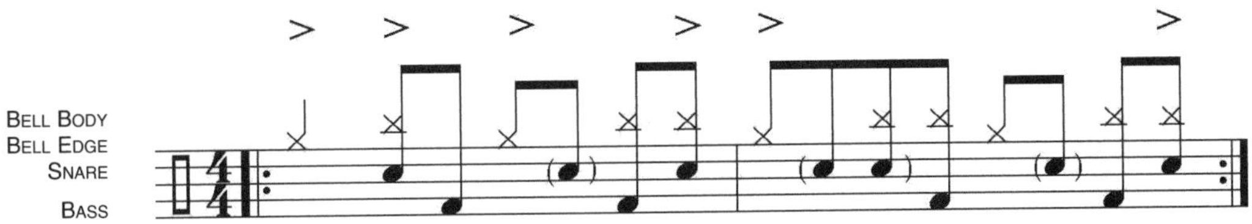

Example 2 (Traditional Songo) (CD 1, Track 37)

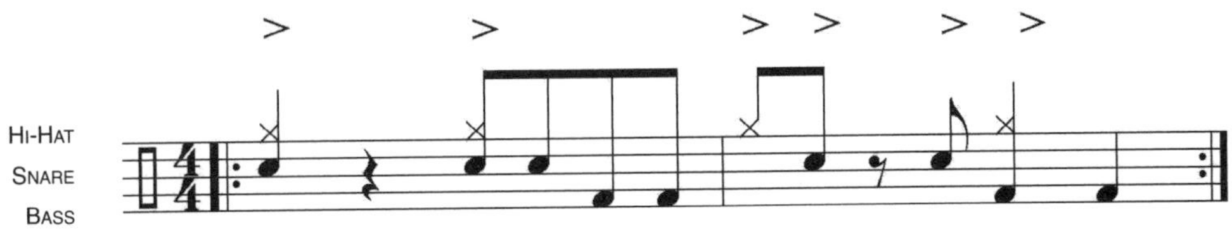

BOMBA

Bomba is the primary Puerto Rican musical style.It has Congolese (Bantu) roots similar to much Cuban music, and it was first brought to widespread popularity by Puerto Rican percussionist Rafael Cortijo in the mid-1950s. Though there are various genres of Puerto Rican music (e.g., Cuña, Lero, Yuba, Grasima), Bomba has become the defining name for all Puerto Rican styles. Puerto Rican musical roots extend back to the 16th century when music and dance arrived from Ghana. These were developed and maintained through sugar plantation slaves' holiday dances. The first written mention of the term Bomba came in 1797 after Andre Pierre Ledru encountered the dance and music in Aibonito. The tradition of Bomba (folkloric instrumentation consisting primarily of percussion and vocals) continues in the 21st century in festivals such as the Santiago Apostol Festival.

The Bomba pattern for drum set incorporates a repetitive bass drum pattern as well as a distinctive bell pattern, played on either the bell of the ride cymbal or a cowbell. It normally does not contain a clave rhythm. **The pattern is usually counted and felt in a quick 4/4 at around quarter note = 180–220 bpm.**

EXAMPLE (CD 1, Track 38)

This features the Bomba bell pattern in the ride hand and a repetitive bass drum pattern. Notice the snare drum accent on the last note of every other measure.

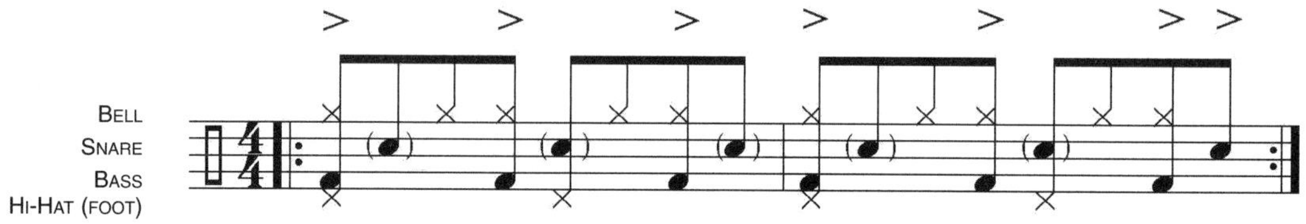

VARIATION

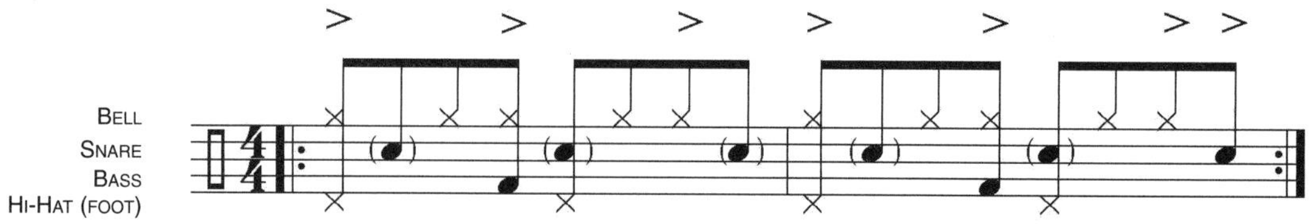

MERENGUE

Merengue is the national dance of the Dominican Republic, officially promoted as such by the dictator Rafael Leonidas Trujillo Molina (in power, 1930–1961). Much like Bomba, Merengue traces its roots back to African slaves. Due to French occupation of the western part of the island (shared by Haiti and the Dominican Republic), the music of the Dominican Republic combined African dance with the French Minuet resulting in the first forms of Merengue in the late 18th to early 19th centuries. Traditional Merengue instrumentation consisted of tambora, guira and accordion. After becoming established as the national dance in the 20th century, it made its way to the United States, primarily through New York City, in the 1950s. It is now a well established form of dance music throughout the world.

The typical characteristic of a Merengue drum set pattern is the recurring floor tom figure (originally played on a conga drum). Notice the use of the floor tom rim as well as a snare drum rim click throughout the pattern. The bass drum pattern is usually a "four on the floor" figure (frequently doubled by the hi-hat foot). **The Merengue is played at a very quick tempo around quarter note = 220–260 bpm.**

Example (CD 1, Track 39)

Notice the sticking (which should be reversed for left handed drummers). For a more advanced technique and sound, "splash" (open) the hi-hat with the foot on the third beat in both measures. Lastly, take note of the "X's" on the floor tom which are played on the rim.

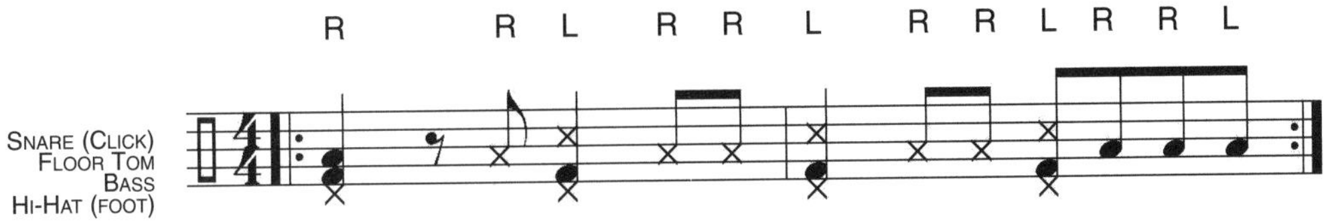

Variation 1

This is a simplified version of a Merengue, most suitable when playing with a conga player. An optional accent can be played on the snare drum on the last eighth note of the second measure.

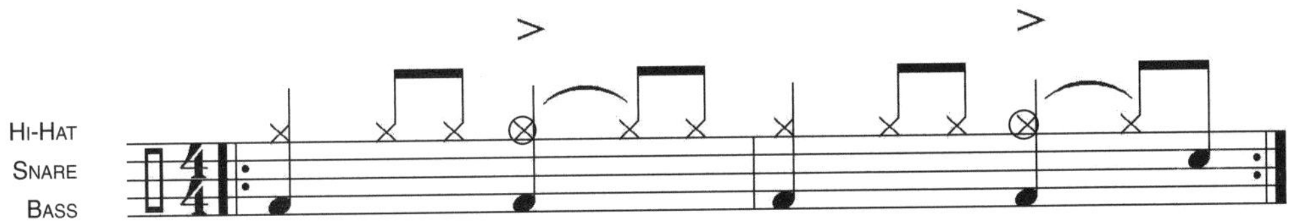

(Circled hi-hat notes are played open)

Variation 2

This is representative of a Merengue subgenre called "Pambiche."

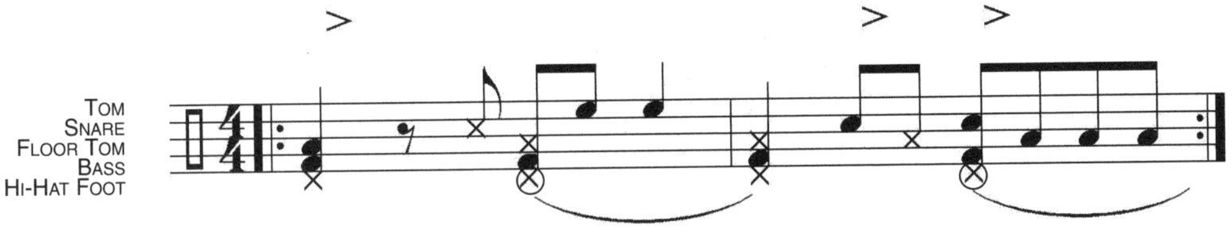

Less Frequently Played Styles

Beguine

First sung in Creole French, the Beguine developed as ballroom music on the islands of Guadeloupe and Martinique. The authentic Beguine found great international success in the late 1940s, though the most famous interpretation of it appeared in 1938 with Artie Shaw's immensely popular rendition of Cole Porter's "Begin the Beguine." The authentic Beguine continued to thrive on the two islands until the 1970s, when Haitian immigrants emphasized their own dance music, which drew attention away from the Beguine.

In addition to the Guadeloupean ballroom Beguine, there is one other primary form of the Beguine: the Martinican drum Beguine, which is more tribal or African-folk oriented than the Guadeloupean Beguine. The more percussive instrumentation of the drum Beguine developed through the slaves and workers on the sugar plantations, while the orchestral Beguine uses the Jazz instrumentation of piano, trombone, clarinet, bass, and drums. The two examples of Beguine below are a commercial version followed by the more authentic rhythm adapted for drum set. **Tempos may range from as slow as quarter note = 112 bpm for ballroom dancing to as bright as quarter note = 280 bpm for the drum Beguine.**

Example 1 (CD 1, Track 40)

This is a Guadeloupean ballroom Beguine pattern for drum set. Played with a combination of rim clicks, standard snare strokes, and the toms, the hands execute a rhythm similar to a wedding Rumba.

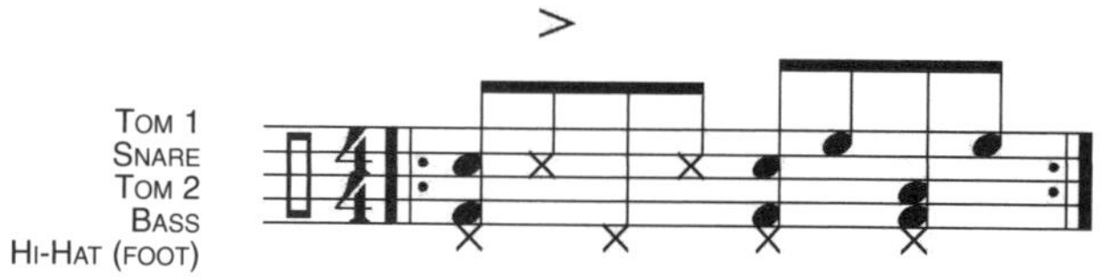

Example 2 (CD 1, Track 41)

This is a Martinican drum Beguine. The hands play a pattern between the snare drum and the floor tom with the same sticking as the second half of the "Baqueteo" pattern, found in the Danzon. When using this sticking, it is necessary to play the snare with the ride hand while the other hand crosses over the top to play the floor tom.

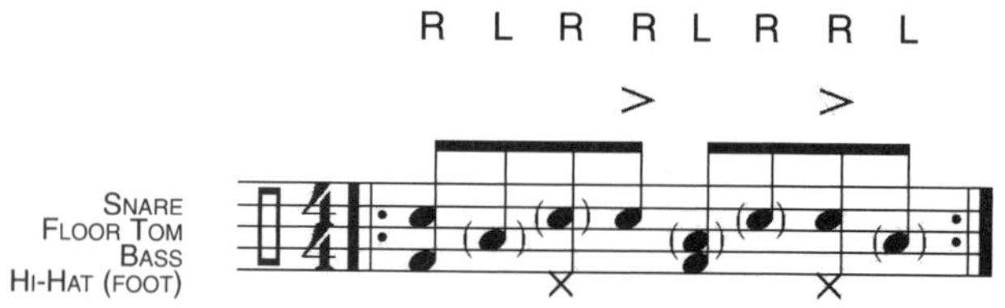

Bolero

The Cuban Bolero dates back over 200 years to Spanish folk dances of love and romance. The term "Bolero" stems from the Spanish verb "Volar," meaning "to fly," exemplified in the elegant moves of the dancers. Around the time that Afro-Cuban musical styles matured, toward the end of the 19th century, Cuban composer Pepe Sanchez composed the first known Cuban Bolero, entitled Tristeza ("Sadness"). By the early 1900s, the immensely popular Bolero reached Mexico and Latin America, eventually gaining recognition in North America by the late 1920s. Additional significant Bolero composers include Guty Cárdenas and Agustin Lara from the early 1900s and, more recently, Jose Feliciano.

Boleros are a ballad style with slow tempos and sentimental lyrics. The signature Bolero rhythm, originally played with a pair of castanets, is now more commonly played by a pair of maracas. Because of this traditional instrumentation, the drum set player has to duplicate the familiar rhythmic sound with sticks, usually playing it on rims and/or hi-hat. **The tempo range is slow at quarter note = 74–120 bpm.**

Example (CD 1, Track 42)

Here, the Bolero rhythm is played on either a tightly closed hi-hat or the rim of a drum.

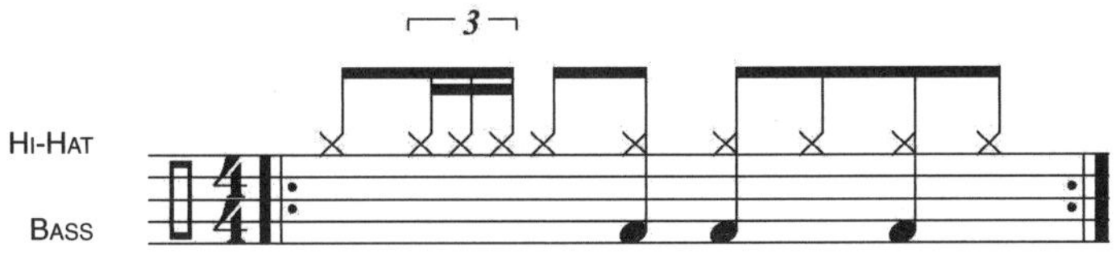

Variation

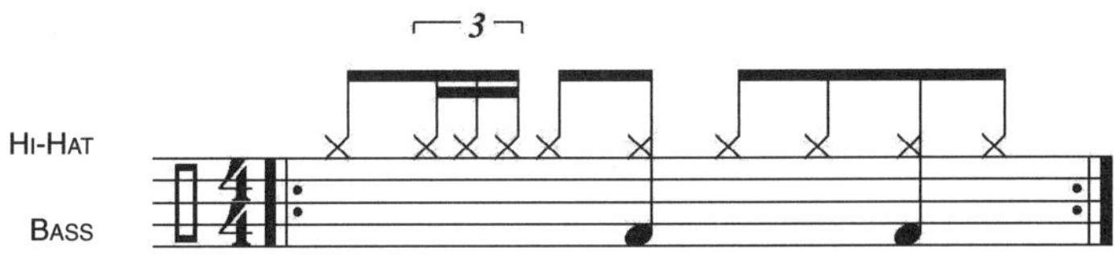

Conga

The Cuban Conga rhythm is played in the "comparsa" ("conga de comparsa"—an ensemble similar in function to the Samba schools of Brazil) during the Cuban carnaval festival. The instrumentation differs depending on whether it's for the Conga Habanera (from Havana) or the Conga Oriental (from Santiago de Cuba, in Oriente Province). Conga Habanera utilizes the requinto, quinto, and conga drums, various-sized bass drums, cowbells, snare drums, trumpets, and frying pans. The Conga Oriental replaces the frying pans with brake drums while also employing the hoe blade, and replaces the traditional trumpet with a corneta china or trompeta china (Chinese coronet or Chinese trumpet). The Conga Habanera features sounds more often found in city life, whereas the Conga Oriental retains a rustic musical character.

Just as the Mozambique is adapted for the drum set from several instruments, the Cuban Conga rhythm for the drum set attempts to encapsulate the rhythms played by many percussionists into the playing of a single individual. Though the rhythmic patterns in the Conga are more numerous than one person can actually play, the following grooves include its most prominent features, capturing its overall feel. **The Conga pattern is played at the very brisk tempo of quarter note = 216–264 bpm.**

EXAMPLE (CD 1, Track 43)

This is a two-measure Conga pattern based on the 2-3 rumba clave rhythm. The ride hand plays a Conga bell pattern between the mouth and body of the cowbell. The snare hand fills in the alternate eighth notes as "ghost notes."

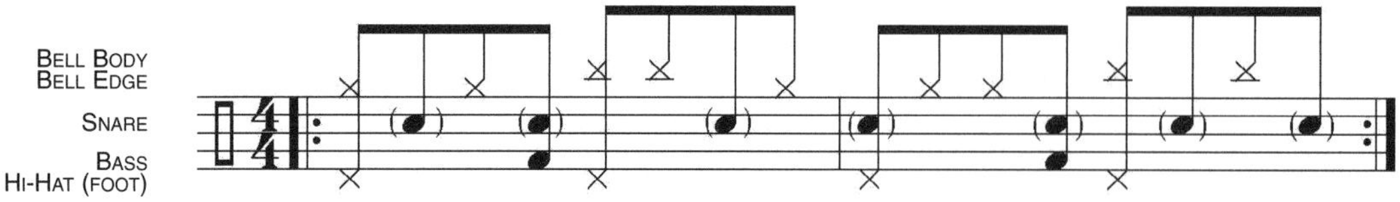

VARIATION 1

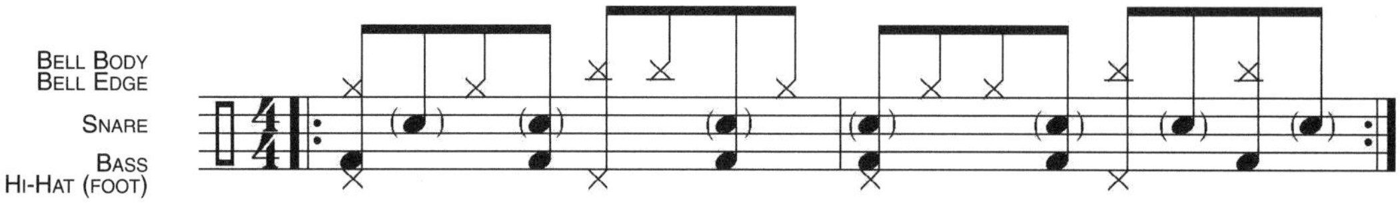

VARIATION 2 (CD 1, Track 44)

This is an authentic march-like rhythm played in the Cuban Comparsa which corresponds to the traditional Cuban Conga pattern. It may be played "in the crack." Refer to the CD for an accurate feel.

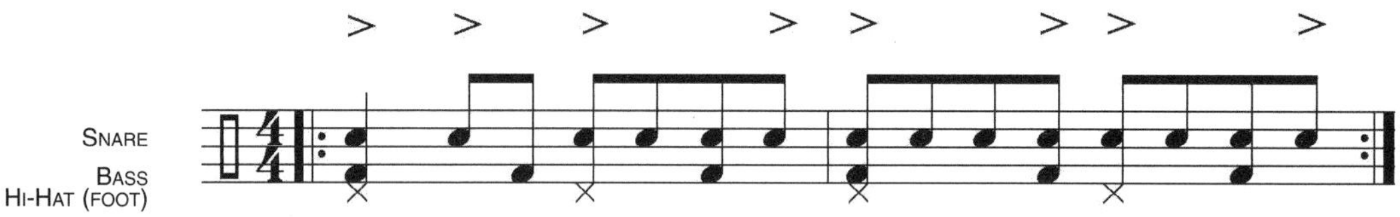

CUMBIA

The Cumbia dates back to the early 1800s and is from the Caribbean coast of Colombia. Its roots can be traced to Gaitero music—folkloric music played on two flutes (indigenous flutes made out of cactus wood), maracas, African hand drums, and other instruments. Similar in evolution to other Afro-Cuban genres, Cumbia developed through the mixing of African slaves and their descendants with local tribes and settlers in the new world.

Rhythmically, Cumbia is characterized by a constant pattern on a high drum, wood block, or bell (seen in the following example) fused with intricate rhythms in the maracas and other hand drums. Over the years, lyrics were added to Cumbia song arrangements, and eventually orchestral and electronic instruments were added. Today, Cumbia is popular throughout North, Central, and South America, and is frequently included in the repertoire of Afro-Cuban ensembles.

The typical Cumbia drum set pattern is characterized by a steady rhythm made up of a quarter note followed by two repeated eighth notes, along with a strong back beat from the snare drum, and a repetitive bass drum pattern usually matching the rhythm of the bass player. Typically, the hi-hat foot accompaniment doubles the snare drum back beat. There is no clave rhythm in the Cumbia style. **The tempo is quick with a double-time feel at quarter note = 160–252 bpm.**

EXAMPLE 1 (CD 1, Track 45)

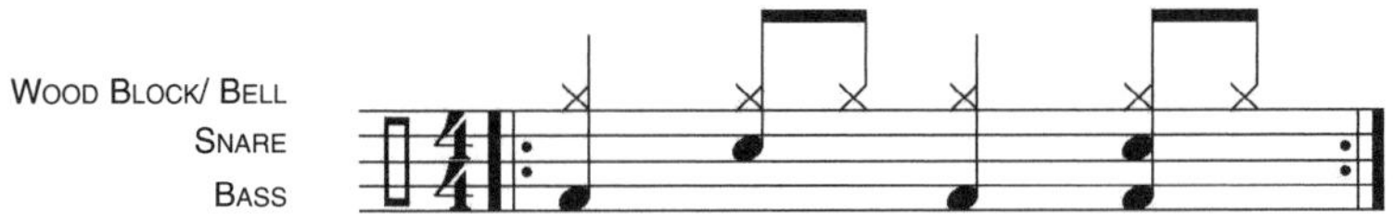

VARIATION 1

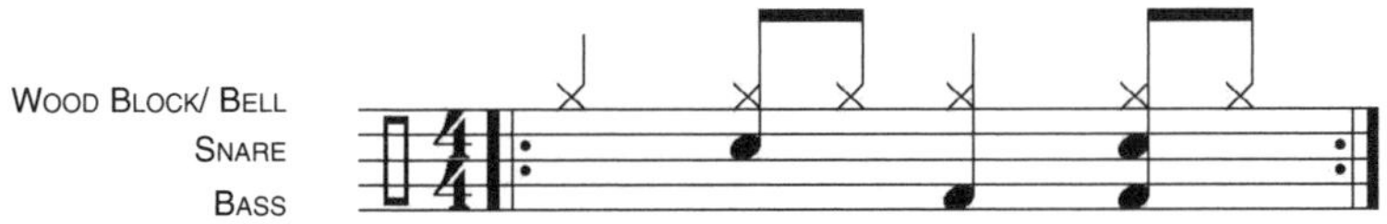

VARIATION 2

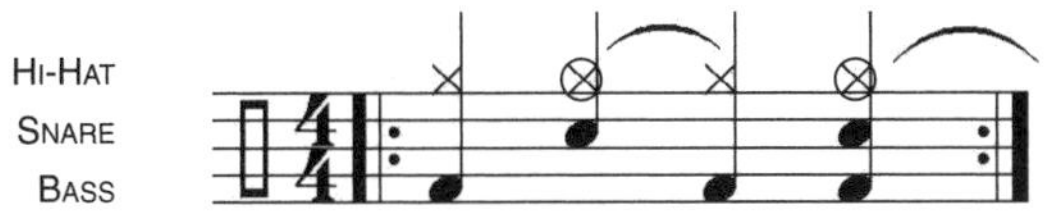

(Circled hi-hat notes are played open)

EXAMPLE 2 (TRADITIONAL CUMBIA)

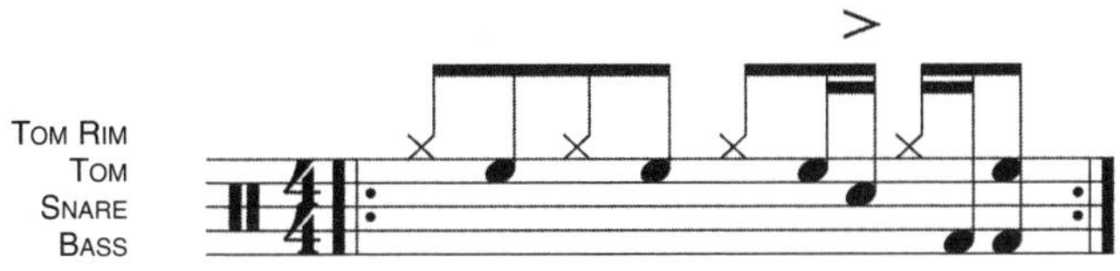

DANZON

Danzon ("Great Dance" or "Grand Dance") arose in the latter part of the 19th century and is the cornerstone of almost all modern Cuban music. Created by Miguel de Failde, the earliest known Danzon ("Las Alturas de Simpson") was performed on New Year's Day in 1879. It developed from the French *contredanse* ("facing dance") which arrived in Cuba between 1790 and 1850 via Haiti and Louisianan immigrants. Similar to an existing Cuban slave dance (couples facing each other in a line), the contradanza found ready acceptance. The normally instrumental contradanza ("San Pascual Bailon" [1803] being the first known example) developed into the "danza," consisting of lyrics, melodies, and intricate rhythms, and eventually into the slower, more relaxed Danzon.

The true Danzon follows this arrangement: the Paseo (prelude), the primary musical theme (played on a flute), the prelude repeated, and a violin section. The addition of the popular Cuban dance music known as Son produced a fourth section, the Mambo (originally called "Nuevo Ritmo"—"New Rhythm"), which introduced improvisation into Cuban music. This new music encouraged the use of the timbales, due to the impossibility of transporting timpani around the island. Finally, the Danzon became the Danzon-cha which led to the Cha Cha. Though it's not played frequently in modern-day ensembles, Danzon characteristics pervade all contemporary Afro-Cuban styles.

Since the timbales were the original percussion instrument used in Danzon and preceded the invention of the drum set, the appropriate method to recreate the timbale sound on a drum set is to play the snare drum with the snares off. The Danzon style requires a meticulous combination of a snare drum rim click, finger tapping, and the striking of the drum with a stick. The following grooves can be effectively interchanged with a Cha Cha or Bolero as a result of the slow tempo of all three styles. **Quarter note = 110 bpm.**

Example (CD 1, Track 46)

This is based on the 2-3 son clave rhythm utilizing a two-measure hand pattern known as a "Baqueteo." The ride hand plays a pattern on the snare drum (with snares off to mimic a timbale) while the snare hand utilizes fingers along with a cross stick to fill in the alternate eighth notes.

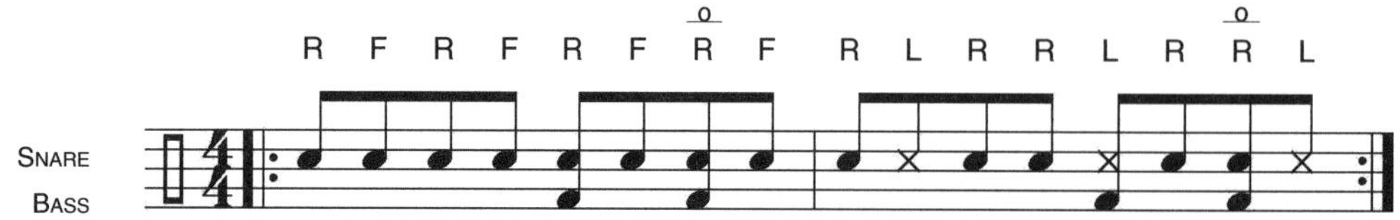

Variation

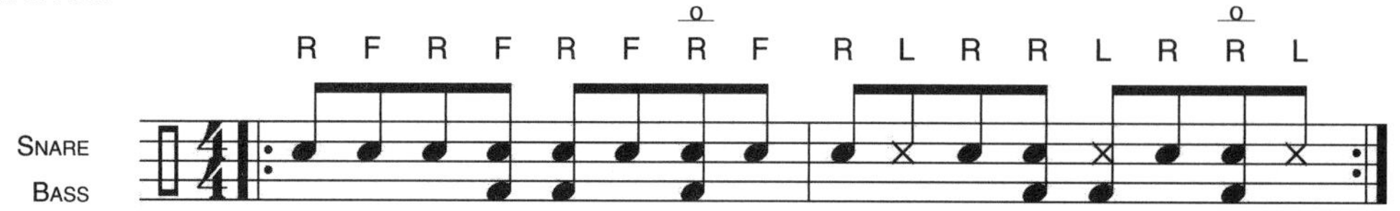

NOTE: Hi-hat foot accompaniment on either all four quarter notes or beats 2 & 4 is appropriate. However, the most traditional way of playing would not include hi-hat foot accompaniment. The "o"s indicate an open, unmuted snare drum tone.

Palito

Palito ("Little Stick") is not a style of music, rather, it is an Afro-Cuban rhythm that was the inspiration for the Cascara pattern (see "Cascara" on pages 14 & 15). The Palito rhythm was originally played on an instrument entitled the gua gua—a hollowed-out piece of bamboo—and was played in Rumbas or during Rumba sections. Currently, the pattern is commonly played on an assortment of surfaces such as the shell of the timbales, different bells, or various pieces of wood, and the rims of hand drums or the drum set.

The Palito pattern originated on percussion instruments only to later find its way to the drum set. It is a two-measure pattern which complements specific sides of the clave. Though it may be played with a 3-2 or a 2-3 clave (rumba or son), the position of the clave remains constant with the notes of the Palito pattern. **This pattern can be played in a wide variety of tempos, ranging from slower feels of quarter note = 120 bpm to brighter tempos of quarter note = 264 bpm.**

Example (CD 1, Track 47)

The Palito pattern is played with two hands between a closed hi-hat and a snare drum rim click. The bass drum plays the Tumbao pattern in both measures. This example is based on a 2-3 rumba clave.

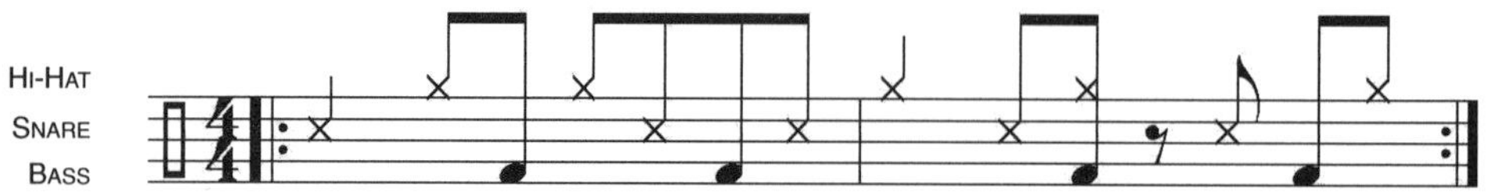

Variation 1

For slower tempos, the ride hand plays the Palito pattern on a closed hi-hat, while the snare hand fills in the eighth notes with a snare drum rim click. The bass drum plays the Bombo note on the "3" side of the clave in the second measure, which falls on the + of beat 2.

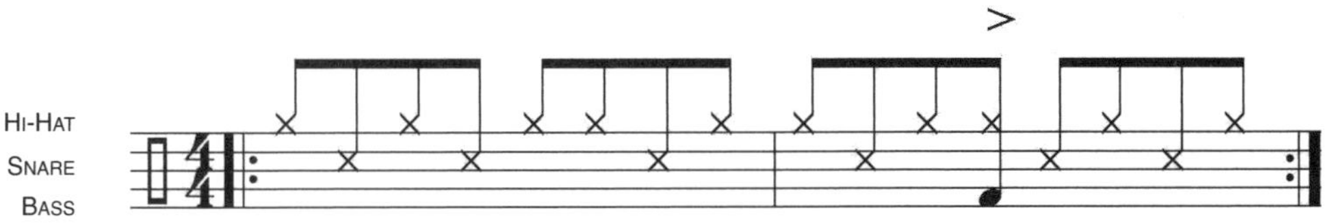

Variation 2 (CD 1, Track 48)

This has the same hand pattern as in variation 1, but integrates the Tumbao bass drum pattern in both measures.

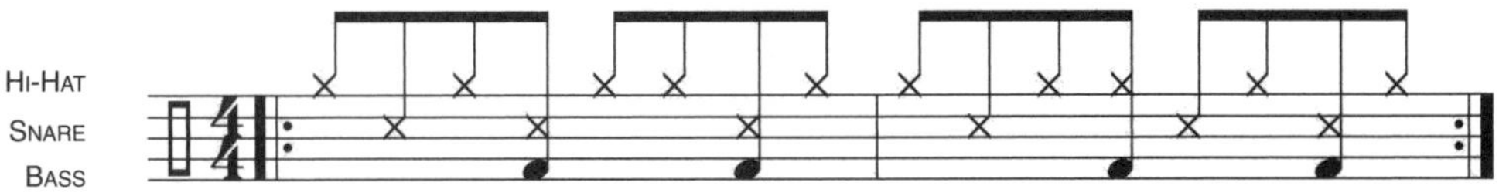

Pilon

Pilon was pioneered in the 1970s in the eastern part of Cuba, most notably by the group Los Bocucos. Its steady rhythm is influenced by the sound of workers pounding coffee beans. Much like the Mambo or the Guaguanco, this two-measure Afro-Cuban pattern has both a signature conga pattern and also a signature timbale melody. When adapted to the drum set, the snare hand commonly plays the timbale pattern while the feet and ride hand play repetitive patterns. The drum set pattern itself has similarities to Cumbia, though the roots of the two styles are not related. The pattern is based on a 2-3 son clave rhythm (not usually played by a drum set player). **The tempo is quarter note = 172–224 bpm.**

Example (CD 1, Track 49)

This has a repetitive ride hand pattern played on either a cowbell or rim of a drum while the snare hand plays the timbale melody on the toms, with snare drum rim clicks, and the feet play half notes simultaneously to augment the steady feel of the pattern.

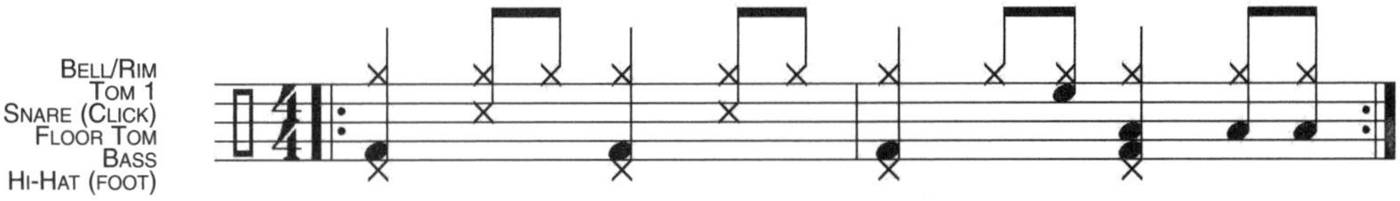

VARIATION

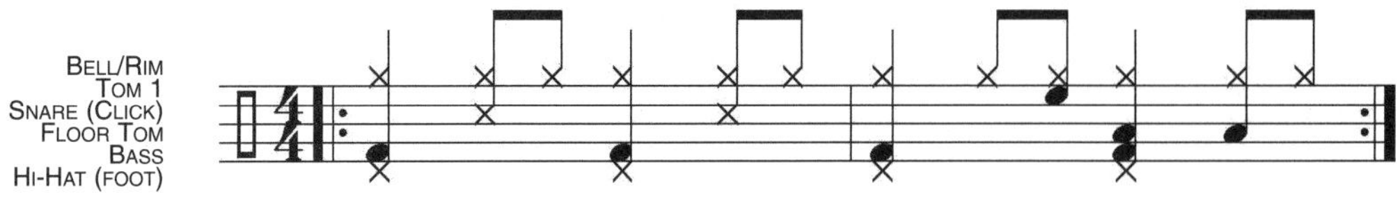

PLENA

Plena ("full") blossomed in Puerto Rico during the latter part of the 1880s, most notably in and around the city of Ponce. Much like Bomba (Puerto Rico's most popular musical style), Plena's roots are in the slaves, sugar cane laborers, farmers and others who migrated to the urban areas of Puerto Rico. The style incorporates characteristics of many cultures, including West African, Spanish, Cuban, and even European. Plena is often referred to as "el periodico cantado" ("the sung newspaper") because its lyrical content reflects local daily news and gossip, and regional historical events.

The genre is a dance-related style which has gained popularity throughout Central America. Many instruments have contributed to the sound of Plena: percussion instruments such as congas, timbales, maracas, guiros, and panderos (similar to a small tambourine minus the metal jingles), as well as the accordion, the cuatro (4-stringed guitar), and, often, large orchestras all contributed to the sound of Plena. Though not an original Afro-Cuban style, Plena influences and sections are frequently found in contemporary Afro-Cuban arrangements. Joselino "Bumbum" Oppenheimer is "the father of Plena," while composer Gary Nuñez and bands such as Los Pleneros de la 21 and Los Pleneros del Batey have contributed to the development of this style.

Though there is no standard drum set rhythm for Plena, the example and variation below are accurate representations of Plena rhythms. A strong characteristic is the simple, quarter-note bass drum pattern found in both the example and variation. The example is appropriate when playing without a conga player. The variation (Soca) is best used when a conga player is present. Notice that the Soca rhythm is only one bar long, and is counted and felt in a medium 4/4 pulse, which takes the same time as playing two bars of a Plena rhythm. Though it's a two-measure pattern, the clave rhythm is not usually played in Plena. **The tempo range is usually swift at quarter note = 208–276 bpm.**

EXAMPLE (CD 1, Track 50)

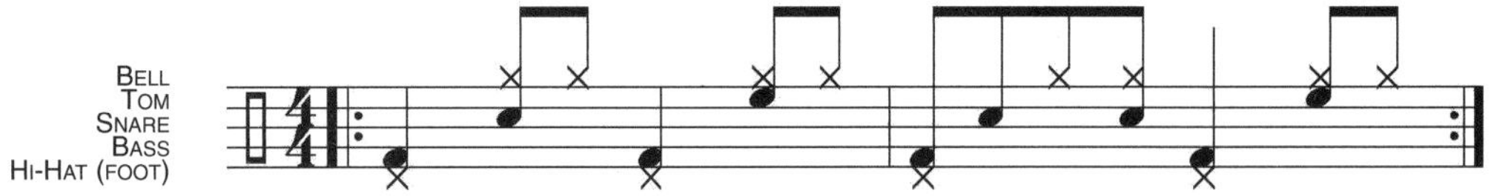

VARIATION (CD 1, Track 87)

This variation is a standard Soca rhythm for drum set (see Soca in the Caribbean chapter). The steadiness of the bass drum mixed with the syncopated accents from the snare drum are appropriate for the Plena style.

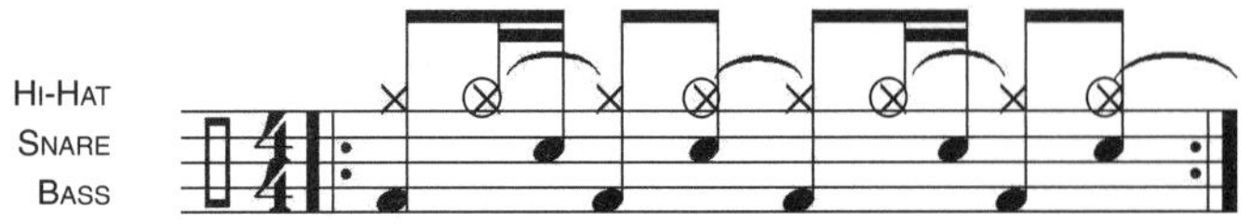

(Circled hi-hat notes are played open)

4 Blues

In the post-Civil War United States, a mixture of field hollers, spirituals, and dance music gave birth to the Blues. By the early 20th century, Blues had emerged as its own genre. However, it was a classically trained musician who first brought Blues to worldwide attention. In 1903, W.C. Handy was waiting for a train in Mississippi and heard a Blues musician. He later called the style "the weirdest music I ever heard." Despite his first impression, Handy was inspired to compose his own Blues songs, most notably "Memphis Blues" and his immensely popular "St. Louis Blues."

Blues' infectious spirit is exemplified through many songs and legendary stories. For instance, upon hearing "Good Night Irene," the governor of Louisiana was so moved that he granted the song writer, convicted murderer Huddy "Leadbelly" Ledbetter, a full pardon. In the 1930s, guitarist/vocalist/songwriter Robert Johnson brought Blues to a higher level of recognition through his recordings for Columbia Records. At about the same time, musicologist Alan Lomax traveled through the southern United States recording a huge amount of Blues music for the Smithsonian Institution. Lomax's work and the popularity of Johnson and other Blues artists, especially Bessy Smith (also recorded by Columbia), brought Blues to national popularity. At this time, Blues was still an acoustic form played by individual guitarists/vocalists (or sometimes piano and vocalist) and occasionally small ensembles utilizing guitar and percussion instruments such as washboard, spoons, and even the musician's own body ("hambone") rather than the drum set.

The Blues changed greatly in the 1940s. Prior to that decade, Blues had been an almost exclusively acoustic music. But in the post-war period, Chicago-based Blues artists such as Muddy Waters, Howlin' Wolf, Elmore James and Willie Dixon, and the West Coast-based T-Bone Walker, began playing "electric" Blues featuring the electric guitar, amplified vocals, bass (still upright bass at the time), and the drum set. By this time, Blues had matured to its standard 12-bar form (4 bars of the I chord, 2 bars IV, 2 bars I, 1 bar V, 1 bar IV, 2 bars I, played in 4/4 swung time) in which the vocal melody and lyrics were organized in an A-A-B structure. A well known song that exemplifies these characteristics is "T-Bone Shuffle," by T-Bone Walker, which has been recorded by innumerable artists. (Of course, there are many Blues songs in nonstandard forms; to cite but one example from this general period, Floyd Dixon's famous "Hey Bartender" is a 16-bar Blues [featuring 8 bars of the I chord at the beginning of the pattern].)

At about the same time, a fusion took place between Swing and Blues, resulting in Jump Blues, which included horns and never strayed from swung time. The most prominent exponents of this enormously popular style were Louis Jordan, Junior Parker, and T-Bone Walker.

By the mid-1950s, Rock n' Roll (which is usually played with straight eighth notes, rather than swung) had begun to achieve mass popularity, and Blues artists such as Chuck Berry and Bo Diddley began to explore the straight feel (while keeping the 12-bar form). An example is Chuck Berry's famous "Johnny B. Goode" (which is also nonstandard in that the V chord at the 9th bar "hangs" rather than descends to the IV at the 10th bar).

In the 1960s, white musicians and bands (especially in England) such as John Mayall, Eric Clapton, Savoy Brown, The Rolling Stones, and (in the U.S.) Paul Butterfield began playing the Blues. Ironically, they had much greater success than the African-American musicians who had pioneered the form. But they did bring Blues to a far wider audience than it had ever had, and some of the established African-American Blues players benefited from this in the form of recording contracts and concert gigs.

With the death of Jimi Hendrix in 1971 and the end of the late-1960s/early-1970s cultural upheaval—despite the arrival of a few exciting new Blues performers such as Son Seals—Blues lost much of its audience. And with the rise of Disco and Punk, it appeared all but dead by the end of the 1970s.

However, in the mid-1980s Stevie Ray Vaughan, with his blistering electric Blues and guitar virtuosity, almost single-handedly brought Blues to greater popularity than ever before. At the same time, Robert Cray resurrected and modernized West Coast Blues, updating the style popularized by T-Bone Walker in the 1940s and 1950s. Despite the death of Vaughan in 1990, Blues has retained its popularity and continues to feature the guitar as its primary instrument. Prominent current guitarists include Coco Montoya, Keb Mo, Susan Tedeschi, Sue Foley, John Mayer, Joe Bonamassa, Debbie Davies, and the lesser known but virtuousic Willie Edwards.

NOTE: The rhythm in standard Blues tunes is always swung, unless otherwise noted. However, shuffles and other Blues patterns are often written as if they're in straight time, that is, with straight eighths on the hi-hat or ride rather than a triplet pattern. (It's a dubious practice, but it's common.) To facilitate ease of understanding, all of the shuffle patterns here are written in 4/4 with a shuffled triplet pattern (eighth-note triplets with a rest between the first and third notes) in the ride hand.

Standard Blues Shuffle

The Shuffle is almost certainly the most common Blues groove. It's a swung pattern characterized by the ride hand's playing the first and third eighth-note triplets of every triplet grouping on every beat in a measure. The downbeats are usually accented louder than the off beats. In addition, the snare drum is played with a strong back beat on 2 & 4, and of course the bass drum (as in almost all styles of music) should be played with conviction. **The tempo of the Blues Shuffle covers a large range of quarter note = 80–160 bpm.**

Example (CD 1, Track 51)

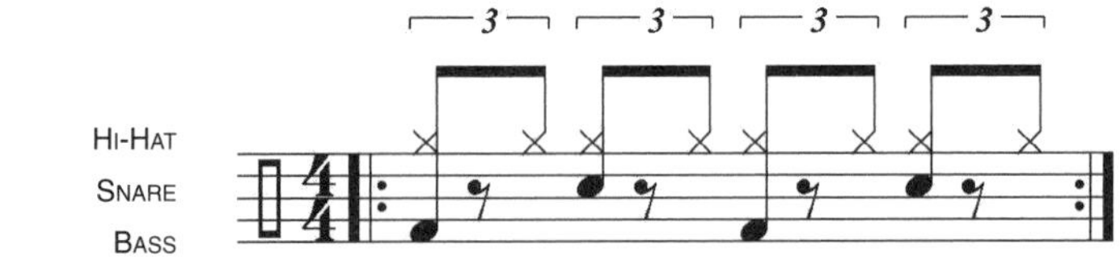

Variation 1

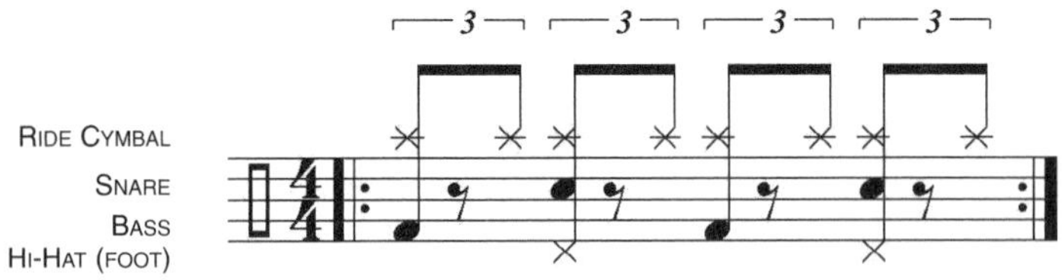

Variation 2

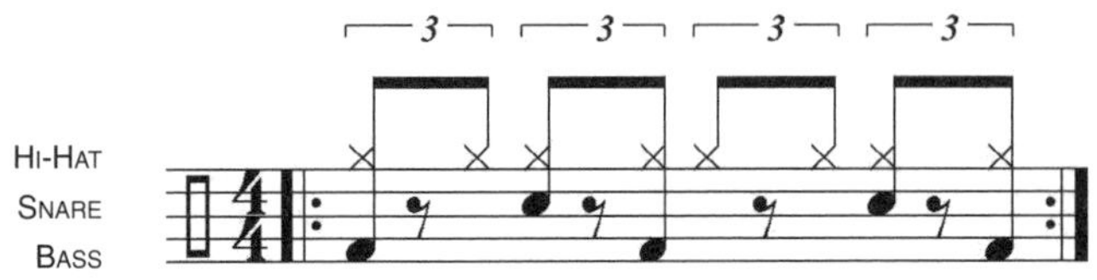

VARIATION 3 (CD 1, Track 52)

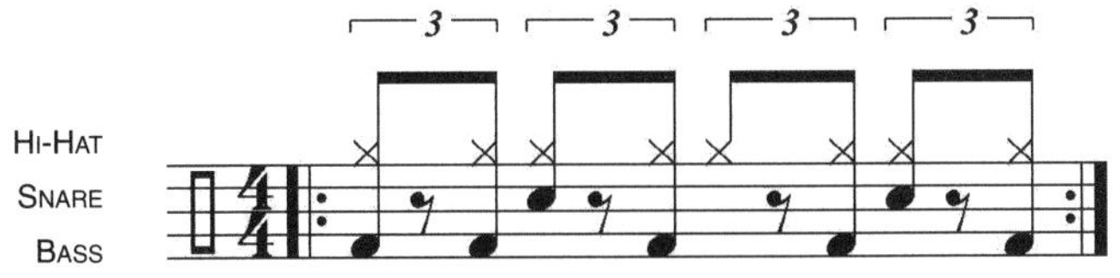

VARIATION 4

This variation generally will sound best during the more dynamic sections of songs or during entire songs that call for high volume.

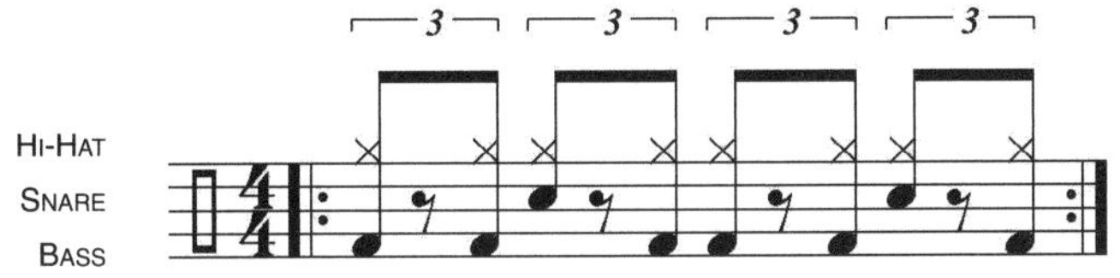

VARIATION 5

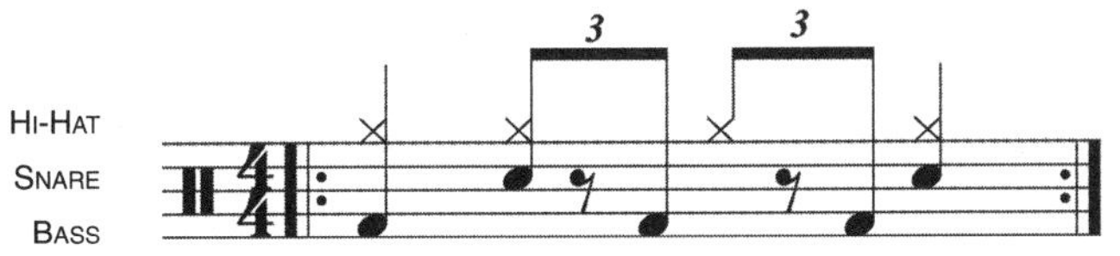

NOTE: Any of the above patterns can be played with the ride hand pattern moved to the ride cymbal and the hi-hat foot on beats 2 & 4. Another practical hi-hat foot pattern is to play all four quarter notes.

CHICAGO SHUFFLE (JAZZ SHUFFLE)

The Chicago Shuffle, also known as the Two-Handed Shuffle, is identical to the Jazz Shuffle with the name corresponding to the style in which it's played ("Chicago Shuffle" for Blues, "Jazz Shuffle" for Jazz). The Chicago Shuffle is one of the earlier shuffle feels, stemming from a combination of Blues and Swing. Having a bigger sound, this style is most practical in a large Blues band (i.e., with horn section) or Big Band setting, but can be used in smaller bands (both Blues and Jazz) during the climactic sections of songs. The execution and timing of the unison hand pattern is the defining element of the groove. **The tempo of the Chicago Shuffle also covers a large range at quarter note = 80–160 bpm.**

EXAMPLE (CD 1, Track 53)

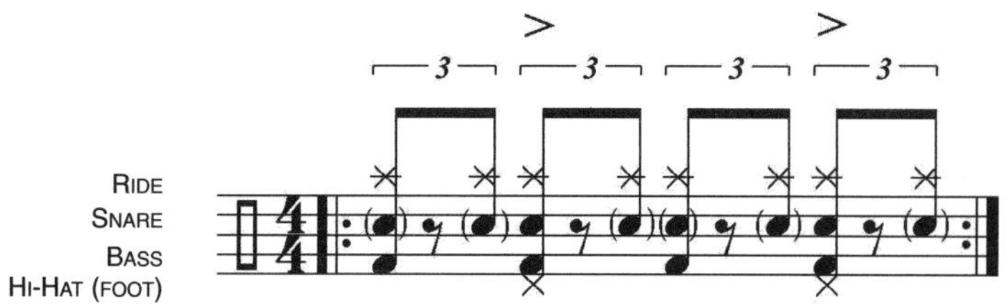

VARIATION 1

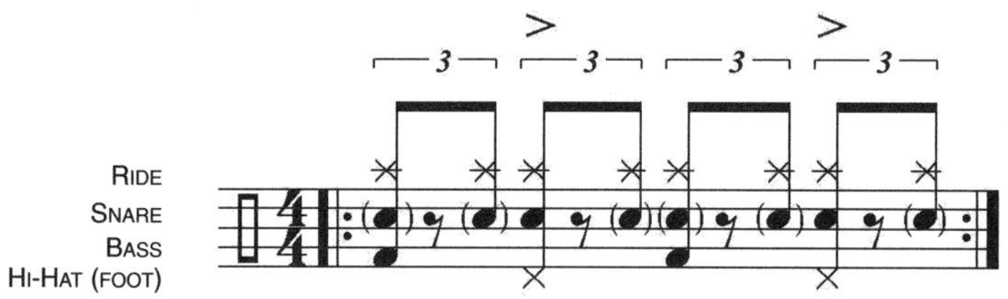

VARIATION 2 (CD 1, Track 54)

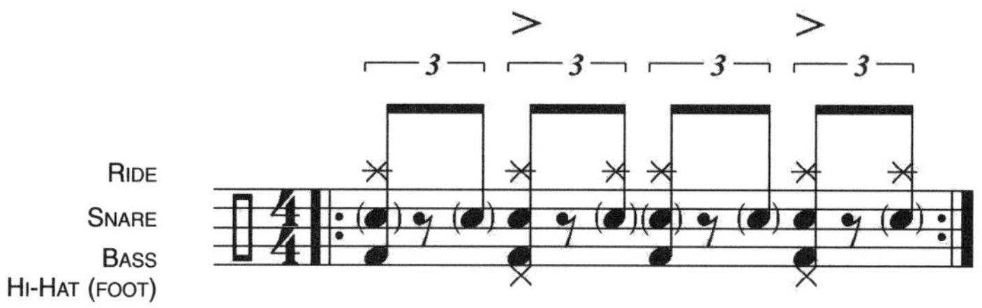

VARIATION 3

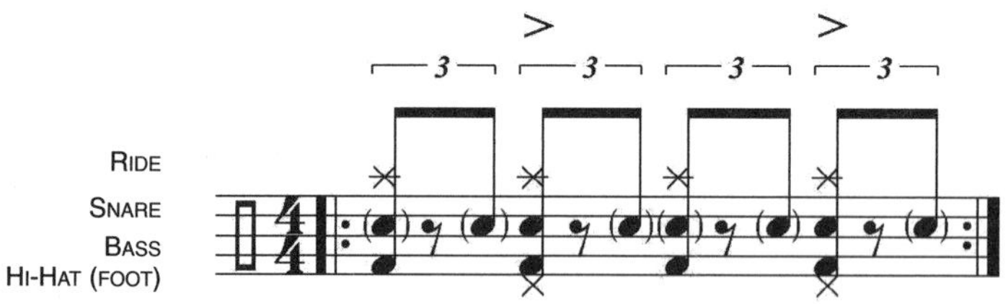

NOTE: Another practical hi-hat foot pattern is to play all four quarter notes.

Backdoor Shuffle

Another useful groove in the Blues genre is the Backdoor Shuffle (sometimes called the "Upbeat Shuffle"). Its predominant characteristic—and the only thing that distinguishes it from the Chicago Shuffle—is the repetitive snare drum note on the last triplet of each beat. A good example of this feel is found in "Midnight Stroll" by Robert Cray (with drummer Kevin Hayes). Just as in the Standard Blues Shuffle, the ride hand pattern can be moved to the ride cymbal with the hi-hat foot on beats 2 & 4. Another practical hi-hat foot pattern is to play all four quarter notes. **The tempo is similar to that of other Blues Shuffles at quarter note = 80–160 bpm.**

Example (CD 1, Track 55)

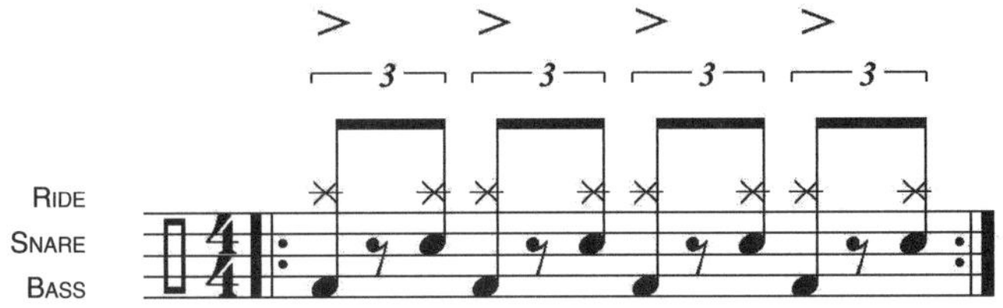

Variation (CD 1, Track 56)

This variation featuring all triplets in the ride hand is most useful as a slower groove.

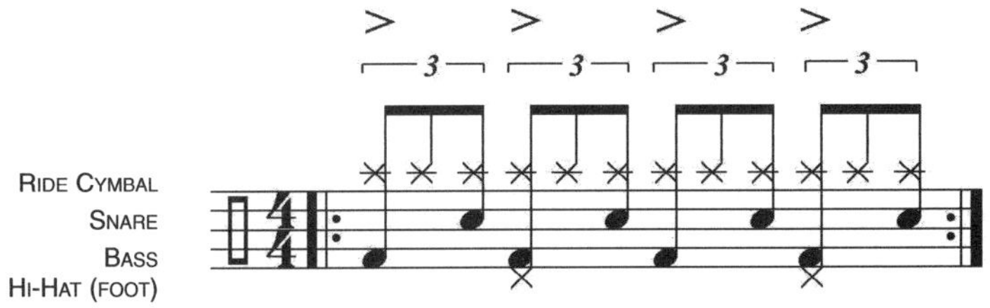

Backbeat Shuffle

The Backbeat Shuffle (which apparently originated in East Texas) is still another useful Blues groove. Its predominant characteristic—and the only thing that distinguishes it from the Chicago Shuffle—is the omission of the bass drum notes on beats 1 & 3. This creates a laid back feel suitable for slower, "loping" songs. A good example of such a tune is Doug Sahm's version of "Honky Tonk" (George Rains, drums). **The tempo range of the Backbeat Shuffle is narrower than that of other Blues shuffles at quarter note = 80–120 bpm.**

Example

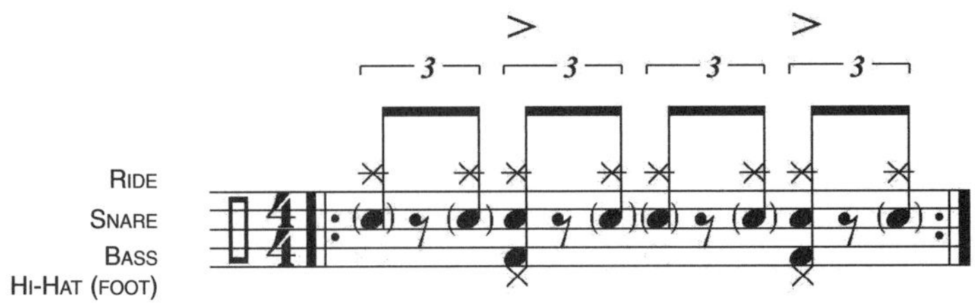

Texas Shuffle

In the late 1950s and early 1960s, Texas R&B became very popular. It is strongly associated with guitarists such as T-Bone Walker, Albert Collins, and Freddie King. The Texas Shuffle is the predominant groove in this style, which is characterized by extremely tight but laid back grooves. Stevie Ray Vaughan's "Cold Shot" and "Pride and Joy" (drummer Chris Layton) provide good examples of this groove.

Its defining characteristic is the ghost note pattern on the snare drum accompanied by either quarter notes or the Jazz ride pattern on the ride cymbal. A strong "four on the floor" pulse on the bass drum and a 2 & 4 pulse on the hi-hat is common in Texas Shuffles. **The tempo range is the same as with other shuffles, at quarter note = 80–160 bpm.**

Example

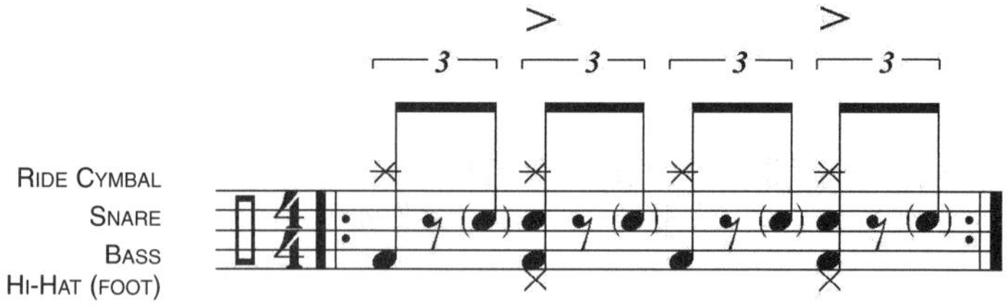

Variation

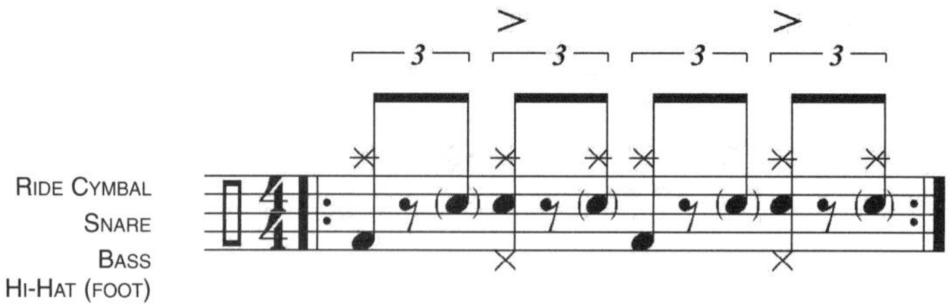

Purdie Shuffle (Ghost Note Shuffle)

This pattern is attributed to Bernard Purdie, an innovative contemporary drummer who combines Blues with Funk. The use of ghost notes and a half-time feel characterize the pattern. Lightly played on the snare drum, the ghost notes blend in well with the sound of the hi-hat, filling out the triplets around the back beat of the snare. Notice that the Purdie shuffle is exactly the same as variation 4 of the Standard Blues Shuffle (earlier in this chapter) with the addition of ghost notes in the snare hand. Generally, the Purdie Shuffle is most practical in a syncopated and/or busy Blues setting. **The tempo of the Purdie Shuffle is quarter note = 100–160 bpm.**

EXAMPLE (CD 1, Track 62)

Ghost notes are played on the second triplet of each beat. Remember to keep ghost notes very subtle.

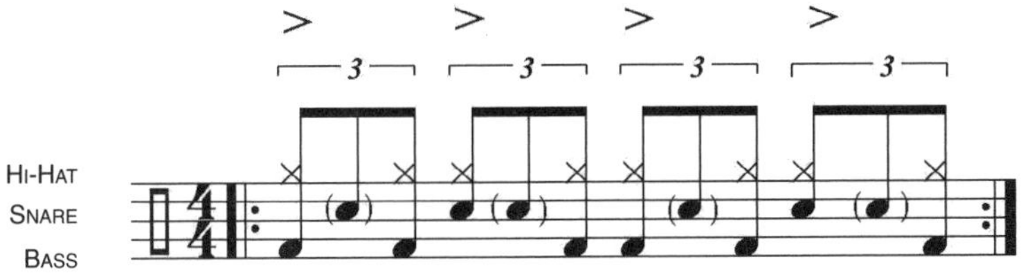

VARIATION (CD 1, Track 63)

Variations of this groove can be found in "Babylon Sisters" and “Home At Last” by Steely Dan (with Bernard Purdie on drums). “Rosanna” by Toto (with drummer Jeff Porcaro), and “Fool In The Rain” by Led Zeppelin (with drummer John Bonham).

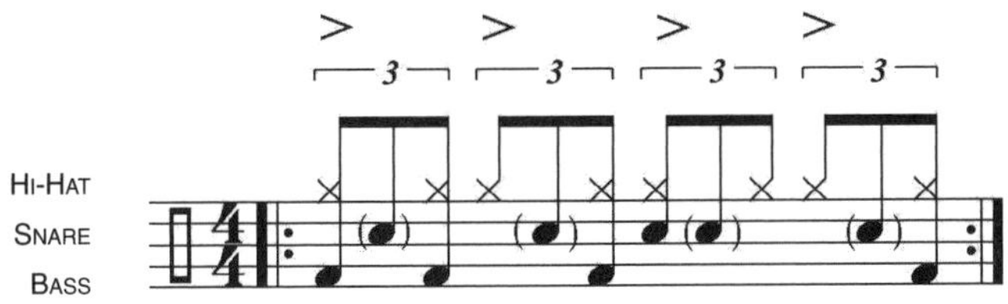

12/8 (SLOW BLUES) PATTERNS

Though usually written in 4/4, slow Blues patterns are felt in 12/8, with all 12 eighth notes played. This pattern's greatest application is (obviously) in slow Blues, but it can also be played at a medium tempo depending on a drummer's hand speed. Once again, it is important to play a strong back beat on beats 2 & 4 with the snare hand and less prominent accents on beats 1 & 3 with the kick foot. **The tempo range for a 12/8 Blues is fairly narrow at quarter note = 50–80 bpm.**

EXAMPLE (CD 1, Track 57)

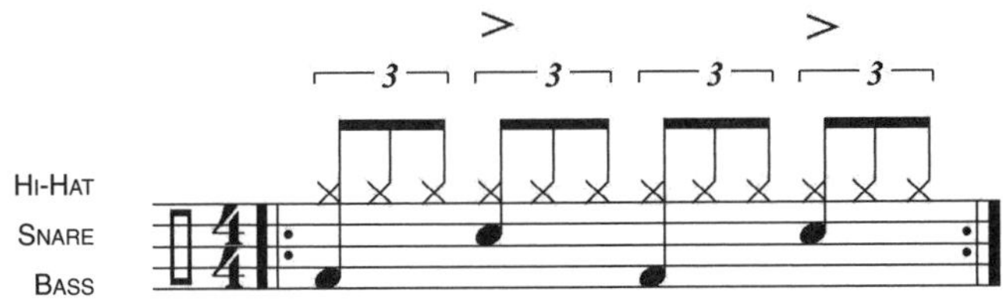

VARIATION 1 (CD 1, Track 58)

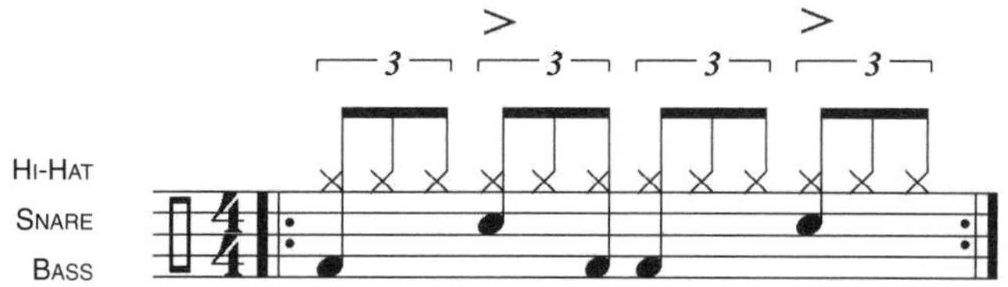

VARIATION 2 (CD 1, Track 59)

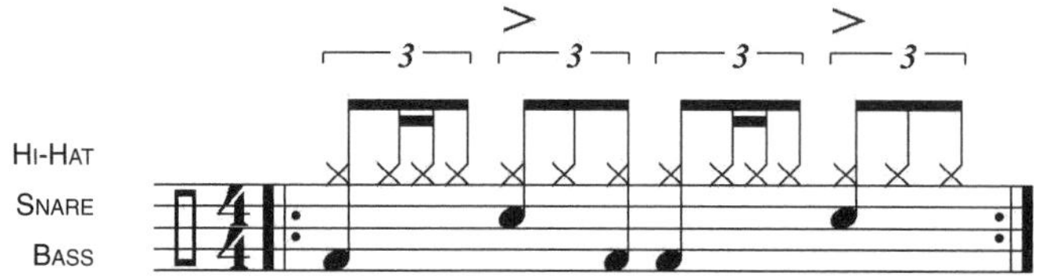

VARIATION 3

This variation is more easily read in 12/8 than 4/4. It's played exactly the same way as it would be if written in 4/4 with 16th-note sextuplet groupings.

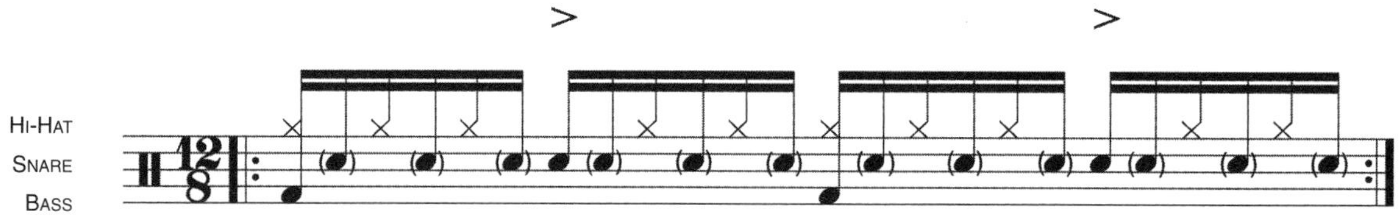

NOTES: 1) The most common way to play variation 2 is to swing the 16th note triplets in the ride hand pattern. However, it's also practical to play the notes straight. 2) Each pattern above can incorporate the use of a snare drum rim click in place of a standard back beat during softer sections of songs. In addition, a large number of bass drum/ride hand variations are possible while usually avoiding beats 2 & 4 on the bass drum. Each of the above patterns can be played with the hi-hat pattern moved over to the ride cymbal, with the hi-hat foot accompanying the snare hand on beats 2 & 4.

STRAIGHT BLUES/ROCK GROOVE

Blues may also be played with a straight feel. This is usually defined by straight eighth notes in the ride hand, played on the hi-hat or ride cymbal. (The snare and bass drums are also played straight.) Though a straight feel is less common than a swung feel in Blues, it is important for a drummer to be well versed in both. **The tempo of straight Blues grooves covers a large range of quarter note = 80–160 bpm.**

EXAMPLE (CD 2, Track 80)

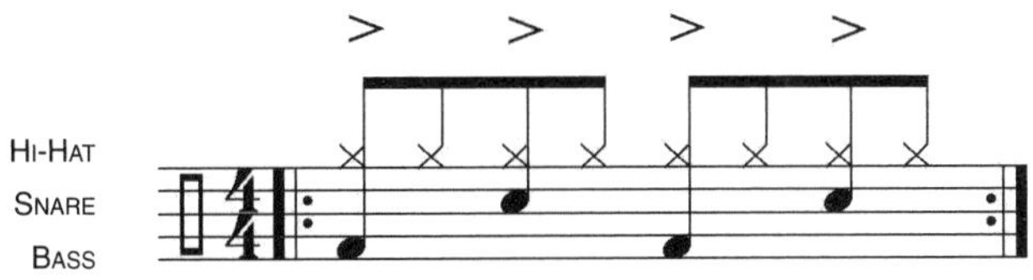

VARIATION 1 (CD 2, Track 81)

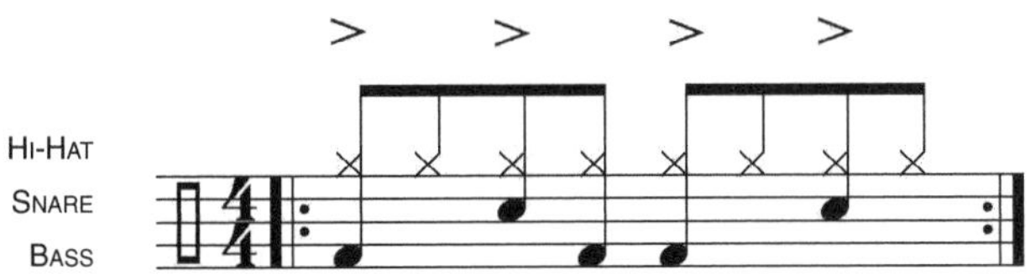

VARIATION 2

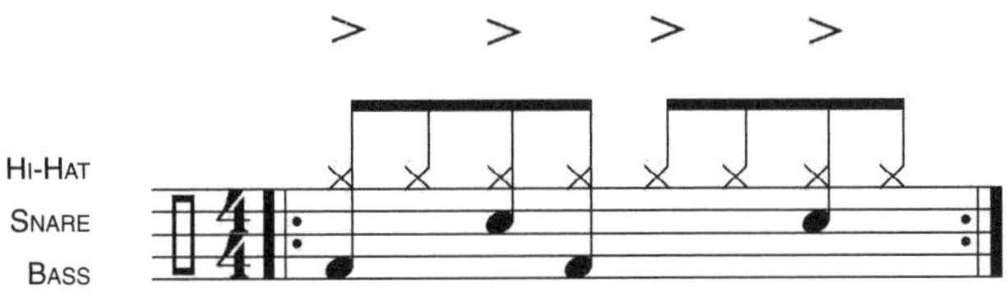

VARIATION 3

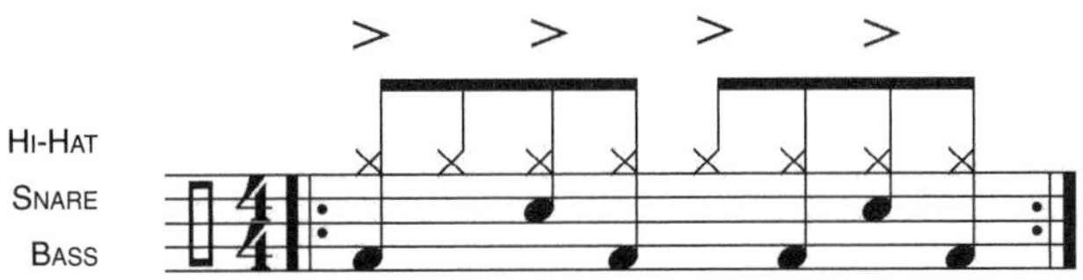

VARIATION 4 (CD 1, Track 60)

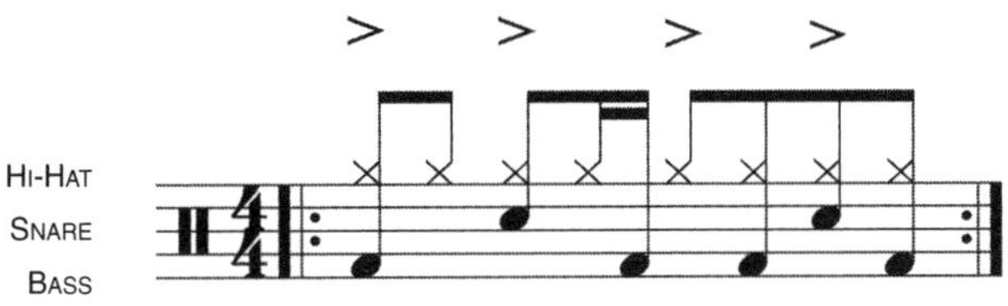

VARIATION 5 (CD 1, Track 61)

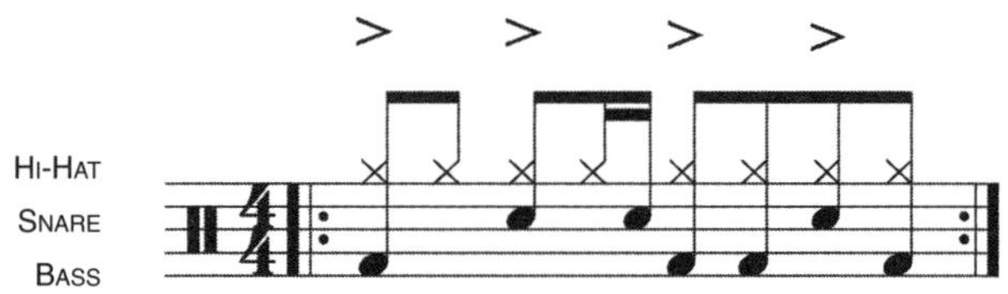

NOTE: For more straight Blues/Rock variations, see the Standard Rock section of the Rock n' Roll chapter. As with the shuffles, the ride pattern can be moved onto the ride cymbal with the hi-hat foot doubling the snare hand on beats 2 & 4.

BLUES RUMBA

Sometimes referred to as the "Blues Mambo," the Blues Rumba utilizes a Cuban-style groove in a Blues setting. The groove itself closely resembles the Wedding Rumba (see Wedding Dances chapter) and contains elements of the Cuban Bolero (see Afro-Cuban chapter). **The tempo range is quarter note = 108–160 bpm.**

EXAMPLE (CD 1, Track 64)

This has a "four on the floor" bass drum pattern. Alternate sticking is the most practical choice.

VARIATION 1 (CD 1, Track 65)

Similar to the main example, this variation employs the same hand pattern but has a syncopated bass drum pattern on beats 1, the + of beat 2 and beat 4. Alternate sticking is again the most practical choice.

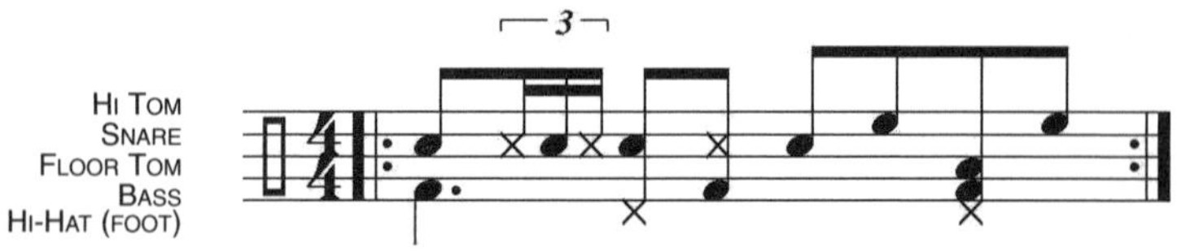

Variation 2

Featuring a slightly different hand pattern than the initial example, this variation is found in Albert King's popular "Crosscut Saw."

NOTES: 1) The Blues Rumba is practical with the snares on or off. 2) The indicated sticking should be reversed by left-handed drummers.

Blues Mambo

Though the Blues Rumba is often referred to as a Blues Mambo, there is a more specific Blues Mambo pattern. It has a double-time feel and closely resembles the traditional Cuban Mambo. The Blues Mambo is a tasteful and sensible choice when a song calls for a syncopated Latin feel, but is played at a fast tempo (which could cause difficulty in playing the Blues Rumba pattern, and make it sound cluttered). A good example of a Blues Mambo is "One Way Out," by Sonny Boy Williamson. The song was covered by the Allman Brothers, using a different Blues Mambo pattern. **The tempo range is quarter note = 180–220 bpm.**

Example

This is very similar to the Cuban Mambo pattern. (See Afro-Cuban chapter.) It shares the mambo bell pattern with the Cuban Mambo, but uses snare drum strokes, rather than cross sticking, and a slightly varied bass drum pattern. The presence of the hi-hat on beats 2 & 4 differentiates the Blues Mambo from the Latin Rock Mambo (which is also used in Acid Jazz).

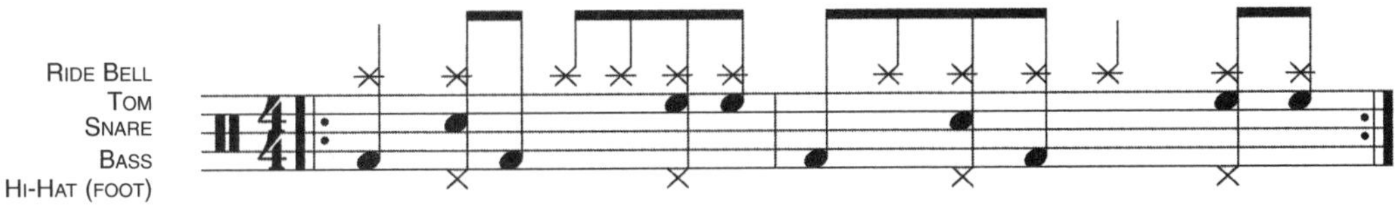

Variation 1

This variation uses a Cascara bell pattern on the ride cymbal bell or cowbell. (The cowbell can be substituted for the ride.)

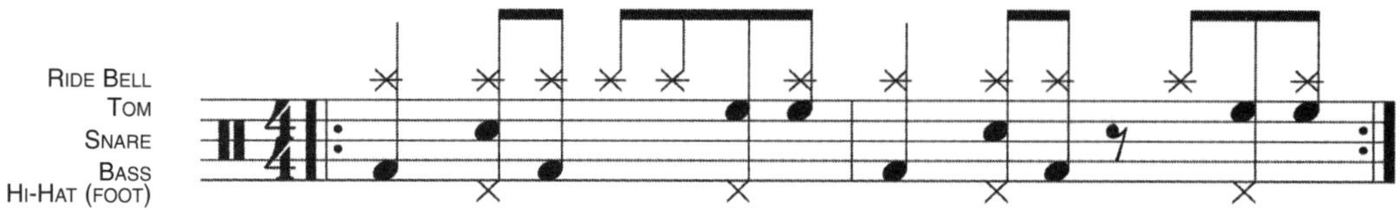

5 BRAZILIAN

IT IS IMPORTANT NOT TO CONFUSE Brazilian with Afro-Cuban drumming. Each has its own distinct characteristics and specific rhythms, and it is important to know what type of rhythmic patterns to play when a song is classified as "Latin." By becoming familiar with the various grooves in this and the Afro-Cuban chapter, a drummer will be able to recognize and play appropriate grooves in almost any Latin style.

The roots of Brazilian music can be traced back over 400 years to when Brazil was a Portuguese colony. To manage the abundant slave population, the government supported the rule of slave kings and queens in each tribe. Their coronation ceremonies and celebrations became known as the "Maracatu." With the abolition of slavery and the end of slave royalty, Maracatu emerged as the musical ensemble and dance for street celebrations in the northeastern Brazilian state of Pernambuco. The festivals evolved to include dancers and a "bateria" (percussion battery). This legacy continues today as Brazilian music is often performed in the tradition of the Maracatu (with instruments such as ago-go bells, repinique, and surdo drums).

With the incorporation of the drum set into Brazilian music, the percussion role often falls on a single player. To approximate the variety of instruments in a bateria, a single drum set player must incorporate the various rhythms of the percussion section. Celebrated Brazilian percussionists/drummers include Airto Moreira, Duduka da Fonseca, Edu Ribeiro, Rafael Barata, Marcio Bahia, Alex Buck, Kiko Freitas, Celso de Almeida. Prominent educators include Adriano Santos, Henrique de Almedia and Alberto Netto. Since the early 1990s, Brazilian music has become much more diverse and now branches into Reggae, Funk, and even Hip Hop. In this chapter, we focus on traditional forms that developed within Brazil.

SAMBA

Samba is the most famous Brazilian musical form. Though often thought of as one style, it actually has many variations: samba rural (rural samba), samba enredo (theme songs of samba schools), samba de roda (circle samba), samba baiana (Bahian samba), and several more. The term Samba is derived from the West African fertility dance ("Semba") meaning "dance of the bellybutton." The styles when applied to the drum set (those presented in this section) are derivatives of the Samba traditions found in Brazilian carnaval celebration.

What we now recognize as Samba developed in the working class culture of Bahia and Rio de Janiero during the early part of the 20th century. Stemming from the tradition of the Maracatu, Samba ensembles had large percussion sections. Samba attained national popularity via Brazilian radio broadcasts in the 1930s. It attained worldwide recognition around 1940 when it became a featured musical style in several Hollywood films, most notably those starring Portuguese singer/musician Carmen Miranda. By the 1950s and 1960s, Samba became accepted within the Jazz genre through artists such as Stan Getz and Sergio Mendez. As a result of this fusion, it has become quite common to play Jazz standards in a Samba style.

The drum set ideas presented here can be applied to Jazz performed in a Samba style or to authentic Brazilian music. The consistent foot pattern (mainly on the bass drum) mimics the rhythm of the surdo drum while complimenting the bass player's pattern in an ensemble. The hands are centered around a Partido Alto pattern. **Samba tempos are generally played quickly, starting around quarter note = 170 bpm.**

Example 1 (CD 1, Track 66)

The snare hand is playing the Partido Alto rhythm (on either the rim or the snare itself).

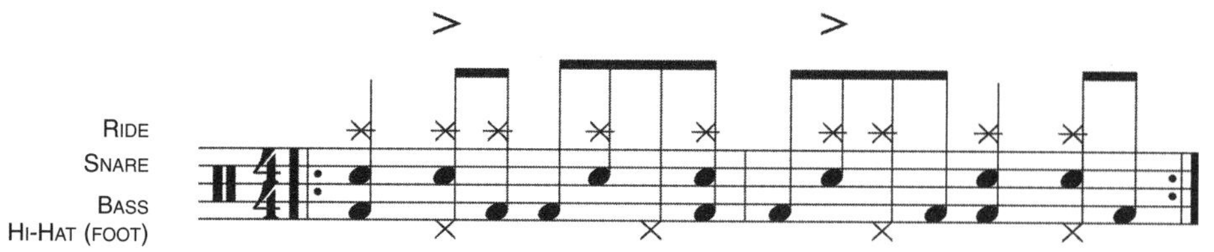

Variation 1 (CD 1, Track 67)

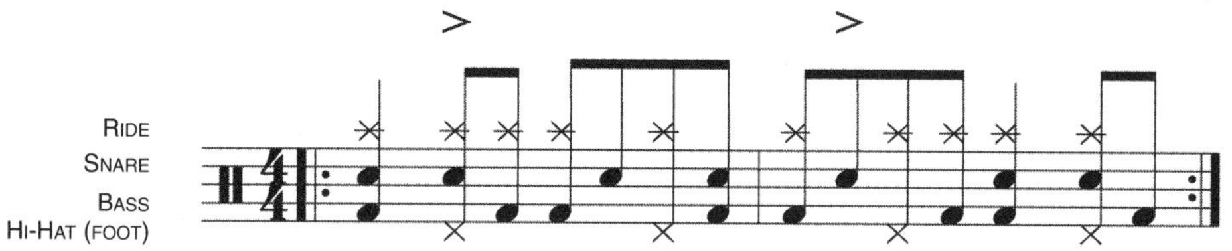

Variation 2

This has a "Jazz Samba" ride pattern. Many ride pattern variations are possible with Samba grooves. Two common ones are all eighth notes or repetitive groupings of two eighth notes followed by one quarter note.

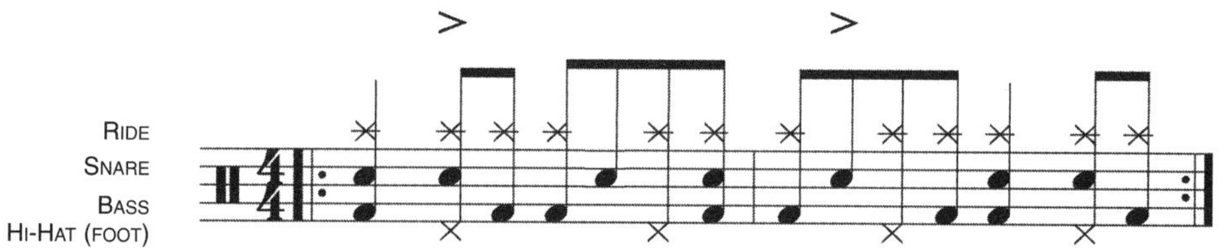

Variation 3 (CD 1, Track 68)

This is the Samba Cruzado. The Partido Alto rhythm is played on the toms by the snare hand.

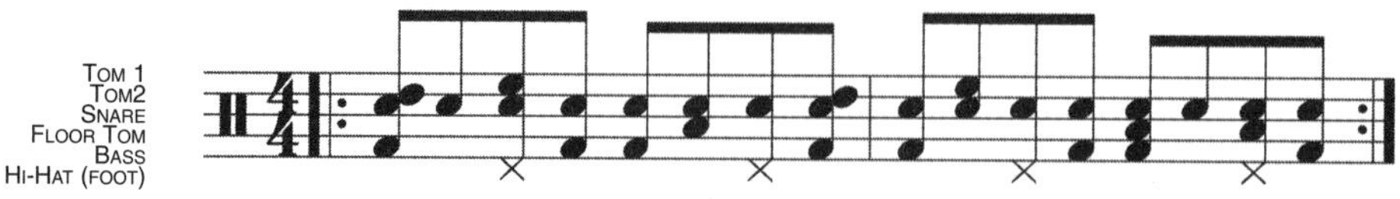

NOTE: It is extremely important to remember that while Brazilian grooves are routinely written in 4/4 in the U.S., they are felt in "two" (with emphasis on written beats 1 & 3).

Variation 4 (CD 1, Track 69)

This final variation is called Samba-Reggae. The pattern of the floor tom mimics the sound of a surdo drum and is influenced by the Reggae style (see Reggae in Caribbean chapter).

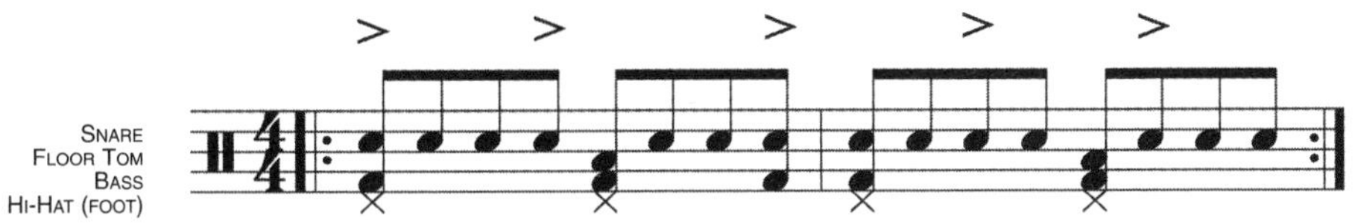

Example 2

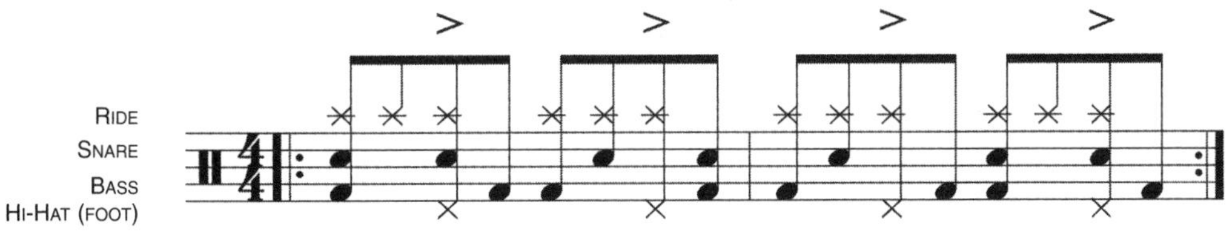

Variation 1

This variation employs a Tamborim pattern on the snare.

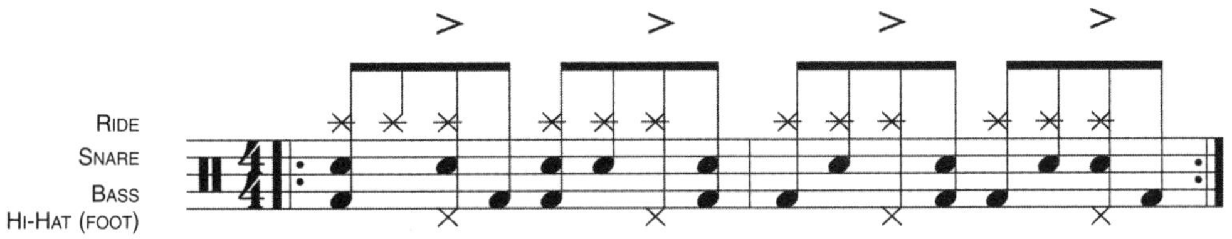

NOTE: The first and second measures can be reversed in all of the above patterns, depending on the feel.

Batucada (Samba Batucada)

The word Batucada (stemming from the West African dance, "Batuque") refers to the percussion rhythms of street Samba from carnaval in Rio de Janeiro and is short for "Samba Batucada" (Samba played solely on percussion instruments). Sometimes used synonymously with the word "Samba," it is comprised of the specific rhythms played on the various percussion instruments within the bateria: repinique, surdo, caixa, ago-go, pandero, tamborim, cuica, and chucalho. The Batucada rhythms presented here are authentic replications of the rhythms played on the instruments just mentioned, particularly the surdo drum, and can be incorporated into an authentic Brazilian Samba. Because these Batucada rhythms create a busier sound than the Samba grooves presented at the beginning of this chapter, it is usually appropriate to play these rhythms during the more climactic portions of a song. **Batucada rhythms start around quarter note = 170 bpm.**

NOTE: To clarify the above description, here are two Batucada rhythms which precede the main drum set example. Generally, the rhythms are played with the ride hand on the floor tom, duplicating the sound of the surdo drum. Notice the X's marking a dampening stroke (muting the drum's ring by pressing firmly on the head with the tip of the stick).

Batucada Surdo Patterns (on floor tom)

1A) Dampen on 1, hit on 3 (in both measures).

(CD 1, Track 70)

1B) Dampen on 1, hit on 3, + of 3 and + of 4 (measure 1); dampen on 1, hit on 3 and 4 (measure 2).

(CD 1, Track 71)

Batucada Drum Set Grooves

Example (CD 1, Track 72)

The pattern of the feet in the main example is identical to that of the main Samba example. The snare hand plays a Partido Alto rhythm, while the ride hand plays Batucada pattern "A" on the floor tom.

Variation 1 (CD 1, Track 73)

Variation 1 retains the same Samba foot pattern while adding a tamborim pattern on the snare and Batucada pattern "B" on the floor tom. Note that the lower accents are on the floor tom.

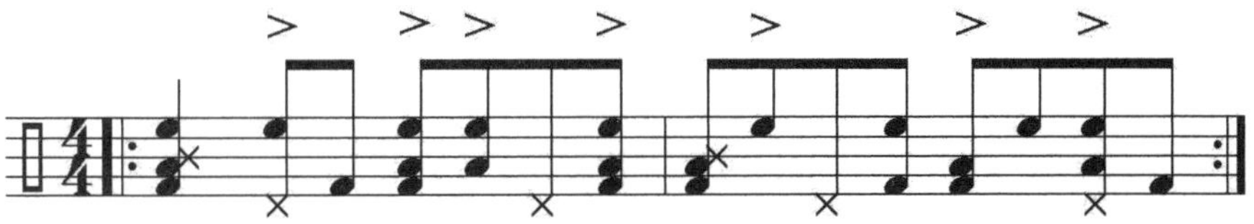

Variation 2 (CD 1, Track 74)

The hands play a march-like pattern on the snare (similar to the rhythms in variation 1 and mimicking an ago-go bell pattern) while continuing to accent the Batucada "B" pattern on the floor tom. Due to the active hand pattern, the bass drum pattern is simpler.

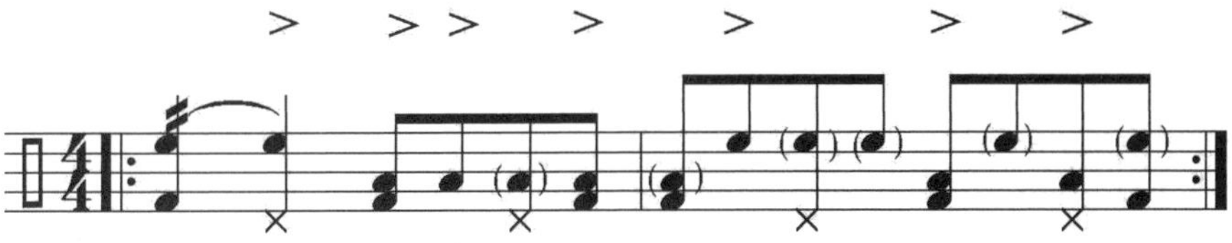

NOTE: The first and second measures can be reversed in all of the above patterns, depending on the feel.

Baiao

The roots of Baiao (pronounced as "by-ow" or "by-own") can be traced back to the northeastern Brazilian state of Paraiba. Though Baiao incorporates the stylized dances of European settlers accompanied by Brazilian instrumentation, it allegedly originated with the dancing of Cangaceiros (Brazilian bandits). As it was originally performed, the primary percussion instrument was a zabumba (a large bass drum) played on both sides in a syncopated rhythm.

Baiao's development was greatly influenced by radio and musician Luis Gonzaga in the 1930s and 1940s. Prior to radio exposure, Baiao was mainly an instrumental form traditionally consisting of the zabumba (large drum), accordion, vocals, pandeiro and triangle. With air play, it achieved popularity throughout Brazil and began to include the guitar. By the 1960s, Baiao rhythms made their way to the United States and into popular music in songs like Burt Bacharach's "Do You Know The Way To San Jose?" Baiao can now be found in American Jazz in compositions by artists such as Joe Henderson and Chick Corea.

Although not created from a fusion of Bossa Nova and Samba, Baiao contains rhythmic elements of both. The prevalent rhythm is identical to the first measure of the Brazilian clave, with a tempo closer to that of Samba than Bossa Nova. **The tempo begins at quarter note = 170 bpm.**

EXAMPLE (CD 1, Track 75)

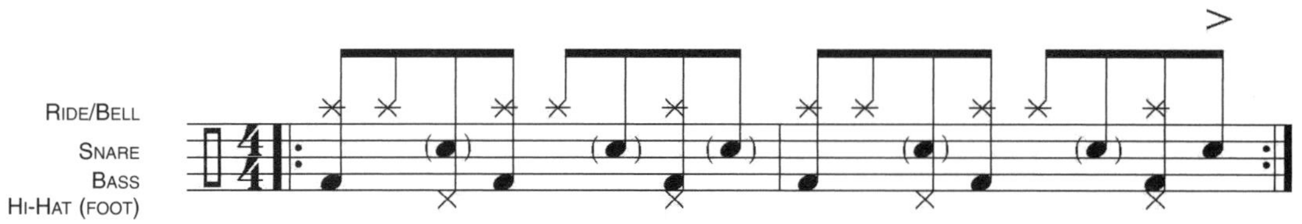

NOTE: The characteristic Baiao bass drum pattern is the same as the characteristic New Orleans Funk bass drum pattern (played on the 1, the "and" of 2, and the 4). (See Funk chapter.)

VARIATION 1

This is similar to a Puerto Rican Bomba (see Bomba in Afro-Cuban chapter) with a slightly different bell pattern.

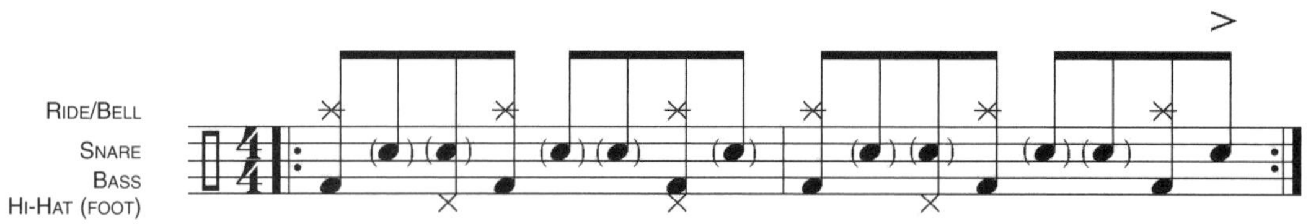

VARIATION 2 (CD 1, Track 76)

This variation is quite different than the initial example. The hands play a march rhythm on the snare containing rolls, accents, and sixteenth notes, with a slight variation in the second measure. This marching hand rhythm above is played "in the crack"—between a straight and a swung feel. (Left handed drummers should reverse the sticking.)

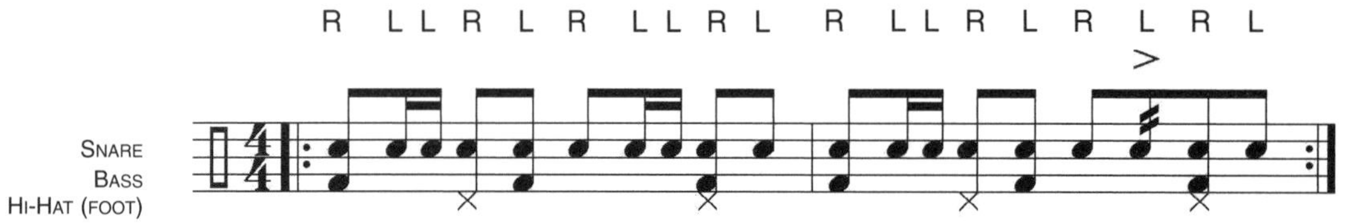

Example 2

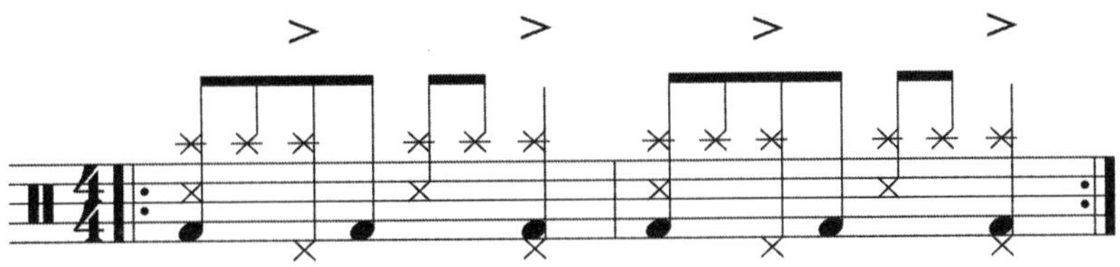

> NOTE: Multiple snare drum rim click patterns are possible in a standard Baiao. However, a good place to start is with downbeat rim clicks as found in the Example above.

Bossa Nova

While Samba music traditionally dealt with the hardships of the Brazilian working class, Bossa Nova focused on the idyllic atmosphere of the prosperous neighborhoods along the beaches of Rio de Janeiro. Similarly, Bossa Nova composers and musicians tended to come from the middle and upper classes. To reflect its theme of a luxurious lifestyle, Bossa Nova borrowed the melodious chord structures found in American Jazz while retaining the drum rhythms of Samba, but at a slower and more relaxed tempo.

With its birth in the 1950s, through guitarists Joao Gilberto and Antonio Carlos Jobim and their songs "Bim Bom" (Gilberto) and, later, "Chega de Saudade" (Jobim), Bossa Nova blossomed within Brazil. (Three early Brazilian drum set players [Edison Machado, Milton Banana and Dom Um Romao] established the Bossa Nova drumming style.) In 1963, one song firmly established the style worldwide: "The Girl from Ipanema" ("Garota de Ipanema"), written by Vinicius de Moraes and Antonio Carlos Jobim. The song attained immediate popularity and since its original release has been covered by over 300 recording artists.

By the mid-1960s, Bossa Nova had become accepted as a prevalent genre within American Jazz and, much as with Samba, American Jazz standards are often composed or played in Bossa Nova style (e.g., "Blue Bossa," by Kenny Dorham). In addition, variations on Bossa Nova can even be found in popular songs such as "Break On Through," by the Doors, and "Aja," by Steely Dan.

The Bossa Nova grooves which follow can be applied to American Jazz standards or authentic Brazilian Bossa Nova. The constant bass drum pattern is identical to the one played in a Samba. The ride hand commonly plays a consistent sequence of eighth notes, while the snare hand plays a rim click pattern often referred to as the "Brazilian Clave." **The style is counted and felt in 4/4 and usually played at a tempo of quarter note = 100–168 bpm.**

Example (CD 1, Track 77)

In the main example, the snare hand plays the familiar "Brazilian Clave" rhythm as a rim click.

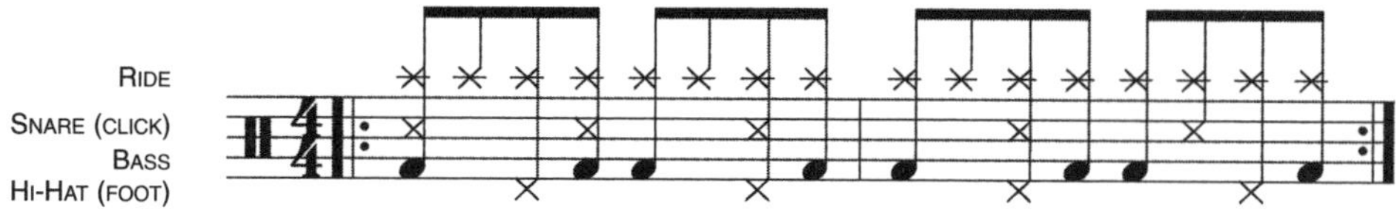

Variation 1

The rim click pattern here is a Partido Alto rhythm.

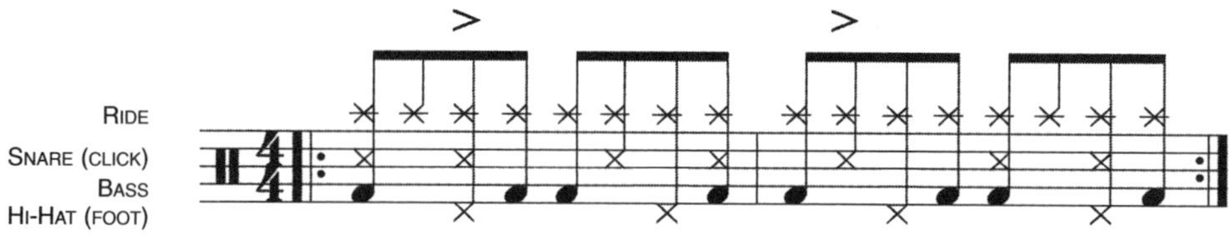

Variation 2 (CD 1, Track 78)

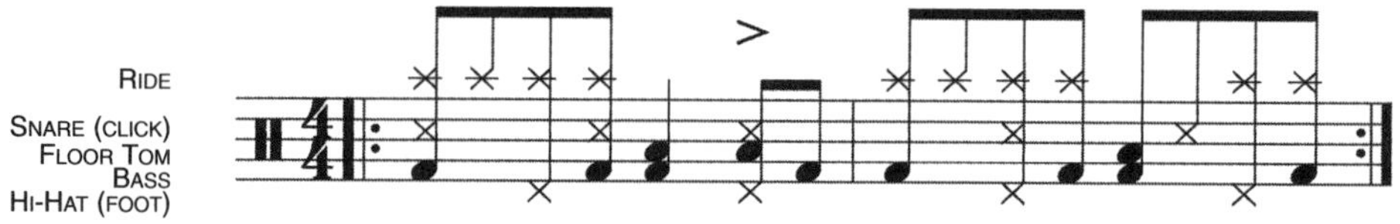

Note: Accent is played on floor tom.

NOTE: All patterns can also be played with the ride hand playing eighth notes on the hi-hat, either completely closed or with the foot striking the pedal on beats 2 & 4 to replicate the rhythm played on the guiro.

Partido Alto

Partido Alto is a samba style whose rhythmic pattern has been incorporated into other Brazilian styles both for percussion and drum set. The roots of Partido Alto lie in the Jongo style, which in turn is rooted in African culture in southeast Brazil. Various drums (candongueiros, angumativas, and caxambus) were used in the Jongo style, and the rhythmic patterns played on these drums highly influenced early Samba styles, with Partido Alto rhythms appearing in Samba in the 1930s. Early Partido Alto composers include Aniceto do Imperio, Nilton Campolino, Geraldo Babao, Clementina de Jesus and Bezerra da Silva. More modern composers include Grupo Fundo de Quintal, Zeca Pagodinho, and Almir Guineto.

Though the full pattern is commonly played on one surface (e.g., the snare, using cross sticking) in Samba settings the Partido Alto drum set pattern is commonly broken up between the snare drum and bass drum. Partido Alto is a syncopated pattern, which usually matches the bassist's rhythmic pattern and sometimes that of other instruments. **Partido Alto rhythms start at about 90 bpm.**

Example (CD 1, Track 77)

The characteristic Partido Alto rhythm is broken up here between the snare and bass drum.

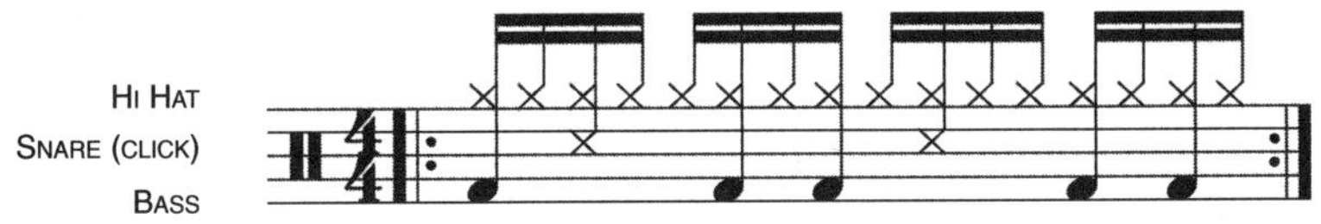

Variation 1

The broken-up 16th-note pattern in the hi hat makes this groove useful at faster tempos.

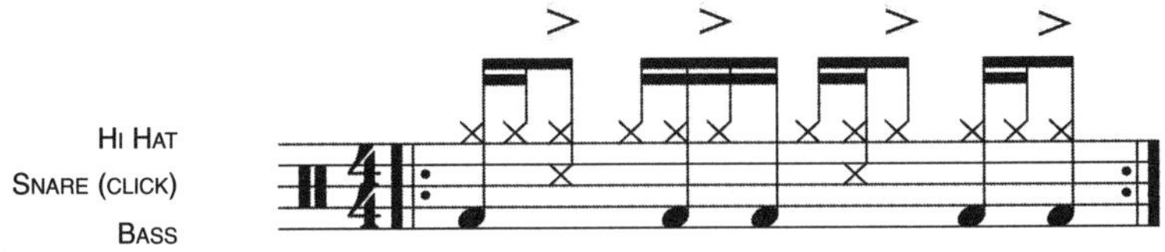

Afoxe

Stemming from Northeastern Brazil, Afoxe is a traditional yet secular style of music of the Candomble religion, originally from Yoruba (Nigeria). In addition, an afoxe is a Brazilian percussion instrument normally comprised of a set of plastic beads wrapped around a circular top which is twisted back and forth to create a shaker sound, similar to that of the Afro-Cuban instrument, the cabasa (which uses metal beads).

As with most Brazilian styles, Afoxe originated primarily on percussion instruments and is performed during the Carnaval festival. The more traditional and accurate forms of Afoxe are performed by the Filhos de Gandhy ("Sons of Gandhi"), a group of Brazilian peace activists formed in 1949 as a reaction to the assassination of the Indian independence leader and nonviolence advocate, Mahatma Gandhi.

The predominant rhythm of the Afoxe is the "Ijexa," which is typically played on agogo bells (which have been incorporated into the drum set example below). **Afoxe tempos start at around quarter note = 90 bpm.**

Example (CD 1, Track 77)

The Ijexa pattern on the agogo bells dominate this pattern. The snare hand cross stick notes can vary depending on the drummer's ability to improvise over the bell pattern.

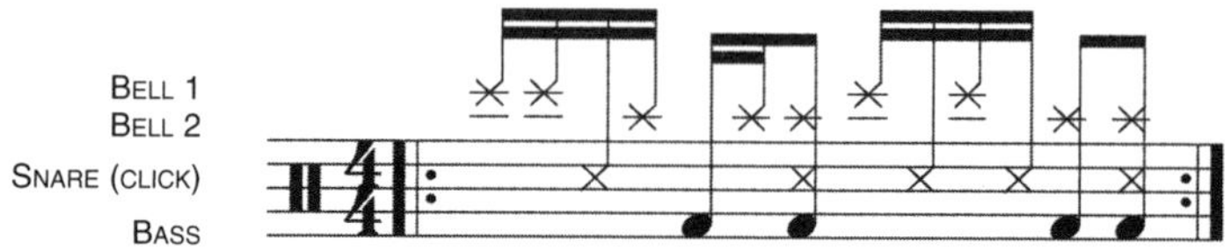

Variation 1

This is a more contemporary Afoxe drum set pattern.

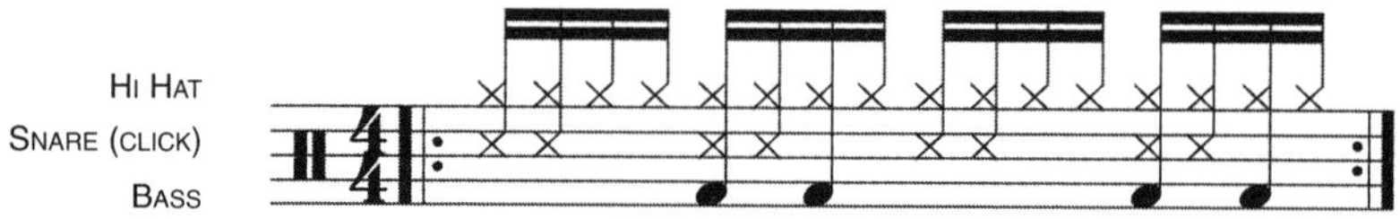

Variation 2

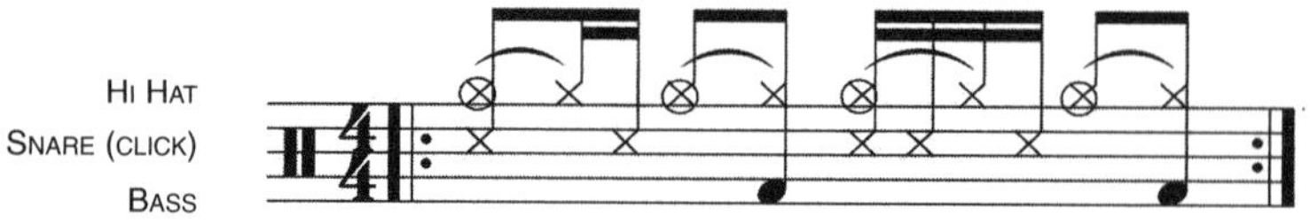

(Circled hi-hat notes are played open)

6 CAJUN / ZYDECO

THE TERMS "CAJUN" AND "ZYDECO" refer to two distinct styles, both stemming from French cultures in southern Louisiana. Traditionalists say "lache pas la patate" ("don't drop the potato"), meaning "don't let go of the old culture," more specifically, don't allow Cajun music to become a hybrid musical form. However, as current Cajun and Zydeco musicians often cover both genres, it's appropriate to include both in this chapter. An appreciation and understanding of the differences between the two will aid in accurate and authentic performance of both.

Cajuns ("Acadians," French-Canadians exiled from Nova Scotia) came to central and southwest Louisiana in the 18th century. Cajun music revolved around the fiddle and the single-row button accordion. Like a harmonica with bellows, the German-style (single-row button) accordion has a fixed and limited range, producing harmonically and structurally simple music.

Traditional Cajun rhythmic accompaniment involved stomping the floor on beats 1 and 3 (in 4/4 time) while playing a homemade triangle called the "tee frere" ("little brother"). In addition to 4/4 tunes, Cajun music includes many songs in waltz time (3/4), often subdivided into a 9/8 feel (3/4 with a triplet pulse) or played as a 3/4 shuffle (with an eighth-note triplet pulse, but with the middle eighth notes omitted).

Zydeco has its roots in African and Caribbean music and the Creole culture (Creoles being the racially mixed offspring of Europeans, American Indians, and Africans). The two leading instruments in Zydeco are the multi-row button accordion (which includes sharp and flat accidentals) or the keyboard accordion, and a percussion instrument called a "frottoir," a rub-board often worn on the chest. Invented in the '40s by Willie Landry and accordion player Clifton Chenier (for his brother Cleveland Chenier), it has become Zydeco's signature rhythmic voice. With the rubboard up front and dictating the rhythm, the style evolved into a more up-tempo music, with the drummer and bass player powerfully driving the band. Zydeco music is predominantly played in 4/4 (shuffled or straight), with fewer 3/4 (and far fewer 9/8) time signatures than Cajun music. The term Zydeco is attributed to the accordion legend Clifton Chenier, who popularized the song "Les Haricots Sont Pas Sales" ("The Beans Aren't Salty"). "Les Haricots" (pronounced "lay zarico") evolved into the term Zydeco.

Though the music maintained marked differences well into the 20th century, Cajun and Zydeco cultures began to blend as far back as the early 1900s when rural African-American laborers invented "Juré," a style which mixed singing, praying, hand clapping, and dancing. Shortly after, Juré began to fuse with Cajun music to form "La La" (Creole French for "House Dance"). These early styles featured percussion instruments such as spoons, washboard with a notched stick, the fiddle, and the accordion.

The influence of Country music and Rhythm & Blues in the early 1950s brought the electric guitar, electric bass, and drum set into the ensemble. Although Cajun and Zydeco music developed separately, by the mid-1980s bands often played both styles, and some Cajun/Zydeco bands earned worldwide recognition. Acclaimed bands and musicians include Beausoleil, Queen Ida, Buckwheat Zydeco, Zachary Richard, Tout Les Soir Cajun Band, Steve Riley and the Mamou Playboys, Dwaine Dopsey, Chubby Carrier and the Bayou Swamp Band, and Zydeco-A-Go-Go.

As both styles are dance music, the role of the drummer is to establish a strong sense of time with a loud back beat. The examples and variations below provide a thorough representation of Cajun/Zydeco drumming, most notably the Two-Step groove found in both styles. The most important characteristic in distinguishing between Cajun and Zydeco is that the Zydeco rhythm section is more active than the Cajun rhythm section. Both Cajun and Zydeco incorporate a standard drum set format with the ride hand primarily playing the ride cymbal. Cajun/Zydeco bands often mix both genres freely when performing, but almost never within the same song. **The tempo range is generally bright at quarter note = 160–240 bpm.**

CAJUN STYLES

CAJUN TWO-STEP

EXAMPLE (CD 1, Track 79)

This features a simple bass and snare drum pattern similar to the Standard Rock Beat, with the ride hand playing all quarter notes on the ride cymbal. **Quarter note = 120–176 bpm.**

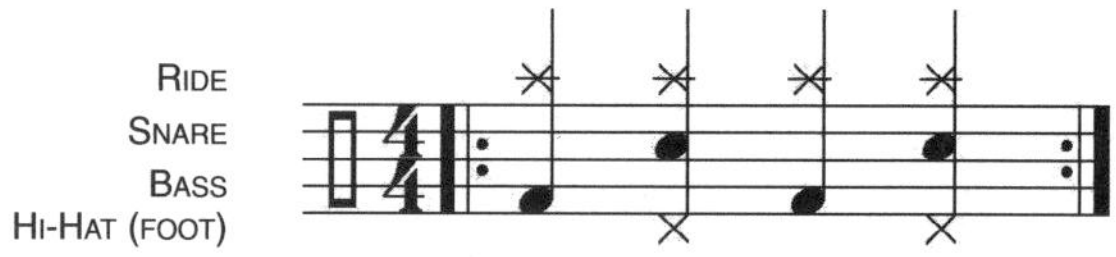

VARIATION 1

This is identical to the main example, but adds eighth notes to the ride hand. The eighth notes are most often played straight, though they're sometimes shuffled.

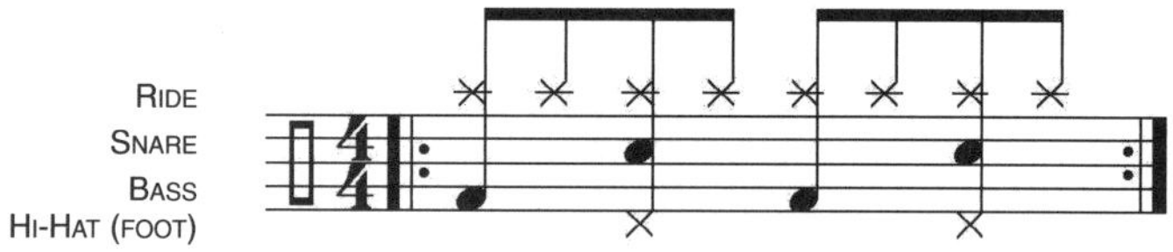

VARIATION 2

This adds a ride pattern that is the reverse of a Standard Swing ride pattern (see Big Band in Jazz chapter, example 1A). The 8th notes are played "in the crack."

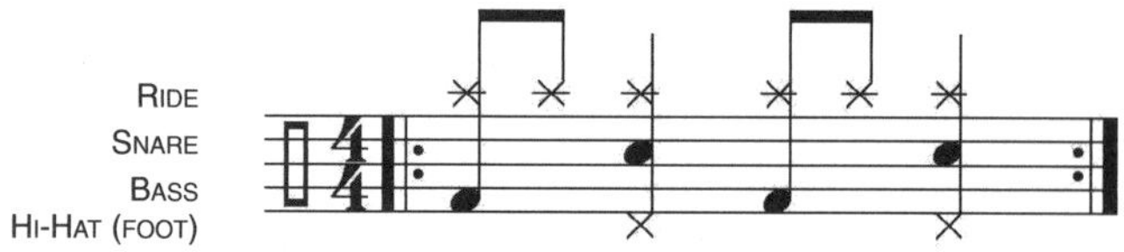

Cajun Waltz

Example (CD 1, Track 80)

This is a typical Cajun Waltz (similar to the Country Waltz) with quarter notes on the ride cymbal.
Quarter note = 126–152 bpm.

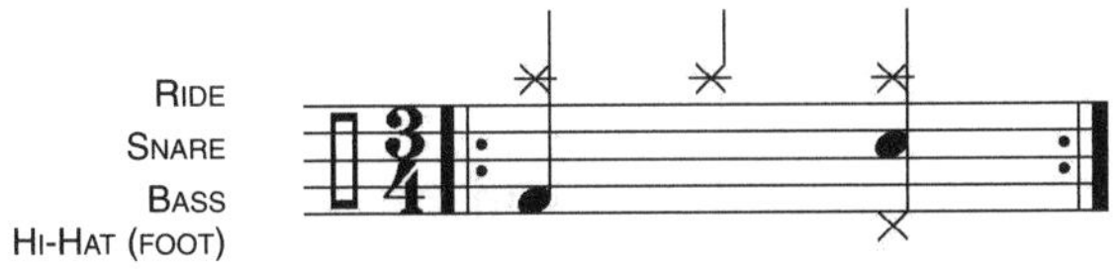

Variation 1

This is identical to the Cajun Waltz, but adds eighth notes in the ride hand. The eighth notes may be played straight or shuffled.

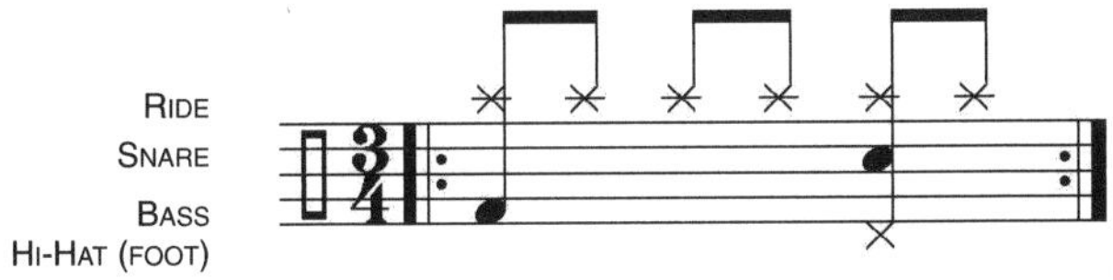

Variation 2

This is identical to the Cajun Waltz, but it adds beat 2 on the hi-hat foot, has a 9/8 or triplet feel in the ride hand, and is generally played at a slower tempo. **Quarter note = 100–126 bpm.**

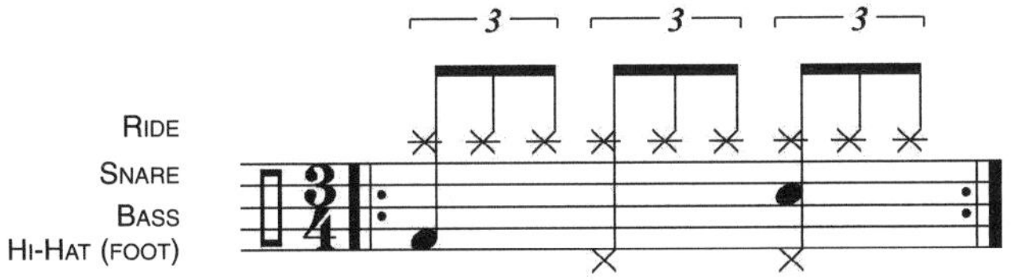

NOTE: Though the Cajun Waltz snare pattern is usually played on the snare drum, it may also be played as a snare rim click.

Zydeco Styles

Zydeco Two-Step

Example (CD 1, Track 81)

This is the Zydeco Two-Step, similar to Cajun Two-Step variation 2, adding additional bass drum and snare drum notes with the ride hand pattern played "in the crack." **Quarter note = 156–235 bpm.**

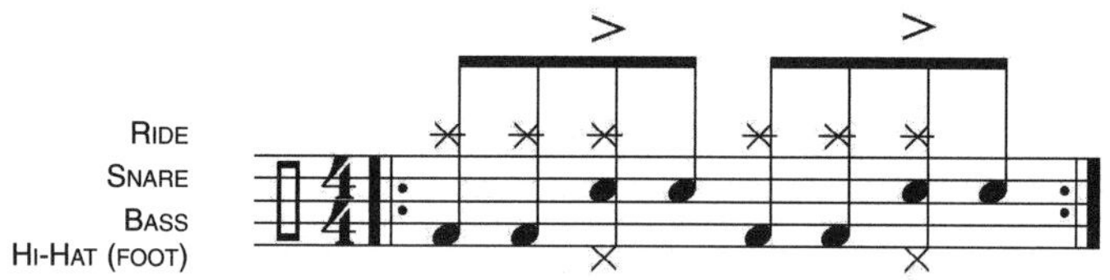

Variation 1

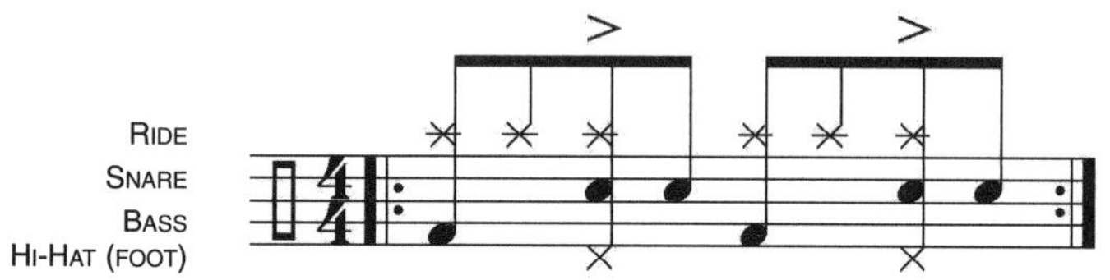

Variation 2

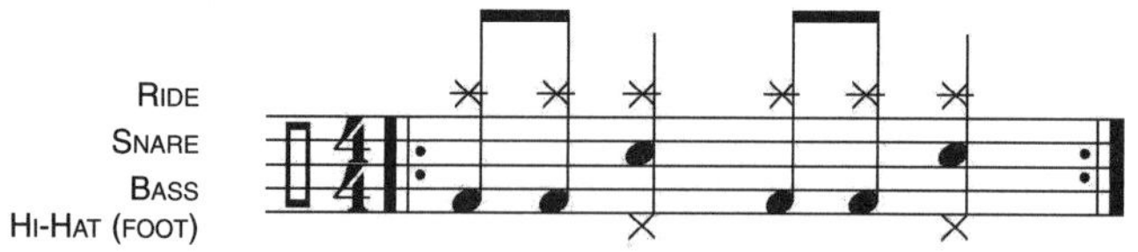

NOTE: All three of the above grooves may be used interchangeably within the same Zydeco song.

Zydeco Shuffle

Example (CD 1, Track 82)

The Zydeco Shuffle is nearly identical to the Blues Shuffle (see Blues Chapter) but with fewer variations of the pattern in Zydeco than in Blues. **Quarter note = 80–160 bpm.**

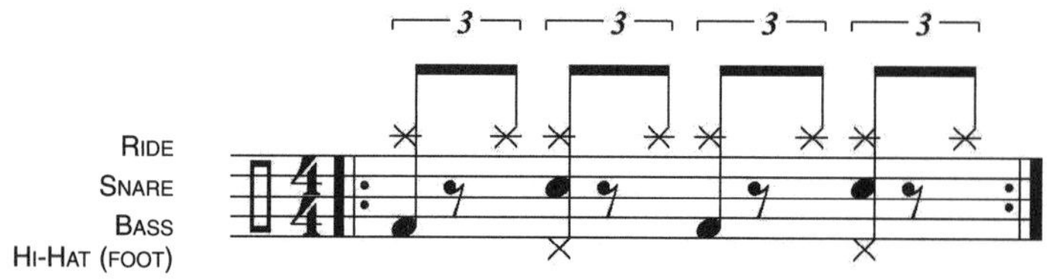

VARIATION

The most common Zydeco Shuffle variation uses the bass and snare drum rhythms from the Zydeco Two-Step.

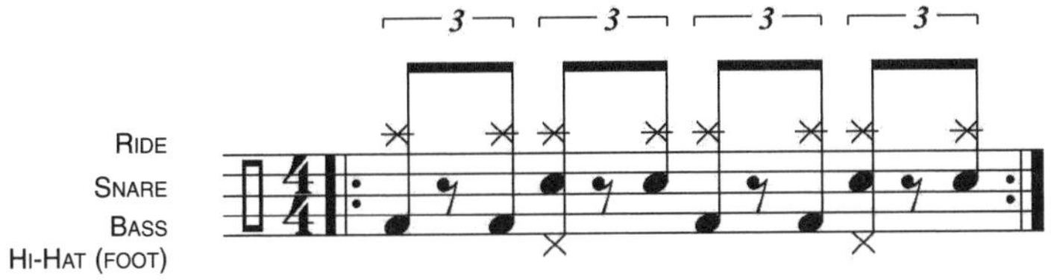

ZYDECO WALTZ

EXAMPLE (CD 1, Track 83)

Not as common as the Cajun Waltz, the Zydeco Waltz features a more active pattern in the bass drum and snare. Played either straight or swung, the tempos tend to be brighter than those of the Cajun Waltz.
Quarter note = 132–160 bpm.

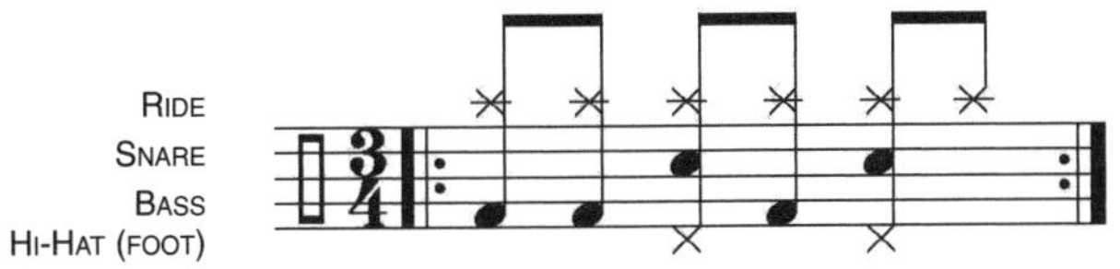

VARIATION

This is most appropriate in faster tempos due to the less active ride pattern, and is played straight or swung.

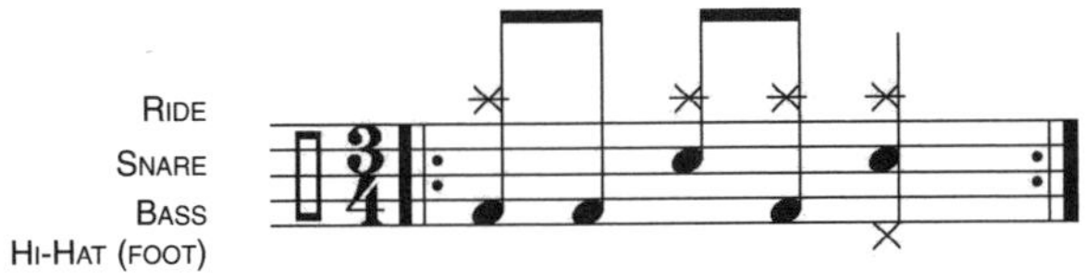

Zydeco Train Beat

Example (CD 1, Track 84)

The Zydeco Train Beat is identical to the Country Train Beat with the notes played either straight as in traditional Country (see Train Beat in the Country chapter), or shuffled (see Rockabilly in the Rock n' Roll chapter) or "in the crack." The notation of this Train Beat is written in eighth notes rather than 16th notes to correspond to the notation and feel of the Zydeco Two-Step. **Quarter note = 176–240 bpm.**

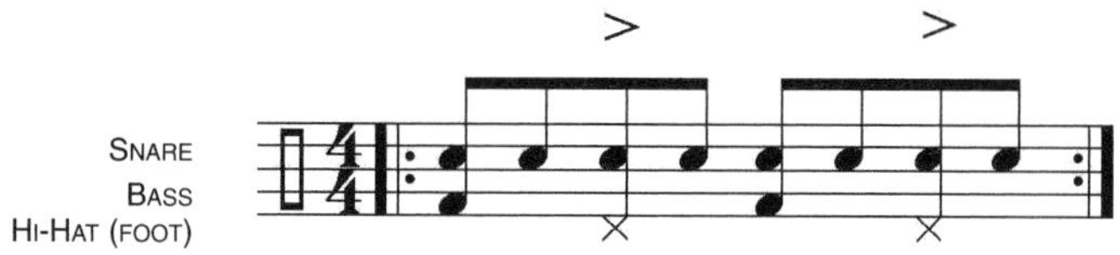

Variation 1

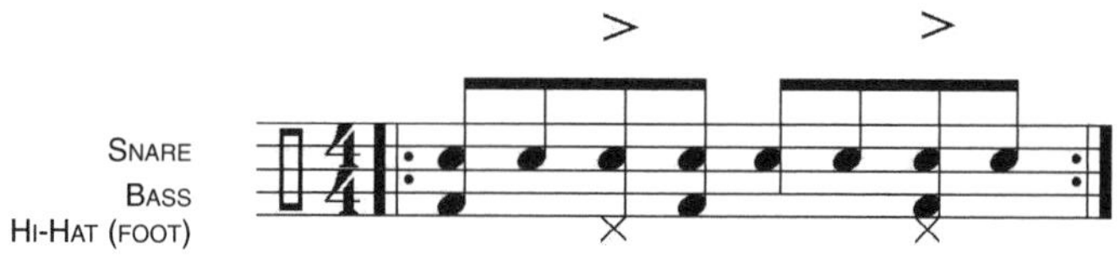

Variation 2

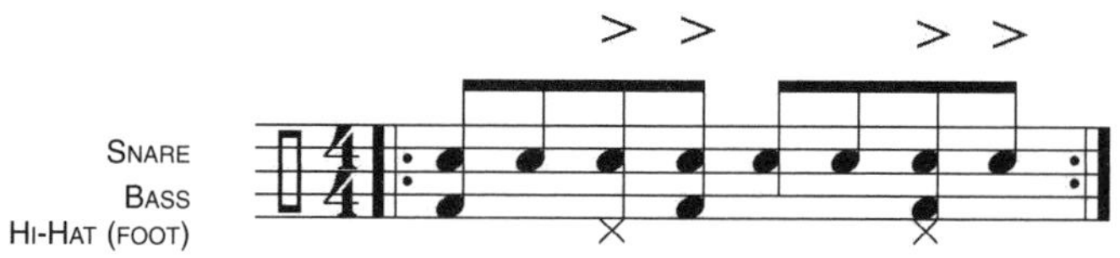

NOTE: Although alternate hand patterns are most common, using RR LR RL RL sticking in Zydeco Train Beat grooves will help you get the "in the crack" feel (between straight and swung time).

Zydeco Rock

Example (CD 1, Track 80)

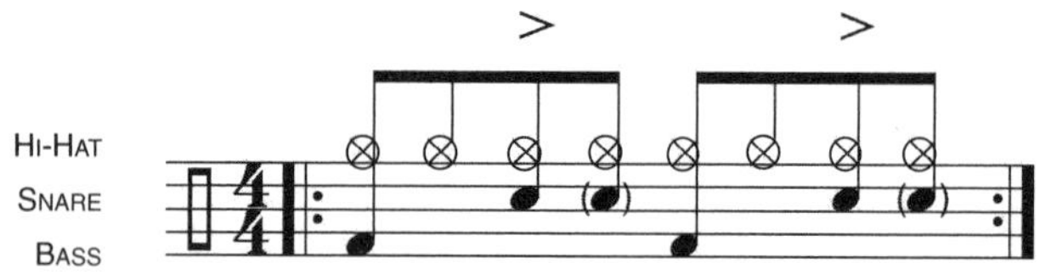

(Circled hi-hat notes are played open)

VARIATION 1

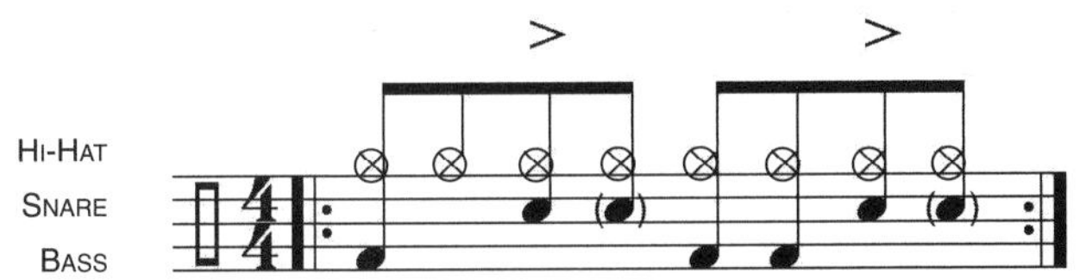

NOTE: The hi-hat eighth notes may be played straight or "in the crack" in both the Example and the Variation.

CAJUN / ZYDECO

Though Cajun and Zydeco drumming grooves usually are distinct, some beats are found in both styles. The following example and variation can be used in both Cajun and Zydeco. **Quarter note = 172–200 bpm.**

EXAMPLE (CD 1, Track 85)

The bass drum pattern here is a direct reflection of the New Orleans Second Line feel.

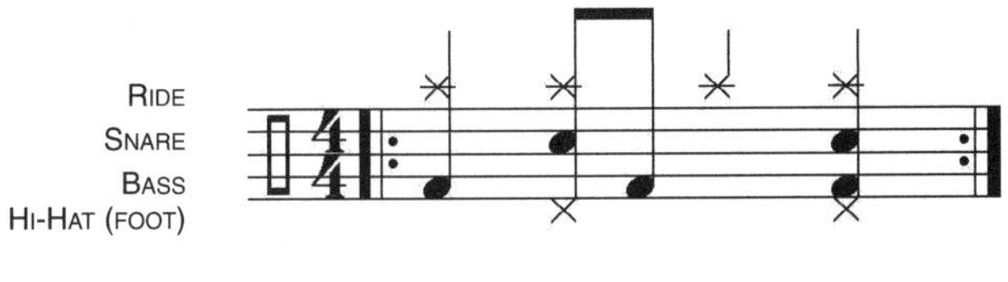

VARIATION

This is identical to the main example but with the Standard Swing pattern in the ride hand, and is played "in the crack."

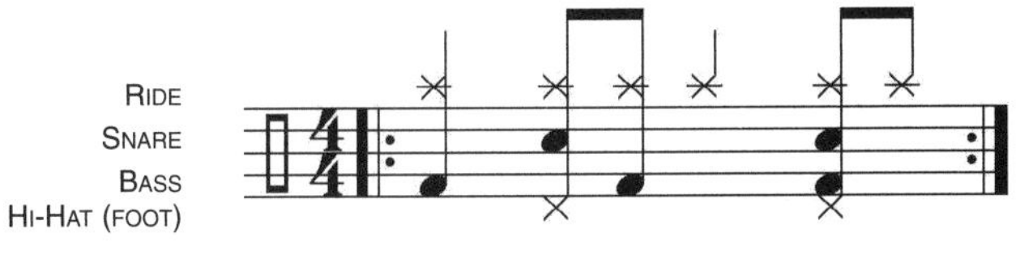

7 Caribbean

Caribbean music is a fusion of many different musical cultures, including South American, Cuban, African (West Indies), North American (U.S. Virgin Islands), and even European (British Virgin Islands); and the compositions, rhythms, and instruments (such as the signature sound of steel drums) which characterize Caribbean music, sometimes referred to as "Island Music," usually reflect a celebratory atmosphere.

This chapter explores the most commonly played varieties within this genre—Calypso, Soca, Ska, and Reggae. The role of the drummer in all types of Caribbean music is based on a strong groove which reflects the music's upbeat mood. Most of this music is rather simple rhythmically and does not usually stray outside of 4/4.

Calypso

Calypso's roots are in the song forms of French Patois culture (a French-Creole dialect in Trinidad and the Caribbean). While Calypso started as a type of folk music, it developed into a verbal "call and response" form, alternating between the leader (the "griot") and the ensemble. While the style originally featured political and social commentary, it has evolved into dance and party music. Trinidadian musician Aldwyn Roberts (popularly known as Lord Kitchener) was a primary exponent of Calypso in its early days, and it attained wide recognition outside of the Caribbean with the success of musician/composer Harry Belafonte in the 1950s and 1960s.

To fully appreciate Calypso (and the related style, Soca), it is important to become familiar with the history of steel drums (which are largely responsible for both genres' characteristic sounds). During British colonial rule of Trinidad in the 1800s, hand drums were used as a form of communication by neighborhood gangs. However, due to a steady increase in violence, the government outlawed the use of these drums in 1886. As a result, Trinidad citizens turned to the use of a variety of materials to take the place of the banned drums. One common replacement was bamboo sticks ("tamboo bamboo") which would be pounded on the ground during parades and ceremonies. These were soon prohibited as well. Regardless, the people continued searching for objects they could use to create music, including garbage can lids, old car parts, and empty oil barrels. Eventually, the combination of these "found" metallic instruments became the foundation of musical gatherings called "Iron Bands." In the late 1930s, it was discovered that a dented section of an oil barrel produced a particular tone, and people began to experiment with different shapes, resulting in the original steel drums which were convex like a dome rather than concave like a dish. Ellie Manette, a steel drum maker still active in the United States, was the first to hammer out a pan and give the drum its familiar concave form. Over many years, steel drum makers have perfected the quality, tone, and appearance of the instrument which has led to its finding acceptance in the present-day percussion family. Two of the most prominent contemporary steel drum artists are brothers Andy and Jeff Narell.

Although its patterns are similar to those of Soca (see below), the bass drum in Calypso plays a slightly more syncopated rhythm while the drum groove is not as audible as in Soca (due to the absence of a constant snare drum pattern). **Typically, Calypso has a tempo range of quarter note = 80–120 bpm.**

Example (CD 1, Track 86)

This is a typical Calypso pattern. Though similar to Soca patterns, the Calypso beat has a more syncopated bass drum pattern and employs a busier hand pattern (minus a snare drum) with consistent hi-hat 16th notes.

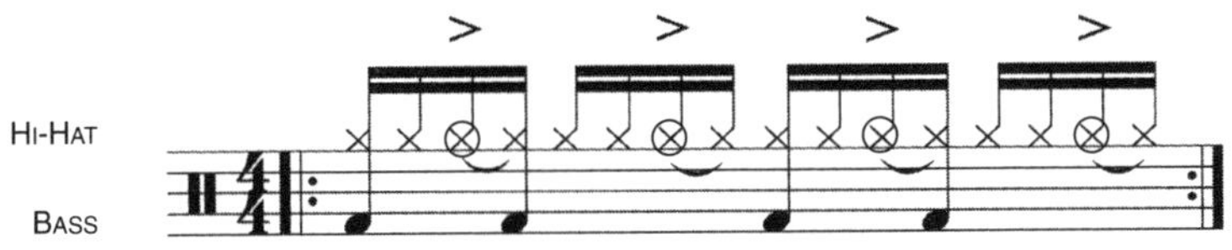

(Circled hi-hat notes are played open)

Variation

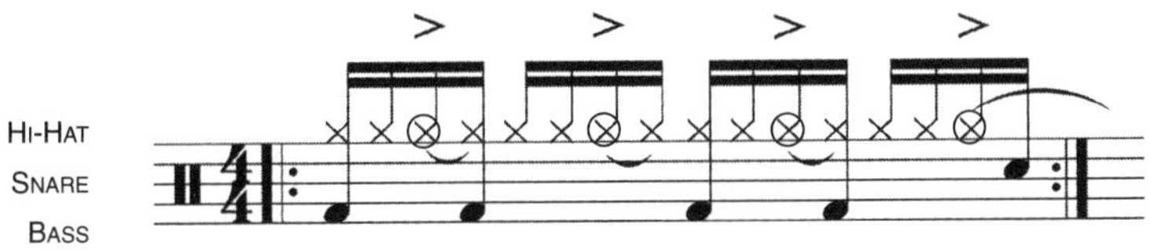

(Circled hi-hat notes are played open)

Soca

Created in Trinidad in the mid-1970s and credited to RAS Shorty I ("Lord Shorty"), Soca incorporates African and East Indian musical elements into Calypso. Initially controversial with purists who considered it a corruption of Calypso, the style has a faster tempo, a heavier beat with a "four on the floor" pattern, and a prominent syncopated snare drum rhythm. However, the party-type lyrical matter of Calypso is retained in the newer Soca style. It found immediate success with its dance audience, and has retained that popularity. Soca now embraces a variety of styles such as Chutney Soca, Ragga Soca and Rapso (a combination of Rap and Soca) all with a similar rhythmic foundation. Popular Soca artists include Super Blue, Iwer George, Colin Lucas, and Ronnie McIntosh.

Soca rhythms, like Calypso rhythms, are commonly found accompanying a steel drum dance band. Notice the steady, driving pulse from the bass drum in each groove. In addition, the repetitive accents or opening of the hi-hat on each upbeat helps propel the grooves. **Soca tempos are faster than those of Calypso, with quarter note = 108–132 bpm.**

Example (CD 1, Track 87)

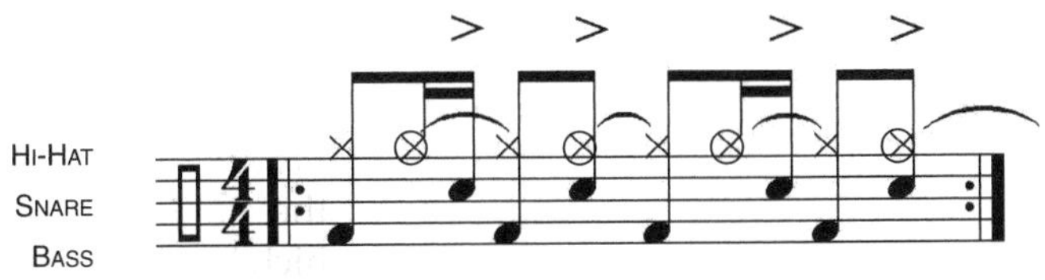

(Circled hi-hat notes are played open)

Variation 1 (CD 1, Track 88)

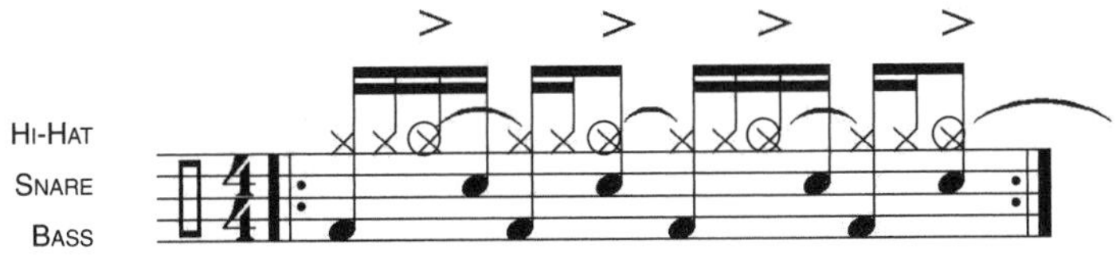

(Circled hi-hat notes are played open)

Variation 2

This is an appealing way to play for one bar at the end of a musical phrase.

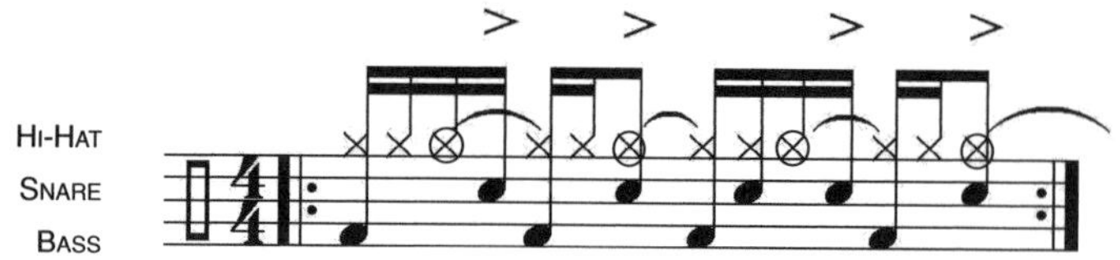

(Circled hi-hat notes are played open)

Variation 3

This is similar to the ending of a New Orleans Second Line groove (see Second Line in Jazz chapter). **Quarter note = 126–152 bpm.**

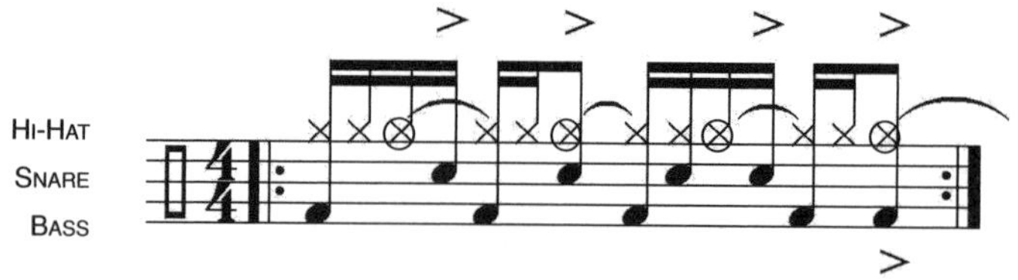

(Circled hi-hat notes are played open)

NOTE: The above patterns can be used interchangeably from section to section in songs. Additional variations are possible through the use of a standard hi-hat accent rather than an "open note."

Ska/Steppers

Jamaican guitarist Ernest Ranglin says that musicians created the word Ska "to talk about the skat! skat! skat! scratchin' guitar that goes behind." Another way that a guitarist might refer to this is "backwards comping," in which the guitar strongly and equally accents all upbeats (the +'s of beats) in comping patterns; this pattern is largely what gives Ska its characteristic sound.

With the popularity of Blues already established in Jamaica, radio broadcasts from New Orleans introduced the music of Fats Domino, Lloyd Price, and other New Orleans singer/songwriters to Jamaica. The influence of New Orleans Second Line along with the sounds of early Rock n' Roll, Jazz and R&B were readily embraced and incorporated into a new Jamaican sound known as Ska in the 1950s. The first successful Ska musicians were Jimmy Cliff, Lord Creator, and Don Drummond and the Skatalites. Bands such as The Police, Men At Work, Madness, and currently No Doubt, 311, and The Mighty Mighty Boss Tones have all continued to popularize Ska.

As with Reggae, a common characteristic in Ska drumming is a rim click on beat 3 of each measure. The outstanding differences between Ska and Reggae are a "straight" feel along with a "four on the floor" bass drum pattern (hence the term "Stepper") in Ska. **The tempo of Ska is quarter note = 116–192 bpm.**

Example (CD 1, Track 89)

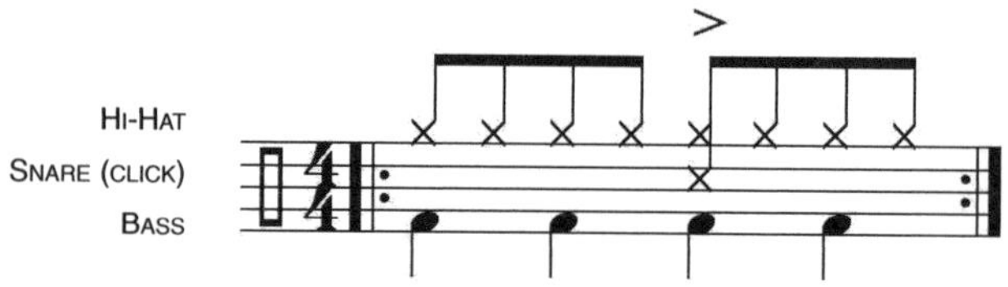

Variation 1 (CD 1, Track 90)

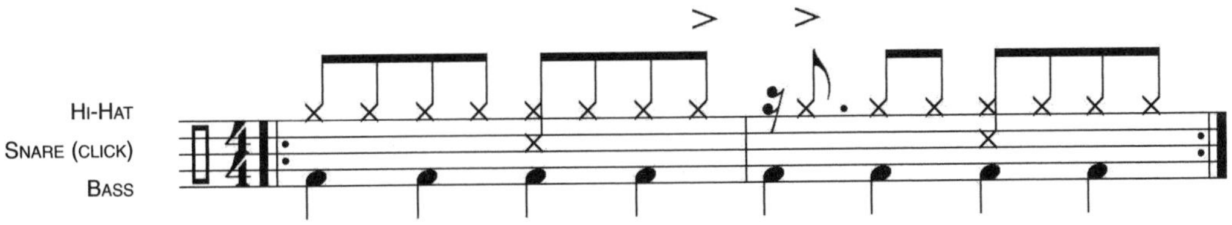

Variation 2

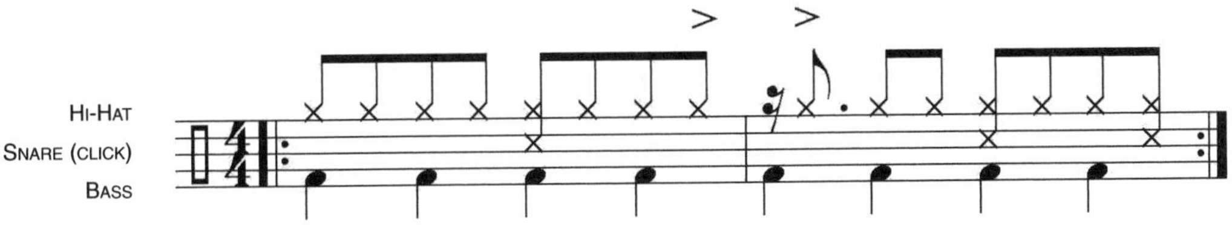

Variation 3 (CD 1, Track 91)

This is a typical up-tempo variation. **Quarter note = 160–208 bpm.**

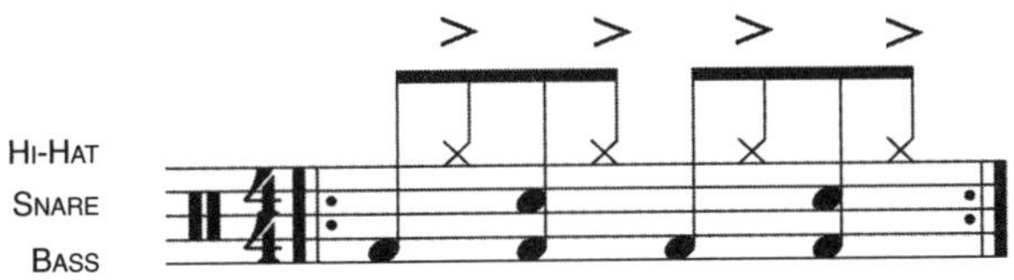

Variation 4

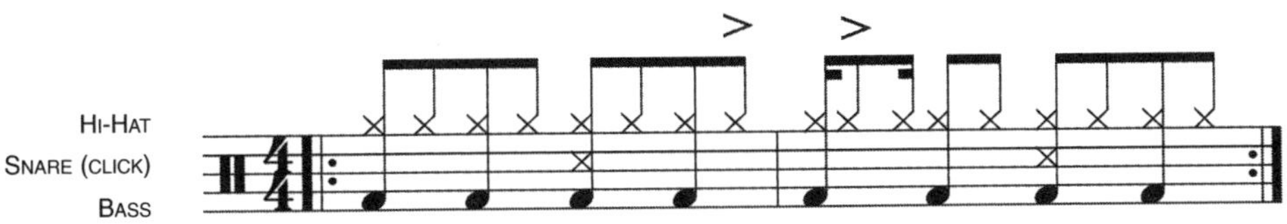

Variation 5

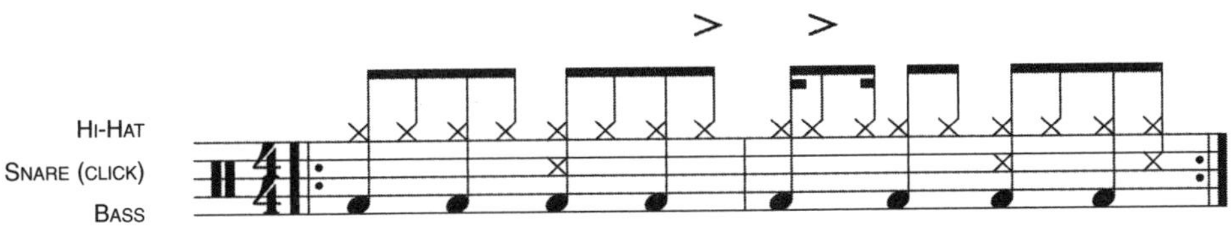

Reggae (One Drop)

The origin of the word Reggae is unclear. Some claim that the word stems from "Regga," which refers to a group of natives from the Lake Tanganyika region in Africa. Bob Marley claimed it was a Spanish term for "The King's Music" (in Spanish, "la musica del rey"), which is unlikely enough that one suspects that Marley was pulling someone's leg—though it is possible that the word "Reggae" is a corruption of the word "rey" (king). Yet another, more likely, explanation is that of Jamaican studio musician Hux Brown: "It's a description of the beat itself. It's just a fun, joke kinda word that means ragged rhythm and the body feelin'. If it's got a greater meanin', it doesn't matter."

Reggae's development closely follows that of Ska, incorporating Rhythm and Blues, New Orleans Second Line "in the crack" feels, African rhythms, Jamaican folk traditions, and Rastafarian culture (a religion developed in Jamaica with allegiance to Ethiopia, and veneration of former Ethiopian emperor Haile Selassie). Though its roots extend back to the 1950s, the genre's success is partially in debt to the breakthrough of Calypso and Ska in the late '50s to early '60s. Reggae gained popularity in the 1960s and 1970s, through musicians such as Alton Ellis, Delroy Wilson, Desmond Dekker, Joe Higgs, Eek-A-Mouse, Burning Spear, Toots and the Maytals, Jimmy Cliff, and, most importantly, Bob Marley and the Wailers (with Marley, even though he died in 1981, still being the leading voice of Reggae). The style was further popularized in the U.S. and Europe by Johnny Nash, Stevie Wonder, Elvis Costello, and Paul Simon. Contemporary artists include Ziggy Marley (son of Bob Marley), Third World, and The Mighty Diamonds, along with a number of those who brought the style to prominence in the 1960s and 1970s, notably Jimmy Cliff, Burning Spear, and Toots and the Maytals.

While other Caribbean styles have largely retained their original forms, Reggae continues to develop into hybrid forms. It influences styles such as Hip Hop and even Latin Rock (Los Fabuloso Cadillacs). Newer styles freely borrow characteristics from Reggae. These styles include Raggamuffin, Raggaeton, Dancehall, and Dub-Reggae.

Reggae drumming resembles that of the New Orleans style. Just as in the Second Line genre, the feel of the music falls "in the crack," which requires playing between a swung and a straight feel. The example below is a standard Reggae/One Drop pattern. The most common distinguishing feature of a Reggae beat is the simultaneous rim click and bass drum played as one note on beat 3 of each measure (creating the name "One Drop"), mixed with the specified triplet shuffle figure written for the hi-hat hand. **The tempo tempo for Reggae is around quarter note = 104–140 bpm.**

Example 1 (CD 1, Track 92)

Remember the "in the crack" rhythmic feel in the shuffle pattern played by the ride hand.

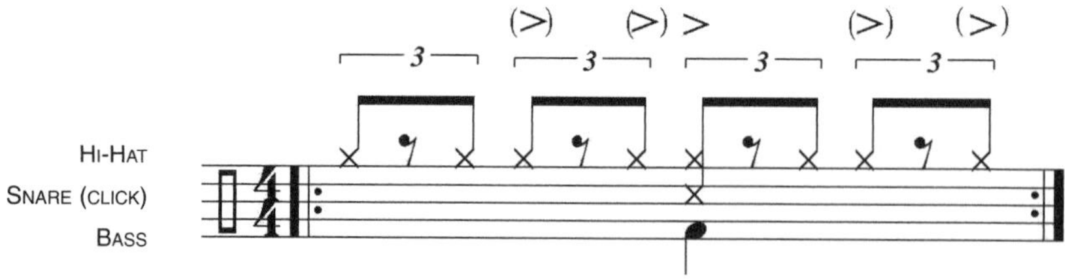

Variation 1 (CD 1, Track 93)

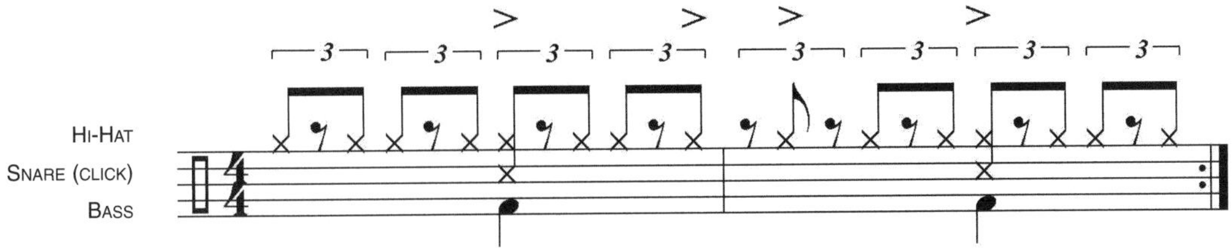

Variation 2

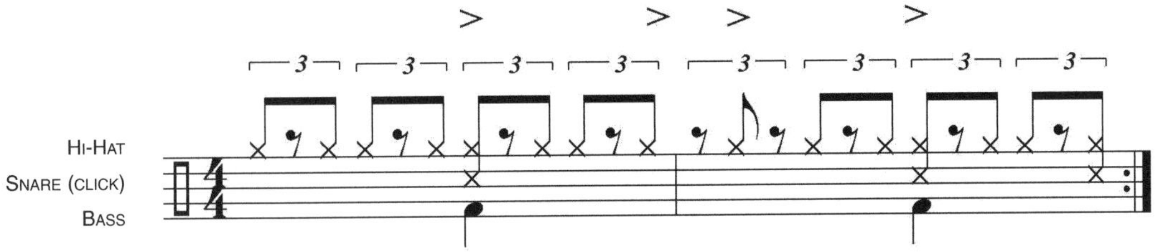

Variation 3

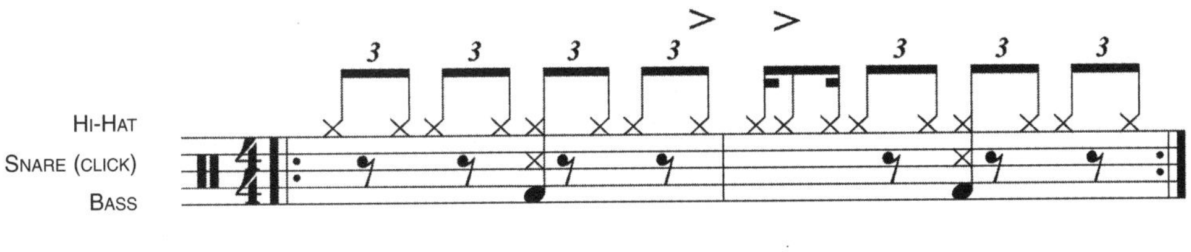

Variation 4

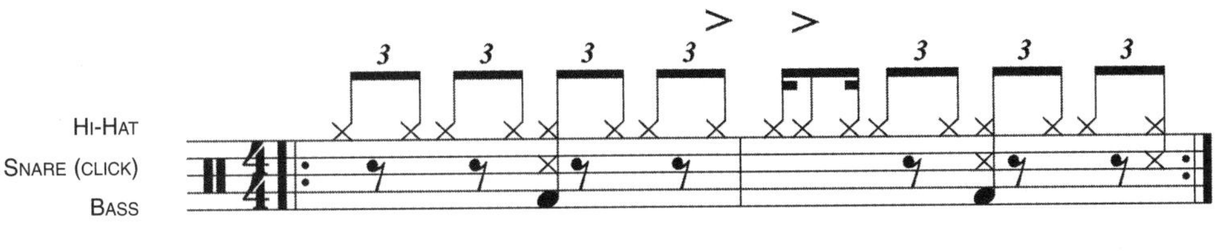

Example 2

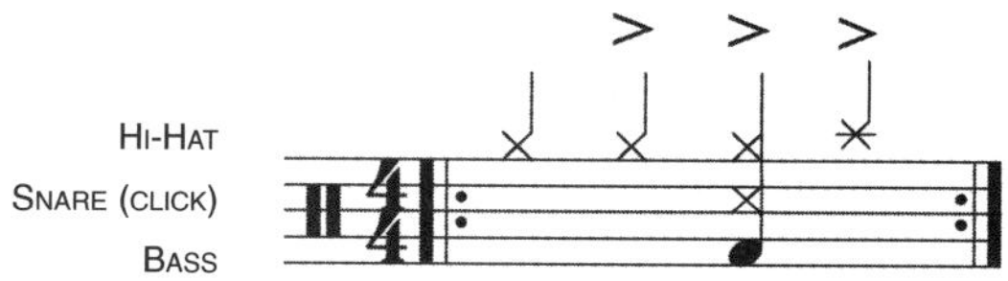

Variation 1

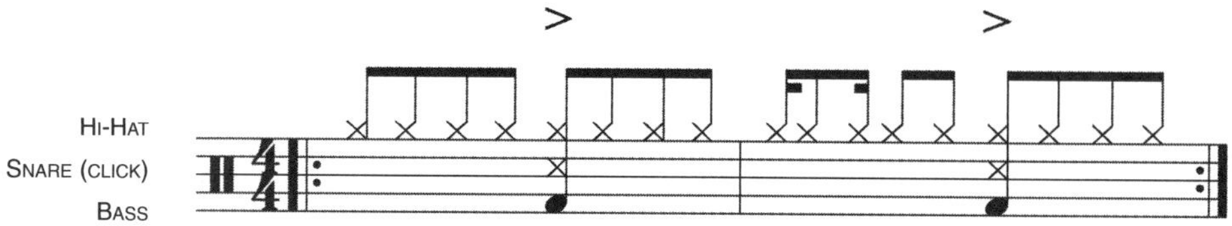

Variation 2

This variation is based on the Jazz ride pattern, but should be played "in the crack."

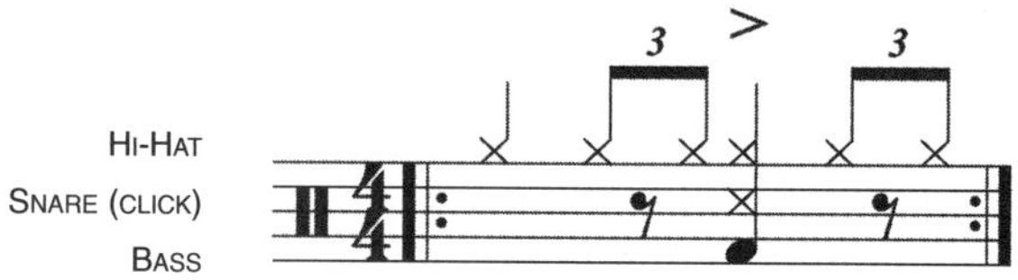

Rockers

The term "Rockers" refers to a style of Reggae that became popular in the mid-1970s, when musicians began to modify rhythms and change bass lines to create a more lively, danceable style of music, calling it "Rockers." Though Rockers sometimes has a more aggressive and syncopated sound compared to other Reggae styles, the overall feel is typically straight-ahead and suitable for dancing and grooving. The most common drum grooves found in Rockers are related to Rock 'n Roll grooves (hence, in all probability, the term "Rockers"). However, the grooves are usually on the slower side and very straight and steady in nature. **The tempo range is quarter note = 62–84bpm.**

Example 1

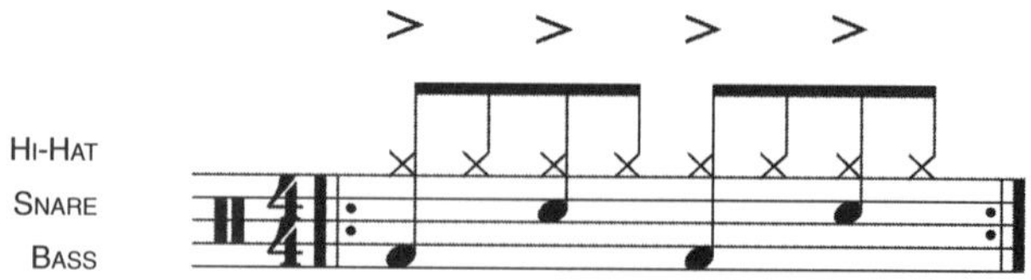

Variation

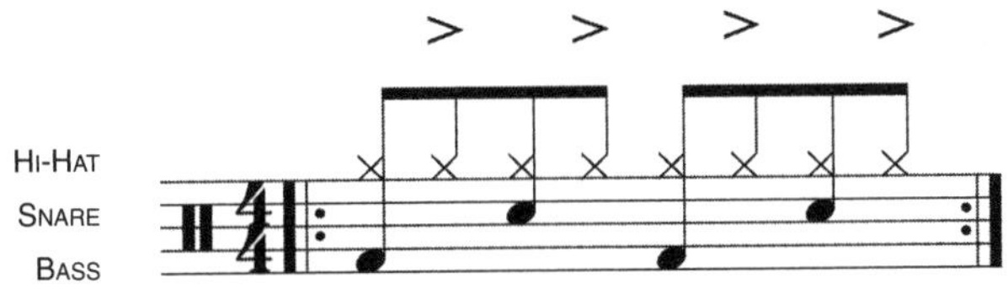

Reggae Steppers

The Stepper (four on the floor) pattern is used in Reggae as well as in Ska. The primary difference between Ska and Reggae Stepper beats is that Reggae Stepper beats are played at slower tempos than Ska Stepper beats. **The tempo rate is quarter note = 108–136 bpm.**

Example

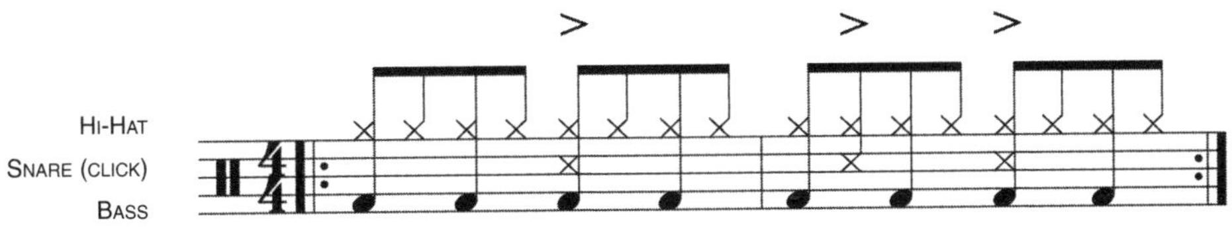

8 Country

Country music is popular around the world and serves an age-old function: storytelling. Its themes of love, heartache, and the promise of redemption in the afterlife are exceedingly popular. It stems from the Appalachian region where during the 18th and 19th centuries a majority of the population were of Scotch or Irish descent. These physically isolated mountaineers performed the Scotch-Irish folk songs of their ancestors. The folk-based musical formula consisted of ABAB rhyming quatrains citing personal experiences combined with the vocal/harmonic characteristics and subject matter of religious hymns.

Appalachian/Scotch-Irish music centered around the fiddle, and this remained so even after the intrusion of railroads in the 19th century brought new musical influences and instruments to the region. Traveling minstrel shows imported the banjo, providing a unique sound to accompany the fiddle, Appalachia's primary instrumental voice. By the early 1900s, now-affordable, mass-produced guitars gave singers a broader chordal and rhythmic base than the less versatile banjo and fiddle. This new arrangement of vocals with primary guitar accompaniment provided the base of contemporary Country music.

In the 1920s, radio broadcasts, most notably Nashville's The Grand Ole Opry (first broadcast in 1925), brought Country music to wide popularity. Recognizing commercial potential, recording pioneer Ralph Peer announced auditions in 1927 in the Bristol, Tennessee newspaper. The indigenous musicians straddling the Virginia-Tennessee border showed up in droves. They included Jimmie Rodgers and The Carter Family.

Drums first appeared in Country music with the recordings of Jimmie Rodgers ("Desert Blues" and "Any Old Time") in 1929, though they were excluded from traditional Country circles, most notably The Grand Ole Opry. They remained largely excluded from Country music ensembles until the 1930s, when Texas musicians, notably Bob Wills (with drummer Smokey Dacus), created "Western Swing," adding drums, other Big Band rhythm instruments, and more complicated harmonies than those of traditional Country music. Also, as the name "Western Swing" implies, the primary feel was "swung," as opposed to the straight feel of most other forms of Country music. When Wills appeared on the stage at The Grand Ole Opry on December 30, 1944, the Opry's ban on drums was lifted exclusively for his performance, and then promptly reinstated.

At about the same time, another relative of Country music appeared in the West, as Roy Rogers and Gene Autry pioneered "Western" music. Western music differed considerably from both Appalachian hillbilly (Country) music and Western Swing in that it downplayed instrumental virtuosity, was primarily vocally oriented, and more especially crooner oriented. The subject matter of its songs differed greatly, too. In place of Country's strange duality of gritty and religious songs, Western performers sang pop songs (e.g., Gene Autry's 1941 version of "You Are My Sunshine") and original Western songs portraying a heavily romanticized West (e.g., "Cool Water" and "Tumbling Tumble Weeds"). Western music's greatest star in the latter half of the 20th century was Marty Robbins ("El Paso"). Western lives on today in nostalgia-oriented groups such as Sons of the Pioneers, though its popularity has diminished. When drums are used in this style (often they're not), they normally play slow Country Shuffle grooves and are very much in the background.

The mainstream of Country music had made its way into the night life of cities and run down bars by the 1940s. And in the latter part of that decade, Country's first post-war "superstar," Hank Williams, developed the "Honky Tonk" style. This featured what has become the standard Country instrumental line-up: acoustic guitar, electric guitar, electric bass, drums, vocalist, and often pedal steel guitar and/or fiddle, and occasionally piano. In the 1950s, following the success of Hank Williams, Ray Price, with drummer Buddy Harman, began using the "Country Shuffle."

Though drums had become much more common by this time, when Buddy Harman appeared with Carl Smith on The Grand Ole Opry Stage he was relegated to playing one snare drum with brushes behind a curtain. Shortly afterward, Opry's new boss, Dee Kilpatrick, banned drums from the stage again.

In the same decade that Price and Harman developed the Country Shuffle, the heavier back beat influence of Rock n' Roll emerged in the style of "Rockabilly." This hybrid style was popularized by Country artists such as Carl Perkins and Johnny Cash, as well as Rock and Rollers such as Jerry Lee Lewis, and, of course, Elvis Presley. However, the louder, more raucous Rock sound tended to overwhelm the Country elements in Rockabilly, and today most Country enthusiasts insist that Rockabilly is a variety of Rock n' Roll rather than Country.

Country went "pop" in the late 1950s with the "Nashville Sound" (which was dominant in Country for decades and, arguably, still is). This was essentially an attempt to reach a mass audience by taking the "twang" out of Country. The distinguishing features of this variety of Country are a very smooth, heavily produced sound, background strings, and vocal choirs. Early examples of this sound are the recordings of Chet Atkins and the more over-produced (by influential producer Owen Bradley) songs of Patsy Cline.

As a reaction against the pop Nashville Sound, and greatly influenced by the Country shuffles of Ray Price and his drummer Buddy Harman, the Bakersfield Sound arose in the early 1960s. Its primary exponent was Buck Owens, who wrote and sang "Tiger by the Tail" and "Act Naturally." The distinguishing feature of the Bakersfield Sound was that the "twang" returned — there were no strings and no vocal choirs. In contrast to earlier Hank Williams-style Country, there was more emphasis on the electric guitar (with a tone owing much to Surf music), and drumming styles included standard Western Swing and Country Shuffle grooves. The primary modern exponent of the Bakersfield Sound is Dwight Yoakam (e.g., "Guitars and Cadillacs"), who, however, covers a much wider range of styles than Buck Owens.

Another reaction against the Nashville Sound was the "Outlaw Movement" of the 1970s. Outlaw music used the sounds of both Hank Williams-style Country and the Bakersfield Sound, differing from them primarily in its lyrical content, which was on the dark side, emphasizing heavy drinking, barroom brawls, and infidelity. Its exponents include Willie Nelson, Waylon Jennings, and David Allan Coe. Predictably, the Outlaw Movement still remains excluded from traditional Country music circles. However, during Outlaw's early years, drums were finally allowed on stage at The Grand Ole Opry when the organization moved to "Opryland" in 1973. Shortly afterward the Opry appointed Buddy Harman as its first regular drummer, while Harman continued to appear on countless Country music hits, including "Ring of Fire" (Johnny Cash), "Bye Bye Love" (the Everly Brothers), "Stand by Your Man" (Tammy Wynette) and even the Rock n' Roll classic "Pretty Woman" (Roy Orbison).

Another notable trend in the early 1970s was the emergence of Country Rock. On the Rock side, performers included pioneers such as The Byrds, Gram Parsons, The Flying Burrito Brothers, Marshall Tucker, and, most prominently, The Eagles. On the Country side, the musicians included Willie Nelson, Waylon Jennings, and Hank Williams, Jr.

Country and Country Rock are still as popular as ever, with performers including Garth Brooks, Shania Twain, Toby Keith, Tim McGraw, Hank Williams III, Kenny Chesney, Brooks & Dunn, The Dixie Chicks, Sara Evans, Faith Hill, Trisha Yearwood, Brad Paisley, LeAnn Rimes, Rosanne Cash, Clint Black, and Reba McEntire.

The distinguishing features of Country Rock are its use of Country harmonies and melodies, both Rock and Country instruments, and Rock drumming grooves. Many of the above-listed performers cross freely between the Country and Country Rock genres.

In the 1980s, still another reaction against the Nashville Sound arose with the New Traditionalists, led by Dwight Yoakam and Steve Earle. These artists returned to the stripped-down sounds of early Country, the Bakersfield Sound, and, to a limited extent, Bluegrass.

A drummer in the Country genre is responsible for a simple and steady beat. Although it appears deceptively easy, Country music boasts some of the best musicians ever to pick up an instrument, drums included. The drumming styles presented in this chapter provide a solid foundation for playing all Country styles. For further information on Country drumming, we highly recommend Brian Fullen's *Contemporary Country Styles for the Drummer and Bassist.*

NOTE: It's common in Country drumming to use a snare drum rim click, often accompanied by a ride pattern played with a brush directly on the snare drum. There are several examples of this technique in this chapter.

Bluegrass

Growing out of the instrumentation of early 20th century string bands and the influence of Blues, Bluegrass (originally called "Old Time Country," "Mountain Music," or "Hillbilly Music") received radio exposure in the 1930s. Developed in Kentucky, it earned Kentucky its nickname, "The Bluegrass State." It became immensely popular after Bill Monroe and his Blue Grass Boys performed at The Grand Ole Opry in 1939, establishing them as the seminal force of this high-energy, primarily instrumental music.

Traditional Bluegrass instrumentation is all acoustic and consists of a 5-string banjo, flat-top guitar, fiddle, mandolin, dobro, and bass. Eventually, the drum set became included in the Bluegrass ensemble as an integral instrument with the music of Lester Flatt and Earl Scruggs. Ricky Scaggs brings Bluegrass up to the present day ("Country Boy" being a good example of his style) along with the Dixie Chicks, Rhonda Vincent, and Blue Highway, while its more traditional forms have had a resurgence of popularity, largely due to the soundtrack from the movie, "O Brother, Where Art Thou?"

Bluegrass songs may—unlike songs in other Country styles—intentionally speed up to add flare to solos ("passing a break," in Bluegrass terms) and a song's finale. Ordinarily, Bluegrass drumming is played with brushes on a snare drum, with faster tempos featuring a "two feel." When Bluegrass's signature groove, the "Train Beat", is used in other genres it may be played with sticks (see "Train Beat" later in this chapter). The Train Beat's main characteristic is the consistent snare pattern accenting the upbeats, reflecting the sound of the 16th notes played on the fiddle and the banjo. **Since the tempo for Bluegrass is fairly fast, it is most easily felt in cut time, with quarter note = 100–160 bpm.**

Example (CD 2, Track 1)

This is the standard version of the Train Beat.

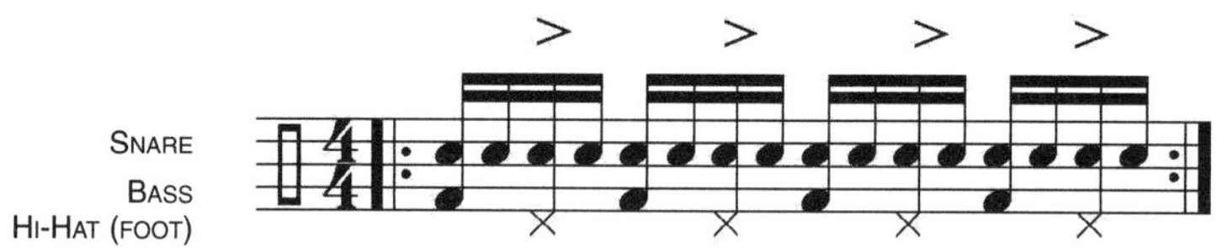

Variation 1

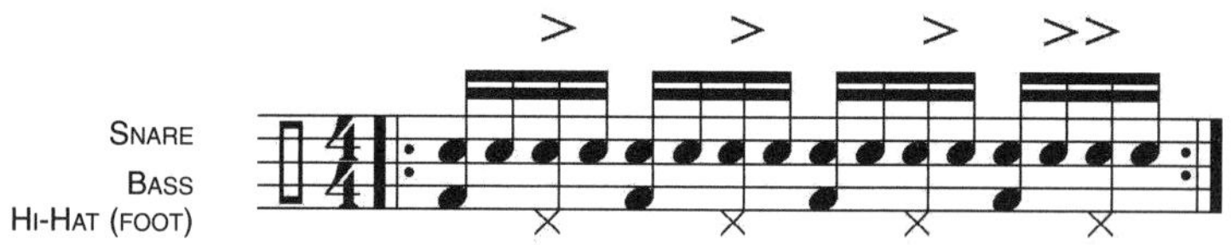

Variation 2

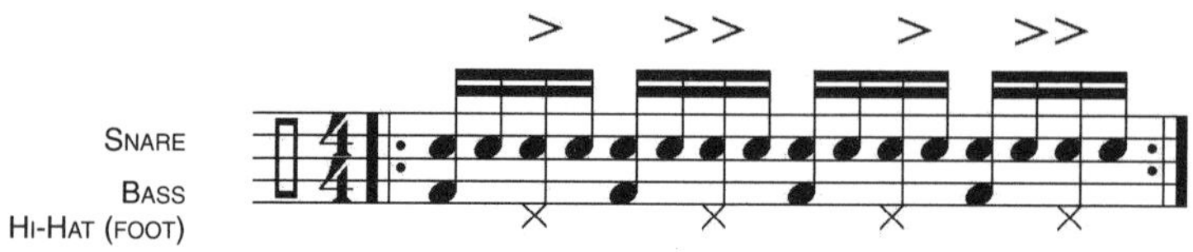

Variation 3

In addition to the Train Beat, another useful Bluegrass groove is the traditional Jazz swing pattern (written in 16th notes for a double time feel). It is written below for the snare with brushes, with the ride hand playing the Jazz swing pattern on the snare drum and the snare hand accenting each upbeat. As a result of the quick tempo, the 16th notes of the ride hand are played closer to straight than swung. This variation is hardly ever played with sticks on the ride cymbal, and the brush pattern is usually played in one spot (i.e., there is no circling around the drum head). **Quarter note = 60–120 bpm.**

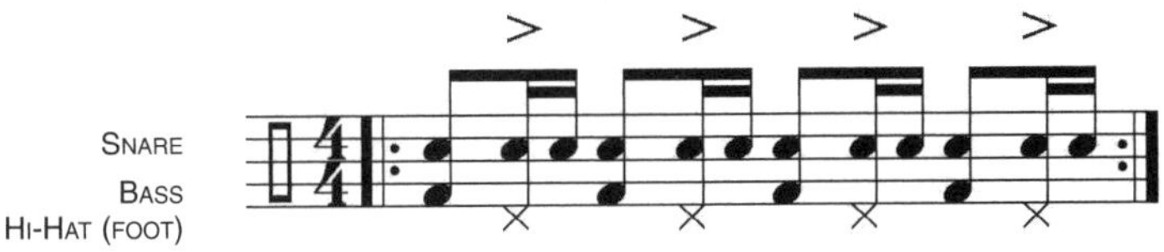

Western Swing

In the late 1930s and early 1940s, Western Swing was popularized by Bob Wills and his Texas Playboys. It featured swung rhythms and Big Band rhythm section instruments, including, for the first time in Country music, the drum set as an integral component (with drummer Smokey Dacus). (Later Wills drummers include Monte Mountjoy and Johnny Cuviello). Western Swing was also the first style to utilize electric guitar, bass, and pedal steel guitar. Fiddle legend Johnny Gimble has kept this style alive for the past six decades, paving the way for modern-day Western Swing musicians such as Asleep at the Wheel and Dan Hicks. In 2011, the Texas Legaslature named Western Swing the official music of the state of Texas.

As in Big Band Jazz, the role of the drummer in this genre is to establish a strong sense of time. In addition, as the name implies, Western Swing invariably has a swung feel. **The tempo is normally quarter note = 132–216 bpm, but may be slower for ballads.**

Example (CD 2, Track 2)

This is based on the Standard Swing Pattern from the Big Band section of the Jazz chapter. The one difference is the use of a snare drum rim click, which is usually more common than an actual snare drum strike, due to the subtler sounds of Western Swing.

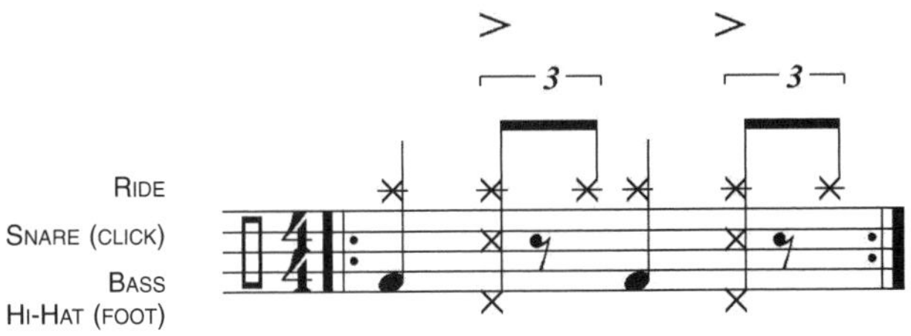

VARIATION

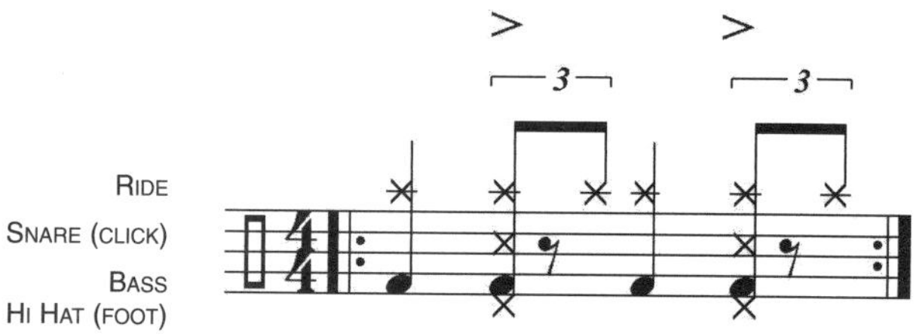

NOTE: The above Western Swing patterns may be played with the ride hand on the surface of a closed hi-hat for softer sections of a song, or with one brush on the snare drum. (The combination of the ride cymbal, hi-hat foot and full snare drum is usually reserved for the louder sections in Western Swing songs.)

ROCKABILLY

Though many Country artists have crossed the line into Rockabilly, the genre appeals mainly to Rock n' Roll enthusiasts. For this reason, Rockabilly drum grooves are listed in the Rock n' Roll chapter.

COUNTRY TWO-BEAT (TWO-STEP)

The Country Two-Beat (Two-Step) is found throughout Country music, ranging from early artists such as Hank Williams, Sr. to contemporary artists such as Reba McEntire and Lyle Lovett. The groove is characterized by a "two feel," emphasizing the upbeat throughout each measure and is often notated in 4/4. **The tempo range is quarter note = 80–132 bpm.**

EXAMPLE (CD 2, Track 3)

This is a Polka pattern (see Polka chapter). In Country, it is often played with a rim click in place of a snare drum note.

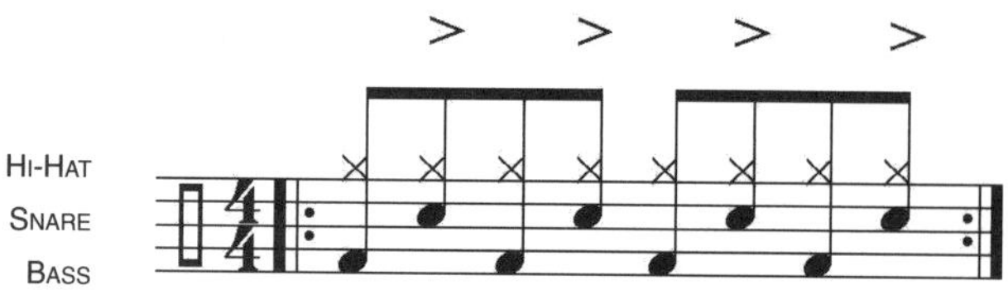

VARIATION (CD 2, Track 4)

The half-time Country Two-Beat emphasizes upbeats on the ride hand with a standard 2 & 4 backbeat on the snare drum.

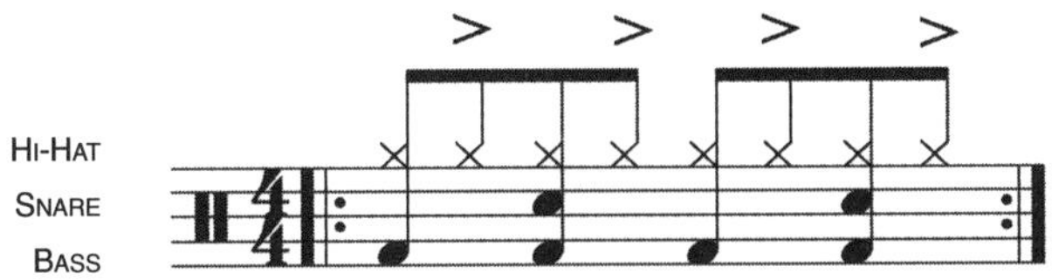

NOTE: The above two patterns may be played with the ride hand moving over to the ride cymbal, and hi-hat foot accompaniment in unison with the snare drum notes.

COUNTRY SHUFFLE

The Country Shuffle is identical to the Standard Blues Shuffle, and differs from it only in name and in its generally slower tempo. As mentioned in the introduction, Ray Price and his drummer, Buddy Harman, were primarily responsible for adoption of this groove in Country music in the 1950s. Since then, the Country Shuffle has come to be used in a variety of musical styles: Honky Tonk, The Nashville Sound, the Bakersfield Sound, and Modern Day Country. Early examples of the Country Shuffle include "Crazy Arms," "City Lights," and "I've Got a New Heartache." **Tempo range is quarter note = 80–126 bpm.**

EXAMPLE (CD 1, Track 51)

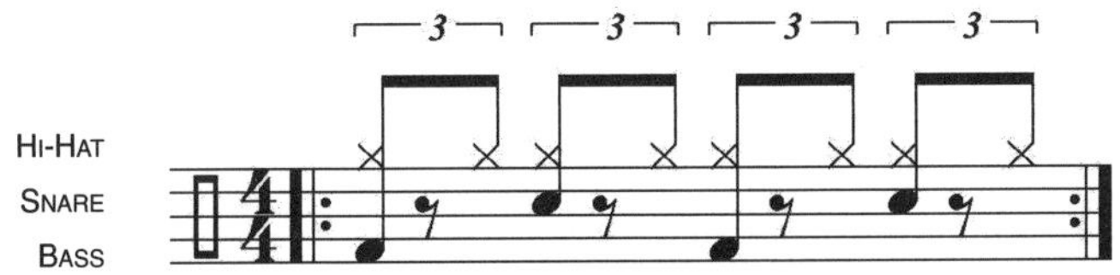

VARIATION 1

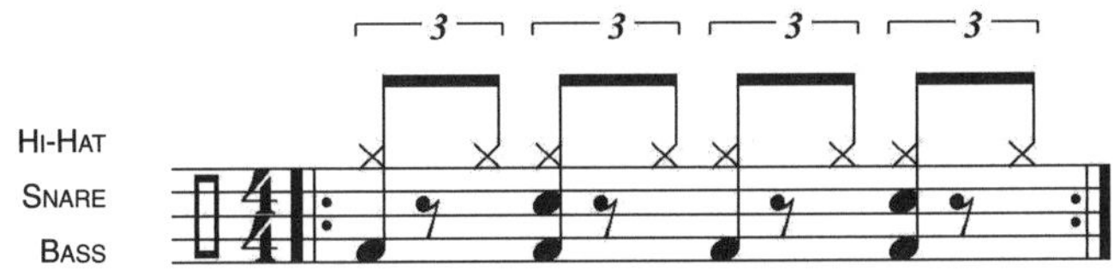

NOTE: The above Country Shuffle patterns can be played with the hi-hat foot accompanying the snare drum on beats 2 & 4, while the ride pattern is played on the ride cymbal or with one brush on the snare drum and a snare drum rim click.

VARIATION 2 (CD 2, Track 5)

This is identical to the Western Swing/Big Band swing pattern, with a snare back beat on 2 & 4. Though technically not a shuffle (beats 1 & 3 aren't shuffled), it is an appropriate groove for this genre as it was used on the earliest Country Shuffle recordings.

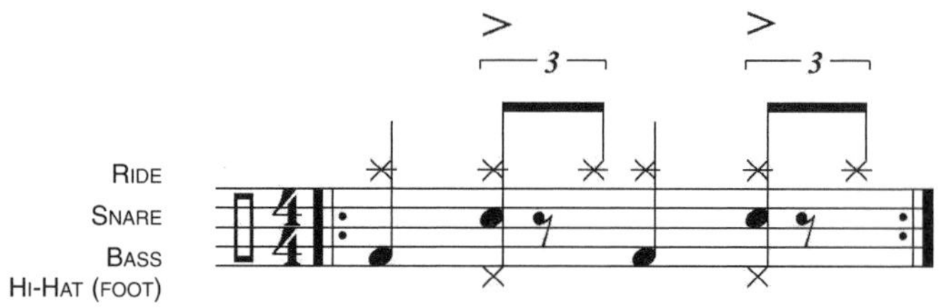

NOTE: Most shuffle patterns tend to be too busy for traditional Country and should be reserved for Country Rock and Modern Day Country. (Refer to additional shuffle variations in the Blues chapter.)

WESTERN

Western Music's initial identification with Country music (as in the archaic term, "Country & Western") stemmed from its sounding somewhat similar to traditional Country and the use of the guitar as the primary instrument. Although it is no longer coupled with Country, a musician may need to play Western songs in a non-traditional Country setting. The Country Shuffle is the primary groove in almost all Western songs, with the distinguishing feature being the slow tempo. **The tempo range is quite narrow, at quarter note = 80–92 bpm.**

While the slow Country Shuffle is the predominant beat, 1930s/1940s-style pop Western songs (e.g., "Wah Hoo") occasionally use the Country Two-Beat, generally in the normal Two-Beat tempo range of quarter note = 80–132 bpm, but occasionally faster than that.

EXAMPLE (CD 2, Track 6)

This is identical to the Country Shuffle example with substition of snare drum rim clicks for snare drum hits.

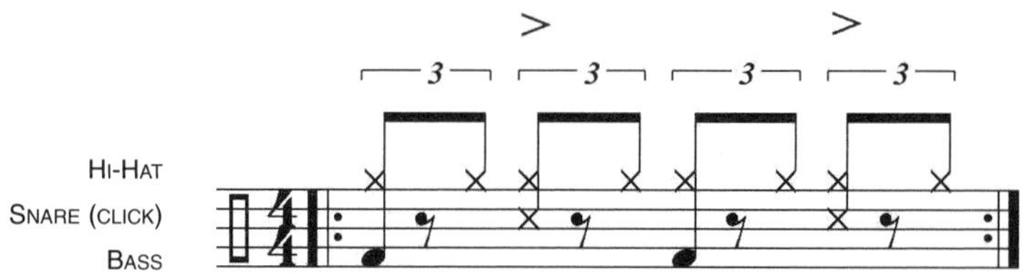

VARIATION

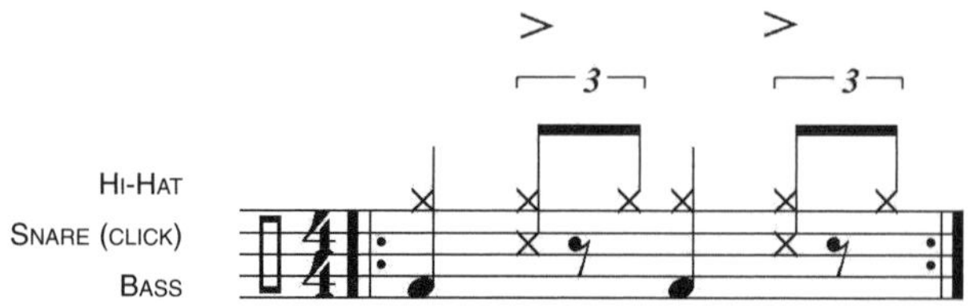

NOTE: Other variations are exceedingly limited, with the ride cymbal almost never being employed. There is similarly almost no deviation from the snare drum rim click. Variations of the shuffle ride pattern may include riding with a brush on the snare drum while retaining the snare drum rim click on beats 2 & 4.

Train Beat

The Train Beat is an indispensable groove at most Country gigs. Though its roots stem from the Bluegrass genre, it is now used throughout Country music. ("On the Road Again" by Willie Nelson is an ideal example.) Just as in Bluegrass, the Country Train Beat's main characteristic is the consistent snare pattern accenting the upbeats. But unlike Bluegrass, in the Country Rock and Modern Day Country genres it may sometimes be played with sticks, the snare drum remaining the exclusive surface. Also, the groove tends to have a slower tempo range than that of Bluegrass, which contributes to its being felt in 4/4 rather than cut time or "two feel." **The tempo range is quarter note = 100–132 bpm.** However, the abundance of snare drum notes simulates a fast, double-time feel.

Example (CD 2, Track 7)

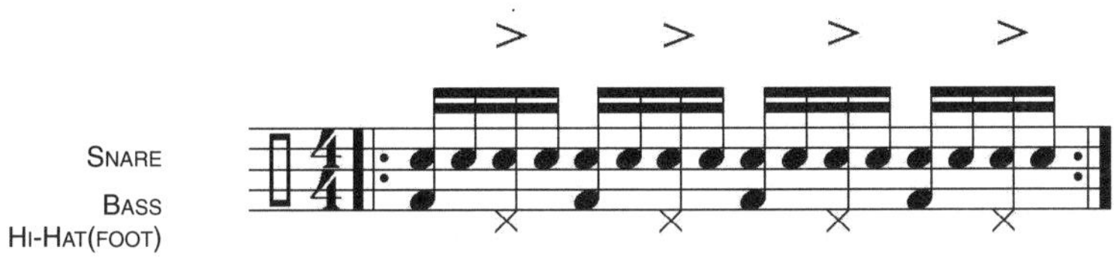

NOTE: For more Train Beat variations, see variations 1 and 2 in Bluegrass, remembering that sticks are appropriate for Country Rock and Modern Day Country, and almost never in traditional Bluegrass.

Country Rock and Modern Day Country

Beginning in the 1970s, Country music began incorporating the sounds and influence of mainstream Rock n' Roll. Artists such as Charlie Daniels, Linda Ronstadt (with drummer Russ Kunkle), Alabama, Willie Nelson, and Waylon Jennings stand as pioneers of this marriage of styles. Current artists such as Garth Brooks, Shania Twain, Faith Hill and Clint Black have attained worldwide popularity outside of normal Country music circles. (Traditional Country music continues to thrive through Modern Day Country artists such as Travis Tritt, Hank Williams Jr., and Winona Judd, with the late drummer Larrie Londin being one of the more notable session musicians of the genre.) As it is heavily influenced by contemporary Rock n' Roll, most Country Rock grooves may be played straight or shuffled (refer to Country Shuffle and the shuffle varieties in the Blues chapter for additional shuffle grooves). The main difference between Country Rock grooves and Modern Day Country grooves is that Country Rock grooves tend to be more active.

Country Rock and Modern Day Country are often included in the same category due to their similar musical characteristics. However, Country Rock tends to incorporate a dynamic rhythm section with loud guitars and bigger drum sounds, similar to those in a Rock n' Roll band. Modern Day Country relies heavily on pop-type grooves and modern production (including drum loops and sequencing). Additionally, there are "crossover artists" that explore characteristics of both styles, such as Tim McGraw and Americana. Similar drum grooves appear in both styles, and both may draw from the more traditional Country drumming styles previously cited in this chapter. **Tempos of both Country Rock and Modern Day Country range from slower ballads at quarter note = 58 bpm (or even slower) to brisk tempos of quarter note = 184 bpm or faster.**

EXAMPLE (STANDARD ROCK BEAT) (CD 2, Track 80)

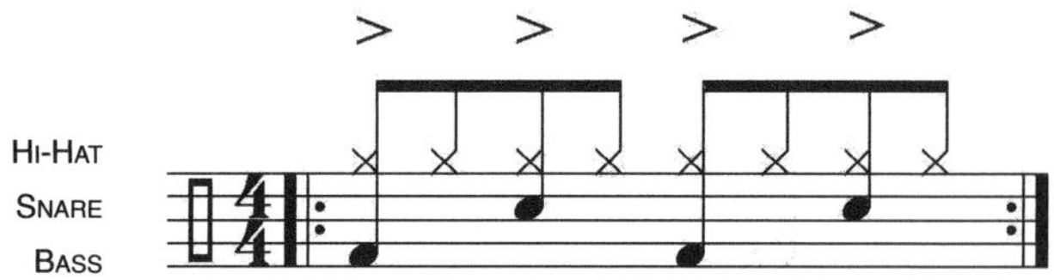

VARIATION

This pattern tends to be used in more aggressive songs or sections of songs and is useful over a narrower tempo range than the Standard Rock Beat. **Quarter note = 92–152 bpm.**

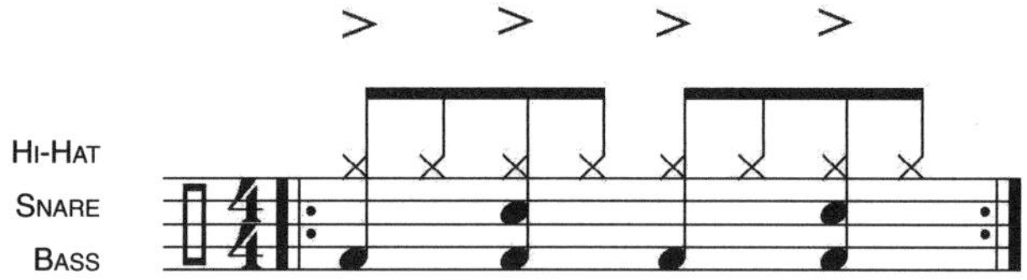

NOTE: As mentioned in previous notes, Country Rock and Modern Day Country may employ the above patterns with the combination of the ride cymbal, hi-hat foot accompaniment and full snare drum as more variations.

COUNTRY WALTZ

The Country Waltz spans the history and range of styles within Country music: traditional Country to Country Rock and Modern Day Country. A crucial characteristic which distinguishes it from the Jazz Waltz, Cajun/Zydeco Waltz and American Waltz is that the snare drum is rarely played on beat 2. The Country Waltz beat is normally found in slower songs or Country ballads. (For more Country Ballad possibilities, see Country Ballad following this section.) **Country Waltz tempos are usually slow, starting around quarter note = 76 bpm , but may range as high as quarter note = 116 bpm.**

EXAMPLE (CD 2, Track 8)

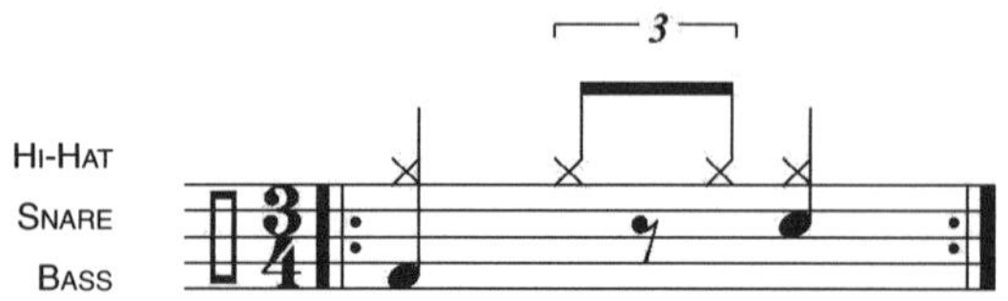

VARIATION 1

This is a busier pattern more commonly played in climactic sections of songs.

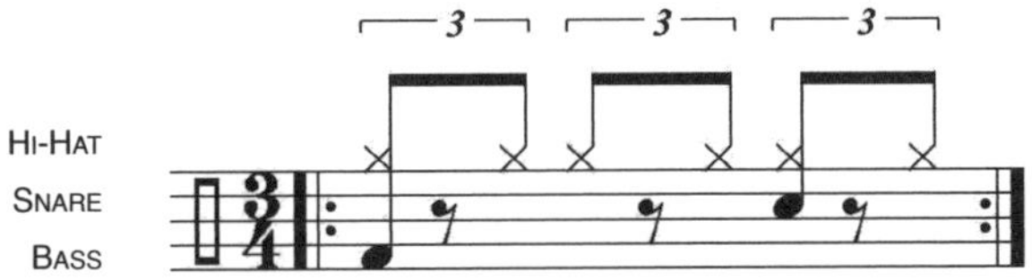

VARIATION 2 (CD 2, Track 9)

Though usually swung, the Country Waltz may also be played straight on very rare occasions, as opposed to the always swung Jazz Waltz. Note the straight eighth notes in the ride hand.

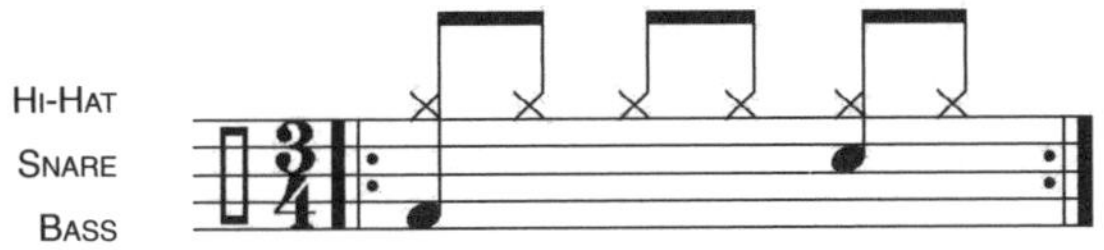

NOTE: The above Country Waltz patterns may be played with the hi-hat foot accompanying the rim click on beat 3, while the ride pattern is played on the ride cymbal or with one brush on the snare drum. (The combination of the ride cymbal, hi-hat, and full snare drum should be reserved for Country Rock and Modern Day Country, though rarely for traditional Country.)

COUNTRY BALLAD

One of the most prominent forms of Country music is the slow ballad, and the grooves below are the most common types. The first groove (12/8 groove—written in 4/4) is used throughout many Country Ballads, including Willie Nelson's hits "Night Life" and "Crazy," written by Willie Nelson, but most famously performed by Patsy Cline. **The tempo has a narrow range of quarter note = 50–80 bpm.**

EXAMPLE

This is identical to variation 1 in the 12/8 Pattern (Slow Blues) in the Blues chapter, but with snare rim clicks.

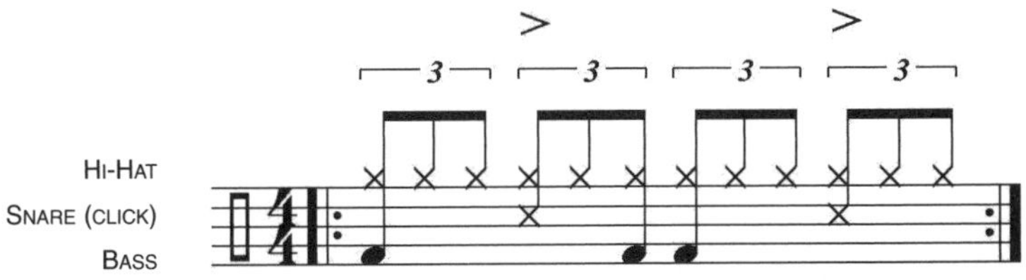

NOTE: Other variations of 12/8 ballads may be used for Country Rock or Modern Day Country, though they would tend to be too busy for traditional Country music.

Variation 1 (Country Rock Ballad)

This is the Standard Rock Beat played at the tempo of a ballad, and with a snare rim click. **Tempo range is quarter note = 60–72 bpm.**

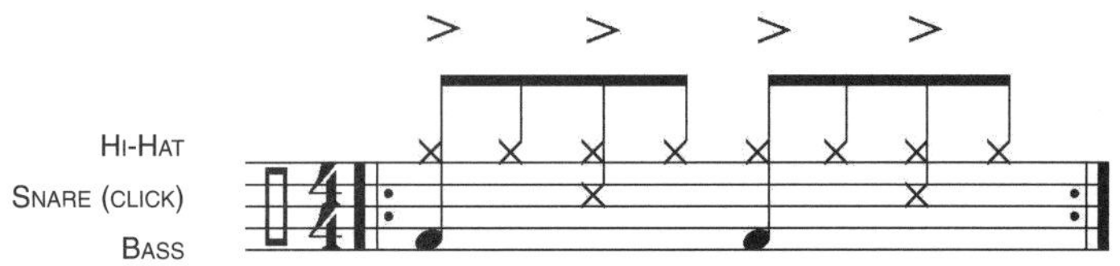

NOTE: Simple variations of the Standard Rock Beat (see Standard Rock in the Rock n' Roll chapter) may be played with ballads in Country Rock and Modern Day Country, but would tend to be too busy for traditional Country music.

Variation 2 (Half-Time Country Ballad)

This is the variation of the Half-Time Standard Rock Beat from the Rock n' Roll chapter. **The tempo range is narrower than that of Half-Time Standard Rock, at quarter note = 60–72 bpm.**

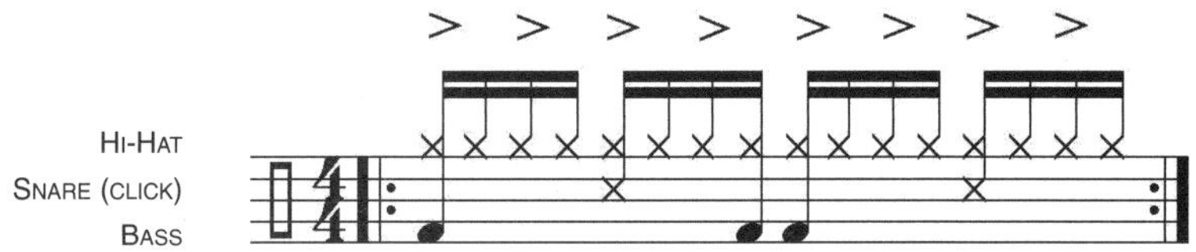

Variation 3 (Half-Time Country Waltz) (CD 2, Track 10)

This final Ballad variation is a two-measure pattern often played at even slower tempos than a Country Waltz. (A good example of the Half-Time Country Waltz is the Eagles' "Take It to the Limit".) **The tempo range is narrower than that of the Country Waltz with quarter note = 76–100 bpm.**

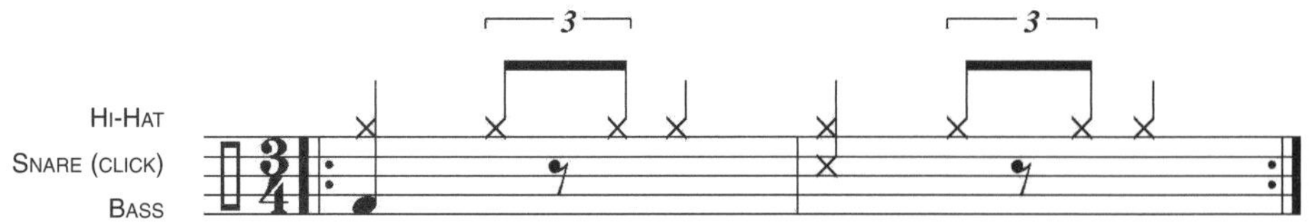

NOTE: The above Country Ballad patterns may be played with the hi-hat foot accompanying the rim click on the appropriate beat(s), while the ride pattern is played on the ride cymbal or with one brush on the snare drum.

9 Disco

Disco incorporates stylistic elements of Rock, Funk and the Motown sound while also drawing from Swing, Soca, Merengue and Afro-Cuban styles. It is above all else drum-driven dance music. Consequently, the role of the drummer is to make the beat prominent and unwavering at all times.

Although some elements of Disco appeared in the music of Funk groups such as Sly and the Family Stone, the style really began to develop in the early to mid-1970s when dance clubs ("Discotheques"), such as the Peppermint Lounge and Studio 54 in New York City began to gain popularity. Major record labels began supplying clubs with dance music on the first known pressings of 12" promo vinyl records (developed by music promoter Tom Moulton), which offered longer mixes ("remixes") of 3-minute standard popular songs. Disco emerged on the radio with a series of early hit singles including "The Hustle" (Van McCoy & the Soul City Symphony), "Love to Love You Baby" (Donna Summer), "Rock The Boat" (Hues Corporation) and "Never Can Say Goodbye" (performed by Gloria Gaynor, written originally by the Jackson Five). The genre reached its greatest popularity in the years 1977–1978, culminating with the movie "Saturday Night Fever," which pushed Disco high onto the music charts and into major concert venues, and greatly contributed to popularizing Disco's fashion and culture. The movie's soundtrack arguably stands as the most thorough compilation of Disco music. The genre began to fade toward the turn of the decade, only to return in the mid-1990s with a trendy "retro revival" in dance clubs, sampling of it on popular songs, and through live Disco/party cover bands.

Since Disco is dance music, the drumming style is simple and consistent. Common drumming characteristics are a "four on the floor" bass drum pattern, a steady 2 & 4 on the snare, and hi-hat patterns such as straight 16th notes or open hi-hat notes on upbeats. **The tempo range of most Disco songs is quarter note = 108–120 bpm.**

Example (CD 2, Track 11)

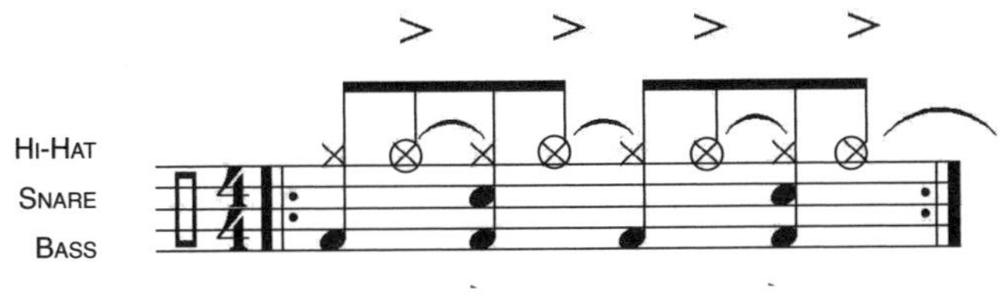

(Circled hi-hat notes are played open)

Variation 1

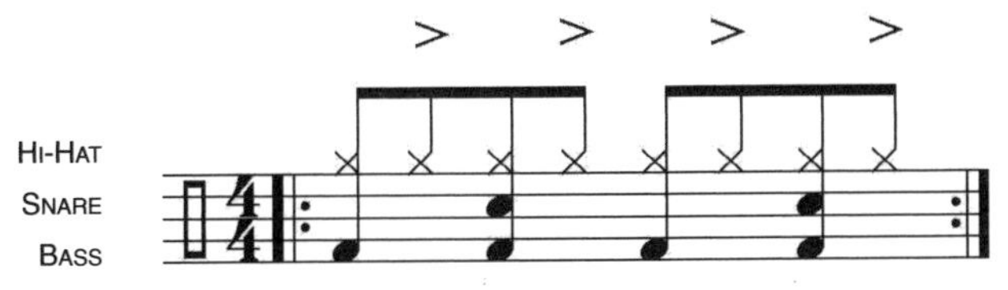

VARIATION 2 (CD 2, Track 12)

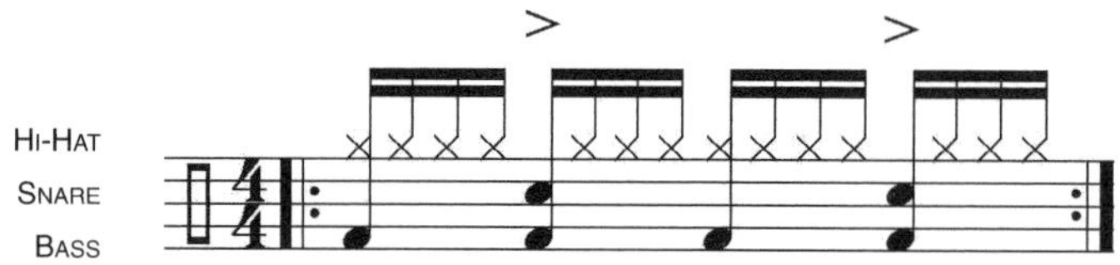

VARIATION 3

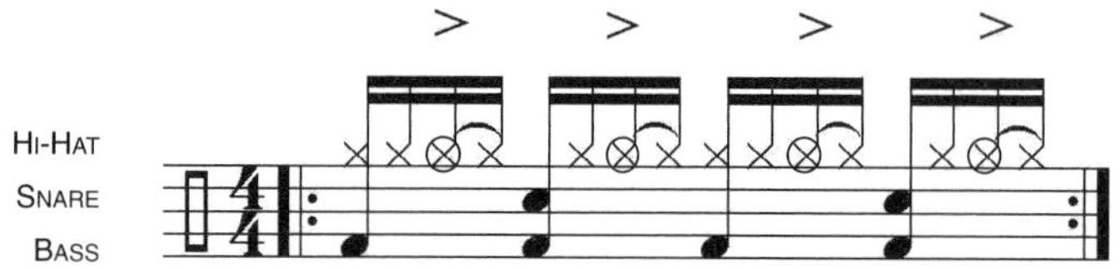

(Circled hi-hat notes are played open)

NOTE: When moving to the ride cymbal, the most common pattern in Disco is to accent the upbeats on the ride bell with hi-hat foot accompaniment on either beats 2 & 4 or on all downbeats.

10 Drum & Bass / Jungle

The history of Drum and Bass / Jungle music is relatively short. It has, however, attained immense popularity within a musical subculture. Jungle was the first of the two styles, emerging around the early 1990s and influenced by the UK hardcore Techno dance scene (specifically the Breakbeat style). Jungle borrowed the frantic, up-tempo electronic rhythms of Techno, while mixing in Reggae bass lines and Raggamuffin-style vocals (rapping with a Reggae accent and rhythm). In addition, the growing popularity of programmed Hip Hop beats and rhythms had a profound effect on Jungle music.

Toward the middle of the decade, Jungle DJs and composers began experimenting with longer songs, fewer vocals, more synthesizer ambience, Jazz and Funk influence, and live drums, eventually leading to the creation of Drum and Bass (often written as "Drum n' Bass"). Drum and Bass provided a more intellectual side for the Jungle musicians, focusing more on the instrumental portion of the music rather than the song-oriented features.

Notable Drum n' Bass composers include Netsky and Squarepusher, and well known Drum n' Bass drummers include Jojo Mayer (with his popular band, Nerve), Tony Verderosa, Akira Jimbo, Zach Danzinger, Guy Licata, and Johnny Rabb (with his popular band, BioDiesel).

As a drummer, it is important to realize that a live player is not always required in this style. Nevertheless, it can be quite challenging to perform as a drum set player in Drum and Bass/Jungle, because a drummer is usually required to emulate the elaborate rhythms programmed into a drum machine or sequencer. The brisk tempos that are common in Drum and Bass/Jungle make the task all the more difficult. In order to reproduce the sounds of Drum and Bass's programmed grooves, it's a good idea to play small drums tuned relatively high, along with small, "trashy" cymbals. It's also a good idea to use electronic drum kits and triggered systems that enable a drummer to combine authentic Drum and Bass electronic sounds with live playing.

The variety of patterns in Drum and Bass/ Jungle is virtually endless. The basic idea is to strive for a creative but also repetitive drum pattern (referred to as a "loop"). Improvisation is also a common element. Below are a few patterns that can be used in Drum and Bass/Jungle. What distinguishes one from the other is the use of broken-up sixteenth notes in the faster patterns of Jungle, as opposed to the simpler/ambient grooves of Drum and Bass. **The tempo range is swift at quarter note = 144–192 bpm.** For further information, we highly recommend Johnny Rabb's *Jungle/ Drum n' Bass for the Acoustic Drum Set."*

Example (CD 2, Track 13)

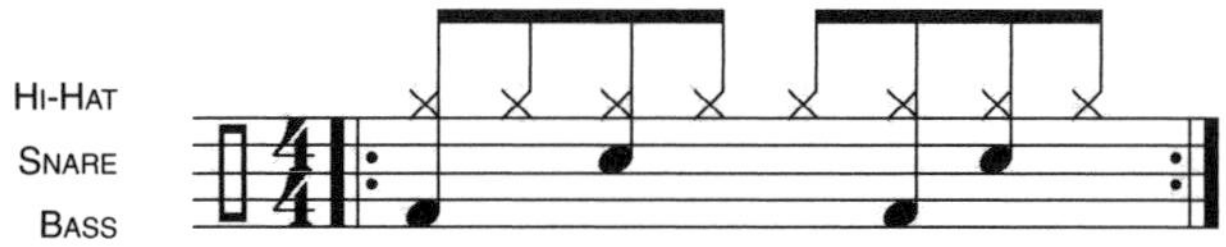

Variation 1 (CD 2, Track 14)

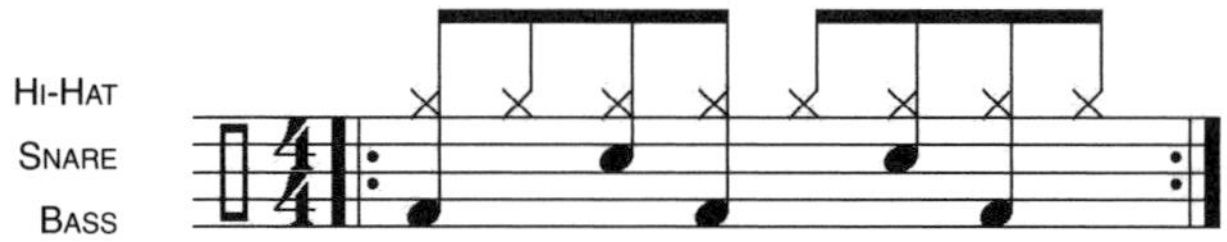

Variation 2 (CD 2, Track 15)

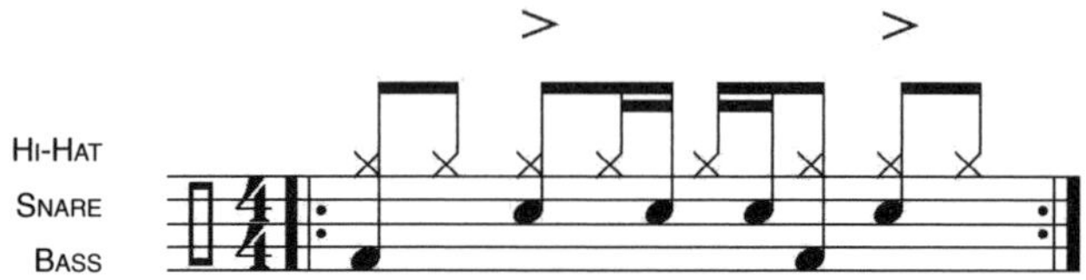

Variation 3

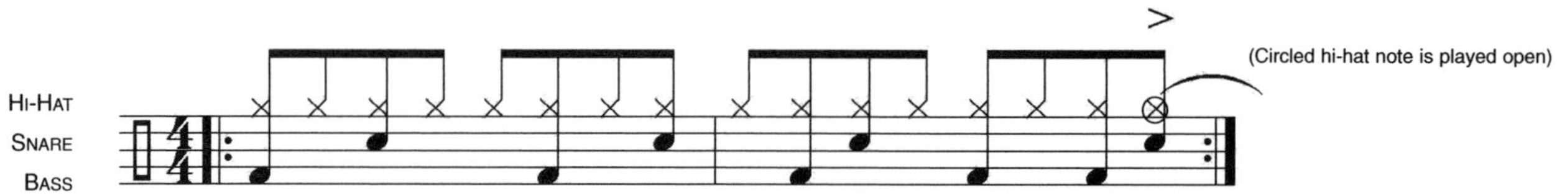

Variation 4

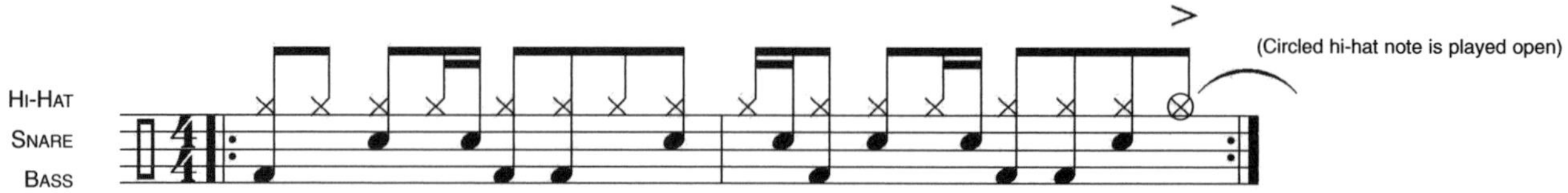

NOTE: The Example plus the first two variations are the most commonly used grooves in Drum & Bass/Jungle.

VARIATION 5 (CD 2, Track 16)

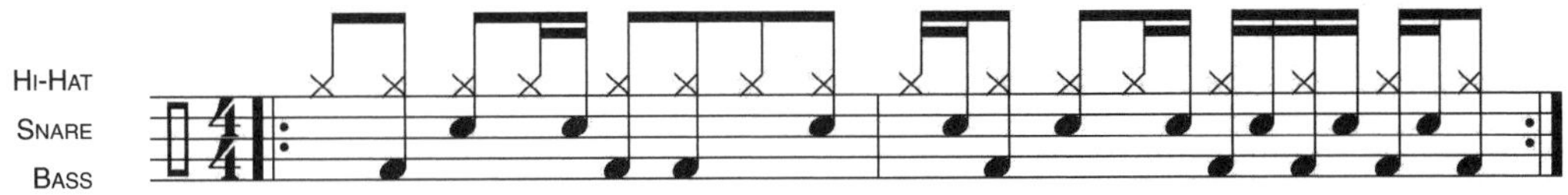

VARIATION 6

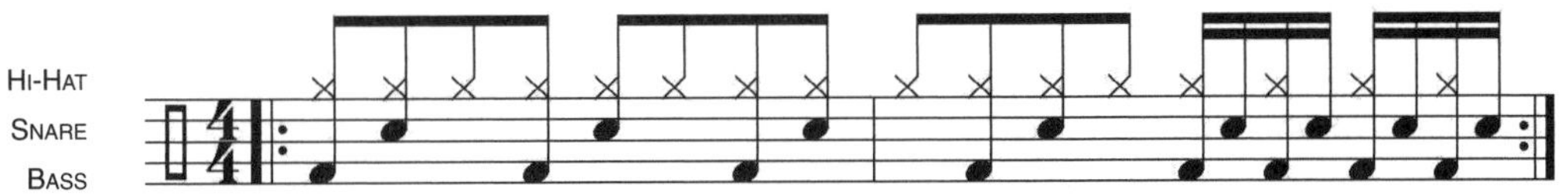

VARIATION 7

VARIATION 8

This is akin to Linear Funk, in which no notes are played simultaneously (see Linear Funk in Funk chapter.)

NOTE: Endless grooves can be created by using the consistent eighth note ride hand, the unison, and the linear approaches, as well as combinations of all three. Though other surfaces besides a closed hi-hat can be played by the ride hand, standard hi-hat foot accompaniment is not usually included.

11 FLAMENCO

FLAMENCO IS A MUSIC AND DANCE FORM that originated over 500 years ago in Andalusia in southern Spain. Early Flamenco blended influences from European and Middle Eastern cultures (Gypsies, Jews, Moors/Arabs, native Andalusians), including Hindu dances mixed with emotional Greek and Roman poems and songs. Flamenco music comes in many forms (3/4, 4/4, 6/8, "12 count," etc.). The most practical traditional forms incorporating drum set are Rumba (Rumba Gitena, not to be confused with the Cuban style of Rumba) and Tangos (not to be confused with the Argentine Tango), both in 4/4.

Traditionally, Flamenco instrumentation includes classical guitar, singing, vocal chanting, and the percussive sounds of staccato hand clapping, castanets, and the sound of the dancers' heels—all supported by an unwavering, steady pulse. Though its development took many centuries, it wasn't until the early 1900s that Flamenco achieved its greatest popularity. Today, artists such as the Gipsy Kings, Rodrigo y Gabriela, and Ottmar Liebert have gained worldwide popularity playing what can be termed "Pop Flamenco," and traditional Flamenco continues to be performed throughout the world and in annual festivals, notably in Andalusia.

Since Flamenco relies heavily on a tradition of modest musical instrumentation, the drum set is not normally used in traditional Flamenco. However, when utilized in Pop Flamenco, drum set patterns are dance oriented, resembling Soca grooves (see Caribbean chapter). Additionally, a Songo groove (Afro-Cuban chapter) is also appropriate. As in many other styles, the drummer's function is to maintain a strong sense of time to accompany the dancers. **The tempo range is generally quarter note = 92–140 bpm.**

TRADITIONAL FLAMENCO

EXAMPLE 1

This pattern is a common Rock/pop groove used in the "Bulerias" Flamenco style. It is written in 3/4, yet can be felt as alternating measures of 3/4 and 6/8.

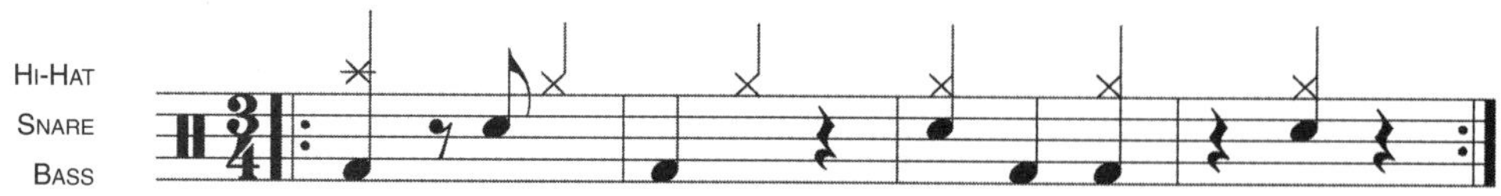

Example 2

This pattern is a typical groove in the "Flamenco Rumba" style.

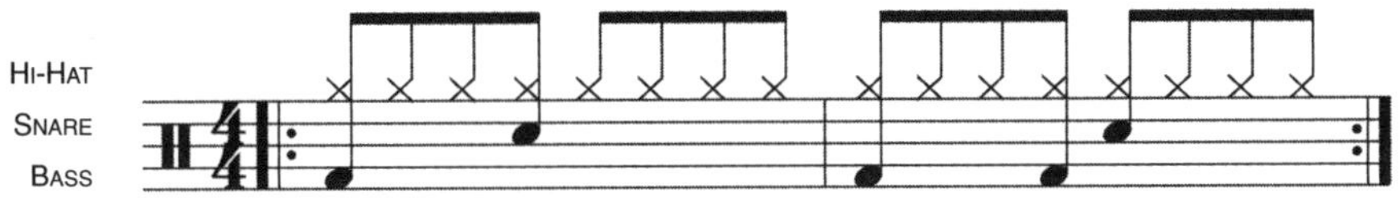

Example 3

This groove is useful in the "Flamenco Tangos" style.

(Circled hi-hat notes are played open)

Pop Flamenco

Example (CD 2, Track 17)

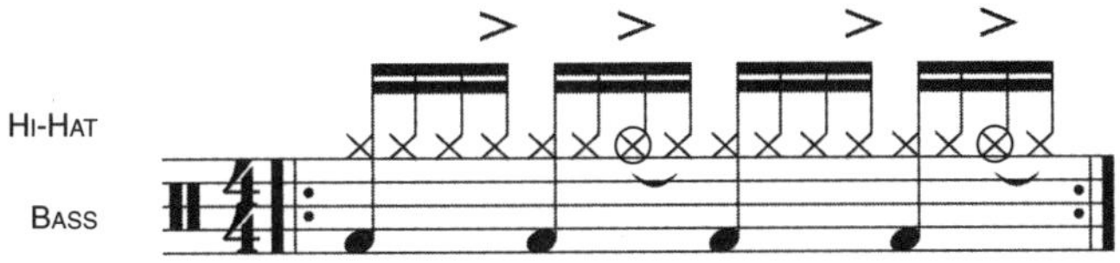

(Circled hi-hat notes are played open)

Variation 1 (CD1, Track 87)

This pattern is the standard Soca groove, with a syncopated snare rhythm along with the bass drum playing the "four on the floor" pattern.

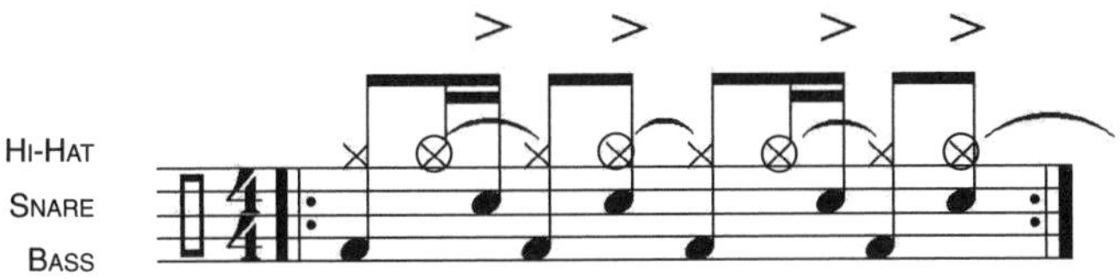

(Circled hi-hat notes are played open)

VARIATION 2 (CD 1, Track 34)

This groove, which is appropriate for traditional Flamenco played in 4/4 (Rumba and Tangos), is the main Songo example. It incorporates a 2-3 rumba clave pattern. (For further variations, see Songo in the Afro-Cuban chapter.)

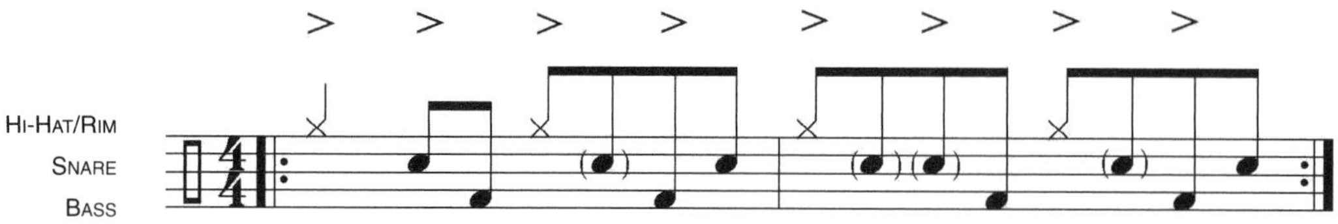

VARIATION 3

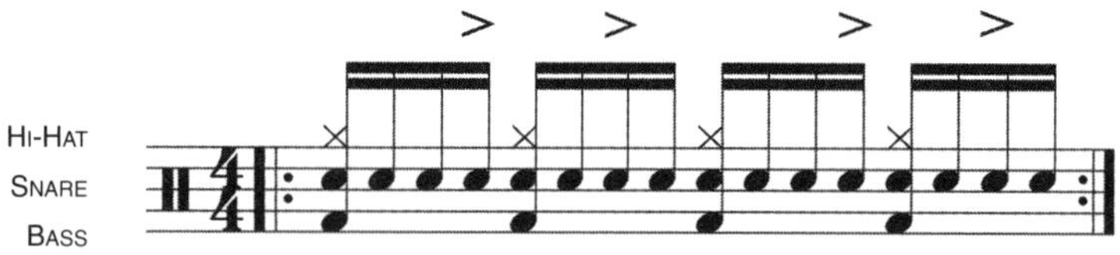

12 FUNK

LIKE JAZZ, BE BOP, AND ROCK N' ROLL, Funk acquired its name from a slang expression with sexual connotations. In musical terms, it originally meant anything that was off the traditional path or something that was "funky." Some of the earliest forms of Funk began in the city that gave birth to Jazz, New Orleans. Along with New Orleans native Fats Domino (whose recordings featured the grandfather of Funk drumming, Earl Palmer), one of the most influential musicians to contribute to this genre is piano player Henry Roeland "Roy" Byrd, popularly known as "Professor Longhair." His style includes the sounds of early Rock n' Roll and Blues with the Afro-Cuban clave influence of New Orleans Second Line (featuring Earl Palmer yet again).

In the 1950s, another primary precursor of Funk arose—Soul Music. It combined elements of Rock n' Roll and Rhythm & Blues, with Ray Charles being among the first to bring this new style to prominence. Near the end of the decade, another artist appeared who would become the driving force of Soul/Funk music for the next 40 years. James Brown ("The Godfather of Soul") created driving dance music which involved advanced musicianship utilizing the syncopated and displaced rhythms which have come to characterize Funk. In addition, in Detroit, beginning in 1960 Motown Records helped create what is now called "the Motown sound." Prominent Motown drummers include Richard "Pistol" Allen, Uriel Jones, and Benny Benjamin. The other prominent Soul label at this time was Stax, whose recordings often featured drummer Al Jackson, Jr.

By the mid-1960s, through the influence of James Brown, Stax, and Motown records, the style had become firmly established. Syncopated rhythms, displaced snare drum notes, and percussive horn arrangements all emerged as defining sounds of Funk and remain essential to the style today. Near the end of the decade, Funk music was further enhanced by the group Sly and the Family Stone, particularly through the innovative "slap" technique of bassist Larry Graham (later of Graham Central Station).

By the early 1970s, Funk began to achieve worldwide popularity. Dr. John, the Meters, and later the Neville Brothers, helped mature the sounds of New Orleans Funk and brought it national exposure. During the rest of the decade Funk music blossomed through the success of artists/groups such as War, Tower of Power (with drummer David Garibaldi), Curtis Mayfield, George Clinton and Funkadelic, Earth, Wind and Fire, The Ohio Players, The Commodores, Stevie Wonder, Barry White, and The Average White Band.

By the 1980s, Funk's extensive popularity began to diminish, though the grooves of the Funk rhythm section had made their way into pop music through artists such as Prince and Kool and the Gang. Even Rock bands of the past 25 years have relied on Funk concepts, Dave Matthews and The Red Hot Chili Peppers being two prominent examples. Throughout the past three decades, the sounds of Hip Hop (see Hip Hop chapter) and modern R & B have also borrowed the rhythms and grooves of traditional Funk. Today the sounds and ideas of Funk pervade all popular music to such an extent that it has become an essential style for the working drummer.

The patterns played by a Funk drummer range anywhere from the simplest Rock grooves to intricate rhythms matching those played by the rest of the band. Additionally, the feels in Funk span from relaxed and laid back ("behind the beat") to intense and driving ("on top of the beat").

New Orleans Funk

The primary components of a New Orleans Funk pattern are the repetitive accents derived from the "3" side of a clave rhythm mixed with the march-style characteristics of a Second Line groove. The distinguishing feature of this style is the cyclical rhythm defined by the drums and augmented by the other instruments. Notable drummers include Earl Palmer (who incorporated street parade drumming into Funk), Idris Muhammad, James Black, Joseph "Zigaboo" Modeliste, Willie Green, John Boudreaux, Johnny Vidacovich, Herlin Riley, Ricky Sebastian, Stanton Moore, Raymond Weber (of Dumpstafunk), Herman Ernest, Chris Lacinak and Joey Peeble, drummer for the newest New Orleans legend, Troy 'Trombone' Shorty. Though easily interpreted in double time, the feel tends to be laid back and relaxed (with the eighth notes often played "in the crack"). **The tempo range is quarter note = 152–208 bpm.**

Example 1 (CD 2, Track 18)

A good example of this pattern is in the song "Hey Pocky A-Way" by the Meters, which is played "in the crack." The same pattern can be played with both sticks on a closed hi-hat instead of the snare drum.

NOTE: Although an alternating hand pattern is typical, the sticking RR LR RL RL is often used with the steady hi-hat and snare drum 8th notes in the above groove. This sticking helps in achieving the "in the crack" (between straight and swung) feel.

Variation 1

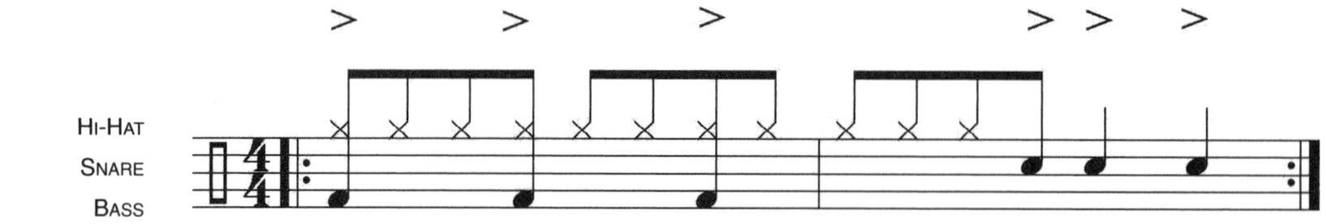

Variation 2

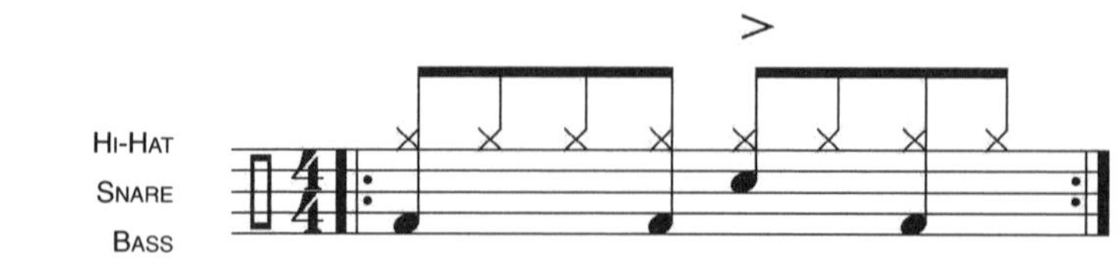

Variation 3 (CD 2, Track 19)

This is the drum pattern from the Professor Longhair classic, "Big Chief." The syncopated snare drum creates a busy sound producing the illusion of a faster tempo. Pay close attention to the buzz stroke in the snare hand on the last eighth note of the measure in this pattern. An option is to leave out beat 1 following the buzz stroke.

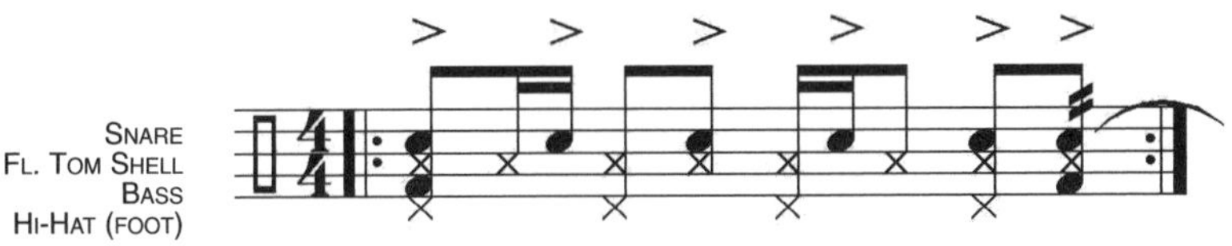

Variation 4

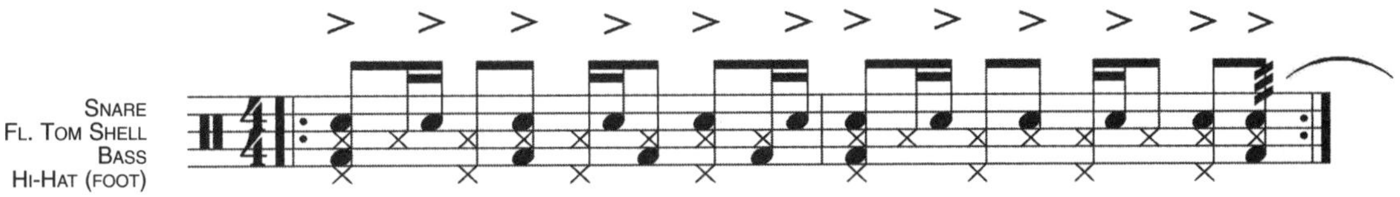

Variation 5

This is the drum pattern for the popular New Orleans Funk groove called the "Magnolia Special."

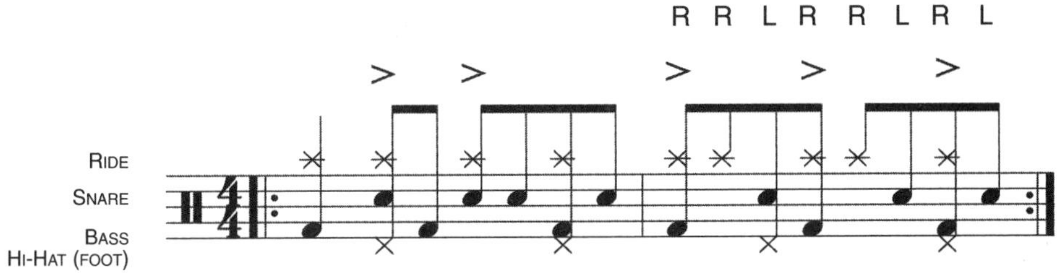

Variation 6

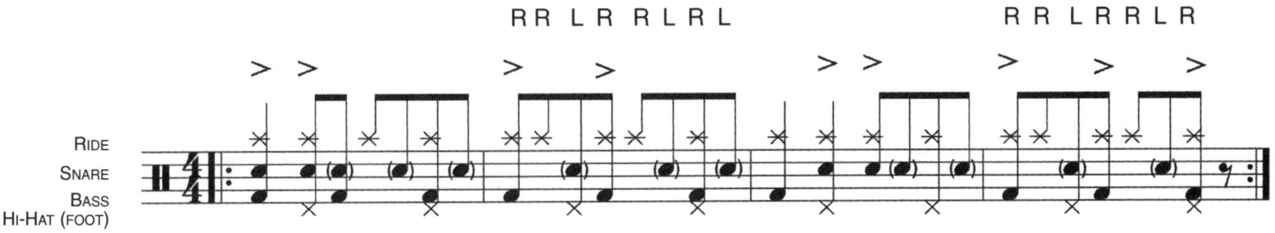

Variation 7

This drum pattern is from the New Orleans Funk standard "Iko Iko." Note the 3-2 son clave pattern in the accented snare notes. (See Afro-Cuban chapter for information on the clave.)

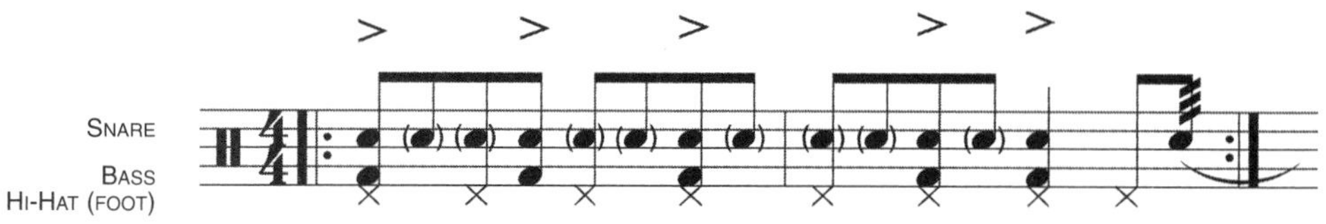

Variation 8

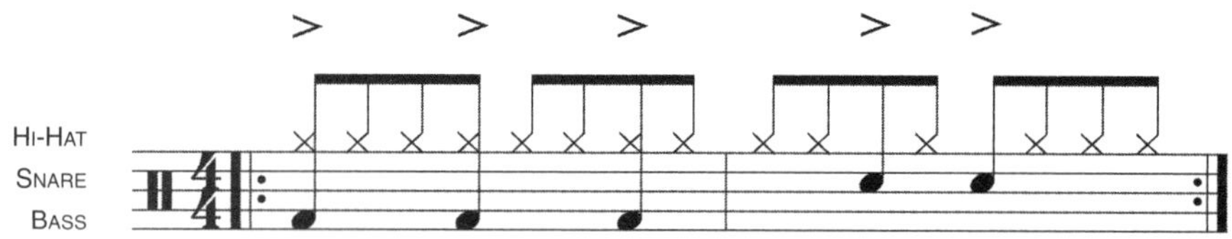

NOTE: Though an alternating hand pattern is most common, LL RL RL RR sticking is often used in the 8th-note patterns in the above grooves. This sticking is helpful in producing the "in the crack" feel and in producing interesting orchestrations when switching between surfaces.

Displaced Funk

"Displaced" refers to playing primary snare drum notes on counts other than the customary strong 2 & 4 back beats. Though creative and sometimes unusual, "displaced" patterns usually retain the repetitive feature of most drumming grooves. An innovative and complimentary pattern may not only be appropriate to a particular song, but can stand as a defining element of the song itself. Songs such as "Cold Sweat" (by James Brown), "People Say" (by the Meters), and "Chameleon" and "Actual Proof" (both by Herbie Hancock and Headhunters) are good examples of arrangements containing memorable Displaced Funk drumming grooves. Drummers of the classic James Brown era, such as Clayton Fillyau, Clyde Stubblefield and John "Jabo" Starks, the Meters' Joseph "Zigaboo" Modeleste, Bernard Purdie, Harvey Mason, Mike Clark (especially on Herbie Hancock's "Thrust" album) and drummers from the Neville Brothers, Stevie Wonder, and the Average White Band all explored the use of "displaced" rhythms. There is no standard Displaced Funk groove. The example and variations below are simply a practical approach to the style. Endless Displaced Funk variations are possible. However, it's good to play at least one snare drum note on a standard back beat (2 or 4) so as not to lose the beat. Whereas New Orleans Funk is usually felt and counted in double time, the patterns in Displaced Funk are felt in 4/4. **The tempo is medium at quarter note = 100–138 bpm.**

Example (CD 2, Track 20)

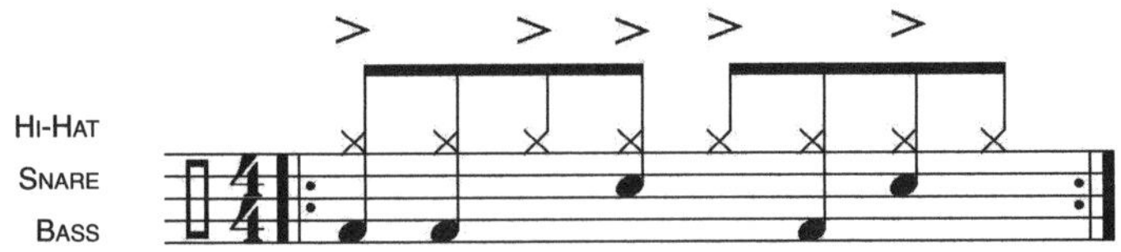

Variation 1 (CD 2, Track 21)

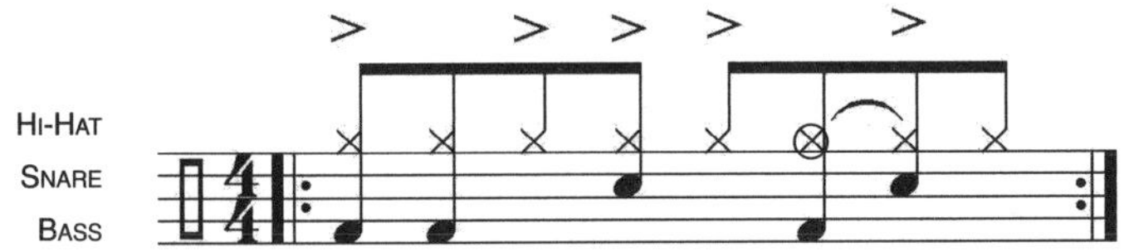

(Circled hi-hat note is played open)

Variation 2 (CD 2, Track 22)

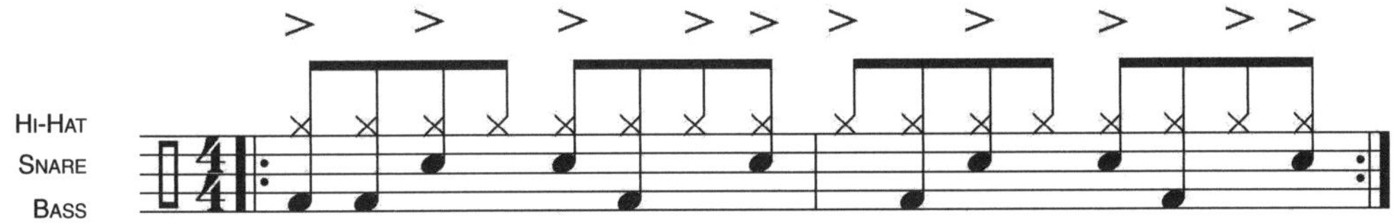

Variation 3

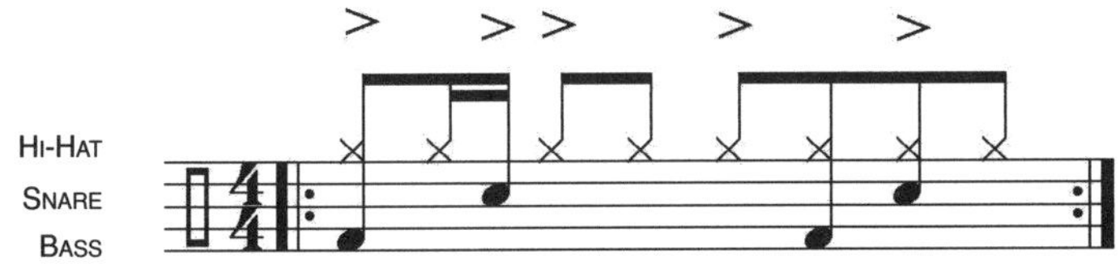

Variation 4

This is the drum pattern in James Brown's classic, "Cold Sweat" (with drummer Clyde Stubblefield). It's a good example of what's known as a "Fat Back" groove.

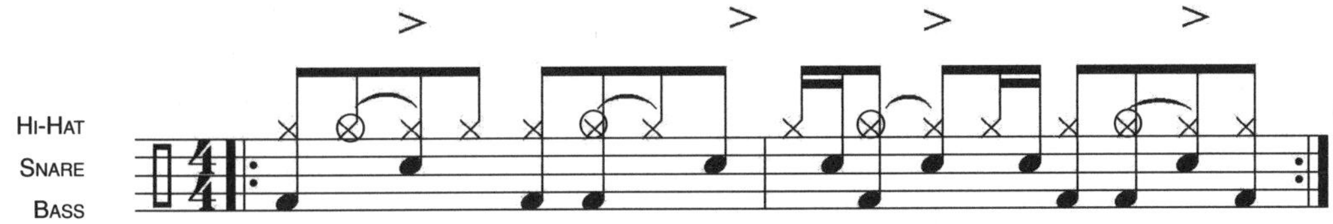

(Circled hi-hat notes are played open)

NOTE: Though not typical, a variation on the above patterns can include playing the ride hand on the ride cymbal with various hi-hat foot accompaniment patterns, such as beats 2 & 4 or all four downbeats. Bass drum displacement is also common in Funk. (Refer to the "Funk Rock" section below.)

LINEAR FUNK

"Linear" describes notes that occur one after another in a "line," with no notes being played simultaneously (that is, no limbs striking at the same time). This creates a lighter sound than the layered approach of Displaced Funk. The Linear approach tends to be quite busy, usually featuring 16th notes throughout an entire measure. Though these patterns can be found in standard Funk (e.g., early Meters recordings featuring Zigaboo Modeleste), they tend to be more prominent in the Fusion genre. Prominent Linear drummers include Billy Cobham, Alphonse Mouzon, Rod Morgenstein, Tony Williams, Mike Clark, and Dennis Chambers. As with Displaced Funk, there is no standard Linear Funk groove. **The practical tempo range for Linear Funk is similar to that of Displaced Funk with quarter note = 100–138 bpm.**

EXAMPLE (CD 2, Track 23)

The following example and variations plus alterations 1A, 1B, and 1C were developed by Mike Clark. The main example and its alterations appear in the song "Slinky" on the CD *The Funk Stops Here* by the Mike Clark Group.

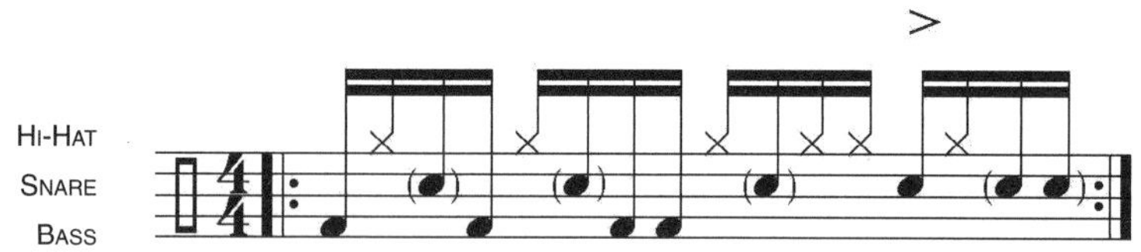

There are several ways to alter this pattern:

1A (CD 2, Track 24)

(•) = A dot placed over a note indicates dividing the value of that note into two 32nd notes. For instance, the example below is written out with a dot placed over two hi-hat notes creating two sets of 32nd notes:

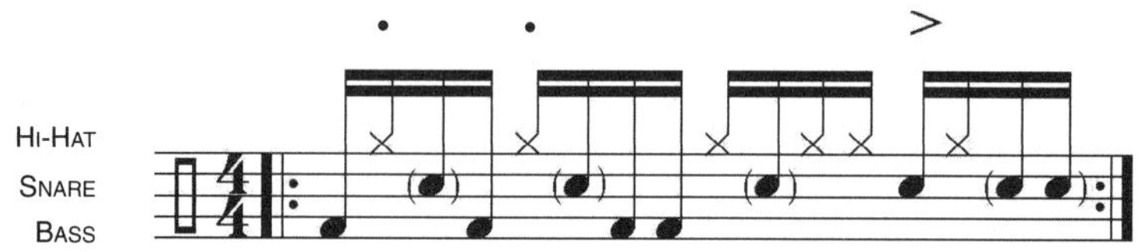

1B (CD 2, Track 25)

(~) = A tilde placed over either a dot or any two consecutive notes indicates a change in "orchestration," which means playing notes on two different surfaces (such as the hi-hat and hi-tom, suggested in the alteration of the example below):

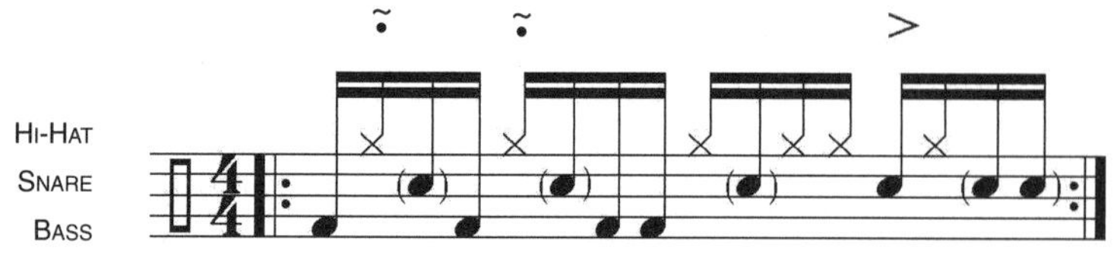

NOTE: The "alteration method" used in this book is for the sake of clarity, and the symbols are not standard. Keep in mind that the symbols themselves are not nearly as important as creating and playing the patterns.

1C (CD 2, Track 26)

(§) = A "double s" placed above any note indicates a rest—not playing that particular note, as suggested in the last alteration of the example below:

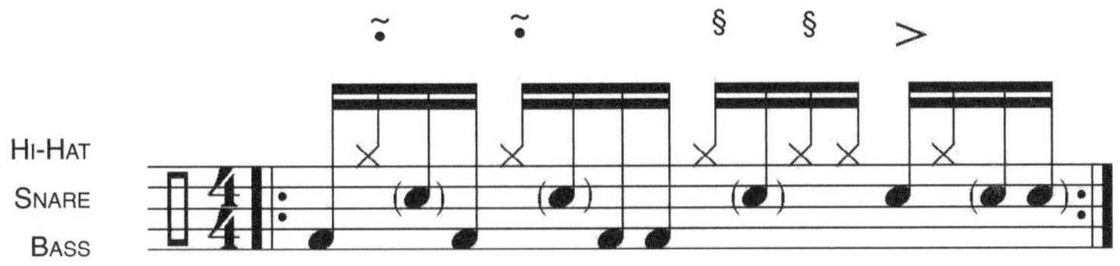

Variation 1

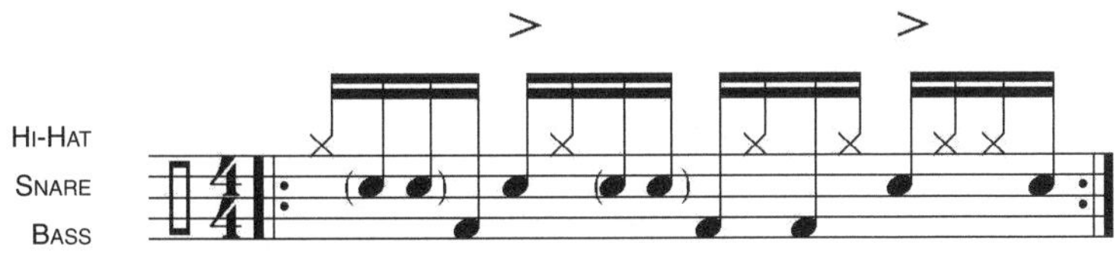

Variation 2

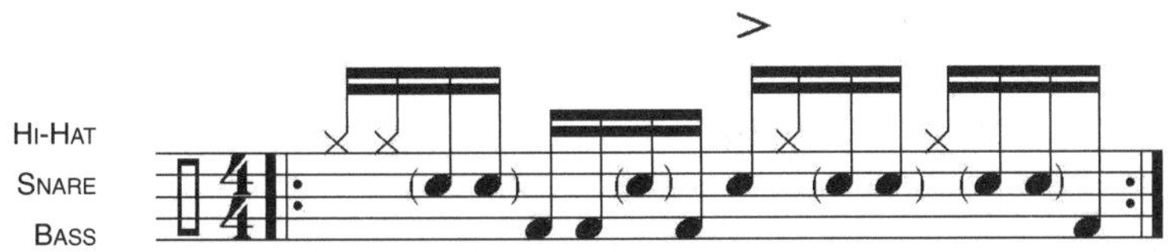

NOTE: The "alteration method" can be applied to the above two grooves as well as any other Linear Funk patterns. However, it is a good idea to have the snare drum play a back beat somewhere in the measure. A final option is to use the hi-hat foot to create four-way-independent "linear" patterns. Other surfaces, such as the bell of cymbals, rims, toms, etc., may also be used for this purpose.

Ghost Note Funk

"Ghost Note" refers to any note that is played very lightly, usually on the snare drum, and is indicated by parentheses surrounding a note. The desired effect is that the ghost notes be heard under the main sound of the groove. This produces a subtle 16th-note feel around a strong back beat or certain accents. As opposed to Linear Funk, the notes of these patterns fall in sync with one another to create a "layered" effect. Prominent Ghost Note drummers include Harvey Mason, Mike Clark, Bernard Purdie, Steve Gadd, and most notably David Garibaldi of Tower of Power. As with the previous styles, there is no standard Ghost Note Funk groove, though the patterns below are common. **Ghost Note Funk patterns are more practical at a slightly slower tempo than those of the above Funk styles with quarter note = 92–126 bpm.**

Example (CD 2, Track 27)

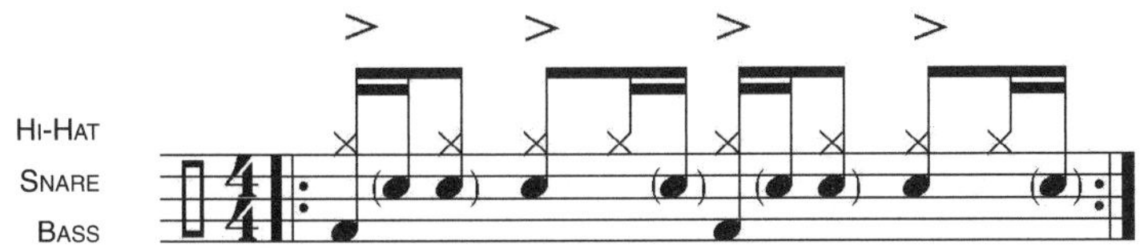

Variation 1

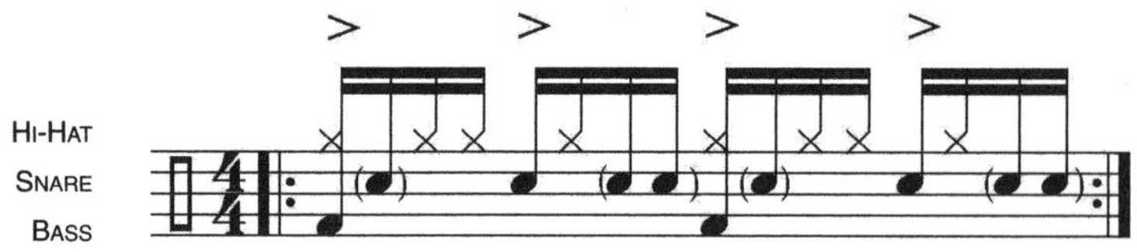

Variation 2

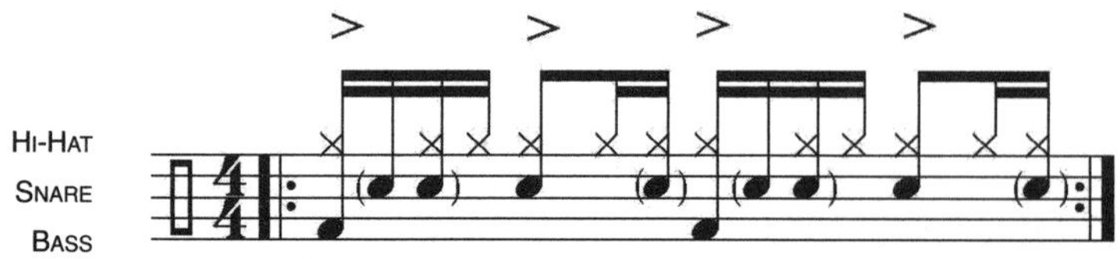

NOTES: 1) For developing musicianship and creativity, try playing bass drum variations with the above hand patterns. Refer to Standard Rock bass drum variations in the Rock n' Roll chapter and the bass drum ideas in Funk Rock. 2) The ride hand may also play the ride cymbal accompanied by the hi-hat foot on all quarter notes, beats 2 & 4, or all upbeats (the +'s).

Funk Rock

Though not technically an established style, the term "Funk Rock" describes music that can be classified as Rock incorporating elements from Funk, such as syncopated rhythms and percussive horn lines. Bands and artists such as Earth, Wind and Fire, The Commodores, Michael Jackson, and Sly and the Family Stone could all be included in both the Funk and Rock genres. As opposed to the above Funk styles, Funk Rock usually has fewer ghost notes, a steady back beat, and an emphasis on bass drum displacement (syncopated bass drum, displaced from the standard strikes on 1 & 3). **The practical tempo range for Funk Rock is similar to Ghost Note Funk at quarter note = 92–126 bpm.**

Example 1 (CD 2, Track 28)

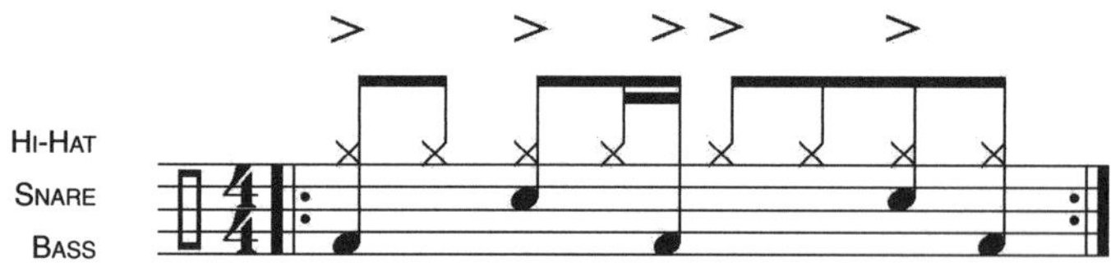

Variation 1

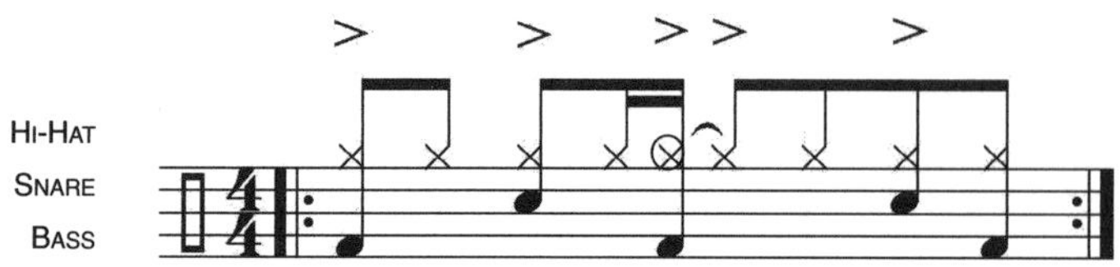

(Circled hi-hat note is played open)

Variation 2

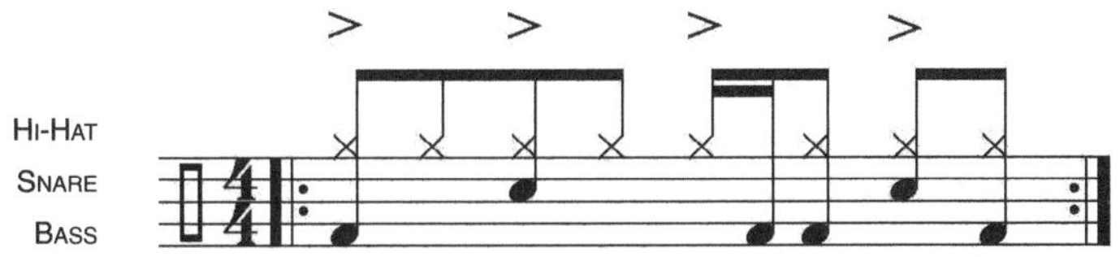

Variation 3

Beat 1 on the bass drum is not played when continuing the groove after the first measure.

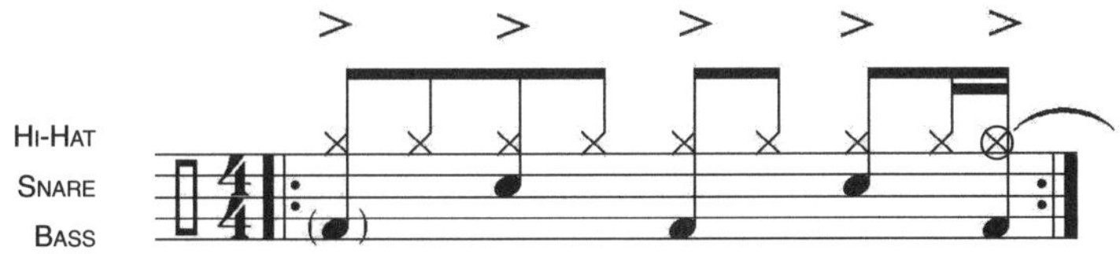

(Circled hi-hat note is played open)

Example 2 (Half-Time Feel)

This pattern can be played at standard tempos (using alternating hand strokes) as well as slow tempos around quarter note = 72 bpm. This is similar to the half-time Standard Rock feel from the Rock chapter.

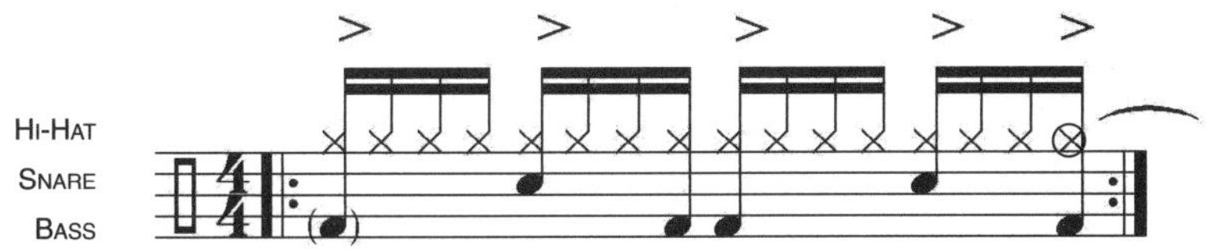

(Circled hi-hat note is played open)

Variation 1

This pattern suggests a half-time feel and is essentially a mix of half-time Rock and New Orleans Funk.

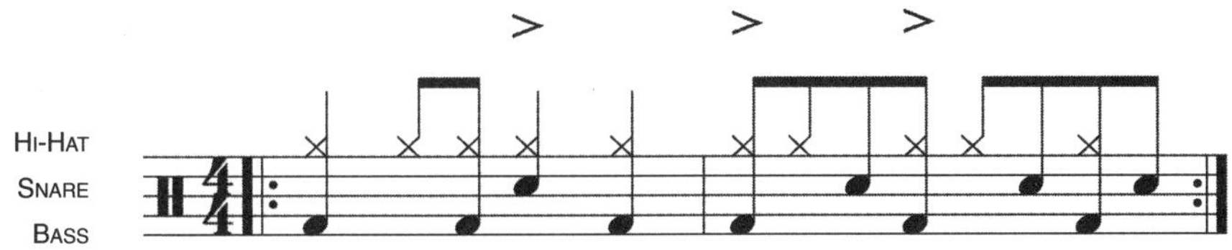

NOTE: As in snare drum "displacement," bass drum "displacement" is virtually limitless, involving 16th note combinations. A common device is playing the last 16th note of any beat, often with an open hi-hat accent (as in variations 1, 3 and 4 above). The ride hand may also play the ride cymbal accompanied by the hi-hat foot on all quarter notes, beats 2 & 4, and upbeats (the +'s). A common pattern is to play the bell of the cymbal on upbeats with the hi-hat foot on downbeat quarter notes.

VARIATION 2

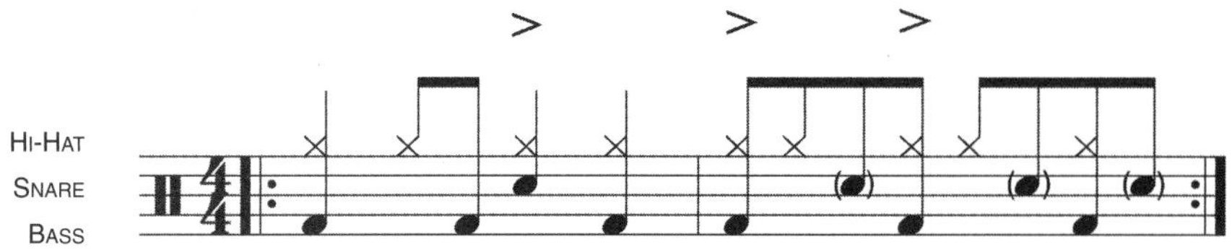

NOTE: A variation on this pattern is to play the hi-hat pedal on 2 & 4 and to move the hi-hat pattern to the ride cymbal.

CASCARA FUNK

Modern Funk is often combined with Afro-Cuban styles. The fusion of the Cascara pattern (see Afro-Cuban chapter) with either steady or displaced back-beat grooves is often found in present-day Funk, Acid Jazz, and Afro-Cuban music (where it's usually called the Timba style). **The tempo range is typically quarter note = 100–136 bpm.**

EXAMPLE

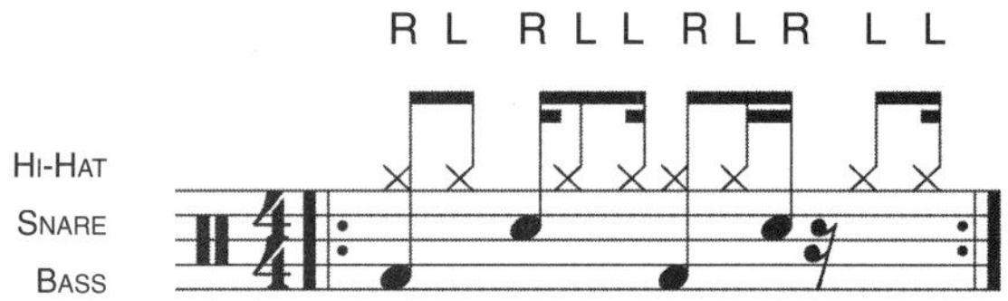

VARIATION 1

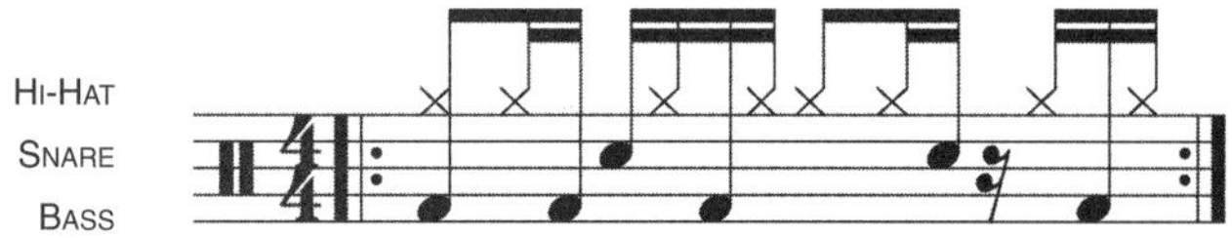

VARIATION 2

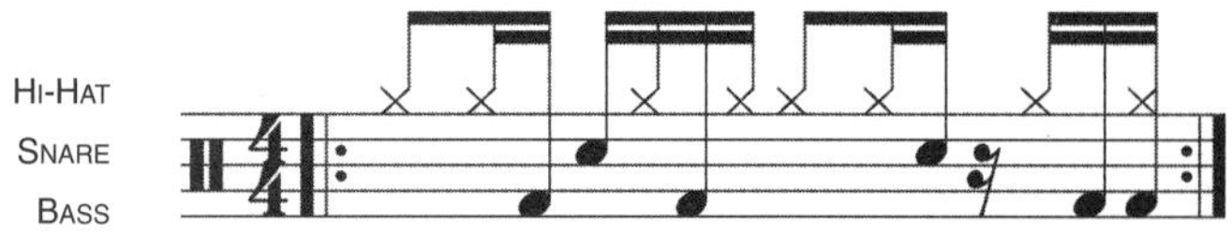

Funk Summary

The ideas from all sections above can be mixed to create grooves with the characteristics of any combination of the five Funk styles. Two of the most acclaimed drummers to accomplish this are David Garibaldi of Tower of Power and Mike Clark of The Headhunters (formerly with Herbie Hancock). The following examples are taken from songs using the Funk patterns presented in this chapter.

Example 1

This is the main drum pattern from Tower of Power's "Soul Vaccination," found on their debut CD entitled *Tower of Power.* **Quarter note = 100 bpm.**

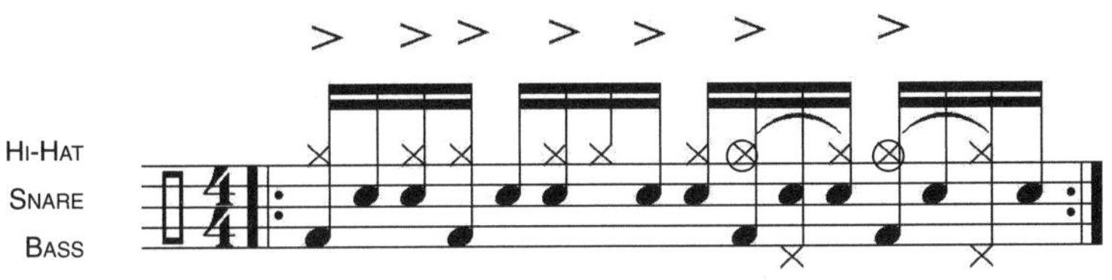

(Circled hi-hat notes are played open)

Example 2

This is the main drum groove from The Headhunter's "Tip Toe" found on the CD entitled *Return of the Headhunters.*

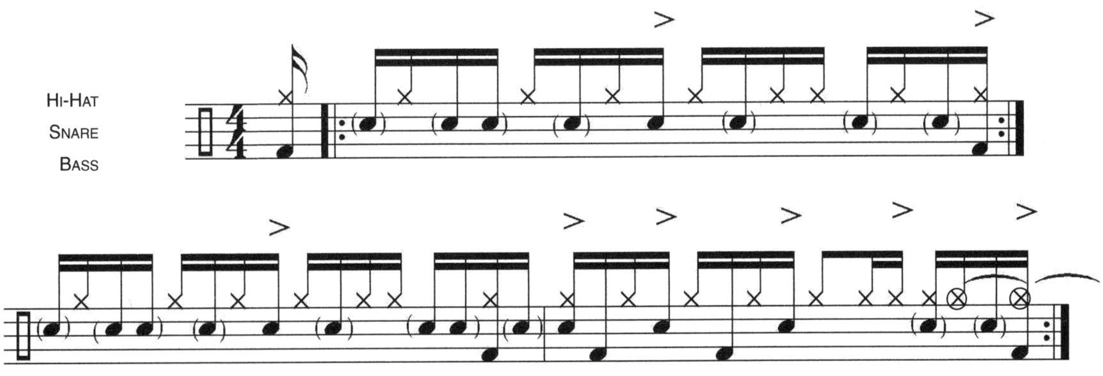

Example 3

This is from the song "Loft Funk" on The Headhunter's CD *Evolution Revolution.*

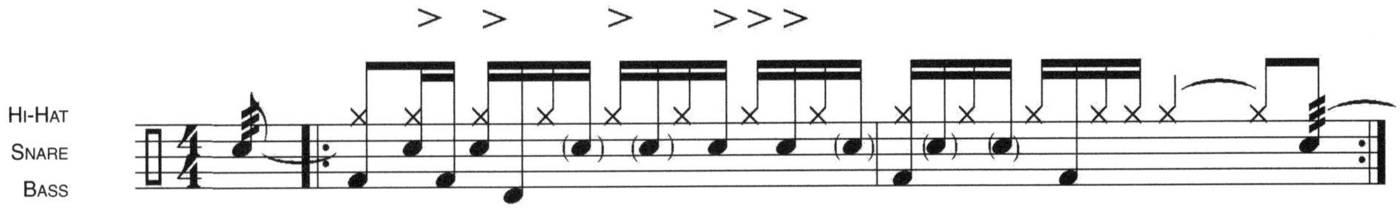

13 GOSPEL

GOSPEL MUSIC brings the tradition of Blues into the music of the African-American Baptist Church. It took the form and name of "Gospel Music" (originally called "Gospel Songs") in the early 20th century through the efforts of a single individual, Thomas A. Dorsey. Born in Villa Rica, Georgia in 1899, Dorsey learned to play piano as a youth in the African-American Baptist Church. As an accompanist for such famed Blues singers as Ma Rainey and Bessie Smith, and after seeing Charles A. Tindley perform at the National Baptist Convention, he became inspired to compose church music with a Blues influence. Though these new sounds were initially rejected by the Baptist establishment, Dorsey continued to promote his music.

After several years of Dorsey's struggling to find acceptance by the church, other singers/musicians such as Mother Willie Mae Ford and Lucy Campbell also began to promote Gospel Music. This, along with Dorsey's persistent efforts, finally led to Gospel Music's acceptance. By 1932, Dorsey had established The National Convention of Gospel Choirs and Choruses, an institution which continues to flourish today. By the time of his death in 1993, Dorsey had written over 800 songs, spanning nearly the entirety of Gospel Music's existence.

Originally sung by large choirs, in the 1930s Gospel Music began to emphasize the solo vocalist. Inspired by Sister Rosetta Tharpe, Gospel singer Clara Ward sang Gospel Music in nightclubs, creating a wider audience; she soon received attention from the recording industry. Her 1950s hit, "Surely God Is Able," is credited as Gospel Music's first million-selling record. By this time, several Gospel singers such as Mahalia Jackson and James Cleveland had emerged as national stars along with such notable Gospel groups as The Caravans and The Soul Stirrers. During the 1950s, Gospel Music and its musicians, along with blues performers, began to create the beginnings of Rhythm & Blues. Composers such as Ray Charles, Little Richard, and Sam Cooke (The Soul Stirrers), and later musicians like Aretha Franklin, Wilson Pickett (The Violinairs) and Ashford and Simpson (The Followers) all created music with strong Gospel overtones. In the last quarter of the 20th century, Gospel continued to thrive in both the secular and sacred worlds, particularly in large ensembles and choirs within the African American Baptist Church.

Gospel is nearly unique in that groups formed as early as the 1920s and 1930s continue to perform today (with, of course, personnel being replaced over the years). Examples of such groups include The Dixie Hummingbirds and The Blind Boys of Alabama.

Recent and contemporary Gospel artists include Sweet Honey in the Rock, Edwin Hawkins, Shirley Caesar, Marion Williams, Kirk Franklin, Vickie Winans, John P. Kee, Yolanda Adams, Christian pop-recording star Michael W. Smith, and R&B legend Al Green.

In the early 21st century, drummers in the Gospel community began to "shed" (trading off ideas between two drummers going head to head, typically in a rehearsal setting). This gave drummers opportunities to share extravagant fills, techniques and grooves with one another. In the first decade of the new millennium, "shedding" became so popular that a series of videos, entitled "Shed Sessionz," was created and successfully marketed by video director Gerald Forrest. Drummers such as Teddy Campbell, Gerald Heyward, Aaron Spears, Tony Royster Jr., Marvin McQuitty, Eric Moore, Chris Dave, and Chris Coleman are just a few of those have introduced this more "extreme" form of Gospel drumming to a wide listening audience.

As always, time keeping is the most important task for the drummer. Supporting the lyrical message of the vocalist requires a drummer to remain in the background virtually at all times, making simplicity another important component of traditional Gospel drumming. Since Gospel adopted ideas from other styles of music, all beats in this chapter can be found in other chapters in this book. The ones presented here are the most practical choices. **Tempos can range anywhere from slow ballads (quarter note = 50 bpm) to fast gallops (quarter note = 280 bpm).**

Example (CD 2, Track 76)

This is a standard Polka or Two-Step groove written in 4/4, and is arguably the most common Gospel drumming pattern. **Tempo is quarter note = 192–280 bpm.**

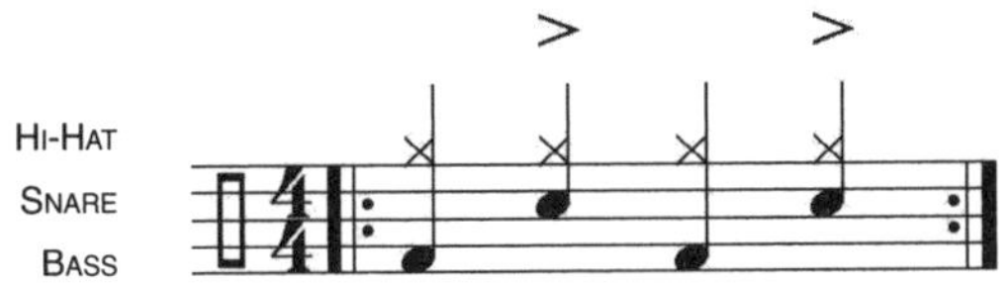

Variation 1

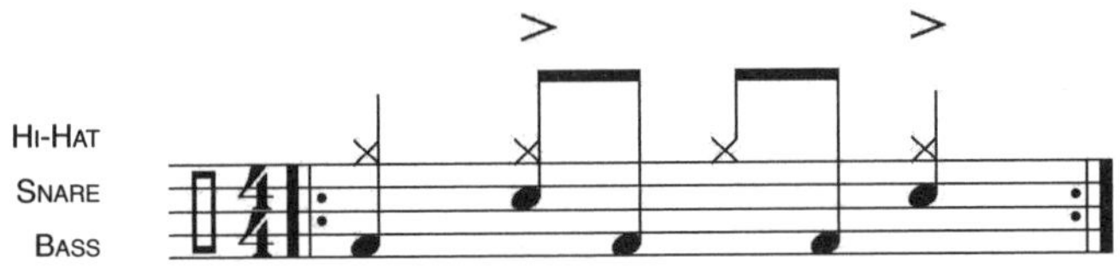

Variation 2 (CD 2, Track 80)

Though many Gospel grooves are frequently played with a double-time feel, a Standard Rock Beat is often employed. This same groove may be used for slower ballads as well. Refer to the Rock chapter for more variations, keeping simplicity in mind. **Quarter note = 60–200 bpm.**

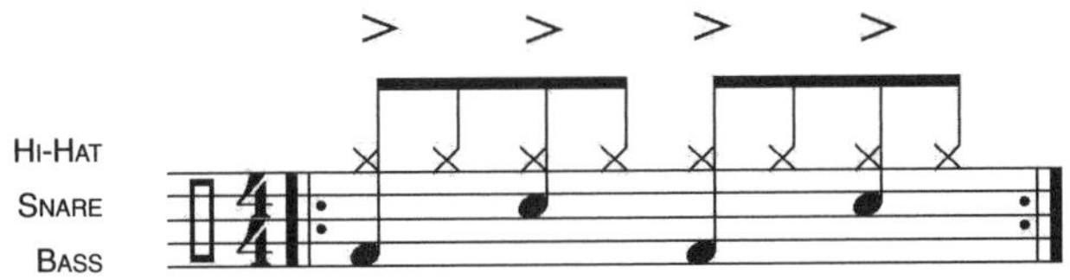

NOTE: Depending on the feel of the song and the desires of the other musicians, the above grooves may be played either with a straight or a swung feel.

Variation 3 (CD 1, Track 59)

This variation is a common 12/8 slow Blues groove (see the Blues chapter). **Quarter note = 50–80 bpm.**

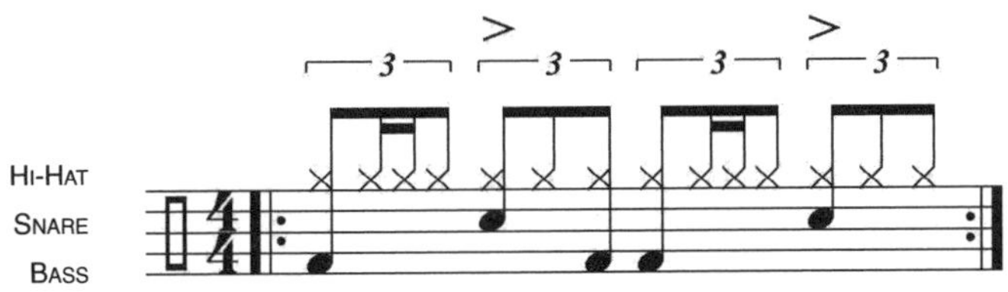

VARIATION 4 (CD 1, Track 51)

This is the Standard Blues Shuffle (for more shuffle variations, see Blues chapter). **Quarter note = 80–160 bpm.**

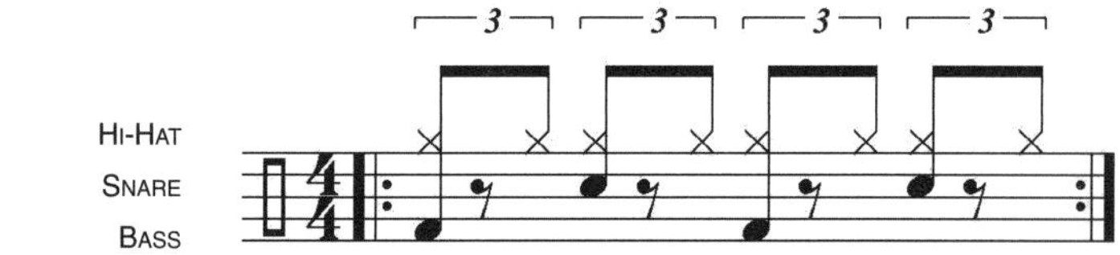

NOTE: Any of the above examples/variations can be further enhanced by playing a ride cymbal in place of the closed hi-hat and by using hi-hat foot accompaniment, usually on beats 2 & 4.

VARIATION 5 (CD 1, Track 80)

This final variation is a common waltz pattern for drum set, utilizing quarter notes on the ride hand, and is the same pattern used for the Cajun Waltz. For more Waltz patterns, see the Country chapter and the Cajun/Zydeco chapter). **Quarter note = 126–152 bpm.**

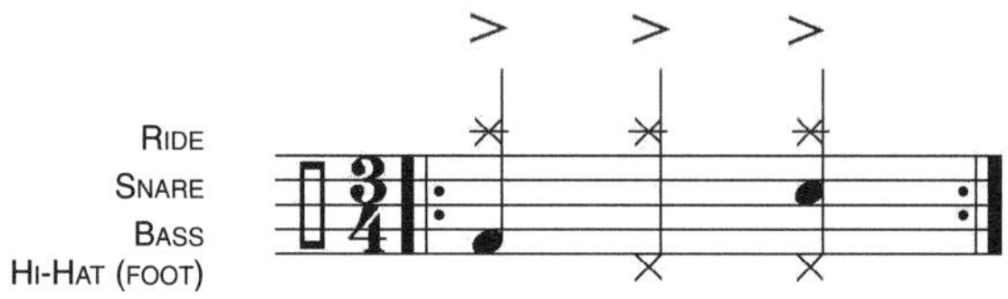

14 Hip Hop / Rap

The popularity of Rap music and the Hip Hop culture has increased immensely over the past 30 years. With its roots in the earliest forms of African-influenced call-and-response vocalizings, Hip Hop/Rap utilizes the advanced technology of electronic sampling and sequencing and has become a leading force in the music industry. Hip Hop/Rap music can be traced back to two sources: spoken lyrics (usually rhyming) and a Rhythm and Blues/Funk musical base.

One of the most prominent early examples of spoken word technique (in a call-and-response format) in a popular song is the chant "Hi-de-hi-de-ho" from Cab Calloway's "Minnie the Moocher" in 1931. By the 1950s, early forms of Rock n' Roll and Do-Wop utilized spoken word technique in sections of songs (e.g., "Little Darlin'" written by Maurice Williams). Within the next few decades, popular songs such as "Alice's Restaurant" by Arlo Guthrie and "The Devil Went Down to Georgia" by The Charlie Daniels Band, not to mention countless Country songs, such as "Phantom 409" and Giddy Up Go," by Red Sovine, had lyrics primarily or exclusively in spoken word format.

In the 1970s, African-American musicians coupled the spoken word format with the sounds of Funk to produce the earliest easily recognizable antecedents of Rap. Artists such as Lou Rawls, Barry White, James Brown, The Brothers Johnson, and Isaac Hayes helped define the early sounds of the style. As well, Jamaican DJs in New York City began improvising rhymes over Reggae music and rhythms. By 1979, the first recordings appeared, "Rapper's Delight" by the Sugar Hill Gang. At the close of the decade, drum machines such as the Linn Drum and slightly later the TR-808 appeared and helped create the first significant electronic grooves to accompany the Rap style.

In the early 1980s, MTV exposed original forms of Rap to a worldwide audience through artists such as Grandmaster Flash, Blondie ("Rapture"), and the immensely popular Run DMC. As well, Rap culture arose with new styles of clothing, images, and dance ("Breakdancing") to accompany this rising new musical style. By the middle of the decade, sampling appeared, a process incorporating a previously recorded piece of music into remixed form. The huge success of the collaboration of Run DMC and Aerosmith, with their revised version of "Walk This Way" in 1986, created the new path which Rap music would follow. The popularity of other sampled songs, such as "Wild Thing" by Tone Loc (borrowed from Van Halen's "Jamie's Cryin'") and "Can't Touch This" by MC Hammer (borrowed from Rick James's "Superfreak"), produced Rap music's first superstars. Later sensations such as Public Enemy and LL Cool J helped elevate Rap to a dominant style in the music industry. The popularity of Rap became so great that by the end of the decade MTV established a program dedicated solely to this style entitled "Yo MTV Raps."

In the early years of the 1990s, as Hip Hop culture became more poprular, with Rap music as a primary component, the term Hip Hop began to replace the more traditional term Rap. By this time, the music had acquired a darker edge, incorporating political, social, and angry (and sometimes misogynistic and scatological) lyrics. Ice T and NWA are among the prominent artists associated with the style of music commonly referred to as "Gangsta Rap." This tougher, more aggressive style continued to evolve through the 1990s with artists such as Snoop Doggy Dog, Tupac Shakur, Dr. Dre, and the successful recording label Death Row Records, owned by Marion "Suge" Knight.

As live musicians began to accompany Hip Hop artists on stage and in the studio, the popularity of sampling and sequencing began to diminish. The latter part of the 1990s and the early 2000s produced drummers able to recreate the electronic rhythms and sounds of Hip Hop music on acoustic drums. Artists such as The Beastie Boys, Meshell Ndegeocello, and especially R&B singer D'Angelo often use live musicians. Drummers include Zoro, John Blackman, and especially Ahmir "?uestlove" Thompson (of The Roots), who regularly appears on *Jimmy Fallon*. Other prominent Hip Hop artists over the years include LL Cool J, Eminem, Queen Latifah, Sean "Puffy Combs, Lil Kim, Lil Wayne, Busta Rhymes, Jay-Z, and 50-Cent.

As in other styles, it is important to play with a strong sense of time. A good suggestion is to utilize high-pitched, small drums to reproduce the sound of programmed loops or grooves. As a result of the fusion between Rock and Funk grooves, the variations available in this genre are virtually endless. Consequently, there is no one standard Hip Hop/Rap groove. However, there are common elements among all the variations. The following grooves accurately represent the more frequently played patterns in this style. Most importantly, each groove can be played with a straight or swung feel, though the swung feel has become more common. **Typically, the tempo range is quarter note = 60–108 bpm for Standard Hip Hop, 60–80 bpm for slow feels, and 132–172 for half-time feels.**

Standard Hip Hop

Example 1 (CD 2, Track 34)

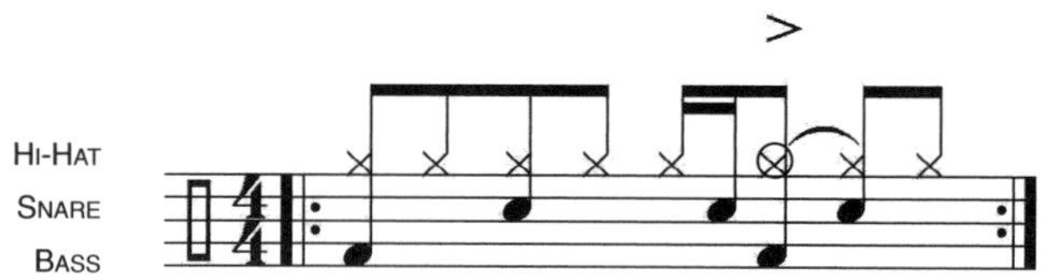

(Circled hi-hat note is played open)

Variation 1

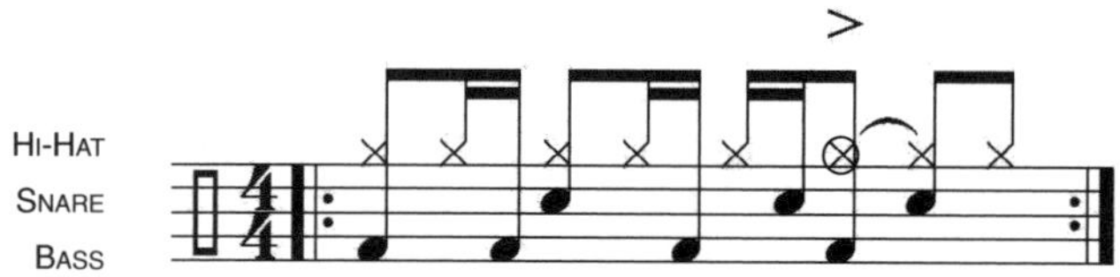

(Circled hi-hat note is played open)

Variation 2

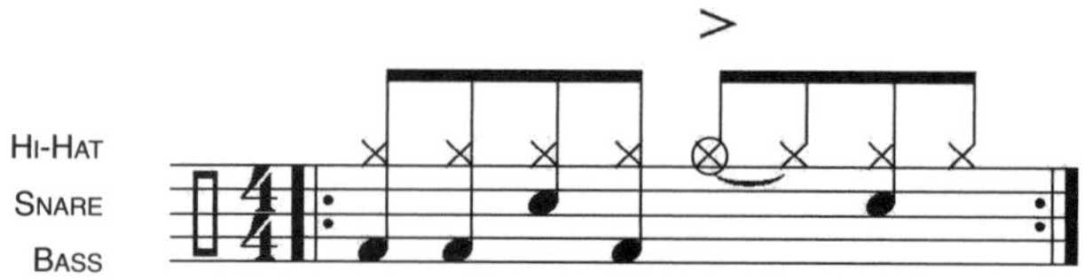

(Circled hi-hat note is played open)

Variation 3

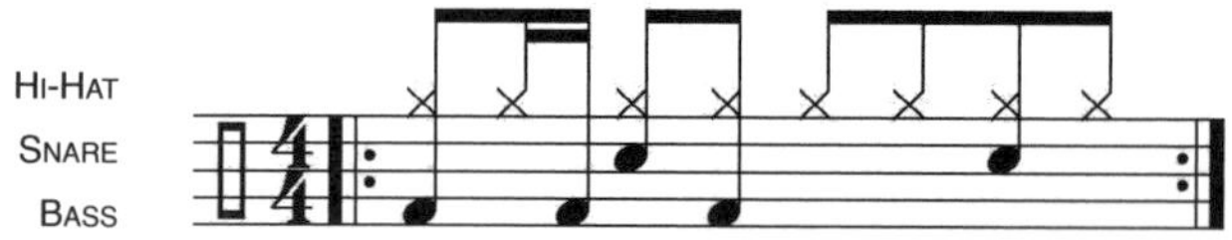

Variation 4

NOTE: The above variations can be played straight or swung by "shuffling" the 16th notes.

Slower Feels

Example 2 (CD 2, Track 35)

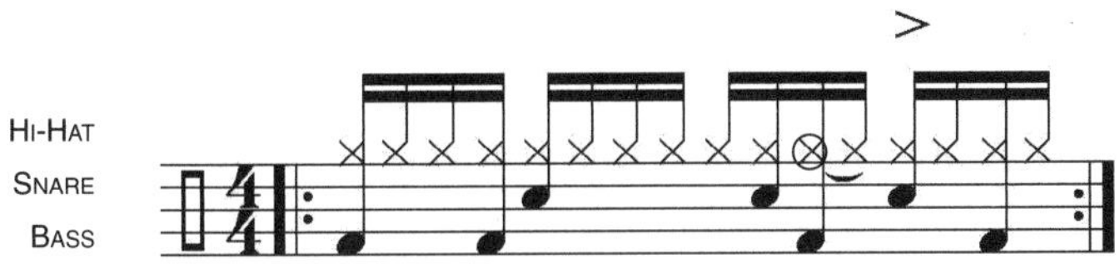

(Circled hi-hat note is played open)

Variation 1

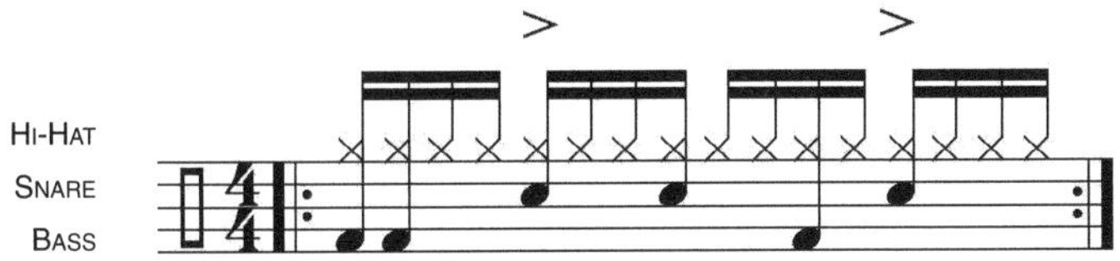

Variation 2

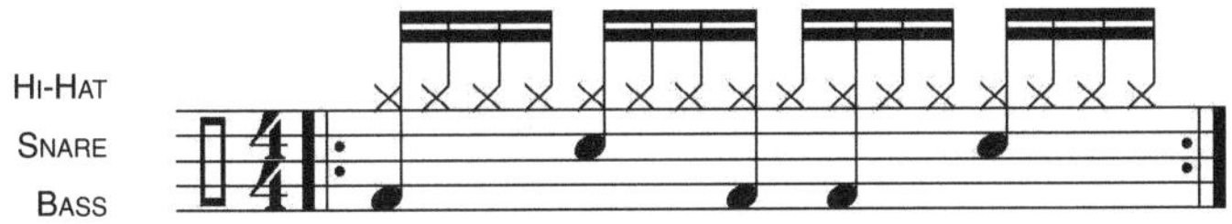

NOTE: The 16th notes in each pattern above may be played straight or swung.

Half-Time Feels

Example 3 (CD 2, Track 36)

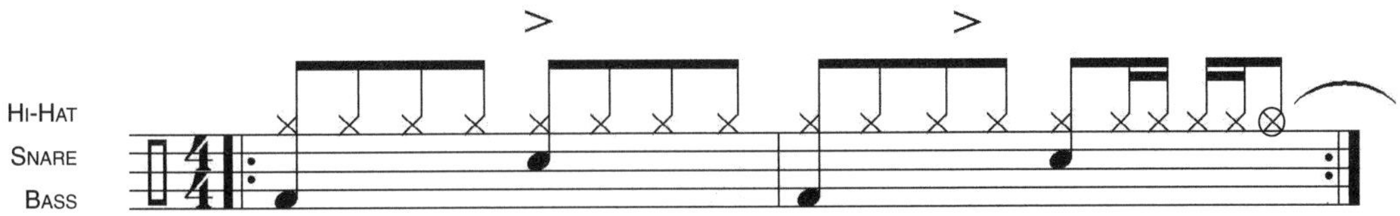

(Circled hi-hat note is played open)

Variation 1

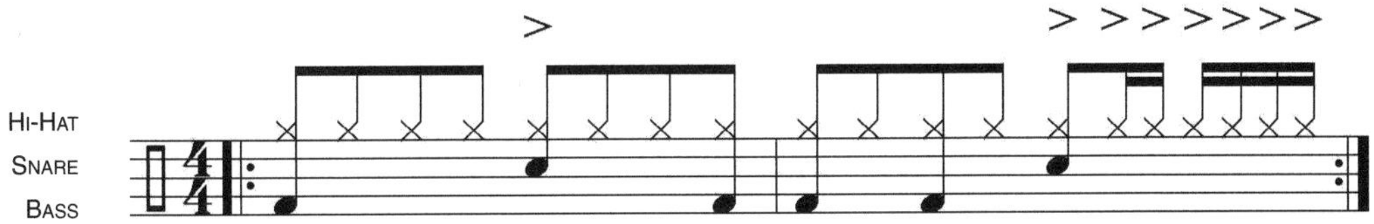

Variation 2

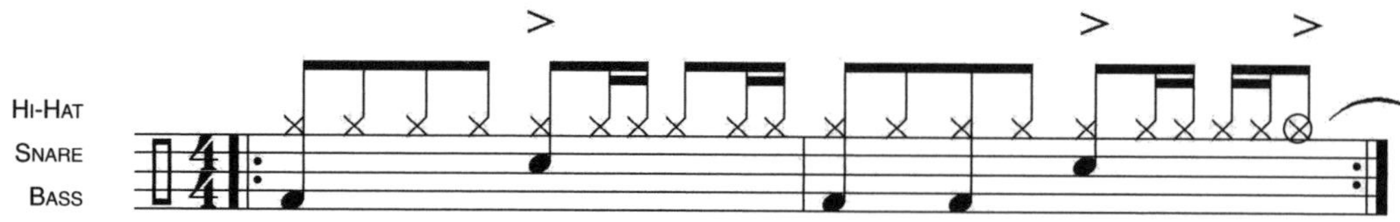

(Circled hi-hat note is played open)

NOTE: In Hip Hop/Rap, most half-time feels are usually played straight rather than swung.

15 Jazz

New Orleans Second Line

Situated at the mouth of the Mississippi, New Orleans has been a major port for nearly three centuries. It's a melting pot of cultures: African, Cuban, South American, European, Caribbean and many others. The fusion of all these cultures created a new style of music, laying the foundation for all types of Jazz which followed.

The end of slavery was a catalyst for a specifically New Orleans-type music, especially what is known as New Orleans "Second Line." In the latter part of the 19th century, funeral and parade bands consisting of former slaves and their descendants became important musical/cultural activities. The first "line" of the funeral consisted of the hearse and immediate family while the "second line" was composed of musicians, dancers, and friends—hence the name associated with this style. The basic drumming feel was triple rather than duple, though it was played "in the crack" (halfway between straight and swung), which is still the defining characteristic of Second Line drumming.

The make up of parade bands in New Orleans was similar to the marching or parade bands that we are familiar with today, consisting of horns with a marching percussion section. In a New Orleans percussion section, it was common to find at least one snare drummer as well as a few bass drummers playing both their bass drums and cymbals simultaneously. Typically, a bass drummer would play his drum with a mallet in one hand, using the other hand to strike a mounted cymbal on top of the drum with a wire hanger. The patterns created by all the drummers when playing together led to the construction of the drum set or trap set (short for "contraption") for a single performer.

When performing New Orleans Second Line drumming today, it's helpful to look back at the drum sets of that era. The trap drum configuration used was not today's familiar five-piece set up. Some of the more common pieces used with a trap drummer's set in the early 20th century were Chinese tom toms (small drums with calfskin heads that were usually tacked on), wood blocks (usually of various pitches), trashy sounding cymbals, a very large bass drum (sometimes up to 40" in diameter!), and a shorter version of the hi-hat known as the "low boy." (The standard hi-hat set up wasn't established until the mid-1930s.)

Second Line drumming transfers the parade-style rhythms to the drum set. Examples of patterns played by parade drummers, but now arranged for a single drum set player, are transcribed in this section. In the example below, notice that the pattern is written out in a two-measure phrase. The role of the bass drum is to project a "1 & 3" feel. Though the first measure sticks to the strong 1 & 3 feel, the following measure has a strong beat 4. That beat acts as a rhythmic "kick" which pushes the music ahead to the next measure. The hi-hat acts as the "answer" to the bass drum pattern, primarily on beats 2 & 4. The foot kicks the hi-hat with the heel for a "splash" sound. Keep in mind that the hi-hat did not exist on a trap kit originally, so the modern day practice of playing the hi-hat here is to mimic the sound of a wire hanger on a cymbal. Finally, the hands should be playing eighth-note patterns with varied accents on the snare against the foot patterns. The trick here is to obtain the correct "in the crack" feel. **The tempo range for Second Line is quarter note = 144–216 bpm.**

EXAMPLE (CD 2, Track 37)

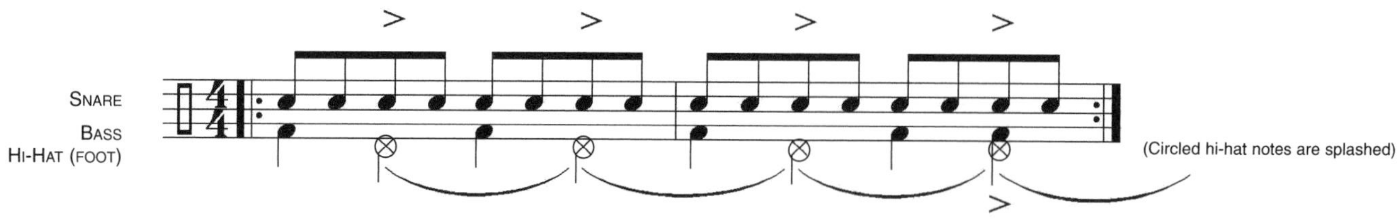

VARIATION 1

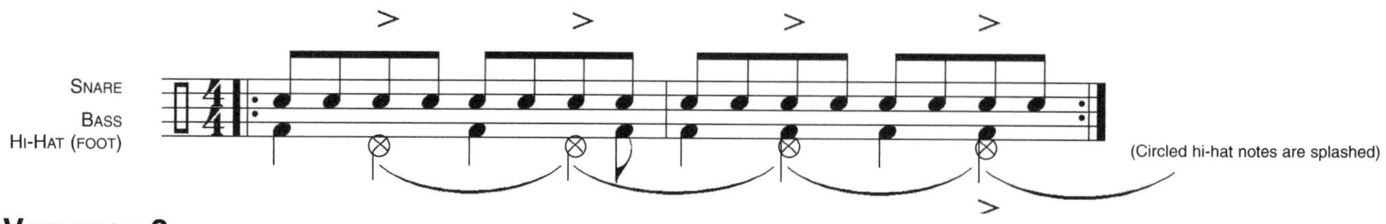

VARIATION 2

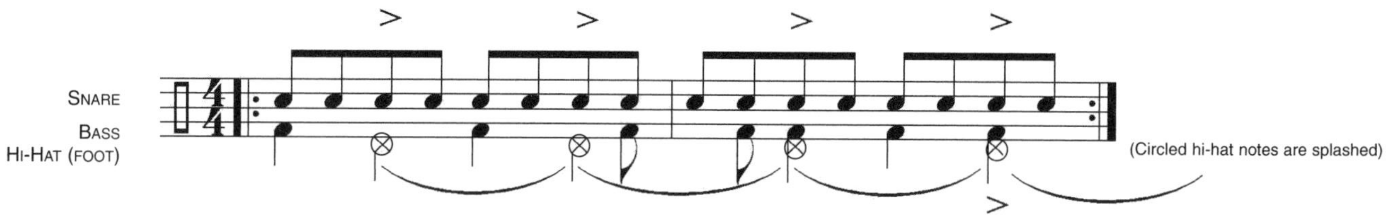

VARIATION 3

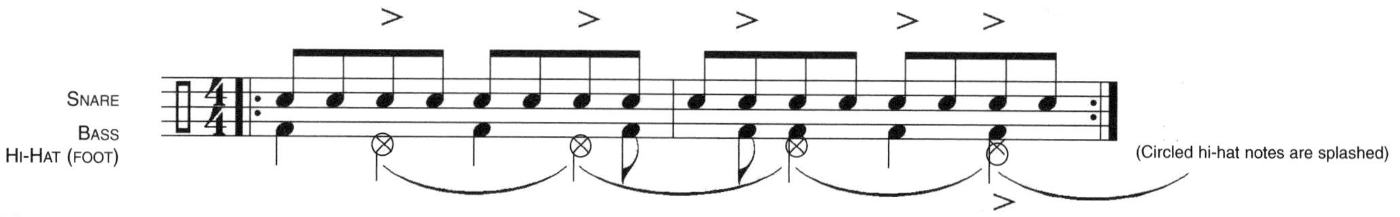

VARIATION 4

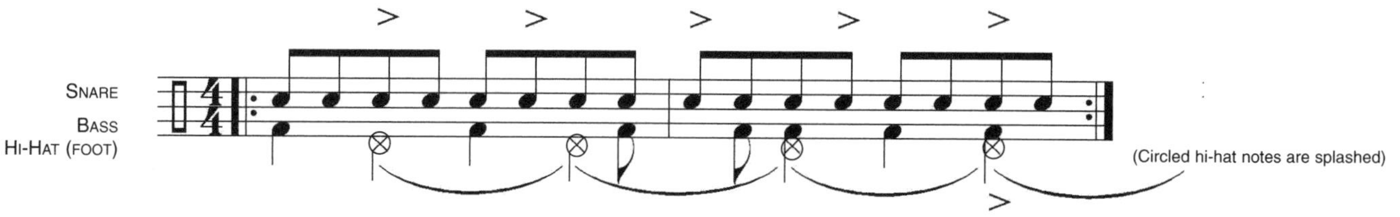

VARIATION 5 (CD 2, Track 38)

This final variation displays an authentic Second Line bass and snare drum marching rhythm. Notice the 2-3 son clave reference in the bass drum pattern (see Clave in the Afro-Cuban chapter).

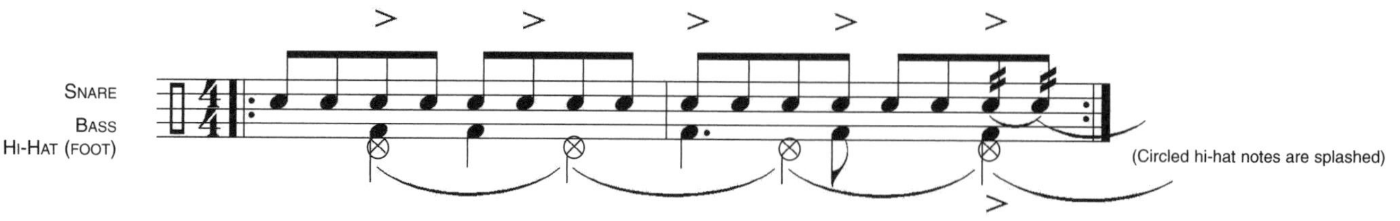

NOTE: There are countless hand and foot variations for Second Line drumming, a style based on improvisation. More variations may be developed through syncopation, accents, and rolls.

DIXIELAND

Dixieland gave birth to traditional Jazz, and served as a bridge between New Orleans music and the Swing/Big Band era. Dixieland drumming is a somewhat simpler style of playing than busy (or improvised) Second Line drumming. In addition, Dixieland has more of a traditional swing feel rather than the "in the crack" feel of Second Line drumming.

"Dixieland" refers to the music that developed in the Storyville (red light) District of New Orleans between approximately 1900 and 1917. Musicians responsible for creating Dixieland include New Orleans natives Buddy Bolden, Ferdinand "Jelly Roll" Morton, Joe "King" Oliver, and Louis Armstrong. Due to the shutdown of Storyville during World War I, musicians migrated north on the Mississippi River and ultimately ended up in Chicago, where the music gained national popularity. It continued to thrive throughout the 1920s as the defining sound of the "Jazz Age." With the legalization of alcohol in 1933, Jazz began to appear in more respectable establishments, giving rise to the Big Band era. This coincided with a diminishment of Dixieland's popularity. But the style has continued to thrive in traditional festivals and Dixieland venues throughout the world, as well as in the cities where it developed and gained popularity.

The configuration of the Dixieland trap set helps bridge the gap between the Second Line drum set-up and those that followed. Usually, the trap set consisted of a large bass drum, a deep snare, and a variety of percussion devices (wood blocks, cowbells, whistles, bird calls). The toms, however, began to show modern features (deeper drums, drum hoops [usually wood], and lugs or tuning pegs) and somewhat smaller cymbals, which produced a crisper sound than in Second Line drumming.

The main example below is a standard groove in Dixieland drumming. Normally, the pattern is to play a Jazz ride pattern on a tight, closed hi-hat while playing beats 1 & 3 on the bass drum, and a strong snare drum rim click on beat 4 of the pattern. It is also quite common to hear variations of Second Line patterns played in Dixieland. The only difference in the execution is that Dixieland has more precise, rolled passages in the hands, similar to those of a snare drum playing a march. In addition, in Dixieland the hi-hat foot normally strikes on beats 2 & 4, rather than "splashing" the cymbals as in Second Line. Overall, Dixieland has more of a solid and definitive sound than the wide open sound of early New Orleans music. Also, note the role of wood blocks in Dixieland. In certain sections (sometimes even during a drum solo), it is quite common to play a snare march-type solo on wood blocks rather than a normal snare drum. **Dixieland patterns are played slightly faster than Second Line patterns at quarter note = 160–264 bpm.**

EXAMPLE (CD 2, Track 39)

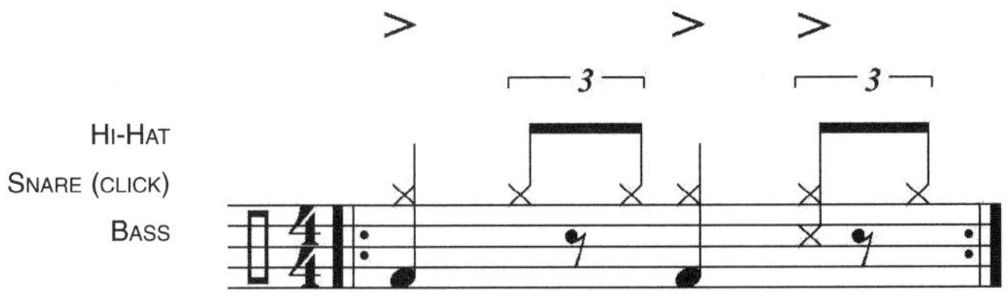

VARIATION (CD 2, Track 40)

This is the "Charleston."

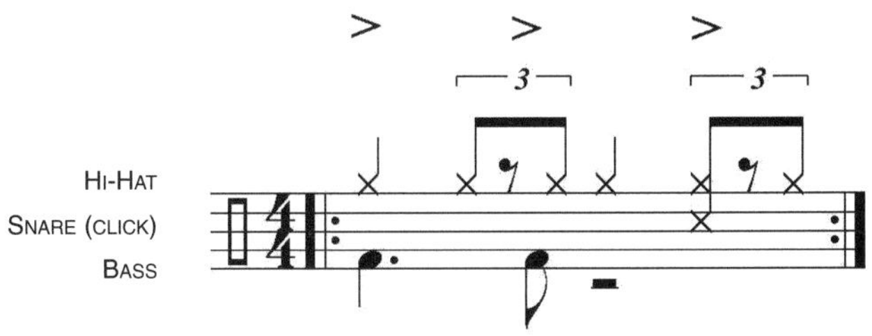

Ending a Dixieland Song

The most common ending to a Dixieland phrase or song is a quick two-bar solo/fill with a splash cymbal hit and choked on beat 4 of the second measure (no bass drum; splash cymbal struck alone, as shown in the following example).

Example (CD 2, Track 41)

Big Band

The Big Band style developed in the 1920s with Fletcher Henderson being the first band leader to attain widespread fame. Also important was band leader and drummer Chick Webb, who brought the drum set into the spotlight and inspired countless Big Band drummers throughout the 20th century. In the 1930s and 1940s, the Big Band genre dominated popular music in recordings, radio, and live settings. Prominent band leaders of this era included Duke Ellington, Count Basie, and Benny Goodman, with prominent drummers including Louie Bellson, Jo Jones, Gene Krupa (with his signature drum solo in Benny Goodman's "Sing Sing Sing"), and, later, Ed Shaughnessy of the Tonight Show Band. Big Band drummers developed powerful and fast technique, which they sometimes displayed through lengthy and frequent solos, the prime example of this being Buddy Rich, who performed this style of music for over five decades.

By 1950, the popularity of Big Band music began to diminish. Though never regaining the prominence it enjoyed in the 1930s and World War II years, it continued to have a strong audience through the 1970s and the 1980s, with the Louie Bellson Big Band Explosion, Buddy Rich Big Band, Maynard Ferguson, Woody Herman (with drummer Ed Soph) and the Tonight Show Band directed by Doc Severinson being its most prominent performers. Big Band had a resurgence of popularity in the mid-1990s through the Jump/Swing revival, most notably in the music of the Brian Setzer Orchestra.

The drummer's role changed with the advent of the Big Band style. Keeping good time became an even more important element, as a Big Band drummer must support a large ensemble (typically ranging from 15 to 18 players). The "time" pattern is the key to the music, placing the emphasis on the ride cymbal and hi-hat foot (see main example below) as opposed to the march-like approach of Dixieland and Second Line drumming. As well, the use of charts in Big Band presents the drummer with another task. The Big Band drummer must play phrases, figures, and accents to accompany and support the other musicians. Given these rigid arrangements, there tends to be less improvisation than in other Jazz styles, with improvisation limited strictly to solos in prescribed places and in choices of set-up figures.

The main example below is the standard time pattern for Big Band drumming. The variations feature different accents, rim clicks, and playing on different surfaces. Following the variations are common Big Band independence and set-up figures, which are a constant in Big Band arrangements. **The wide tempo range for standard time patterns is quarter note = 60–255 bpm (and even beyond) depending on musicianship.**

EXAMPLE (CD 2, TRACK 42)

This is an example of the primary standard "time" pattern played between the ride cymbal and the hi-hat foot. Note the accents on beats 2 & 4 on the ride cymbal. These accents double with the hi-hat foot pattern, defining a strong "pocket" and a relaxed groove.

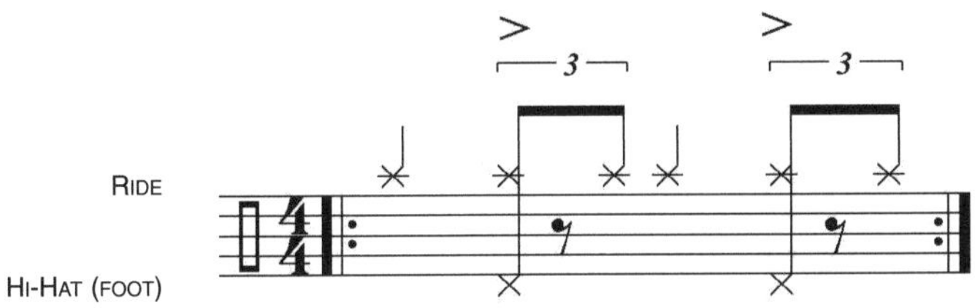

NOTE: In some charts, the ride hand pattern is written out with notation variations (see figures 1A and 1B below). Usually, the time pattern and feel do not change. However, depending on the arranger and/or composer, the notation could suggest how a drummer can phrase the ride cymbal time:

FIGURE 1A

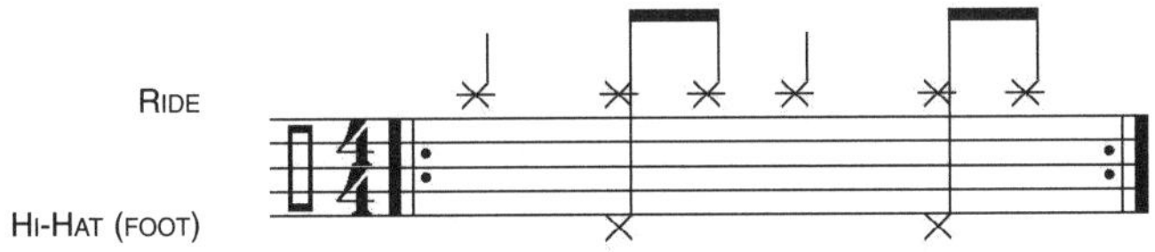

FIGURE 1B

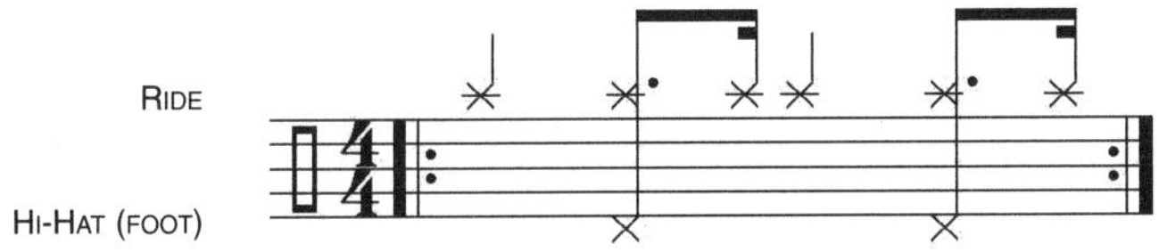

VARIATION 1

This variation has accents on the + of beats 2 & 4 on the ride cymbal. These new accents create a difference in the "time" pattern by creating an overall tighter feel which helps propel the groove. Alternating between the main example and variation 1 will bring out the difference between the two feels.

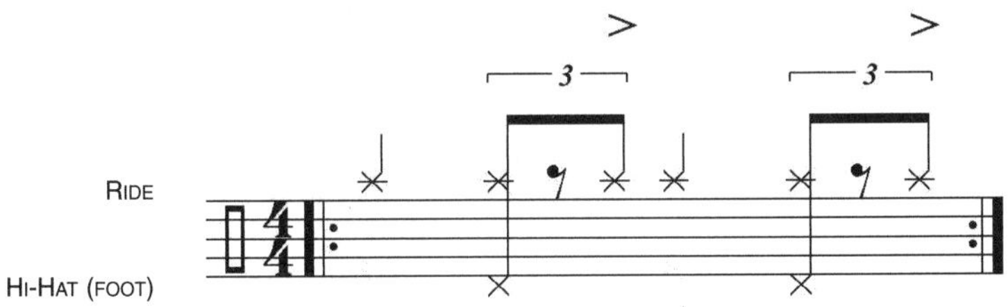

Variation 2

Usually, this type of pattern is played during a solo, a quiet section, or a soli section of a tune (an arranged melody and/or harmony line for a specific horn section).

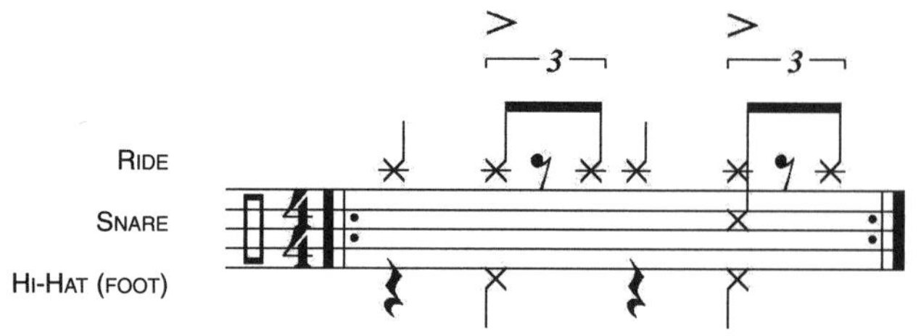

Variation 3

The time pattern is played on the surface of the hi-hat while the foot depresses the hi-hat pedal on beats 2 & 4. This creates an open sound. Like variation 2, this pattern is frequently used during quiet or solo sections.

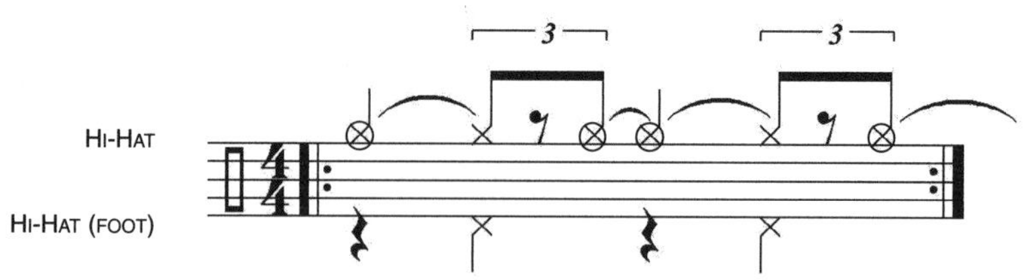

(Circled hi-hat notes are played open)

Variation 4

This "four on the floor" pattern has quarter notes on the bass drum on all four beats, simulating a "doubling" of the walking bass line. This can be played in many sections of a song. However, it is very important to execute this foot pattern softly as it can easily interfere with the bass line and other figures from the band.

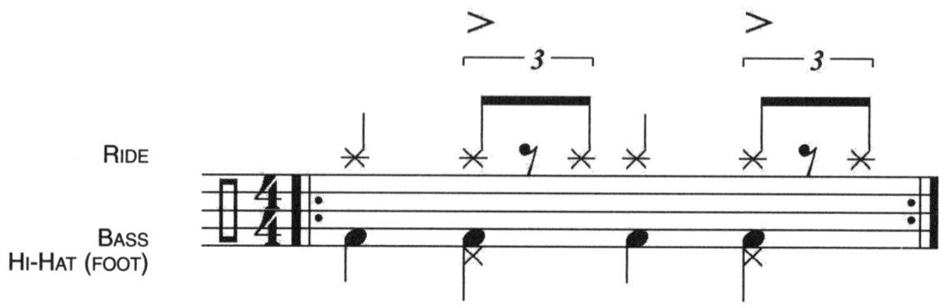

Variation 5

During the louder parts of an arrangement (usually toward the ending chorus or some other climactic point in the tune), a back beat on the snare drum strongly played on beats 2 & 4 will drive the song. Also, note the "four on the floor" bass drum pattern.

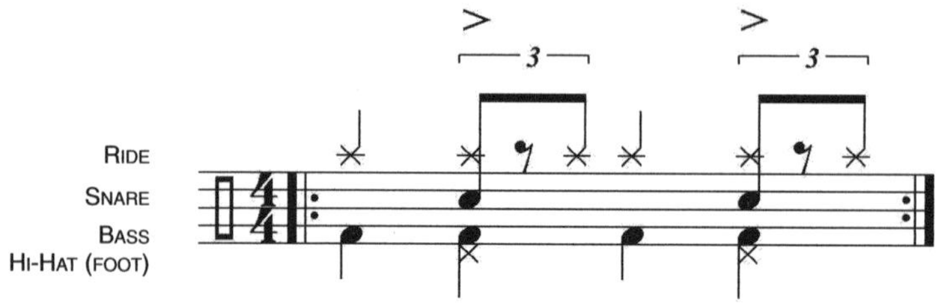

Variation 6 (Jazz Shuffle—CD 1, Track 53)

This final variation is an example of the Jazz Shuffle, which is identical to the Chicago Shuffle (see Blues chapter for more variations). The name corresponds to the style in which it's played (i.e., Jazz Shuffle for Jazz, Chicago Shuffle for Blues). Most practical in a Big Band or Blues (with horn section) setting, it can also be used in smaller bands (both Blues and Jazz) during the climactic sections of songs. The execution and timing of the unison hand pattern is the defining element of the groove. **The tempo of the Jazz Shuffle covers a large range of quarter = 80–160 bpm.**

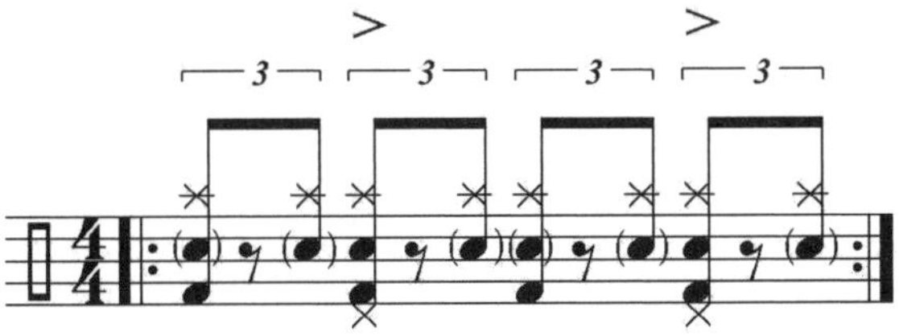

NOTE: It's good to switch between or combine any of the above variations when appropriate (e.g., eight measures of variation 3 followed by eight measures of variation 4).

Big Band Independence and Set-Up Figures

Big Band drummers need to know how to properly execute tied and long notes. Tied notes and notes with a value greater than a quarter note should be played on a cymbal and a bass drum (or cymbal and snare drum) simultaneously, duplicating the longer tone sustained by the band. Such "long sounds" are frequently set up by the drummer with a note (or a drum fill) directly before the long note itself. While long notes are found both on downbeats and upbeats, set up notes usually fall on the preceding downbeat of a figure. Notes without ties and with values of a quarter or less are considered "short notes" and are commonly played with the snare hand (though sometimes with the bass drum foot—often played with a choked hi-hat or cymbal) against the standard time pattern. Like long notes, short notes are also found on both downbeats and upbeats, but rarely have set-up notes.

There are a wide variety of figures in Big Band compositions. Though it's virtually impossible to include every variation, the following are the most likely figures to appear on a consistent basis from chart to chart.

Variation 1

This variation has an eighth note without a tie on the + of beat 4. This is considered a "short note" and is commonly played on the snare drum or occasionally the bass drum along with a time pattern.

VARIATION 2

This is an example of a pattern with a tied note on the + of beat 4. It is usually considered a "long note" due to the tie, and is usually played with the longest sound on the drum set (hence the above suggestion of striking a cymbal along with either a snare drum or bass drum). One would normally play a set-up note when playing this figure. (See the Set-Up variations below for setting up "long notes.")

VARIATION 3

This variation has an eighth note without a tie on the + of beat 2. A drummer would approach this note the same way as in variation 1.

VARIATION 4

This variation has an eighth note with a tie on the + of beat 2. A drummer would approach this note the same way as in variation 2.

VARIATION 5

This variation features a half note on beat 2 and a quarter note on beat 4. This is an example of a short note and a long note within the same measure. The half note will be played as a long note while the quarter note will be played as a short note. Remember to set up the half note!

Set Up Variations

The following are the most commonly played set up figures.

Figure A — Standard Quarter Note

Figure B — Standard Drag

Figure C — Standard Flam

Figure D — Single Stroke Four (Four Stroke Ruff)

Summary Example (CD 2, Track 43)

Here is an eight-measure phrase that could show up in a Big Band arrangement. It illustrates all of the preceding techniques and practices. (CD tempo is quarter note = 134 bpm.)

Small Band Jazz (Be Bop, Cool Jazz, Avante Garde)

Following the Swing era, the size of Jazz groups decreased from large Big Band orchestras to much smaller bands. This trend began in the early 1940s and became increasingly pronounced in the late '40s and early '50s. Jazz terminology reflected this shift: terms such as "trio," "quartet," and "quintet," and styles like Be Bop, Cool Jazz, and Avante Garde all suggest a small band (some other later styles include Hard Bop, a more intensified form of Be Bop, and Soul Jazz which featured a Blues & Funk influence). These bands usually consisted of a lead horn player along with a full rhythm section (drums, bass, and piano) and sometimes an additional horn player. One of the biggest changes in the music was in the approach to improvisation. Though there is improvisation in Big Band music (horn solos or even drum solos in prescribed places), the Big Band genre is primarily based on highly organized, charted arrangements. A small band, however, tends to follow the form of a song rather than a chart, which leaves a lot of room to stretch.

It's important to learn the characteristics of "Jazz form" when studying the small band format. Each song has a melody (the "head") normally played by a horn player and supported by chords on the piano and a walking bass line. After the melody is played, members of the band solo or improvise over the chord progression that supported the original melody. One common form of improvisation here is "trading fours," alternating four-bar improvisations between soloists, one of whom is often the drummer. Following the solo sections of the song, the melody is normally played again, with the tune usually coming to an end following the final statement of the melody.

The driving force behind the development of the small band ensemble was the team of saxophonist Charlie Parker and trumpeter Dizzie Gillespie. Their approach to Jazz focused on improvisation by all instruments. The hallmarks of this new style, known as Be Bop, were very fast tempos, very fast, complicated harmonic changes, and the use of complex chord extensions. Be Bop featured drumming pioneers such as Max Roach, Roy Haynes, and Philly Jo Jones.

By the mid-1950s, musician/composer Miles Davis created what came to be known as Cool Jazz (a more relaxed form of Jazz featuring slower tempos, fewer harmonic changes, and extended songs and solos). Art Blakey, Max Roach, Tony Williams (Miles Davis Quintet), and Joe Morello (Dave Brubeck Quartet) are just four of the drum legends associated with this era.

Shortly after, in the early 1960s, saxophonists John Coltrane, Sonny Rollins, and Ornette Coleman led the improvisation-based Avante Garde movement, and employed such famed drummers as Elvin Jones and Billy Higgins. The emphasis here was mostly on improvisation, and the "songs" played by Avante Garde groups were often improvised on the spot.

The drumming for Be Bop, Cool Jazz, and Avante Garde has much in common and makes use of many of the same musical ideas. However, the approaches to the three styles are different. Be Bop usually has busy drumming, tempos ranging up to quarter note = 300 bpm, and a fairly consistent approach. Cool Jazz usually requires fewer drum notes, more open space for soloists, and slower tempos, though again it requires a fairly consistent drumming approach. This is important during extended solo sections, especially when the soloist is playing "across the bar." Though Avante Garde utilizes the ideas of the previous two styles, it requires more technically advanced drumming, because the time pattern is usually less apparent and is sometimes deliberately obscured or even omitted entirely (as with much of the music of Cecil Taylor). As well, tempos may exceed even those of Be Bop; Avante Garde drummers often use polyrhythmic figures; and the form of a song is sometimes abandoned entirely—if there was a form to begin with (that is, if the playing isn't based on pure improvisation). Finally, with the popularity of Funk/Fusion, Jazz came to include straight as well as swung feels (e.g., Herbie Hancock's "Maiden Voyage").

Today, a Jazz drummer may utilize any of the styles and ideas of the previously mentioned eras. The role of the drum set player in Jazz continues to be to establish the swung or straight feel, with improvisation on the drums complementing the other instruments. The following patterns, featuring time variations and bass/snare drum variations, are only the beginning of countless possibilities for improvisation. To increase your improvisational vocabulary, refer to books such as *Modern Reading Text in 4/4*, by Louis Bellson and Gil Breines, *Syncopation for the Modern Drummer*, by Ted Reed, and *Advanced Techniques for the Modern Drummer*, by Jim Chapin. **The tempo range in Small Band Jazz is wider than that in any other Jazz genre with quarter note = 60–304 bpm.** (The only exception is the Jazz Ballad [see next section] which is played very slowly.)

Time Patterns

Example (CD 2, Track 42)

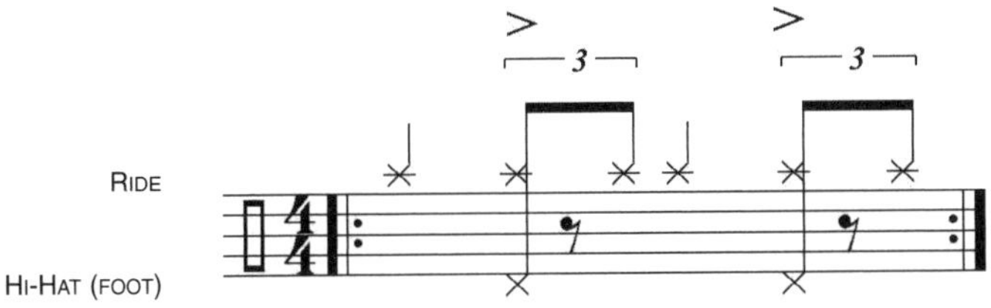

Variation 1

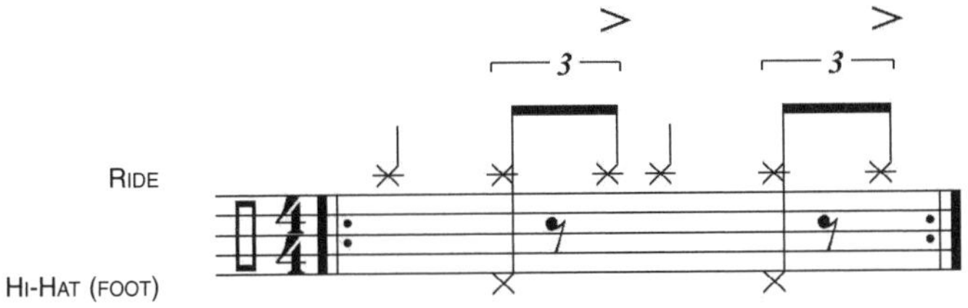

Variation 2

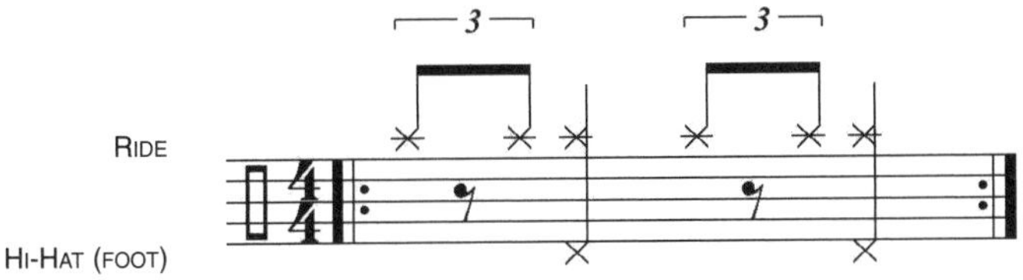

Variation 3

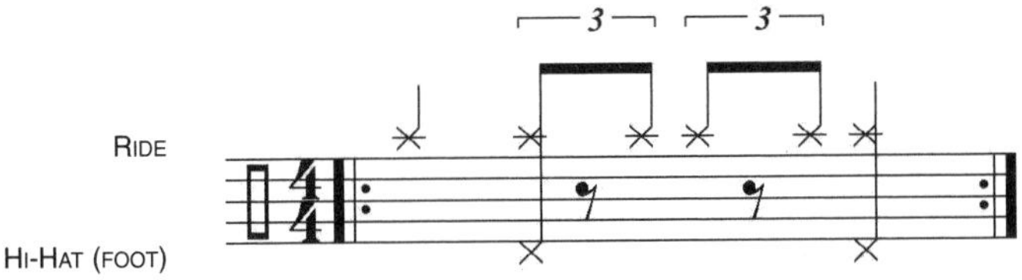

Variation 4

This simple pattern is most appropriate as an introduction to solos and in quiet sections.

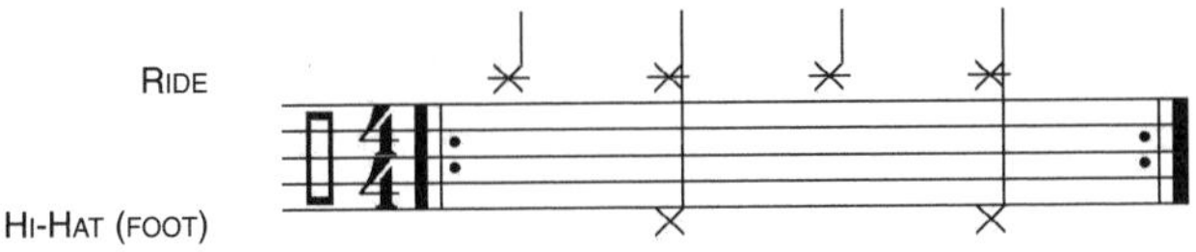

NOTE: All of these time patterns can be applied to the independence figures found below, though the most common and practical time pattern is the Standard Time Pattern in the main example. All of the above patterns may also be mixed with one another to create endless variations. Likewise, the hi-hat foot need not necessarily play beats 2 & 4; hi-hat foot variations are more commonly found in the Avante Garde genre.

Independence Figures

Example 1 (CD 2, Track 44)

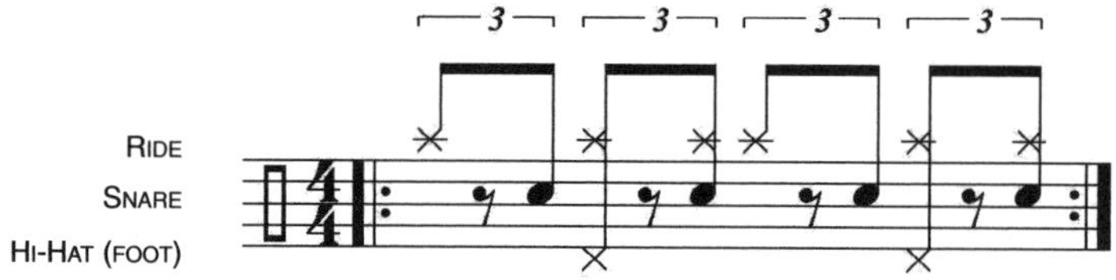

Variation

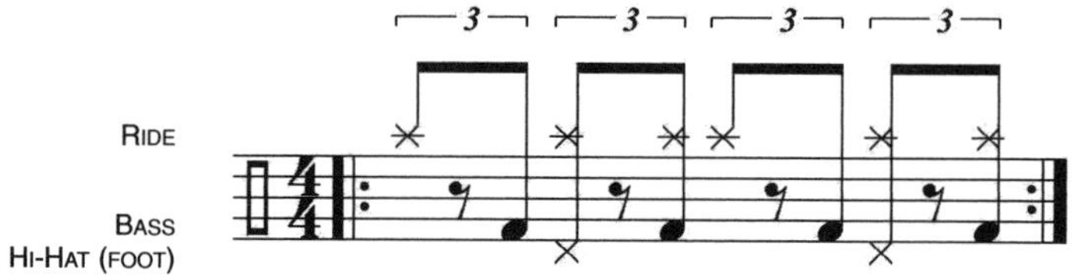

Example 2 (CD 2, Track 45)

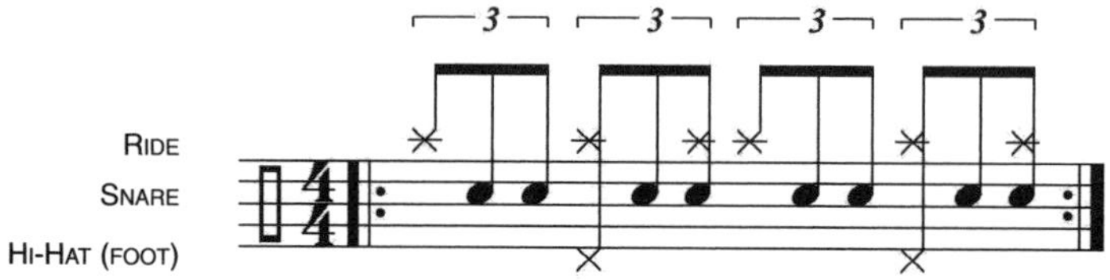

Variation

This variation is the same as example 2, arranged between the snare and bass drums. Leaving out groupings from this pattern can be an effective variation as well.

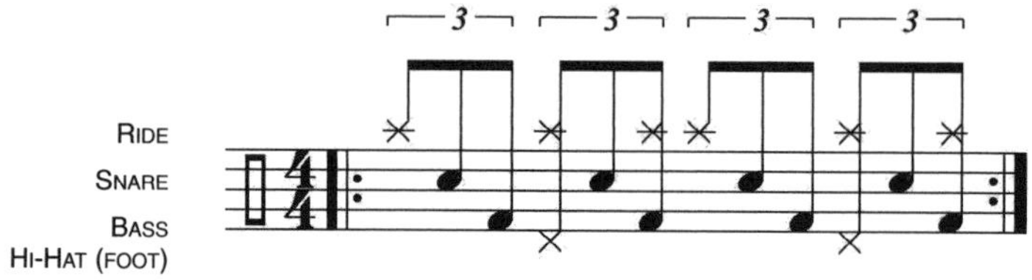

Example 3 (CD 2, Track 46)

Example 3 has a snare pattern that creates a polyrhythmic figure.

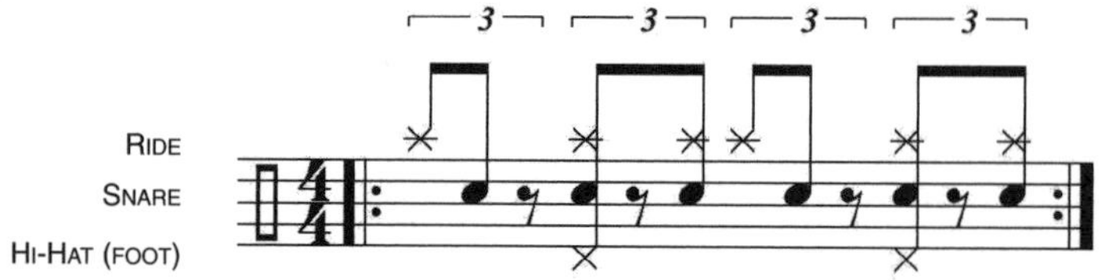

Variation

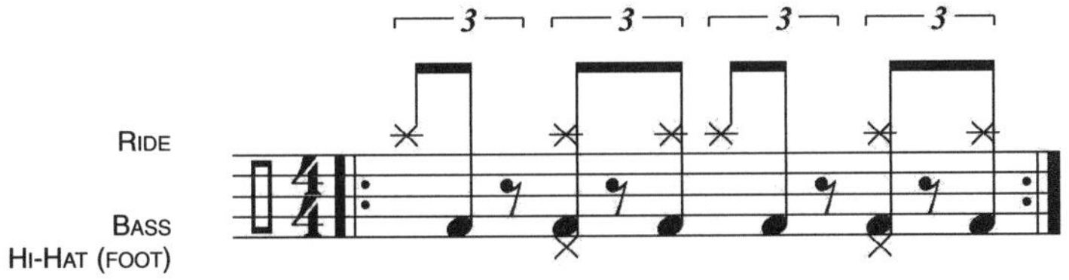

NOTE: The above example and variations are the same rhythmically but are played on different surfaces. For countless variations on this theme, play any combination of notes in the above rhythm tastefully between the bass drum and snare drum. Leaving notes out can be an effective variation.

Fast Swing Independence Figures

Example

Tempos for these figures are typically 190 bpm and above.

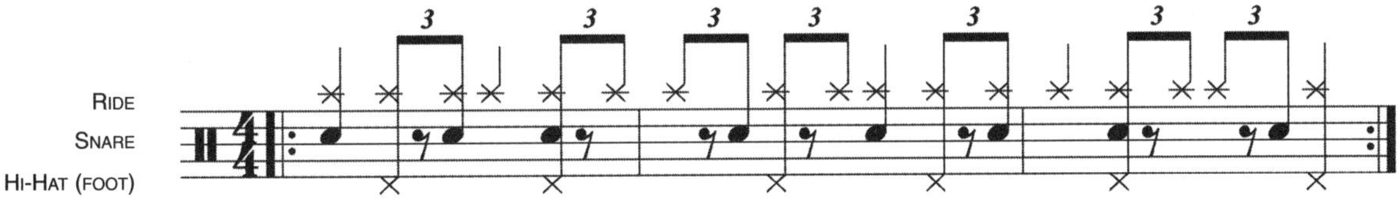

Variation 1

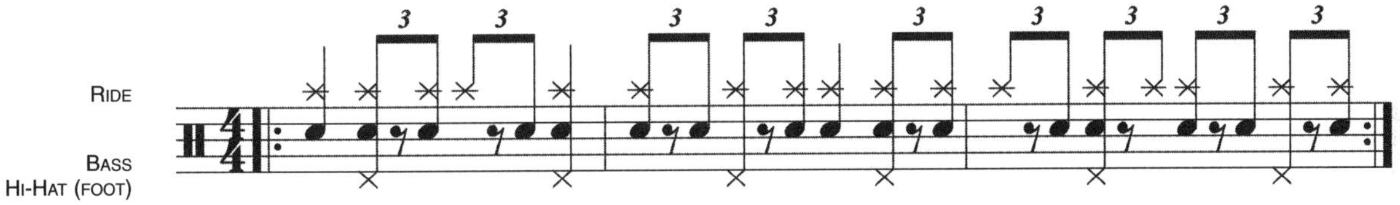

Variation 2

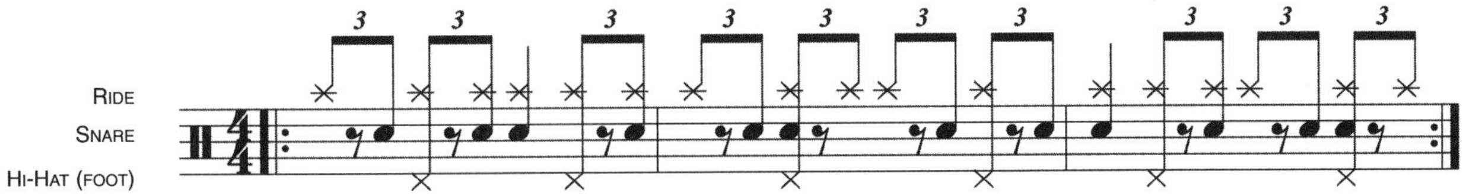

Small Band Summary

All of the above ideas can be used in small band Jazz styles such as Be Bop, Cool Jazz, and Avante Garde. Improvisation is wide open, and any combination of rhythms is possible. The following example incorporates many of the ideas from this chapter, and is simply intended to provide an idea of the wide-open improvisational possiblities in this style. **The tempo on the CD is quarter note = 138 bpm.**

EXAMPLE (CD 2, Track 47)

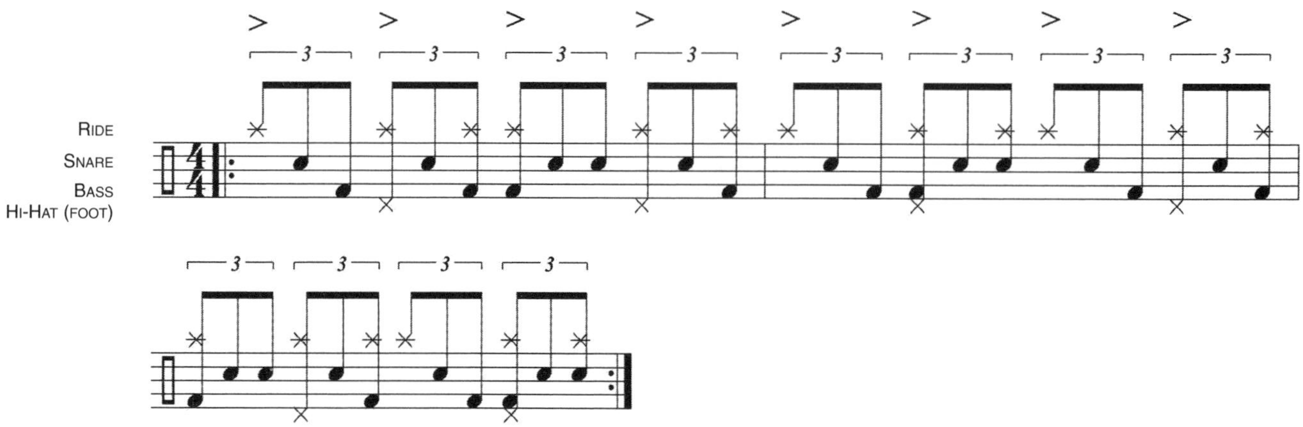

JAZZ WALTZ

The primary musical characteristic of the Jazz Waltz is the 3/4 time signature, though it's almost always played swung. The Jazz Waltz is found in both Big Band and small band arrangements with Max Roach's "The Drum Also Waltzes" among the most prominent drum compositions. Any of the improvisational figures found in the preceding section can be applied (suitably modified for 3/4 time, of course) to a Jazz Waltz. As with the previous styles, there are countless variations on both time and improvisational figures. Below are some of the most useful for the Jazz Waltz. **The large tempo range is quarter note = 100–255 bpm.**

EXAMPLE (CD 2, Track 48)

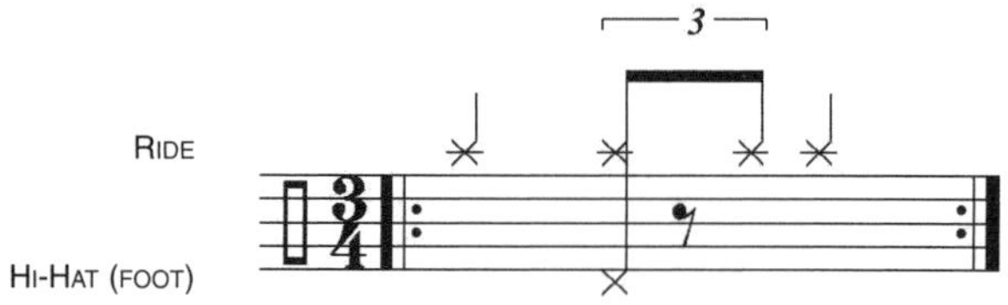

VARIATION 1 (CD 2, Track 49)

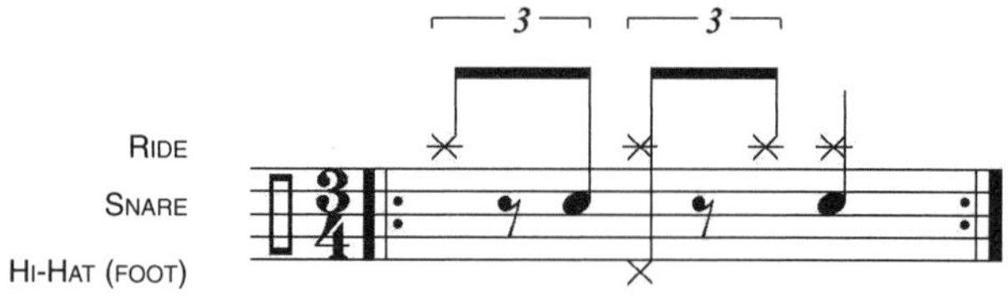

VARIATION 2

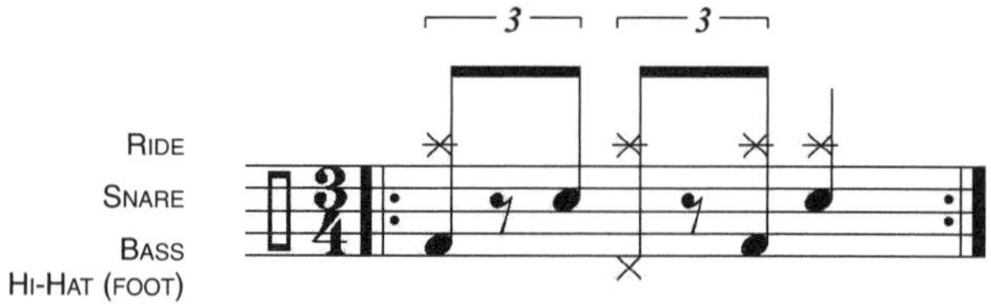

NOTE: The above patterns may include hi-hat foot strokes on any beat(s), though the most practical combinations are strokes on beats 2 & 3, just beat 2, just beat 3, or even the + of beat 2.

JAZZ BRUSHES/BALLAD

One of the distinct sounds of Jazz drumming is the use of brushes, both in standard-tempo songs and, especially, in ballads. The primary brush technique is to drag ("swirl") the snare hand in a clockwise circular motion on the snare while playing a consistent time pattern with the ride hand on the same surface. This requires careful coordination between the two hands.

The snare hand, circling as a hand of a clock, will arrive at ten o'clock on beats 1 and 3, and four o'clock on beats 2 and 4. The time pattern of the ride hand will strike beat 1, the + of beat 2, beat 3 and the + of beat 4 at four o'clock and beats 2 and 4 at ten o'clock, crossing over the circling snare hand (see Diagram 1A, below).

When performing a ballad with brushes, another way to play is the "figure eight" method. Both hands perform a figure eight on the snare drum, swirling and rarely leaving the surface. Generally, the ride hand starts on beat 1 at the upper portion of the drum while the snare hand is placed toward the lower portion on the same beat. The hands move in contrary directions to each other, both in figure eight patterns, and end up on opposite sides of the drum on beats 2 & 4 (see Diagram 1B). This enables a drummer to lightly accent all four beats of a measure with both hands simultaneously. Following the diagrams, musical transcriptions of each style are written out. (Note that a left-handed drummer would reverse motions for the following patterns.) **Tempos are slow for Jazz ballads with quarter note starting at 50 bpm.**

DIAGRAM 1A

Snare Hand

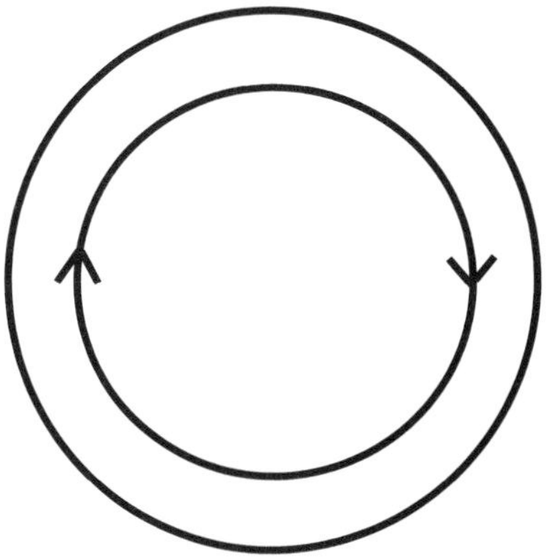

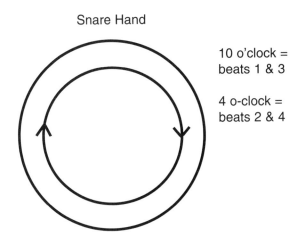

10 o'clock =
beats 1 & 3

4 o-clock =
beats 2 & 4

Ride Hand

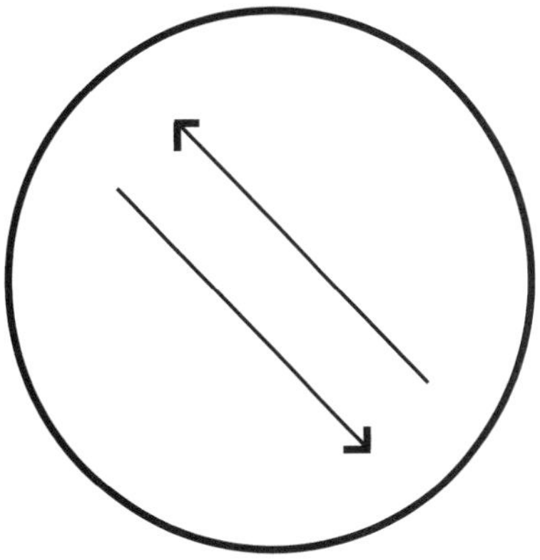

10 o'clock =
beats 2 & 4

4 o'clock =
beat 1, the +
of 2, beat 3,
and the + of 4

DIAGRAM 1B

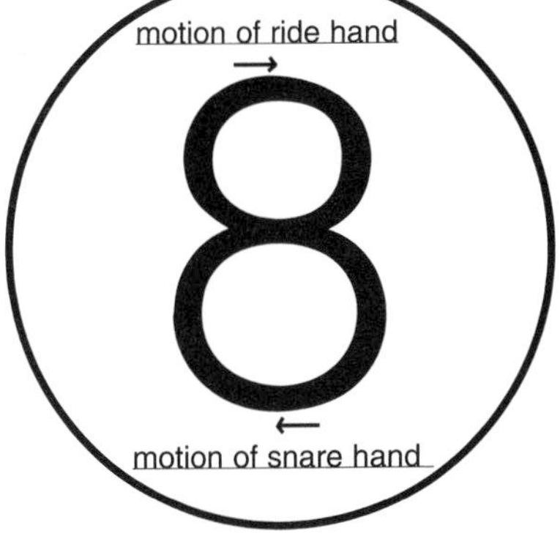

Example (CD 2, Track 50)

This has the ride hand time pattern played on the snare drum as well as a marking for the circular motion for the snare hand. The hi-hat foot accompanies the pattern on beats 2 & 4.

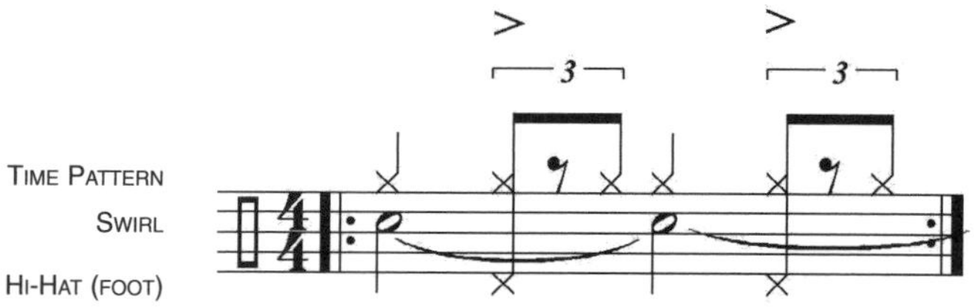

NOTE: The standard brush pattern can be used at any tempo, though it's most useful at a tempo marking above quarter note = 88 bpm.

Variation 1 (CD 2, Track 51)

This variation is the slower tempo/ballad "figure 8" pattern. The tied quarter note markings define the feel and the slight accents for the pattern while the hi-hat foot accompanies the pattern on beats 2 & 4.

Variation 2

This variation is a brush pattern in 3/4 time. The snare hand continues to swirl in a clockwise pattern, but more slowly so as to complete the circle in 3 beats rather than 2 beats. The ride hand plays a typical 3/4 time pattern on the snare head surface with beats 1, the + of beat 2 and beat 3 at four o'clock and beat 2 at 10 o'clock. The hi-hat foot is played on beat 2.

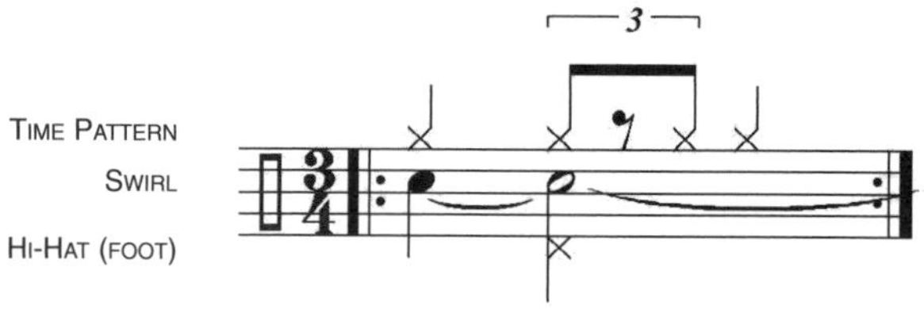

NOTE: On rare occasions, the bass drum may accompany the above patterns on all quarter notes. Remember not to overpower the lighter sound from the brushes. Any ideas for improvisation can be used from the previous sections in this chapter. When improvising with brushes, the ride hand plays the ride pattern on one area of the snare drum head, usually the four o'clock position, rather than crossing over the other hand.

16 KLEZMER

THE TERM KLEZMER comes from the Hebrew words, "kley" and "zemer," meaning "musical instrument." The first written documentation of Klezmer dates from the 16th century, while its creation and development stems from the Jewish population exiled to Poland, Romania, Ukraine, Belarus, and Lithuania (all of which came to be referred to as "the Pale of Settlement").

Many medieval governments and societies restricted Jewish musicians to specific instruments (flutes and stringed instruments among the most prominent), and music itself was one of the few occupations Jewish people were allowed to practice. Thus, every major European city possessed highly skilled, professional Jewish bands. These bands, along with Rom (gypsy) bands, traveled in order to earn a living.

Forced out of Spain, Portugal and Central Europe (Germany in particular), 17th-century Jews found themselves relocated to the Ottoman Empire in the Pale of Settlement. There, foreign musicians traveling on trade routes injected Jewish music with Turkish, Greek, Armenian and Middle Eastern influences, contributing to the formation of early Klezmer. It was characterized by: 1) an extremely high level of musicianship; 2) unique instrumentation; 3) Middle Eastern polyrhythms.

Initially restricted to the quieter instruments clarinet and violin, Klezmer musicians adeptly explored their musical capabilities, developing an emotional depth and expression patterned after the human singing voice (a prominent characteristic still inherent in Klezmer today). With the 18th-century Hasidic tradition (worship through heightened emotion) and the release of Jews serving in the Tsarist army bringing in more militaristic instruments, (trumpets, trombones, concert snare or "little" drums ["tshekal"], mounted bass drums ["puk" a.k.a "poik" or "baraban"], cymbals ["tats"], tambourines, woodblocks, cowbells and other percussion effects) the sounds of modern Klezmer began to emerge.

When 19th-century European governments imposed yet even more hardships upon the Pale of Settlement, emigration to the United States became the logical choice for much of the Jewish population. During the years 1880–1924, Jewish immigration to America (specifically New York City) exceeded more than two million people, bringing Klezmer to the New World. By the early 20th century, several Klezmer musicians came into prominence, among the most respected being clarinetists Naftule Brandwein and Dave Tarras. Additionally, band leaders such as Harry Kandel produced a wealth of Klezmer recordings, making Klezmer accessible for future generations and furthering the Klezmer tradition via Bulgar, Freylakhs, Hora, Khosidl, Terkisher, and other dances.

Since the 1920s, Klezmer's popularity has fluctuated, though it has been routinely performed in wedding ceremonies, parties, and theater productions. After the founding of the Israeli state in 1948, the younger generation felt the need to modernize its culture, causing Klezmer's popularity to diminish further. However, a resurgence began in the latter part of the 20th century in Europe and the United States, with Klezmorim ("musicians") from Berkeley, California and Kapelye ("bands") from New York City leading the way. As the number of young European musicians eager to learn the style rapidly grew, one of Klezmer's primary markets became, of all places, Germany. Musicians from the United States (many with Rock n' Roll experience) found excited students and audiences in Berlin, with Brave Old World (with bassist Stuart Brotman, formerly of Canned Heat and Kaleidoscope), the Klezmatics, and the Klezmer Conservatory Band among the most prominent groups.

Continually evolving, contemporary Klezmer music has accepted the drum set. The grooves listed below offer a wide range of practical choices for playing authentic Klezmer music on the drum set.

Please note that dancers sometimes perform different dances to the same series of songs, and the choice of drum pattern depends on which dance the dancers are performing.

BULGAR originates in Bessarabia (present day Moldova) and is quite similar to the Israeli Hora (a dance performed in a circle, in line, or in couples—not to be confused with the Klezmer Hora found below). Bulgar music may be divided into many parts, though a two-part arrangement is the most common form. **Quarter note = 112–152 bpm.**

FREYLAKHS (pronounced Fray-locks) is similar to Bulgar and is another Jewish circle dance, this one originating from Romania, with a Two-Step feel. It differs from the Bulgar in its slightly faster tempo, more syncopated drum rhythm, and single-section form. **Quarter note = 112–152 bpm.**

HORA (from Romanian and Moldavian cultures, not to be confused with the Jewish Hora danced to "Hava Nagila"—see Wedding Dances chapter) is a circle dance usually written in 3/8 meter as a reminder to avoid phrasing it like a waltz, with the most important characteristic being the lack of emphasis on beat 2. However, its melodic phrasing can range from straight 3 to a "5 against 3" polyrhythm, and it can have an "in the crack" quality. **Eighth note = 112–184 bpm.**

KHOSIDL is a Hasidic folk dance written in duple meter (either 2/4 or 4/4) which usually speeds up to a frantic climax, **starting at quarter note = 120 bpm.**

TERKISHER, also of Romanian origin, is a march-like rhythm with similarities to a Greek "Sirto" rhythm (both similar to that of a Tango—see Wedding Dance chapter). **Quarter note =108–168 bpm.**

BULGAR

EXAMPLE 1 ("A" SECTION) (CD 2, Track 52)

Quarter note = 112–152 bpm

EXAMPLE 2 ("B" SECTION) (CD 2, Track 52)

The "B" section has a "double time" feel. There is sometimes a third section of a Bulgar known as the "Sirba," in which the melody is played in a 6/8 rhythm. However the drumming groove would remain as the quick "two beat" feel.

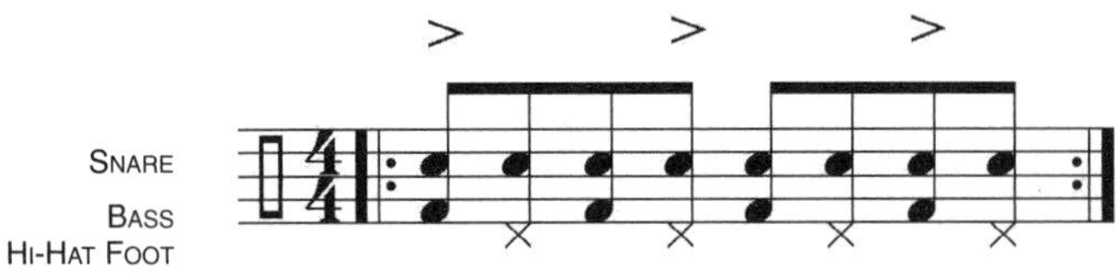

Quarter note = 112–152 bpm

NOTE: Another appropriate choice for the hands is to improvise on a woodblock or the rim of the snare drum (against the above foot pattern) as a counterpoint to the melody.

Freylakhs

Example (CD 2, Track 53)

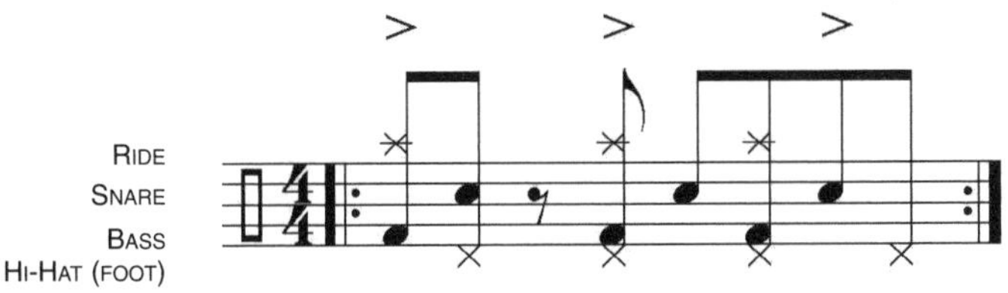

Quarter note = 112–152 bpm

Hora (also Hore, Jok, Zhok, or Gas Nign)

Example (CD 2, Track 54)

Quarter note = 112–184 bpm

(Circled hi-hat note is splashed)

Khosidl

Example (CD 2, Track 55)

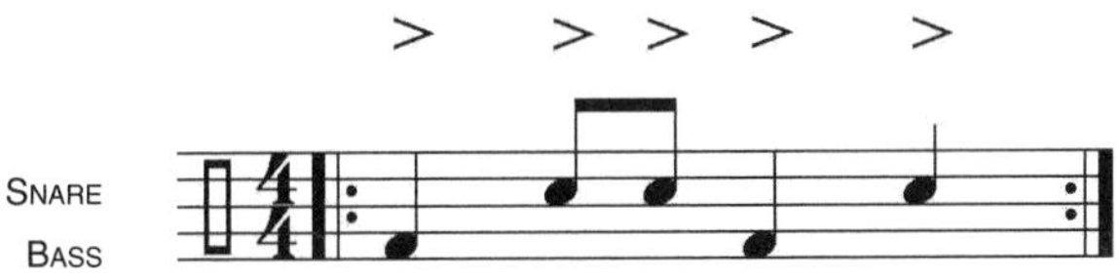

Quarter note = 120 bpm

Terkisher

Example (CD 2, Track 56)

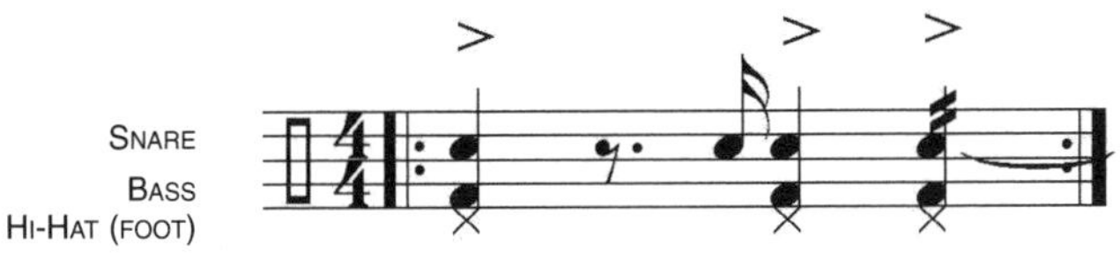

Quarter note = 108–168 bpm

17 Latin Rock

Latin Rock incorporates rhythms from Afro-Cuban and Brazilian music into a Rock format, while often utilizing percussion instruments from all three styles. Though the Afro-Cuban and Brazilian chapters contain grooves which can be used in such early Latin Rock songs as "Tequila" (by The Champs), this style normally uses less authentic and often simplified drum set patterns.

The late 1960s saw the emergence of Carlos Santana, probably the most important musician to popularize the Latin Rock genre. His band featured the use of Afro-Cuban percussion instruments in a Rock music setting. His impact on this style has spanned well over four decades, as he remains a popular figure world wide. Other later, successful Latin Rock artists include Los Lobos and Miami Sound Machine (featuring Gloria Estefan), as well as more recent artists such as Ricky Martin, Marc Anthony, Los Hermanos, Los Tres, La Ley, Mana, and Shakira.

Much as with patterns from the Afro-Cuban and Brazilian chapters, the drum set rhythms are often simplified in Latin Rock to avoid duplicating the parts of other percussionists. When playing alone, the Latin Rock drum set player may expand on the simplified grooves to approximate a more authentic sound. The grooves presented below combine Afro-Cuban, Brazilian, and Rock patterns to offer a wide variety of practical options. **The tempos range from those of most Standard Rock songs at quarter note = 110–120 bpm to that of a double time Afro-Cuban/Brazilian feel at quarter note = 200–232 bpm.**

Latin Rock (Standard Rock)

Example (CD 2, Track 57)

This combines a Standard Rock groove with an Afro-Cuban Cha Cha.

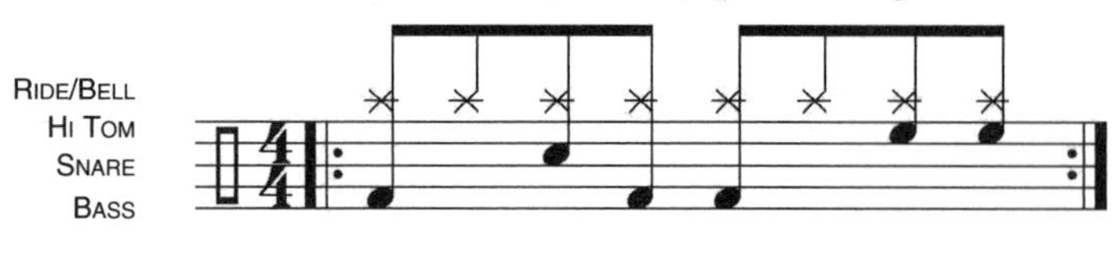

VARIATION 1 (CD 2, Track 81)

This is the first bass drum variation in the Standard Rock section of the Rock chapter. Notice the similarity of the bass drum pattern to that in the previous example.

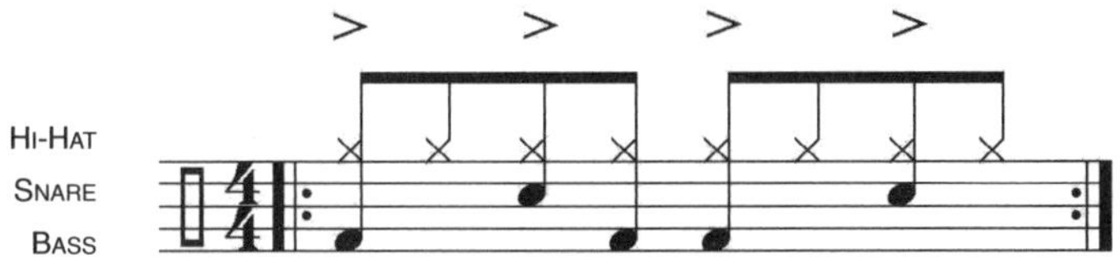

VARIATION 2

Variation 2 is similar to variation 1 with the snare hand playing all quarter notes on a cowbell.

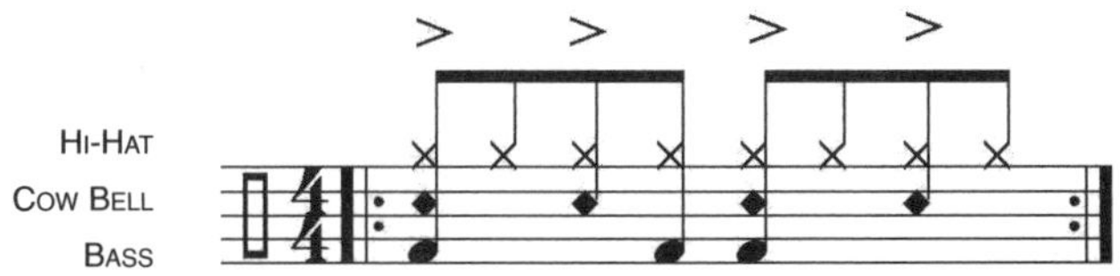

NOTES: 1) All standard Rock beats can be applied to Latin Rock when appropriate, depending on the instrumentation and/or rhythms played by other musicians. 2) The hi-hat foot can accompany the pattern on all four quarter notes, beats 2 & 4, all eighth notes, or all upbeats. The ride hand can also play all quarter notes on a cowbell.

LATIN ROCK (BAIAO)

EXAMPLE 2 (CD 2, Track 58)

This resembles a Brazilian Baiao mixed with a Rock feel. The hands play an alternating 16th note pattern with accents on a closed hi-hat while the bass drum foot matches the hand accents throughout the measure. For variety, the hand pattern can be played on a floor tom or a snare drum with the snares off. **The tempo is again quarter note = 110–120 bpm.**

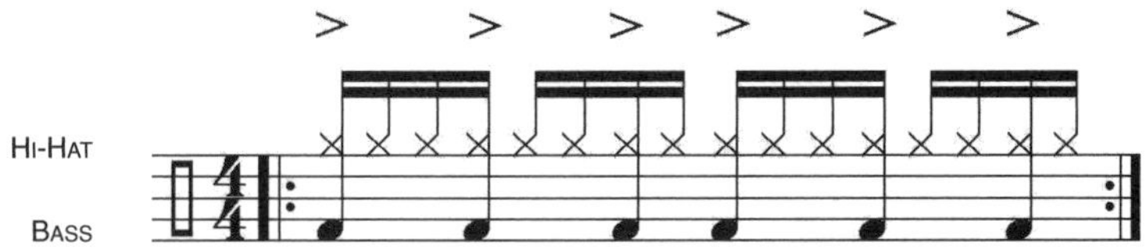

Variation 1

This variation utilizes the same Baiao bass drum pattern while incorporating quarter notes on the cowbell and a 2 & 4 back beat on the snare drum.

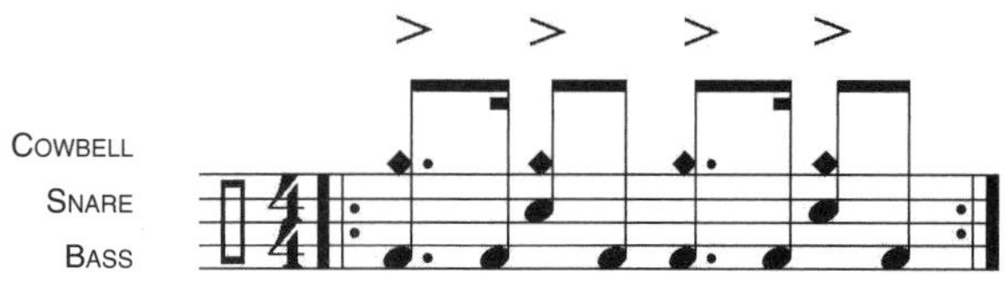

Variation 2

This pattern is most practical for a pop music setting. It retains the 16th-note feel on the hi-hat, while breaking up the bass and snare drum patterns and includes an additional floor tom note on beat 4.

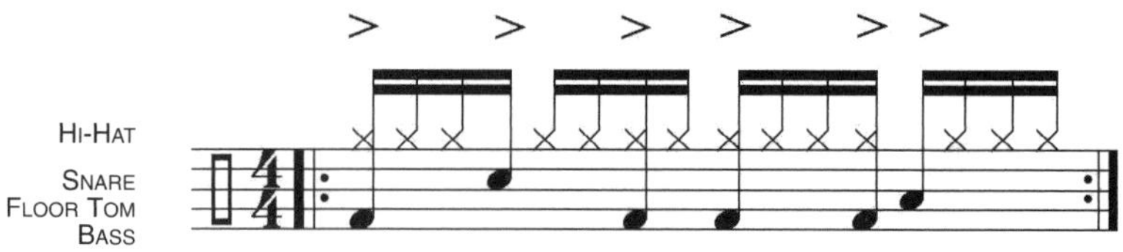

Latin Rock (Mambo)

Example 3 (CD 2, Track 59)

This is similar to variation 1 in the Mambo section of the Afro-Cuban chapter. The only difference is the change of the bass drum pattern to emphasize beat 1 of both measures. **Tempo is quarter note = 180–220 bpm.**

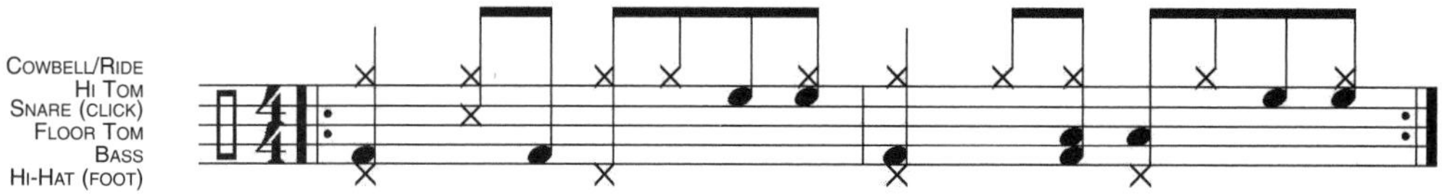

Variation

This variation is the same pattern as the main Blues Mambo example. **Quarter note = 110–120 bpm.**

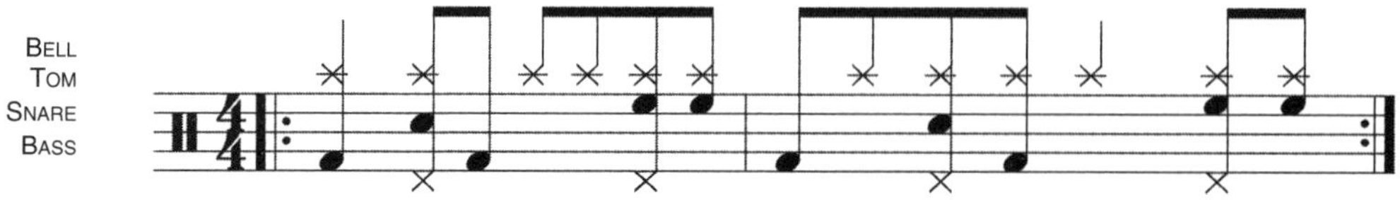

Latin Rock (Rumba)

Example 4 (CD 1, Track 64)

This is the same pattern as the main Blues Rumba example. **Quarter note = 180–220 bpm.**

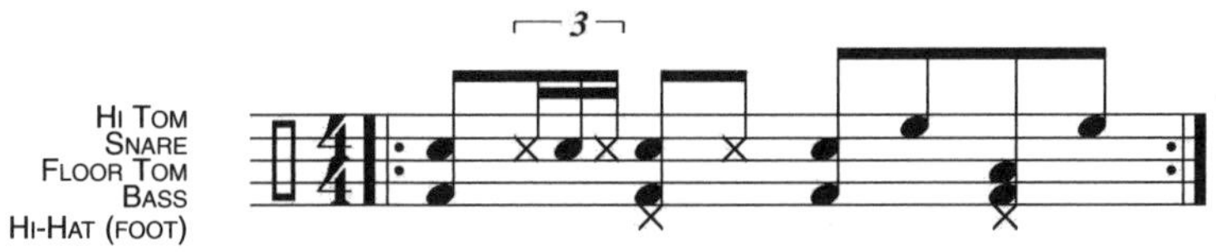

Latin Rock (Soca)

Example (CD 1, Track 87)

This is the same pattern as the main Soca example. It is used in many modern Latin Rock/Pop songs from artists such as Shakira. **Quarter note = 108–132bpm.**

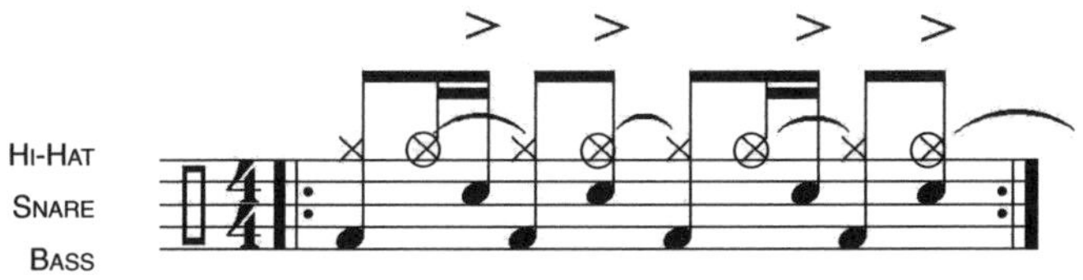

(Circled hi-hat notes are played open)

18 March

The roots of march music extend into the distant past, with modern march music beginning to take form in the European military bands of the early 1500s. A major step toward modern march music occurred after Polish and Austrian armies drove the Turks out of Vienna in 1683; Turkish instruments (drums, cymbals, horns) quickly became incorporated into European military music. This contributed greatly to the beginning of the modern military band, consisting of brass, wind, and percussion sections.

By the time of the American Revolutionary War (1775–1783), military bands had become commonplace, and the music had become standardized in three forms: slow/parade march; quick march; and double quick or attack march. By the second half of the 19th century the march caught on with the general public, and it reached its peak of popularity in the mid-1800s to early 1900s. By the early part of the 20th century march music thrived as the preferred music for outdoor entertainment and even dancing, as the march became the standard accompaniment for the Two Step. During the height of march popularity, its most outstanding composer appeared: John Philip Sousa. His compositions and arrangements still stand as the definitive sound of the march genre.

Marches also played a major role in civilian life. At gatherings, processionals and parades, drummers dictated the tempo of a parade formation. This was especially common among the descendants of African slaves and their descendants in Brazil, Cuba and the southern United States, especially in New Orleans.

By the early 1920s, marching bands evolved further, into "drum and bugle corps" (marching ensembles consisting of percussion and brass sections with no woodwinds), which played marches along with other types of music. Today traditional marching bands function as entertainment at sporting events, military events, and as an indispensable element of celebrations such as Mardi Gras and Carnaval. In addition, virtually every major university has a marching band. The armed forces also maintain a number of orchestral military bands (that is, Sousa-style bands with woodwind sections), which typically appear at 4th of July celebrations. The popularity of drum and bugle corps has led to the establishment of organizations such as Drum Corps International (DCI), promoting competition and tradition within the style.

The most prominent march characteristics are: 1) a solid discernible beat; 2) establishment and development of immediately memorable musical themes; and 3) precise, careful orchestration. Though a marching percussion section typically contains several percussionists, a single individual can reproduce the general sound of march-style percussion on a drum set. Having a general knowledge of rudiments (e.g., flams, double stroke rolls, etc.) will enable a drummer to execute march drumming fairly easily (see Rudiments appendix). **Marches are most often performed at a tempo of quarter note = 120 bpm.**

Standard Marches

Example (CD 2, Track 60)

(Circled hi-hat notes are splashed)

Variation 1

The emphasis in this variation is on the bass and snare drums trading off notes. Note the flams on every upbeat ("+").

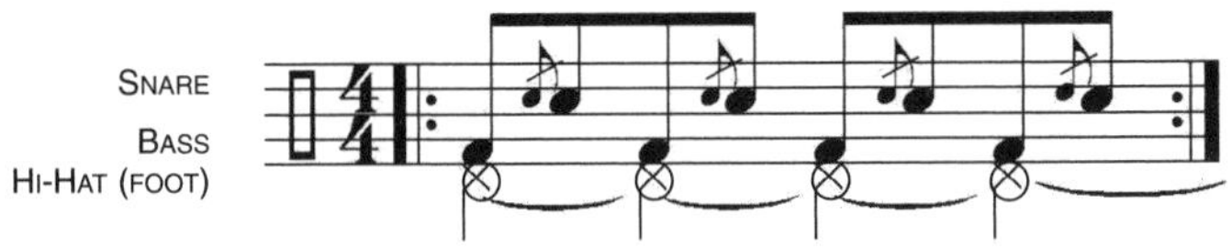

(Circled hi-hat notes are splashed)

Variation 2

This variation utilizes flams and has a swung feel.

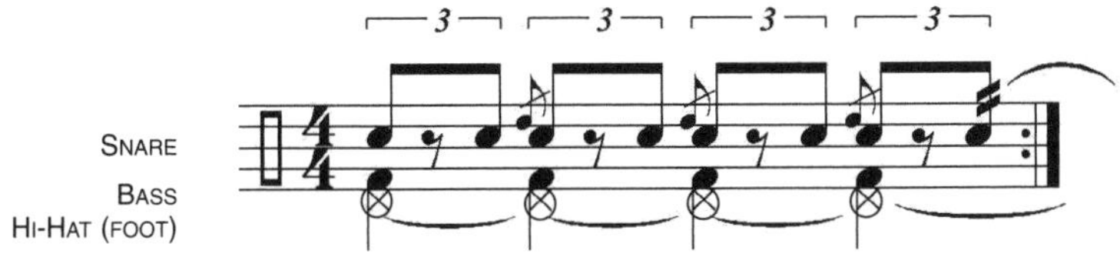

(Circled hi-hat notes are splashed)

New Orleans Second Line

Example (CD 2, Track 37)

This is the main example of a New Orleans Second Line groove from the Jazz chapter. For further ideas, refer to variations 1–5 for Second Line drumming. **The tempo is faster here at quarter note = 144–216 bpm.**

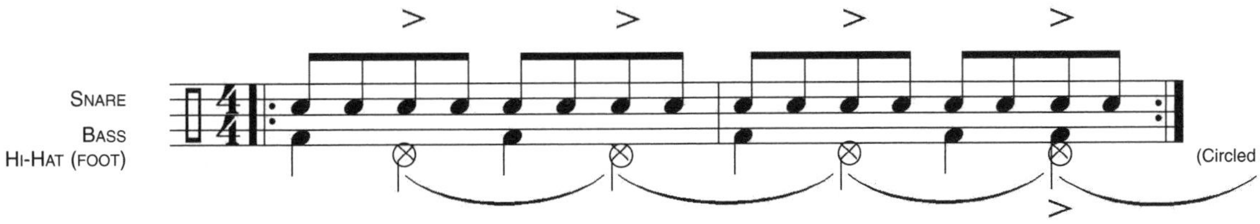

(Circled hi-hat notes are splashed)

Cuban Comparsa

Example (CD 1, Track 43)

This is an authentic march-like rhythm played in the Cuban Comparsa which corresponds to the traditional Cuban Conga pattern (see Conga in Afro-Cuban chapter). This pattern is based on a 2-3 rumba clave. **The tempo is very fast at quarter note = 216–264 bpm.**

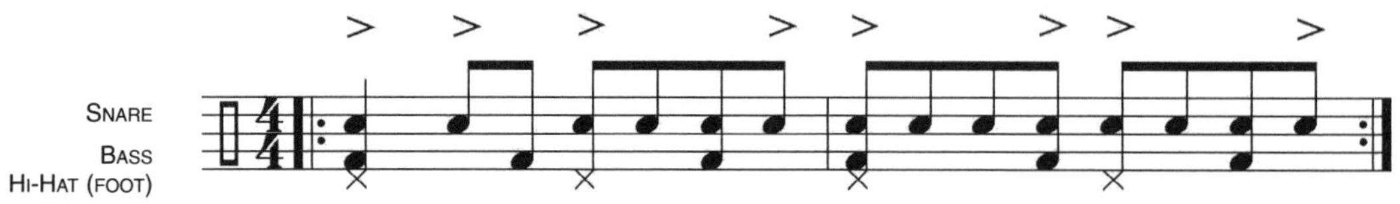

Brazilian Baiao

Example (CD 1, Track 76)

This is the march variation (variation 2) of Baiao from the Brazilian chapter. **Tempo is quarter note = 102 bpm.**

Drum Pattern for *50 Ways to Leave Your Lover*

This is a transcription of the famous drum pattern from Paul Simon's "50 Ways to Leave Your Lover," created and played by Steve Gadd. By breaking up march rhythms and playing them on different surfaces, it reveals many possibilities for using marching patterns to create a unique groove. Play the pattern "open handed," with the left hand on the hi-hat and the right hand on the snare drum (reverse sticking for left handed drummers). **The tempo is quarter note = 102 bpm.**

Example

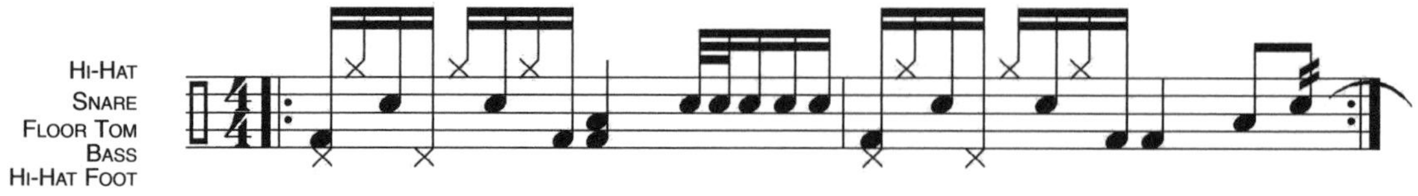

19 Metal

Metal music (originally called "Heavy Metal") has been a driving force in Rock for over 40 years, and continues to develop and expand. The roots of the style can be found in late 1960s/early 1970s Hard Rock and Blues Rock bands. Since then, it has evolved into music featuring exceptionally fast, technically challenging rhythms and heavy drumming, frequently accompanied by growling vocals, heavy, blistering guitar tones, and rapid-fire double bass patterns. The style usually requires an exceptional amount of endurance from the musicians playing it. Terms associated with contemporary Metal are "Death Metal," "Goth Metal," "Black Metal," "Speed Metal," and "Thrash," which all suggest its sound.

Bands such as Led Zeppelin, Deep Purple, Black Sabbath, solo artist Alice Cooper, and California-based Blue Cheer are among Metal originators. Even at its inception, Metal featured louder, harsher guitar, more active bass and drum parts, and darker lyrics than in standard Rock. Another feature of Heavy Metal is that many of its artists put on live concerts involving elaborate stage sets, intricate light shows, pyrotechnics, and outrageous costumes (e.g., Kiss). The Metal sound initially relied on high-pitched singers (e.g., Robert Plant of Led Zeppelin), but has since evolved to embrace lower-range, roaring or growling vocals.

In the late 1970s, the "New Wave of British Metal" raised the bar higher for new Metal musicians. Bands such as Iron Maiden, Motorhead, Venom, and Saxon used even heavier sounds and faster tempos. (The song "Overkill" by Motorhead is perhaps the first popular Metal song to feature the consistent double bass pattern.)

These bands paved the way for many bands that branched out into different Metal styles. Thrash Metal, performed by bands such as Metallica, Megadeth, Pantera, Anthrax, Slayer, Sepultura, and Overkill, is perhaps the most popular of the Metal subgenres. Death Metal, another popular subgenre, is exemplified by Napalm Death, Carcass, and Cannibal Corpse. More recently, still more Metal subgenres have emerged: Deathcore, (Black Dahlia Murder, Veil of Maya, Suicide Silence); Metalcore (Underneath, All That Remains, Bullet for My Valentine, Shadows Fall); Melodic Death Metal (At The Gates, In Flames, Nevermore); and Progressive Death Metal (Hate Eternal, Meshuggah, Nile, Opeth, Origin).

Metal drummers need to develop the considerable speed, coordination, and dexterity necessary to play the intricate patterns, most notably double bass drum patterns, inherent to this style. Typically, Metal drummers use two bass drums in their set up, though a similar double bass effect can be achieved with a double pedal playing one bass drum. The example and variations below move from simple to more complex patterns, and are only an introduction to authentic Metal drumming. The most advanced Metal drumming grooves can also incorporate ideas and patterns from Fusion and Linear Funk. **Tempos range from quarter note = 60 bpm to speeds exceeding quarter note = 300 bpm.**

EXAMPLE (CD 2, Track 29)

This is the Standard Rock Beat, utilizing a loud, half-open hi-hat in the ride hand. Keep in mind that the entire groove is meant to be played loudly and aggressively. All standard Rock variations (see Rock n' Roll chapter) can be played with this technique as well, widening your choices. In addition, moving the ride hand over to a ride cymbal or even a crash cymbal (with various hi-hat foot accompaniments) is common. **Quarter note = 100–200 bpm.**

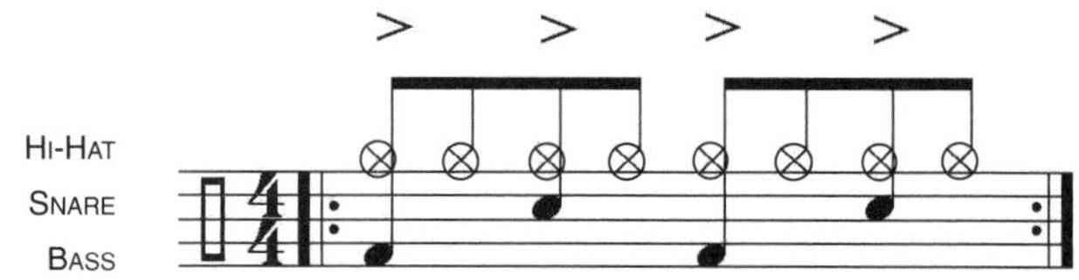

(Circled hi-hat notes are played half-open)

VARIATION 1 (CD 2, Track 30)

Considered the standard Thrash beat (often referred to as the "Skank" beat), this groove is similar to a Two-Step or a Polka groove with an embellished bass drum pattern and a half-open hi-hat. This variation is most practical for quick, double-time feels. **Quarter note = 126–192 bpm.**

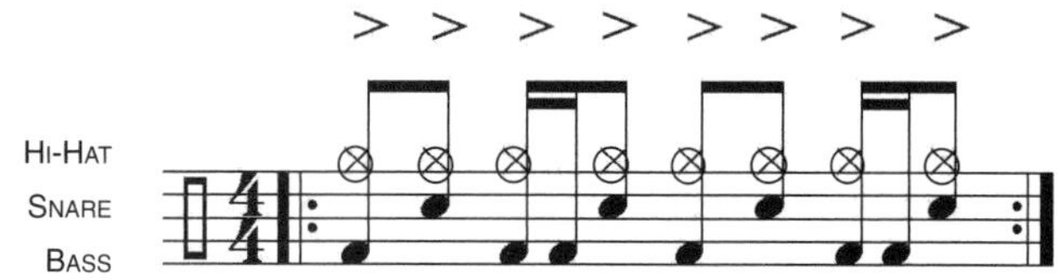

(Circled hi-hat notes are played half-open)

VARIATION 2 (CD 2, Track 31)

This is often called the "Traditional Blast Beat." The hands alternate consistent 16th notes between a half-open hi-hat and the snare drum with the bass drum doubling the notes of the ride hand. This particular groove utilizes extremely fast 16th notes. *Every note is accented!* **Quarter note = 200 bpm.**

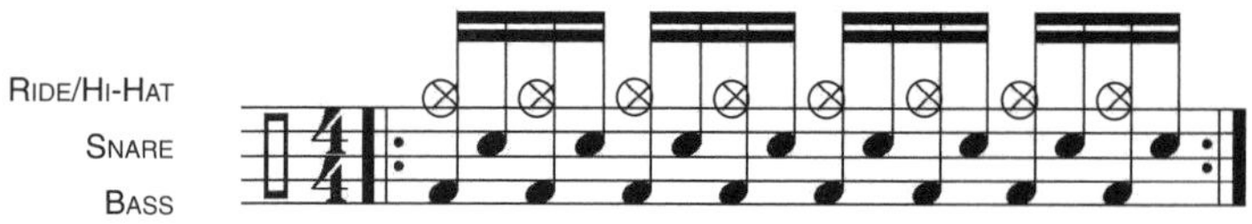

(Circled hi-hat notes are played half-open)

Variation 3

This pattern is a variation of the Blast Beat. The hands (this time, played simultaneously on a half-open hi-hat and the snare drum) alternate with the bass drum foot to play consistent, extremely fast 16th notes. **Quarter note = 200 bpm.**

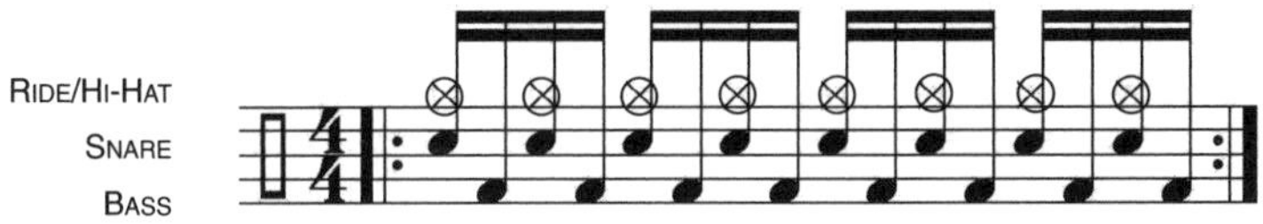

(Circled hi-hat notes are played half-open)

Variation 4

This is often called a "Unison Blast Beat" or a "Hammer Blast Beat."

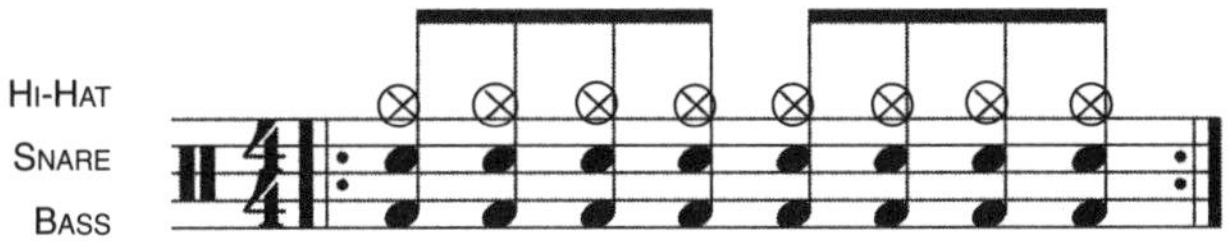

(Circled hi-hat notes are played half-open)

Variation 5

This is often called a "Bomb Blast."

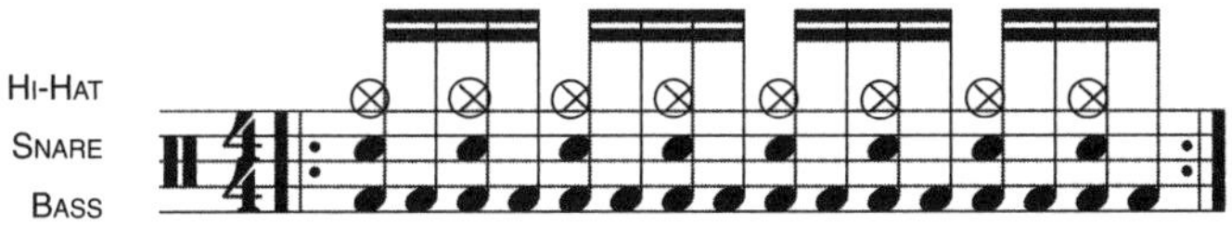

(Circled hi-hat notes are played half-open)

Double Bass Playing

As mentioned in the introduction to this chapter, double bass playing is a strong characteristic of Metal. Skilled double bass drummers can perform anything from extremely fast alternating 16th note rhythms to polyrhythms to syncopated rhythms to rudimental-style drumming with their feet (e.g., double stroke rolls, flammed rudiments, etc.—see Rudiments appendix). Be aware that it's necessary to have patience developing the dexterity, control, and strength required for double bass drumming. Unlike the majority of musical styles covered in this book, double bass drumming is primarily based on muscular development, and it takes ample time to become a well-versed double bass drummer. The grooves presented below are just the beginning—but include some essential patterns—of this style of drumming. **Quarter note = 100–200 bpm.**

EXAMPLE (CD 2, Track 32)

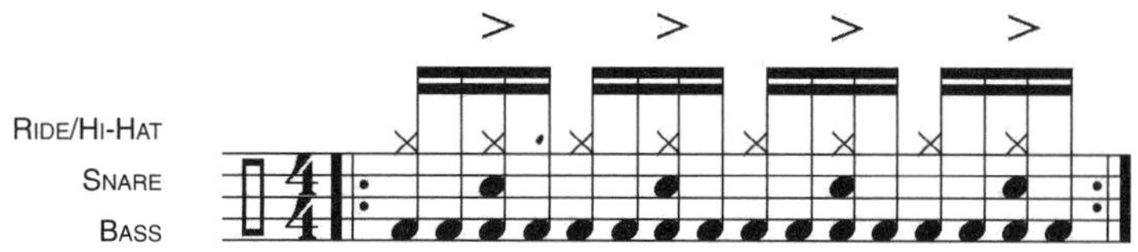

VARIATION 1

The snare drum notes played on beats 2 & 4, create a half-time feel.

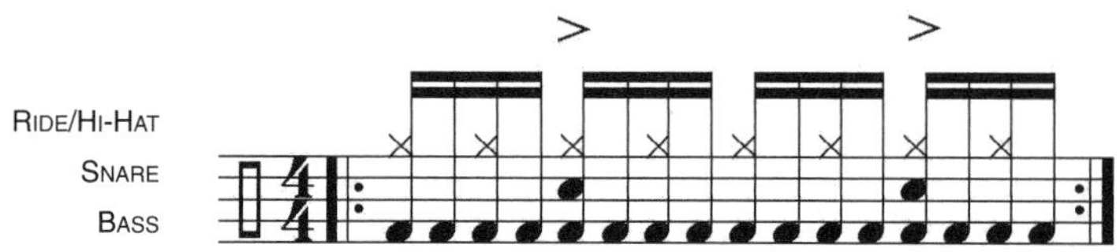

VARIATION 2

This variation displaces the snare hand to beat 3, creating the illusion of a slow groove.

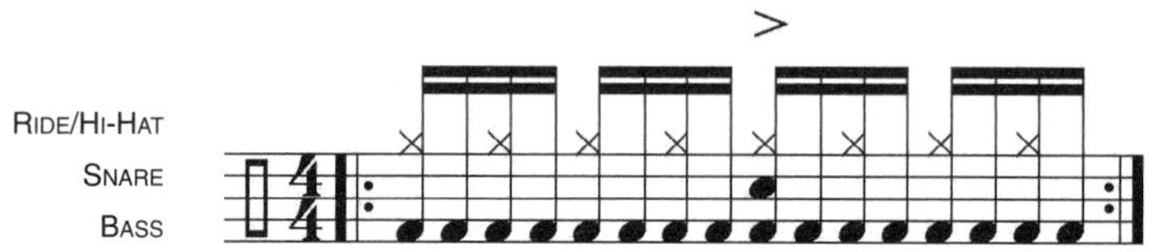

VARIATION 3

This has a gallop-like figure on the feet as well as a displaced snare drum on beat 3.

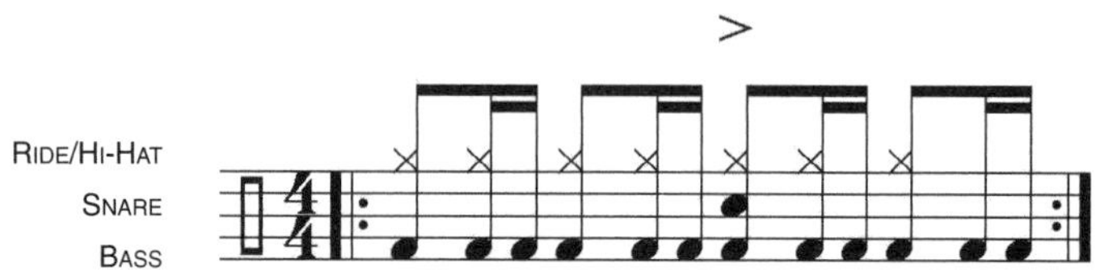

VARIATION 4 (CD 2, Track 33)

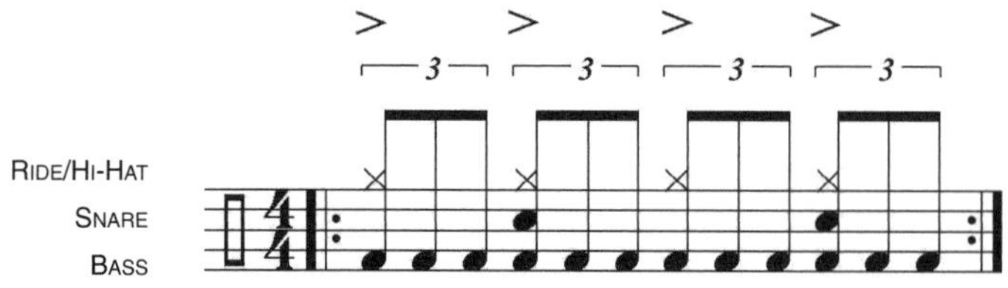

NOTES: 1) For the above double bass grooves, the ride hand can be played on various surfaces. Common choices are a ride cymbal, a second hi-hat (mounted, open or closed, next to or below the ride cymbal), or even a crash cymbal. 2) For developing more dexterity and control with double bass playing, a good suggestion is to extract 16th note or triplet rhythms (syncopated, broken up, etc.) from *Modern Reading Text in 4/4,* by Louis Bellson with Gil Breins, and/or from *Syncopation,* by Ted Reed.

20 MIDDLE EASTERN

THE MUSIC OF THE MIDDLE EAST and the Arabic nations dates back thousands of years, and has influenced countless other musical traditions. Contemporary Middle Eastern music combines the traits of traditional Eastern folk music with elements of Western popular and classical nusic. Ghazal, Qawali, Maghrebi, Kahleeji and Arabic Pop are just a few of the numerous styles of music emanating from Egypt, Morocco, Algeria, Tunisia, Saudi Arabia, Turkey, and the Persian Gulf.

In the music's early modern forms, Middle Eastern composers integrated their folk styles with Western-influenced orchestras, though currently the trend has turned back toward smaller ensembles. (Pre-Western Middle Eastern music utilized smaller ensembles.) Instruments such as the Oud (a pear-shaped stringed instrument), Persian Tars (a plucked/strummed instrument, similar to an Oud, with a soundboard of stretched skin rather than wood), Neys (wind instrument), Qanouns (horizontal instrument with many strings, resembling a dulcimer) and Kamenches & Rebabas (both fiddle-like, bowed instruments) still characterize this musical genre. Notable Arabic musicians include Kazem el-Saher, Nawal el-Zoughbi, Najwa Karam, Assi el-Hillani, George Wassouf, Amro Diab, Nancy Ajram, Ramy Ayach, Kadim al-Sahir, Hatem al-Iraqi, and Lara Iskander.

Middle Eastern rhythms were originally devised in antiquity on frame drums, the Arabic tabla, the doumbek, the darabuka, finger cymbals, and other traditional percussion instruments. Though an authentic Middle Eastern ensemble still contains such instruments, the drum set is often used in modern-day Middle Eastern ensembles.

Traditional Middle Eastern rhythms cover a wide array of odd-time signatures. However, as a result of Western music's influence, a large portion of contemporary Middle Eastern music is composed in duple or other meters containing even numbers. Thus, the first two following drum set patterns are written in 4/4. Their overall sound and rhythm serve as accurate examples of traditional Middle Eastern music adapted for the drum set.

Middle Eastern Pop (almost all in 4/4) is also an important subgenre of Middle Eastern music, as is Algerian Rai music (again, almost all in 4/4). The history and stylistic characteristics of both are covered in their subsections in this chapter.

TRADITIONAL RHYTHMS

EXAMPLE 1 (CD 2, Track 61)

This is a 3 + 3 + 2 Middle Eastern ("Saudi") rhythm. This particular rhythm has a double time feel. For more grooves and information regarding breaking up 4/4 rhythms (for example, 3 + 3 + 2, 2 + 3 + 3, etc.), see the Odd Time chapter. **Quarter note = 220 bpm.**

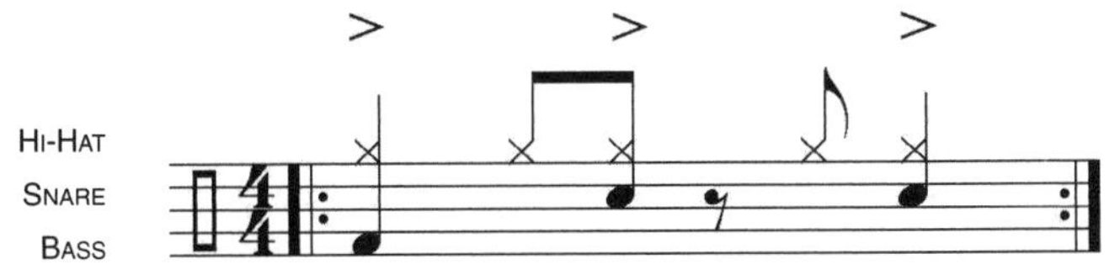

Example 2 (CD 2, Track 62)

This is a Sayyidii rhythm, from the Maqsuum family of rhythms. It's a good idea to turn the snares off in order to mimic the sound of a hand drum. Other surfaces besides the closed hi-hat (such as the ride, the rims of the drums, other cymbals, or mounted tambourine) may be used for the ride hand patterns. **Quarter note = 120 bpm.**

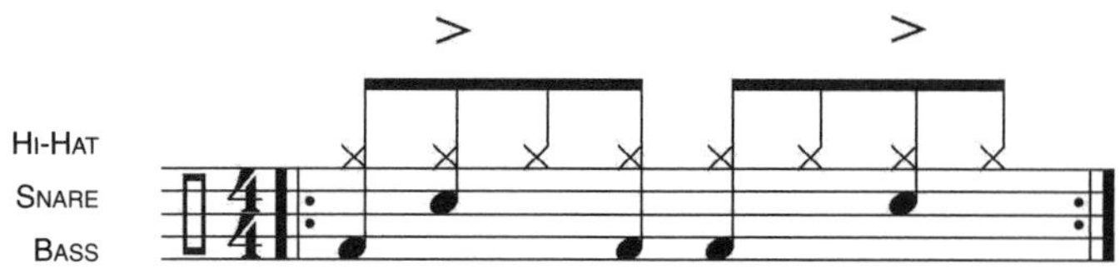

Variation

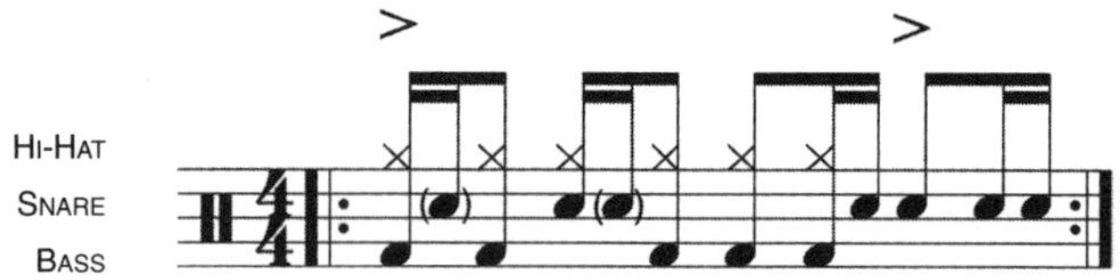

Example 3 (CD 2, Track 67)

This is a standard grouping of 2 + 2 + 3 in a 7/8 time signature and is called a "Laz" rhythm; it's of Turkish/Arabic origin and is used in Greek folk songs as well as Middle Eastern music. **The tempo range for this and the following odd-time examples is eighth note = 192–320 bpm.**

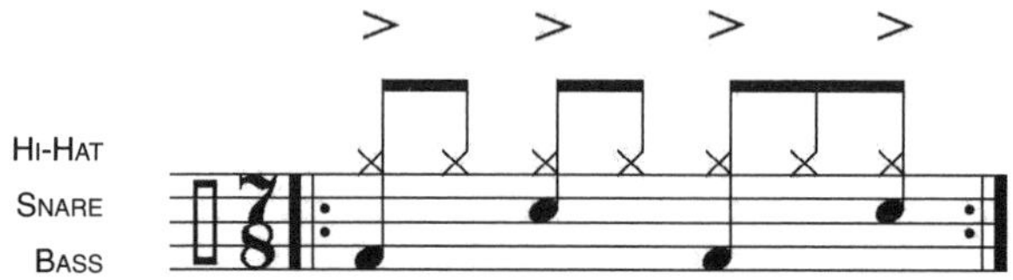

Variation

Example 4 (CD 2, Track 71)

This is the common 2 + 2 + 2 + 3 breakdown of a 9/8 meter. It's called a "Karsilama" rhythm, is of Turkish origin, and is from a large family of 9/8 rhythms known as Aqsaaq rhythms.

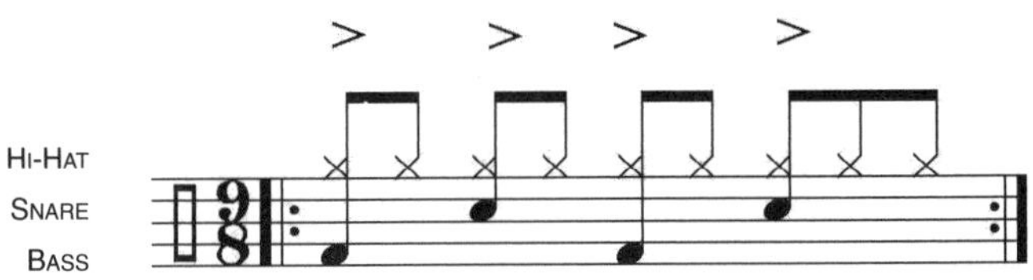

Variation

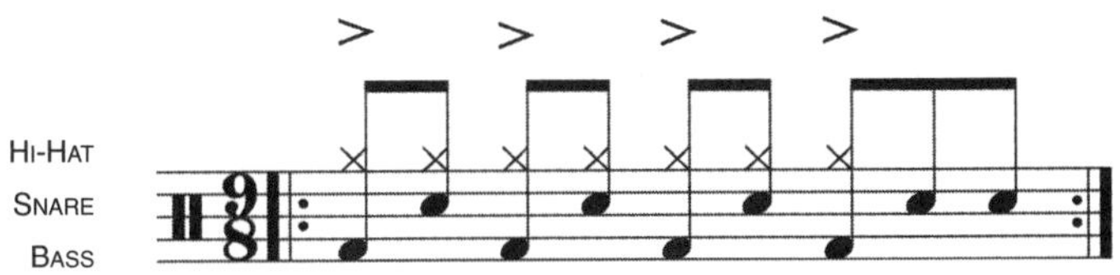

Example 5 (CD 2, Track 72)

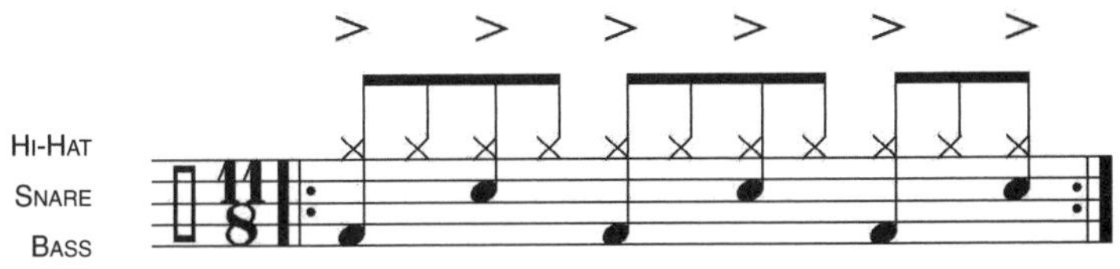

Example 6

This is a northern Iranian groove known as a "Lezgi" pattern.

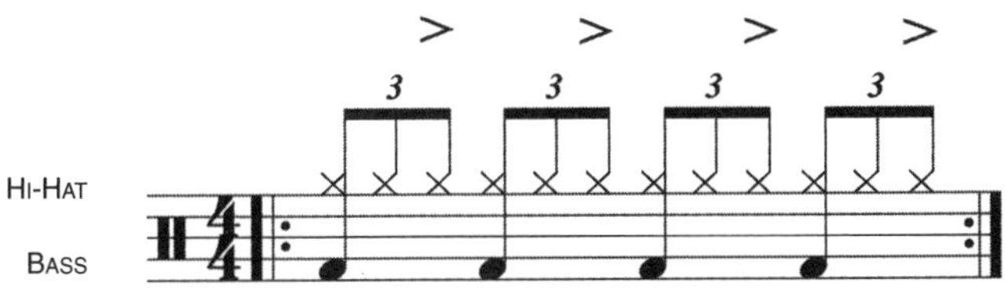

Example 7

This is a central Iranian groove known as a "Babakaram" pattern.

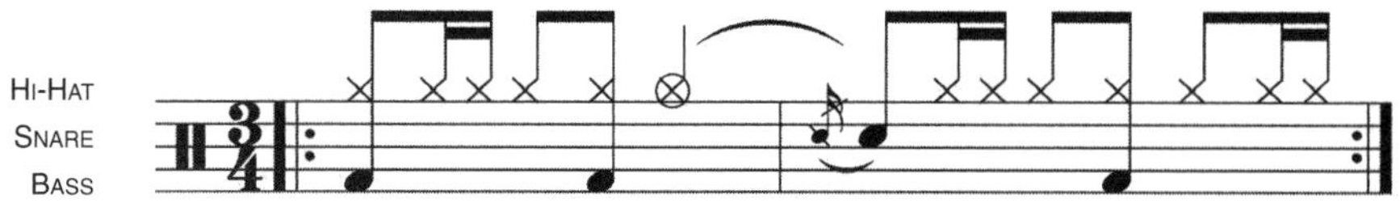

(Circled hi-hat note is played half-open)

Example 8

This is a southern Iranian groove known as a "Bastaki" pattern.

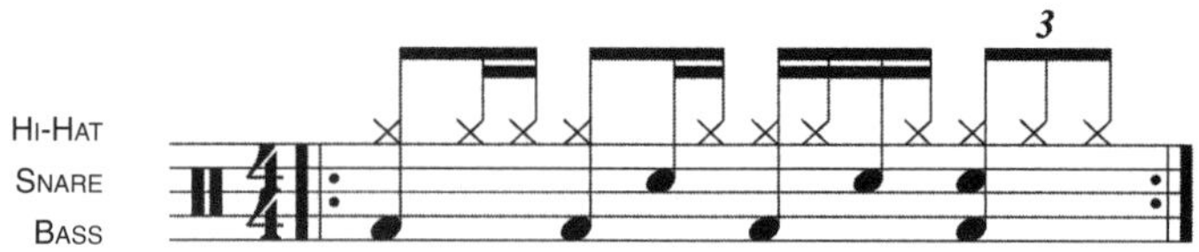

Middle Eastern Pop

Middle Eastern pop music fuses the rhythms of Western music with the scales and quarter-tone melodies of Middle Eastern music. Rhythmically, Middle Eastern Pop draws from Flamenco, Soca, Techno, Reggaeton, and other Western pop styles. However, there is a strong tendency toward snare displacement in Middle Eastern Pop, as well as frequent use of tom patterns (simulating the sounds and rhythms typically played by Middle Eastern/African drums such as the doumbek, djembe, and darabuka). A predominant characteristic of Middle Eastern Pop, adopted from Western pop music, is the use of straight, common time signatures (4/4 or 6/8) rather than the multitude of odd-time signatures often found in more traditional Middle Eastern music.

As in all forms of pop music, Middle Eastern Pop boasts many superstars. Amr Diab, Nancy Afram, Nawal Al Zoghbi, and Haifa Wehbe are just a few of these multi-platinum recording artists. **The average tempo range for this genre is quarter note= 90–110 bpm.**

Example

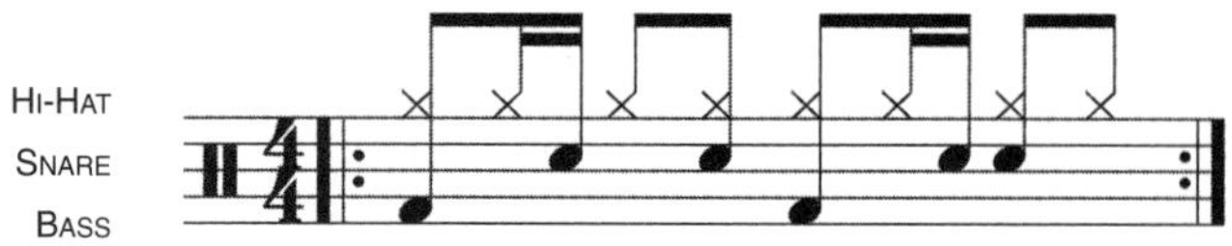

Variation 1

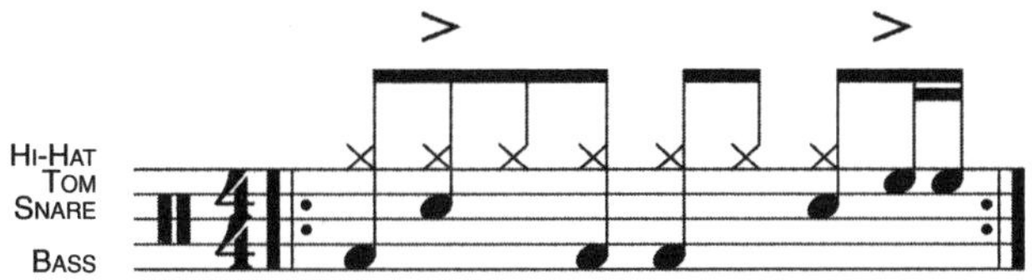

Variation 2

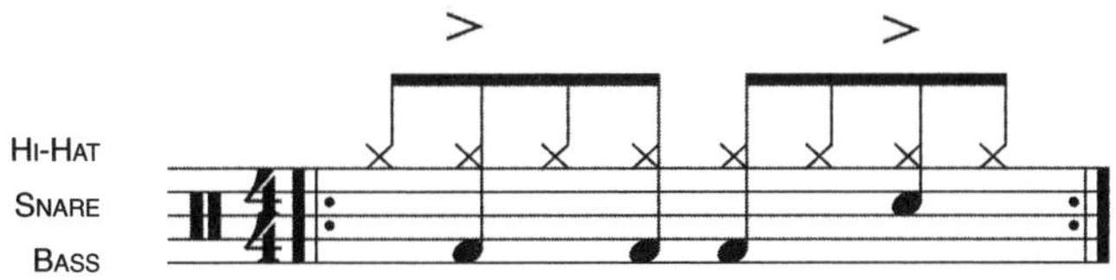

Variation 3

Thisi s a common Middle Eastern pop groove that is found throughout Iran as well surrounding countries.

Rai

Rai developed in Northern Africa, primarily in Western Algeria in the port city of Oran. It's a form of Maghreb music (North African region), and its roots go back to the early 1900s when the folk music of nomadic North African tribes was combined with romantic Arabic poetry. As 20th century pop music spread, Western Algerian culture incorporated its sounds and ideas into its own indigenous music. Rai is influenced by such diverse styles as Funk, Rock, Ska, Reggae, Jazz, Techno/House, and Afro-Cuban combined with the quarter-tone scales of Arabic music. Prominent Rai musicians include Bellemou Messaoud ("the Father of Rai"), Khaled Hadj Brahim ("the King of Rai"), and Cheb Mami ("the Prince of Rai").

Drummers find that playing Rai involves any number of contemporary grooves. Since Rai music draws from many genres, the grooves for the styles mentioned in the previous paragraph can be (and are) used for both traditional Rai/Maghreb and contemporary Rai music. The tempo depends on the style of music being played in a particular song.

Traditional Rai / Maghreb

Example (CD 1, Track 1)

The main example is a style of Maghreb felt in 6/8, but written in 4/4. **Tempo is quarter note = 100–132 bpm.**

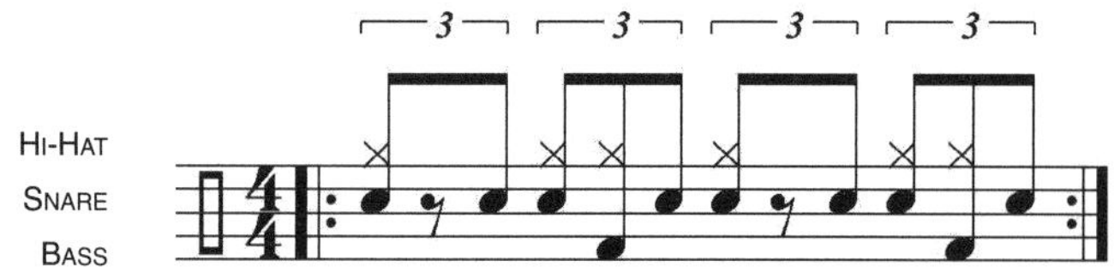

Variation

This variation is a 16th-note-based groove utilizing accents on the hi-hat. **Quarter note = 100–132 bpm.**

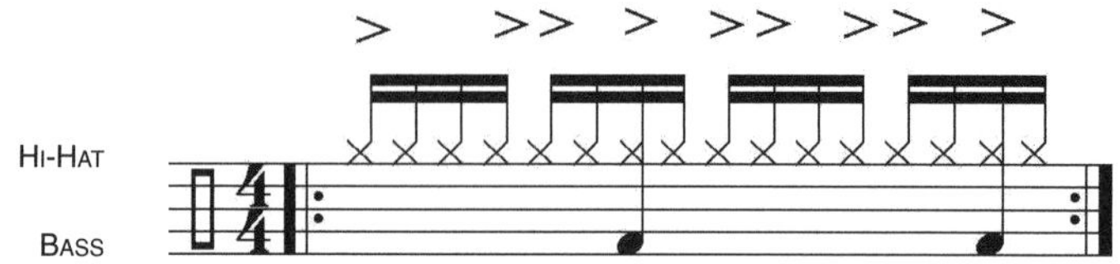

Contemporary Rai (Nontraditional Maghreb)

Example (CD 1, Track 87)

This is the Soca groove, found in the Caribbean chapter. **Tempo is quarter note = 108–132 bpm.**

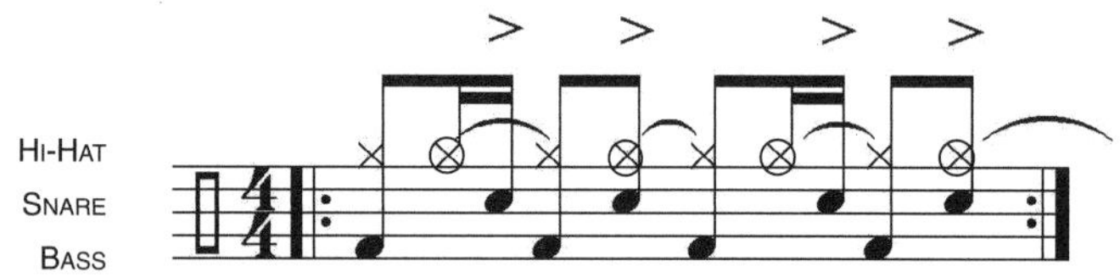

(Circled hi-hat notes are played open)

Variation 1 (CD 2, Track 11)

This is the main example from the Disco chapter (also used for House music; see Techno chapter). **Tempo is quarter note = 108–120 bpm.**

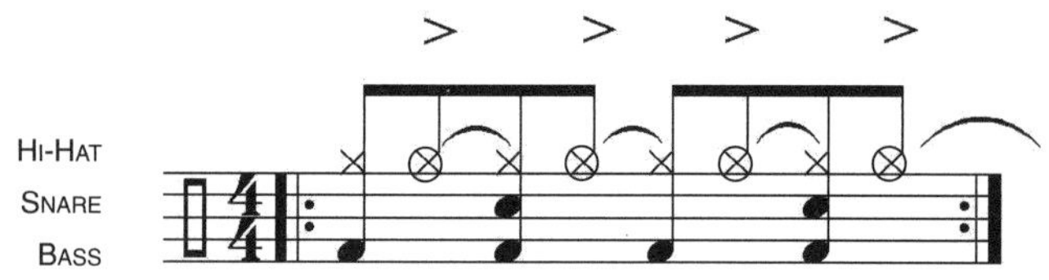

(Circled hi-hat notes are played open)

VARIATION 2 (CD 1, Track 92)

This is a Reggae "One Drop" groove (see Reggae in the Caribbean chapter). **The tempo starts at quarter note = 116 bpm.**

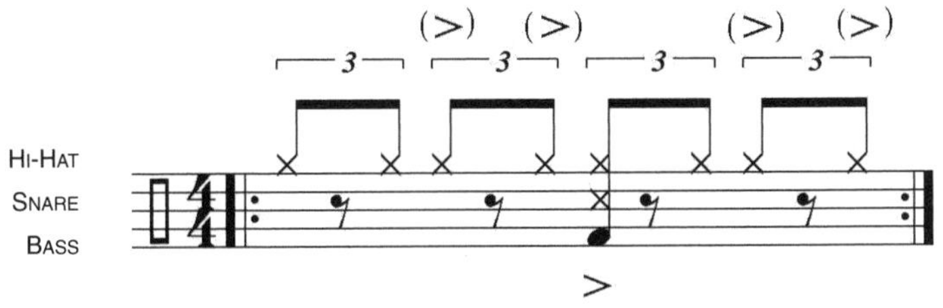

NOTE: See the variations on the above grooves found in their respective chapters.

21 Odd Time

Though most music is composed and played in common time signatures (2/4, 3/4, 4/4, 6/8, 9/8, 12/8), it's not unusual to find music played or composed in odd time signatures (5/4, 5/8, 7/4, 7/8, 11/8, etc.).

For thousands of years, odd time meters have added richness to musical genres in every part of the world. This chapter explores the history of odd time meters in popular music, their role in music today, and the correct approach to understanding and playing them.

It is important to understand time signatures, that is, what the numbers in them mean. The top number tells how many beats there are per measure, while the bottom number tells what kind of note lasts for one beat. So, in the most common time signature, 4/4, the top "4" indicates four beats per measure, and the bottom "4" indicates that a quarter note lasts for one beat. Further, the top number may be any number within reason, while the bottom number is restricted to a small range of even numbers (i.e., 2, 4, 8, 16, and less commonly 32, 64, and even 128), with "2" representing a half note, "4" representing a quarter note, etc.

In the early periods of Jazz and Rock n' Roll, songs were almost always composed and played in common meters. However, by the middle of the 20th century, odd time meters were often employed in Jazz. The Dave Brubeck Quartet was among the first to compose songs with odd meters (e.g., "Take Five," by Paul Desmond). Another pioneer was Don Ellis, who used odd time signatures in his Big Band Jazz compositions, such as "Strawberry Soup." The early 1970s saw a handful of "Progressive Rock" groups use a wide variety of odd time meters. Kansas, Rush, Yes, Emerson Lake and Palmer, King Crimson, Genesis, Gentle Giant, and Frank Zappa and his Mothers of Invention are a few of the pioneers who continue to influence countless musicians (e.g., Sting with Vinny Colaiuta on "St. Augustine in Hell" and "Seven Days"). Bands such as Dream Theater, Queensryche, Spock's Beard, Fates Warning, King's X, Soundgarden, and Tool all use odd time meters today. In addition, New Age artists such as Yanni and John Tesh expose a very different audience to such meters. With odd time meters, the role of the drum set player continues to be to establish a strong groove with solid time. (For more information regarding odd times through the use of odd groupings, see Polyrhythm chapter.)

Prominent Odd Meters

5/4

There are two practical approaches to counting the 5/4 time signature: subdividing the measure into familiar time signatures or counting all five beats within the measure. In subdividing, the most common approach is to divide the five quarter notes into groups 2 and 3 or 3 and 2. A less common, but appropriate method in some songs (primarily Progressive Rock), is to count 4 and 1 and/or all five quarter notes. Included below are not only rock patterns but perhaps the most famous odd time Jazz drum pattern (by famed drummer Joe Morello, from "Take Five"—see variation 4). **The practical tempo range for 5/4 time is roughly quarter note = 100–132 bpm.**

Example (CD 2, Track 63)

This is a 2-beat plus 3-beat (2 + 3) standard Rock pattern. Note that all five beats are accented, with the bass drum falling on beats 1, 3 and 5 while the snare drum falls on beats 2 and 4.

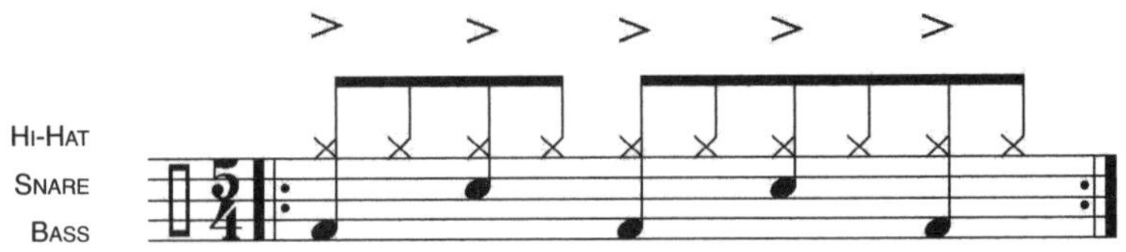

Variation 1

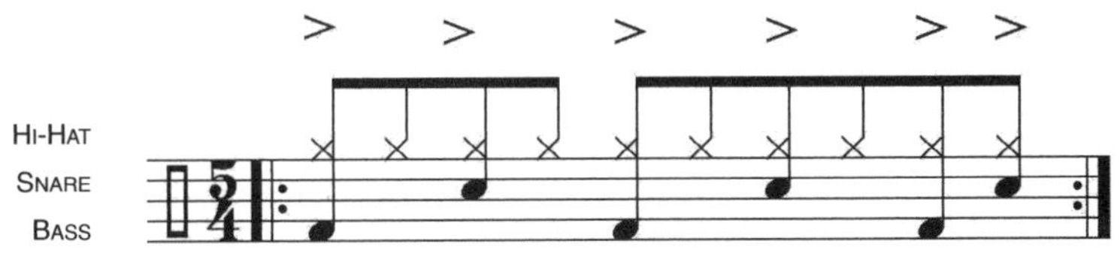

Variation 2

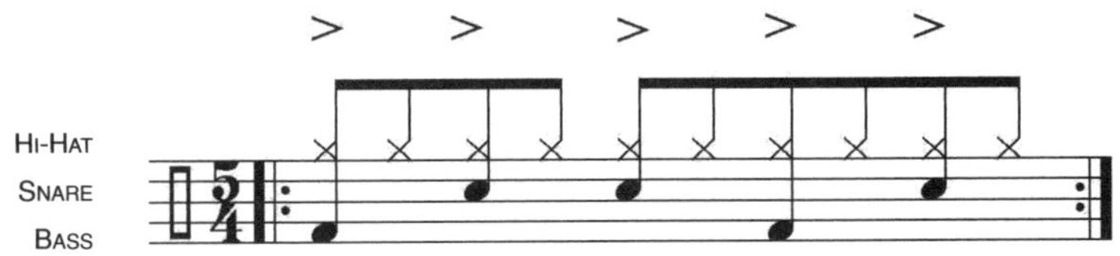

Variation 3 (CD 2, Track 64)

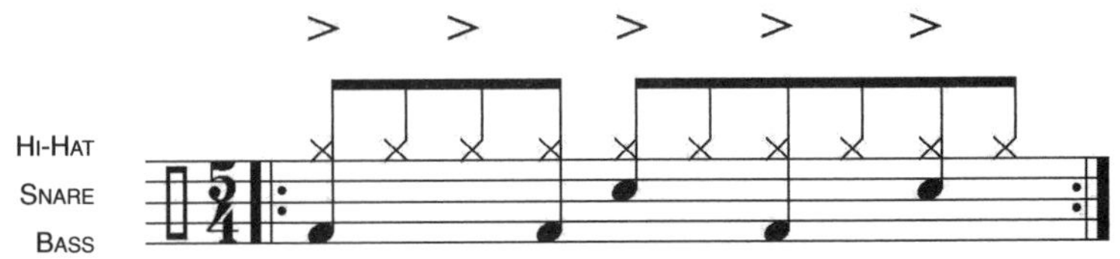

Variation 4

This is the same as the Example at the top of the page, but it's broken down into 3 + 2 rather than 2 + 3.

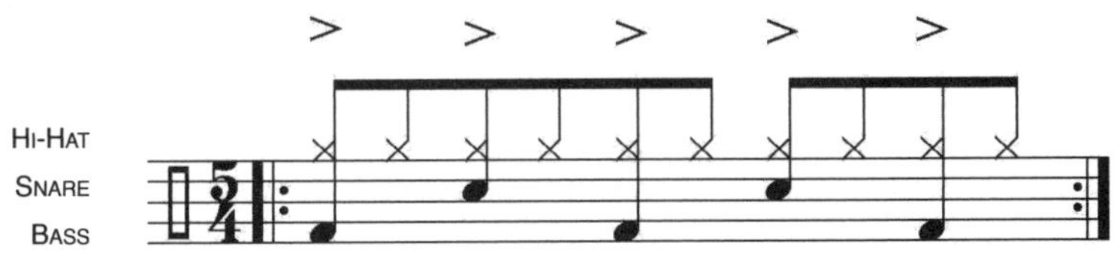

NOTE: The above patterns can be played with the ride hand moving over to the ride cymbal and the hi-hat foot playing different accompaniment patterns, such as doubling the snare or playing all quarter notes.

Variation 5

This is the opening groove for "Take Five." Unlike the Rock 5/4 patterns above, the "Take Five" pattern is most easily felt by breaking it down into a Jazz waltz followed by two extra beats. **Quarter note = 152–160 bpm.**

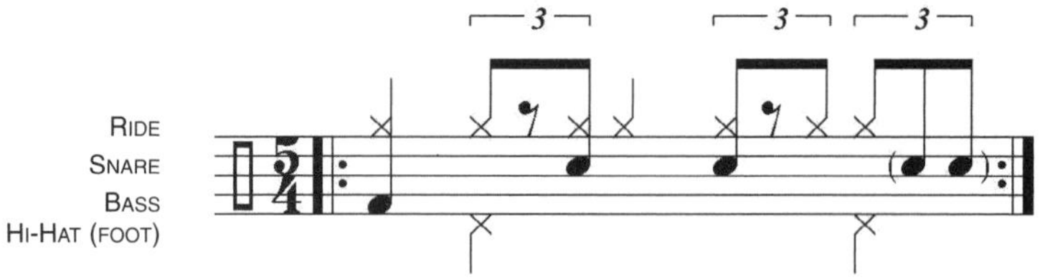

7/4

Like the 5/4 time signature, 7/4 meter is relatively easy to count. It's normal to count a song in 7/4 in one of three ways: 1) count all seven beats per measure; 2) count a measure of 4/4 followed by a measure of 3/4; 3) count a measure of 3/4 followed by a measure of 4/4. Probably the most famous rock song written in 7/4 is Pink Floyd's "Money" (drum groove included as the variation below). As with other styles, there are countless variations and embellished drum grooves to play in 7/4. Below are two practical patterns. **The tempo range is similar to that of 5/4, with quarter note = 100–132 bpm.**

Example (CD 2, Track 65)

This is a standard Rock groove in 7/4. Note that all seven beats are played either on the bass drum or snare: the snare drum plays on beats 2, 4, and 6, while the bass drum plays on beats 1, 3, 5 and 7. This example can be played with the ride hand moving over to the ride cymbal and the hi-hat foot playing different accompaniment patterns, such as beats 2, 4, and 6, all quarter notes, etc. This groove can, of course, also be broken down into 3 beats + 4 beats groupings.

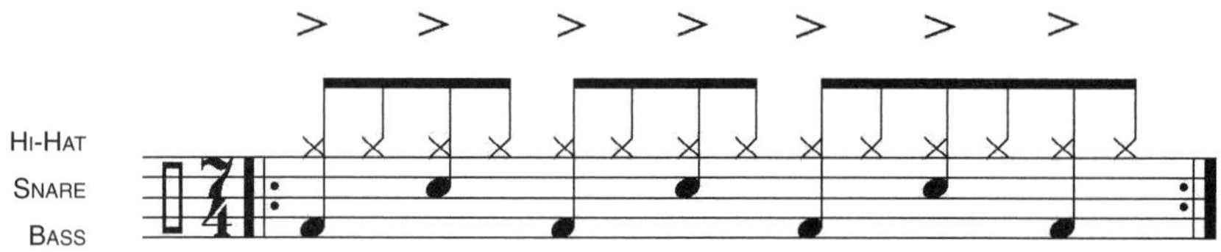

Variation

This is the groove from Pink Floyd's "Money." **Quarter note = 120 bpm.**

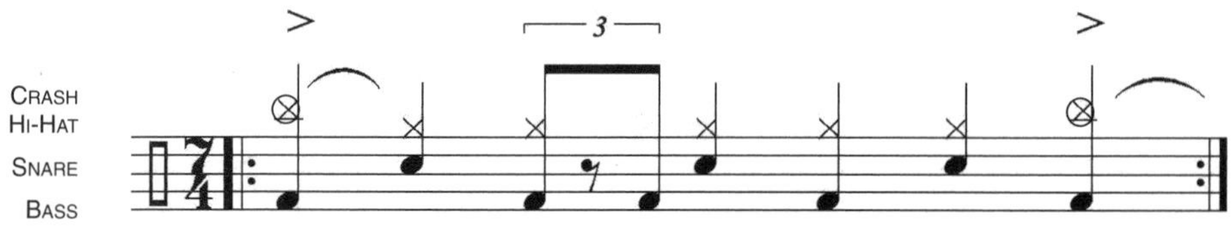

5/8

The 5/8 meter is often more difficult to feel than 5/4 or 7/4 because it's normally played at a faster tempo. One practical way of counting this meter is to sound out all five eighth notes per measure. However, due to its faster tempo, it may be more practical to break down the meter into two separate groupings, either a 3 + 2 grouping or a 2 + 3 grouping. **The pulse of 5/8 meter is often brisk, with eighth note = 192–320 bpm.**

Example (CD 2, Track 66)

This is a common 5/8 groove, with a 3 + 2 grouping. Note that the bass drum and snare do not play all five beats: the bass drum falls only on beat 1 and the snare drum falls only on beat 4.

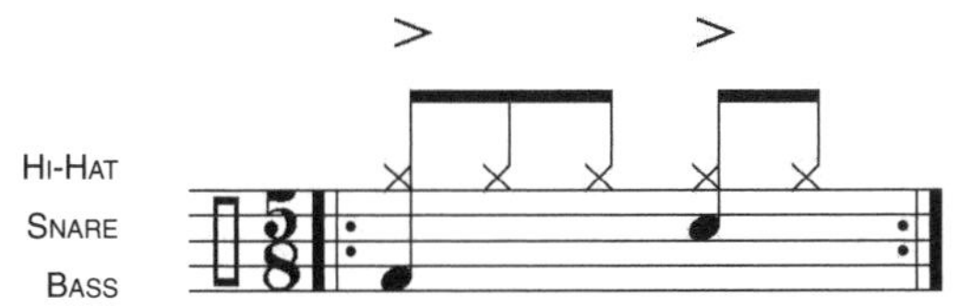

Variation 1

This is similar to the above example, but with a 2 + 3 grouping. Playing the snare drum on beat 3 (rather than beat 4, as above) changes the feel.

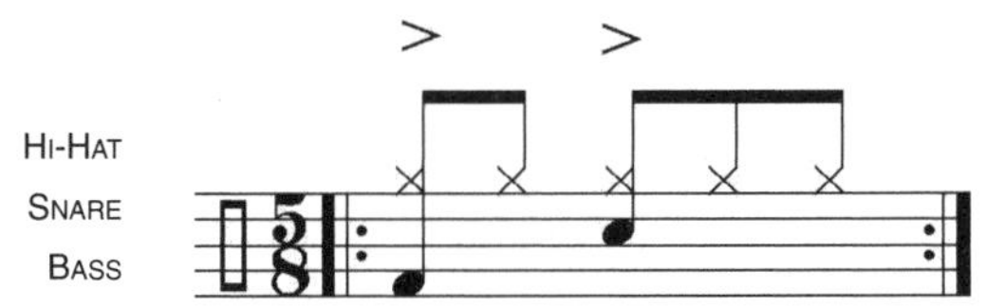

Variation 2

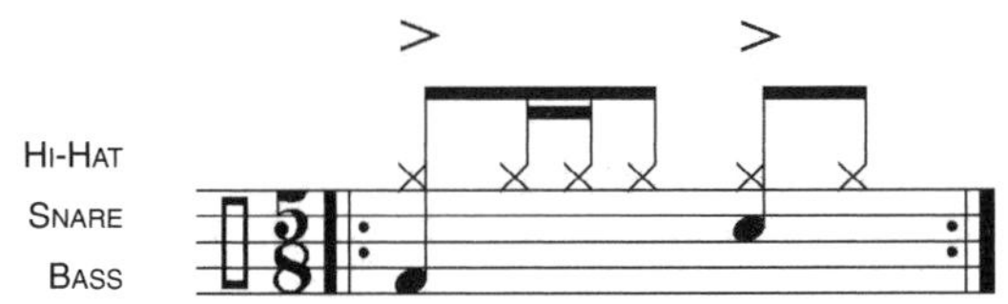

NOTE: Any of the above patterns may incorporate the ride cymbal as well. However, hi-hat foot accompaniment may cause independence issues due to the fluctuating downbeat. One suggestion is to initially double the hi-hat foot with the snare drum. For more challenging limb independence, attempting steady quarter notes against the meter over two measures will flip the feel of the hi-hat foot and will introduce polyrhythms into the patterns (see Polyrhythm chapter).

7/8

Similar to 5/8 meter, 7/8 is usually played at a quick tempo. The most practical way to count this meter is the breakdown method, dividing it into groupings of 2 + 2 + 3 or 3 + 2 + 2. **As with the 5/8 meter, the tempo range is eighth note = 192–320 bpm.**

EXAMPLE (CD 2, Track 67)

This is a standard grouping of 2 + 2 + 3 in a 7/8 time signature. Note that only beats 1, 3, 5, and 7 are played on the bass drum or snare: the bass drum plays beats 1 and 5 and the snare drum plays beats 3 and 7.

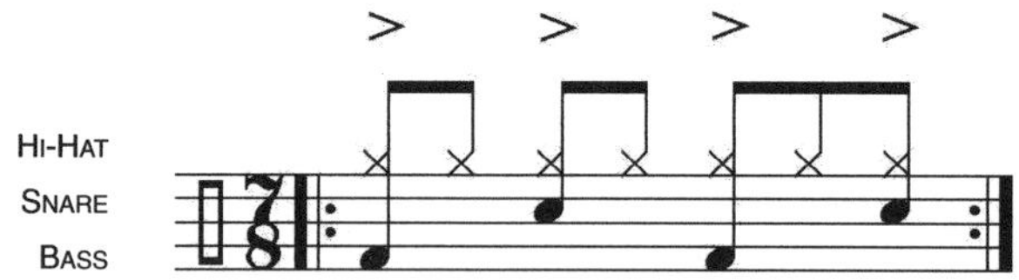

VARIATION 1

This is similar to the above, but has a 3 + 2 +2 breakdown. Note that the bass drum plays only on beat 1 and that the snare drum plays beats 4 and 6.

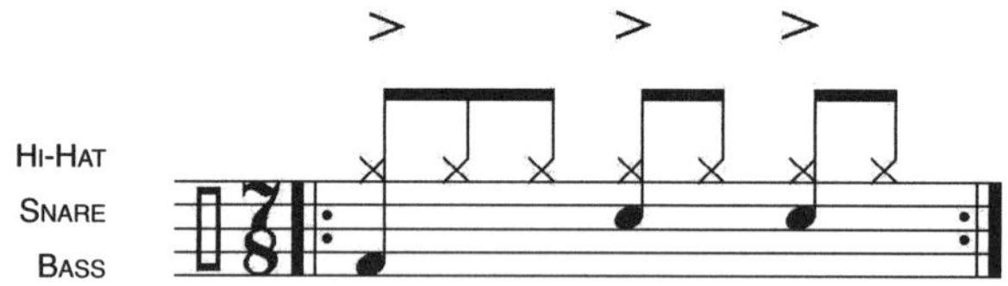

VARIATION 2 (CD 2, Track 68)

Here, the bass drum and snare drum suggest a half-time feel. Note that the bass drum plays beats 1, 3, and 7 and the snare drum only beat 5.

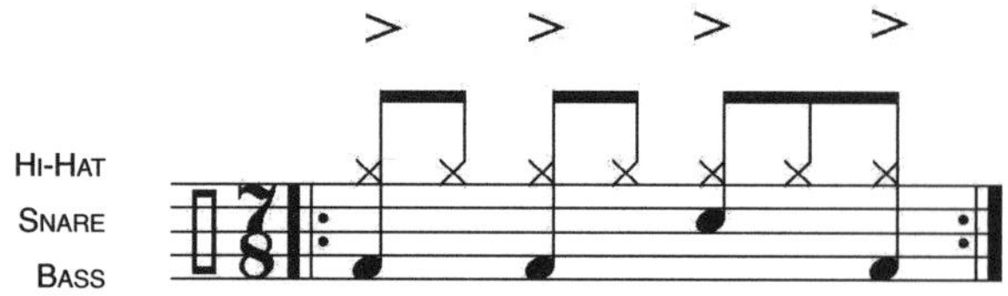

NOTE: Any of the above patterns may incorporate the ride cymbal as well. However, hi-hat foot accompaniment may cause independence issues due to the fluctuating downbeat. One suggestion is to initially double the hi-hat foot with the snare drum notes. For more challenging independence, attempting steady quarter notes against the meter over two measures will flip the feel of the hi-hat foot and will introduce polyrhythms into the patterns (see Polyrhythm chapter).

Breaking Up Standard Meters into Odd Groupings

3/4

Dividing a 3/4 measure into two groups of three eighth notes is the most common way of breaking up 3/4 into a non-standard grouping. This creates what is essentially 6/8. It's fairly common in tunes where this is done by some instruments (especially drums) for other instruments to continue playing in standard 3/4 (broken up into three groups of two eighth notes); this creates a polyrhythmic feel (3 against 2, with eighth notes, of course, being of equal duration). **The tempo markings can range from quarter note = 88 bpm up to 192 bpm.** The two measures of 3/4 below show the feel changing from 3/4 to a suggested 6/8.

Example (CD 2, Track 69)

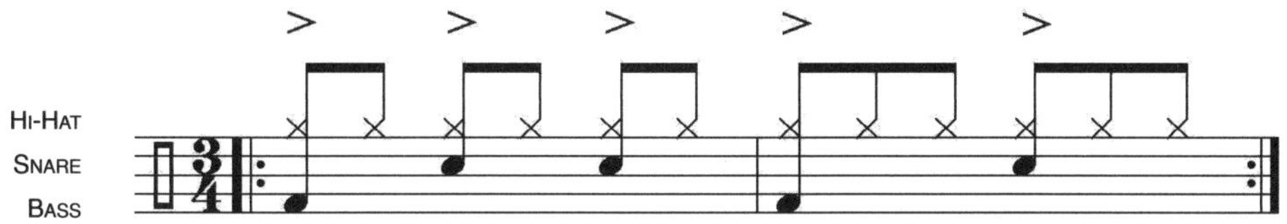

4/4

Though the 4/4 meter is usually played straight or swung, it can be divided into groupings which create an odd time feel. What is probably the most common nonstandard breakdown of this time signature, dividing it into two groups of three eighth notes and one group of two eighth notes, hides the 4/4 pulse and makes the time sound like a compound meter, that is, 3 + 3 + 2/8 (see Middle Eastern chapter). Of course, other breakdowns are possible, with 3 + 2 + 3, 2 + 3 + 3, 3 + 5 and 5 + 3 being the most practical choices. There are no standard grroves for these breakdowns. Four possible ones follow. **Tempos range from quarter note = 60 bpm for slower ballads to over 200 bpm for energetic feels.**

Example (CD 2, Track 70)

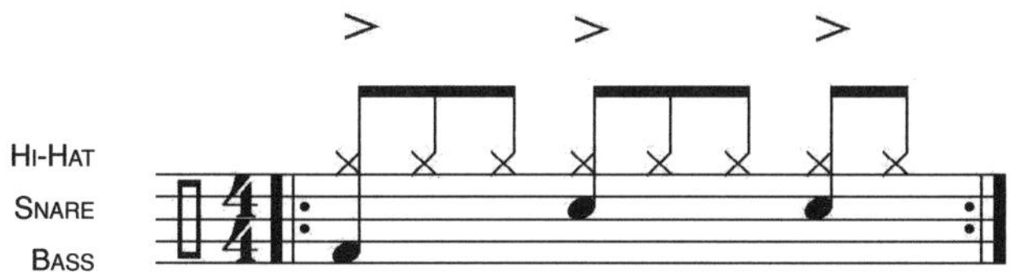

VARIATION 1

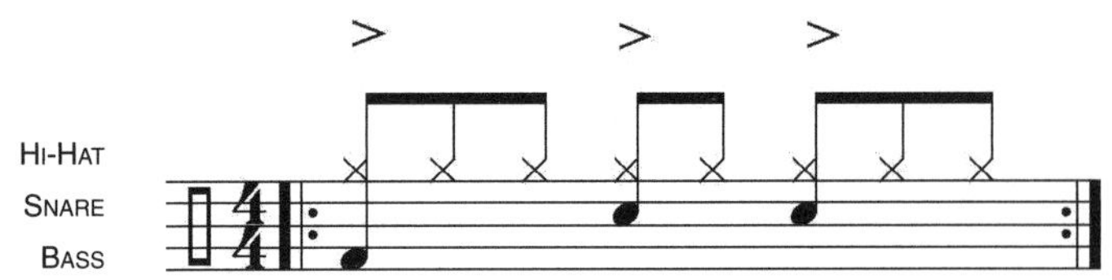

VARIATION 2

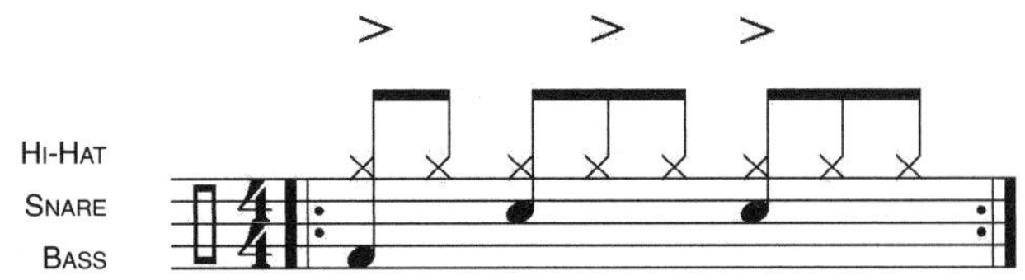

VARIATION 3

This is a more obvious odd-time suggestion than the previous examples.

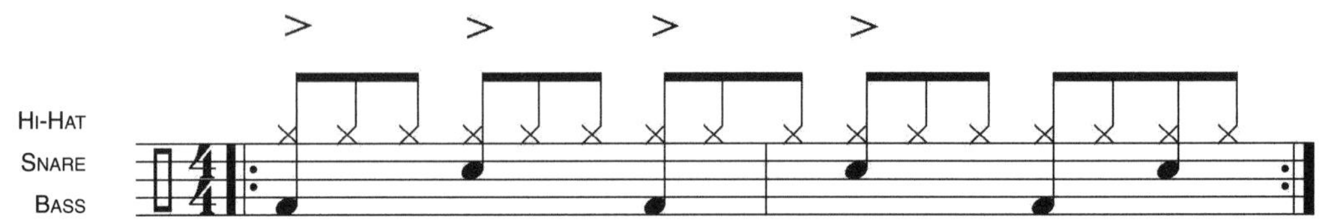

9/8

The standard way of playing 9/8 is to count it as having three beats per measure, with three eighth notes equaling one beat. Another fairly common way to feel 9/8 is to have a predominant duple feel throughout the measure accompanied by one triple grouping of eighth notes at the end, essentially making it 2+2+2+3/8. This approach is often found in Middle Eastern rhythms (Dave Brubeck's "Blue Rondo a la Turk" being a perfect example of Turkish influence). When counted in this way, the count changes to 9 beats per measure and the 8th note pulse remains brisk. Another common way of breaking down 9/8 is 3 + 2 + 2 + 2. Of course, there are other ways of breaking down 9/8, but 2 + 2 + 2 + 3 and 3 + 2 + 2 + 2 are the most practical options for the duple emphasis. **As with the previous time signatures, the practical tempo range remains at approximately eighth note = 192–320 bpm.**

EXAMPLE (CD 2, Track 71)

This is the common 2 + 2 + 2 + 3 breakdown of a 9/8 meter.

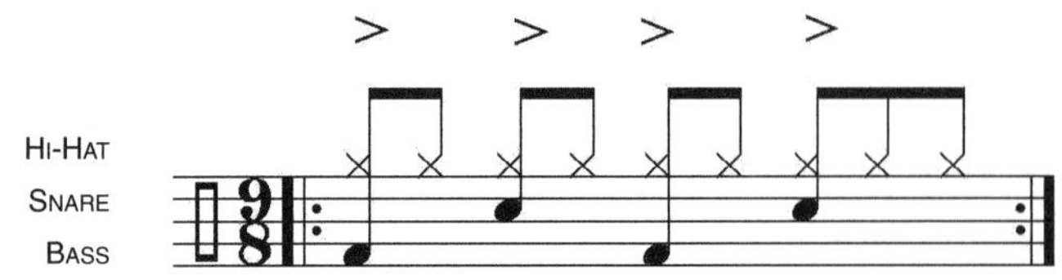

Variation 1

This is a 3 + 2 + 2 + 2 breakdown of a 9/8 meter.

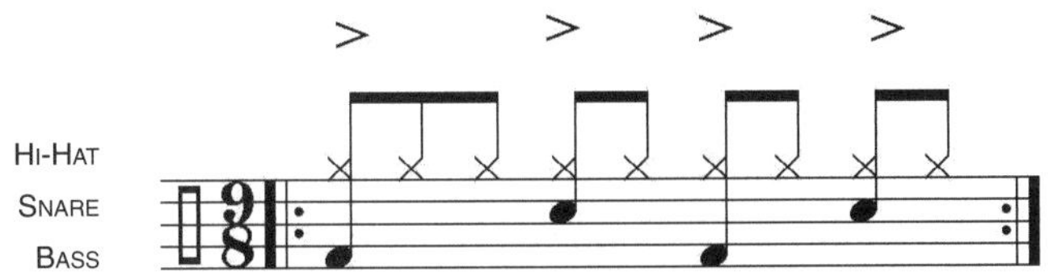

NOTE: The above example and variation may incorporate the ride cymbal as well. However, hi-hat foot accompaniment may cause independence issues due to the fluctuating time. One suggestion is to initially double the hi-hat foot with the snare drum notes. For more challenging independence, attempting steady quarter notes against the odd eighth note meter will flip the feel of the hi-hat foot and will introduce polyrhythms into the patterns (see Polyrhythm chapter).

Variation 2

This is a four bar phrase played by Jazz drumming great Joe Morello from "Blue Rondo a la Turk," written by Dave Brubeck. Notice the duple and triple groupings within this phrase.

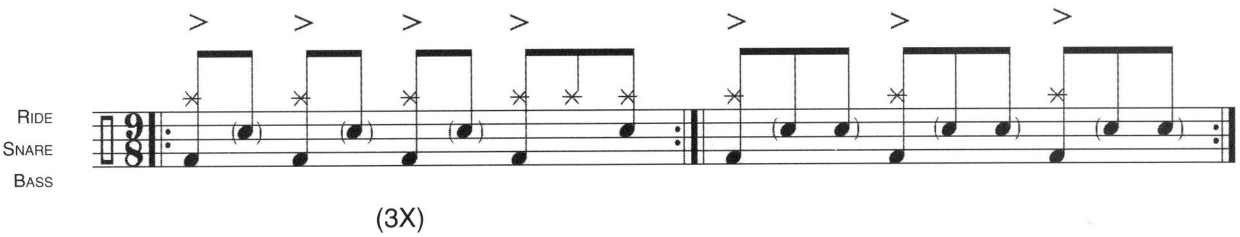

Creating Additional Odd Time Meters

In order to play in meters such as 11/8, 15/8, 19/8, etc., take any of the previous odd meter examples and add an even number meter to it (e.g., adding 4/4 to 7/4 gives you 11/4). However, the more common approach is to add an odd grouping of eighth notes to a measure of 4/4 (e.g., adding a measure of 3/8 to a measure of 4/4 gives you 11/8). Likewise, odd time meters utilizing a 16th note pulse can be created by changing the bottom number of any of the previous meters to "16" (e.g., 5/8 becomes 10/16). As a result, the tempo would increase by 2 to 4 times relative to the previous meters. The examples below present some additional odd time possibilities. All, with the exception of the 11/8 variation—from "Whipping Post," by the Allman Brothers, which is broken down 3 + 3 + 3 + 2—were created by adding odd groupings of eighth notes to a 4/4 meter. **Because the primary pulse becomes the eighth note, the practical tempo range remains the same as for the previous examples with an eighth note pulse at eighth note = 192–320 bpm.**

Example 1 (11/8) (CD 2, Track 72)

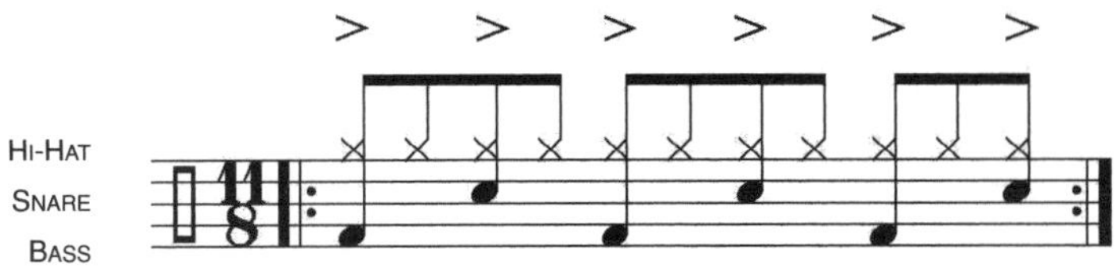

Variation (11/8)

This is the 11/8 (3 + 3 + 3 + 2) pattern from the Allman Brothers' "Whipping Post." Please note that the crescendo marking applies *only* to the snare drum notes. **Eighth note = 196 bpm.**

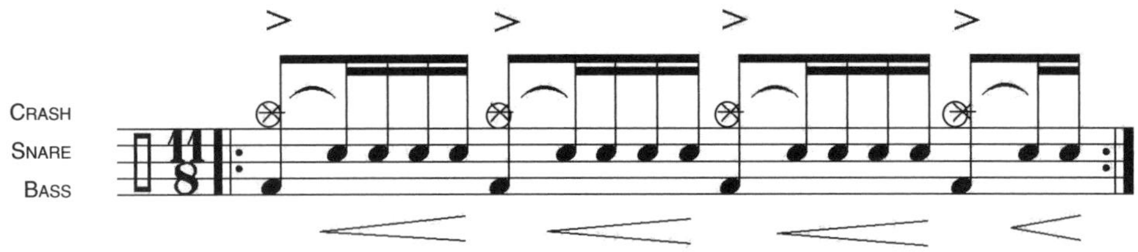

Example 2 (13/8) (CD 2, Track 73)

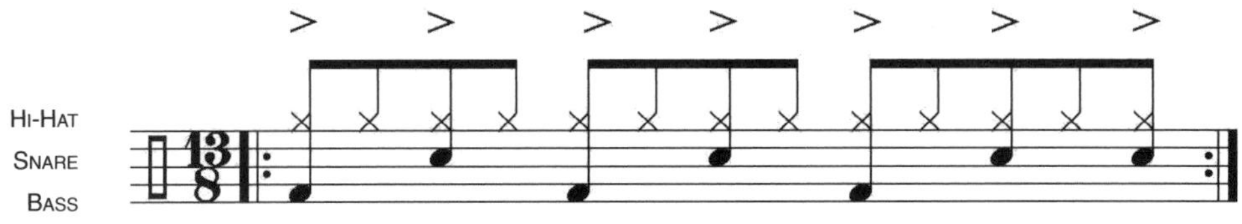

Example 3 (15/8) (CD 2, Track 74)

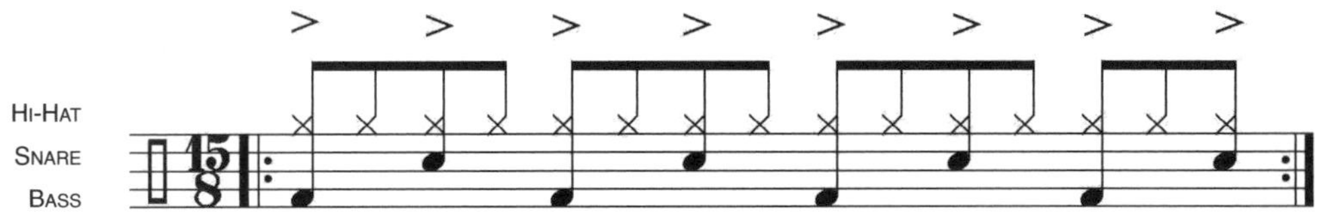

Example 4 (19/16) (CD 2, Track 75)

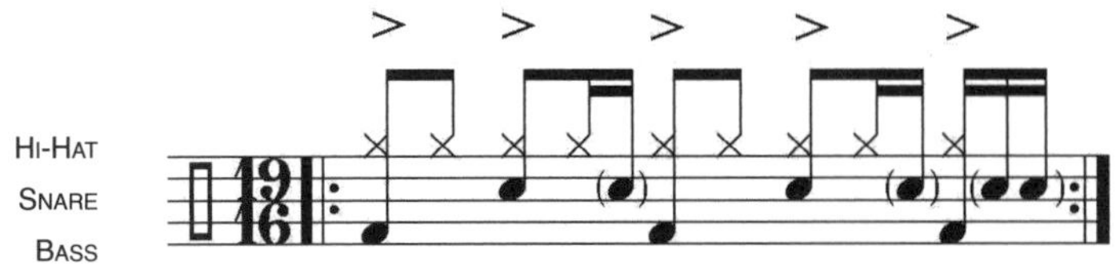

NOTE: Any of the above examples can be rearranged by inverting the location of the odd 8th/16th grouping added to the measure of 4/4 (i.e., placing the odd grouping before the measure of 4/4 rather than after), creating a different feel within the same odd time signature.

22 POLKA

POLKA ORIGINATED IN THE EARLY 1800s in what is now the Czech Republic. The term probably stems from the word "pulka," which refers to the short half-steps integrated into the dance. Toward the middle of the 19th century, the musical style spread to other European countries, including France, Germany, Austria, and especially Poland. Primarily composed and felt in 2/4, the genre is an upbeat, celebratory music traditionally played on an accordion, concertina, and fiddle accompanied by a rhythm section. Currently the instrumentation often includes clarinet, trumpet, tuba and saxophone.

Contemporary artists such as Frankie Yankovic, Lawrence Welk, and the Texas-based Brave Combo are a testimony to Polka's enduring popularity. In addition, a large number of drum scores for show tunes utilize the Polka rhythm (commonly referred to in a chart as a "Two Beat"). Other important current Polka bands and artists include Polkacide (Punk Polka), Six Fat Dutchmen, Jimmy Sturr, and oddly enough and still going strong, Weird Al Yankovic, whose parody albums almost always include at least one Polka song.

Perhaps as a result of its simplicity, the primary drum set rhythm for Polka has influenced the rhythmic approach in many other genres of music including Country, Rock n' Roll, Gospel, Metal, Punk, Norteño, and Tex-Mex. Polka drum patterns can be found in all of these styles, and are a defining feature of the final three. **Tempos for Polka are usually very bright at quarter note = 192–280 bpm (in 2/4 time).**

EXAMPLE 1 (CD 2, Track 76)

This is a standard Polka rhythm. Though usually felt and written in 2/4, it can also be written in 4/4 or "cut time."

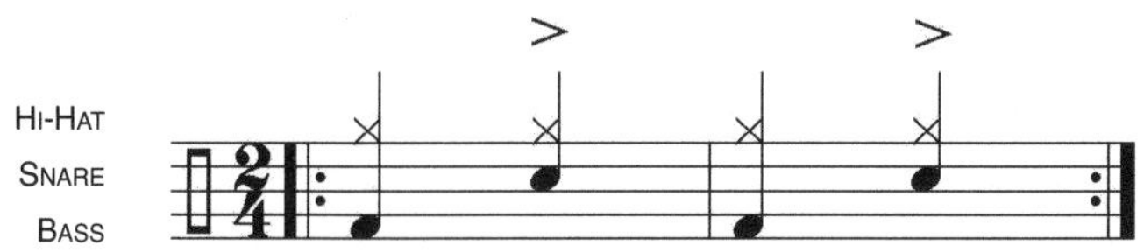

EXAMPLE 1A (CD 2, Track 76)

Though written in 4/4, this example is played exactly the same as the above example in 2/4.

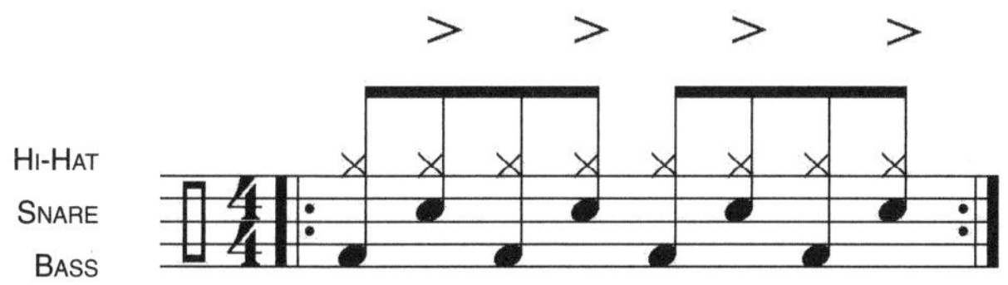

NOTE: The ride hand can play the ride cymbal with hi-hat foot accompanying the snare drum back beat in all of the above patterns.

Variation 1

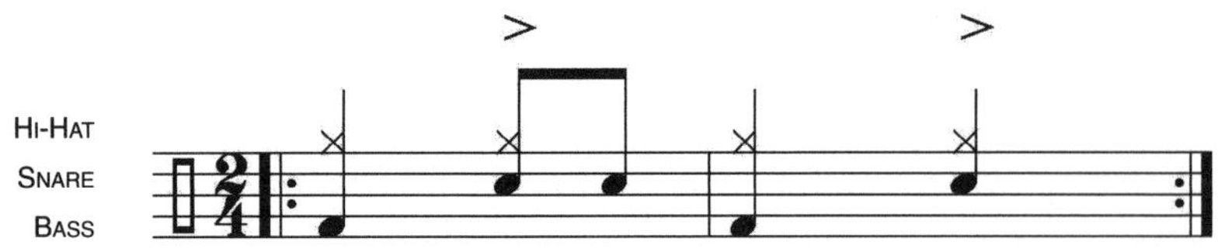

Variation 2

Variations 2 & 3 can be used to "kick it up a notch," and can be considered a combination of Polka and Rock.

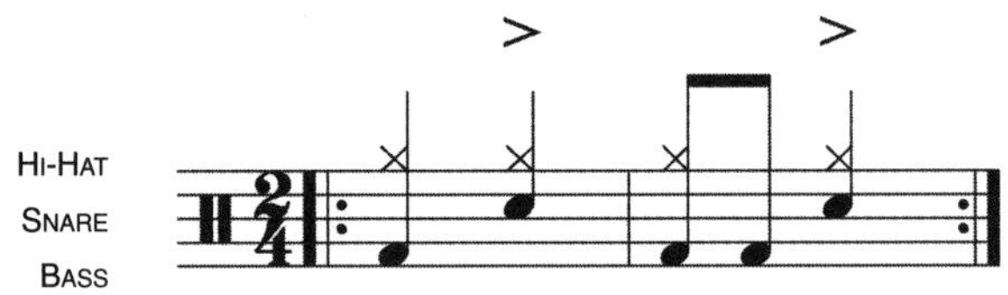

Variation 3

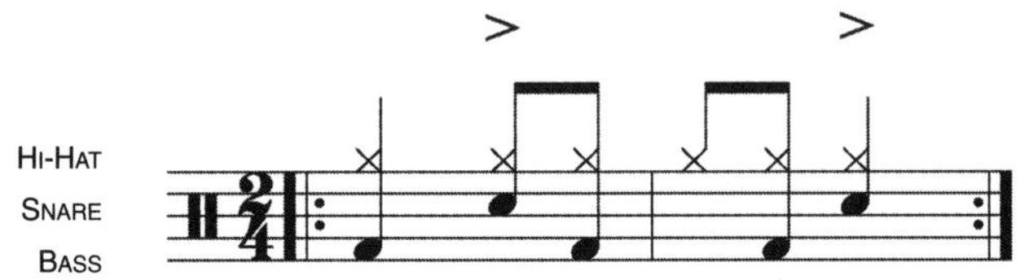

Variation 4

The standard Jazz ride pattern works perfectly when swinging a Polka.

Variation 5

This is a "Polka Mazurka." It's similar to a Waltz, but with a heavier accent on beat 1.

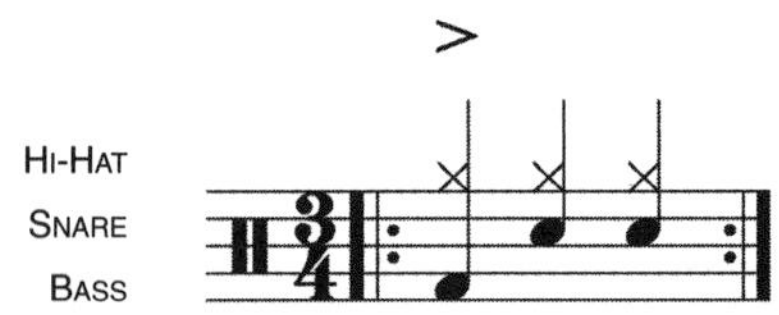

23 PUNK

The punk attitude/musical approach began to manifest itself in the mid to late 1960s in, arguably, UK Rock n' Roll groups such as The Rolling Stones, The Who, and early Kinks, and especially through the American groups MC5, The Stooges (fronted by Iggy Pop), The Velvet Underground (with Lou Reed), the very raw sounding The Seeds, and, again arguably, The Count Five and Blue Cheer. In the early 1970s, The New York Dolls (of the short-lived "Glam" punk movement) and the Velvet Underground continued the trend. By the mid 1970s, The Ramones were playing high energy music which concentrated on rebellious posturing, both musically and lyrically.

In 1977, the British group The Sex Pistols receivedworldwide recognition for their pivotal album, "Never Mind the Bollocks Here's the Sex Pistols," firmly establishing the genre of Punk music—and (hearkening back to MC5) bringing to it overt political content. At the same time, the even more overtly political The Clash debuted with their influential "garage"-sound album, "The Clash." The rebellious style of the Sex Pistols and The Clash gave rise to countless other UK and North American groups in the next wave of Punk known as "Hardcore," with bands such as the very political (anarchist) Dead Kennedys, MDC (Mega-Death Corporation), The Germs, Circle Jerks, and Black Flag leading the pack.

In the 1980s, Punk entered the mainstream through groups like Generation X and the still-active, more polished-sounding The Clash. Perhaps, paradoxically, *because* of this mainstream acceptance the musical momentum of Punk soon dissipated, in spite of the 1984 hit movie "Repo Man" and its popular, all-Punk soundtrack. Despite Punk's musical eclipse in the mid-1980s, the Punk subculture continued to flourish throughout the decade, providing Punk bands with a supportive (in spirit, if not financially) audience.

Punk music and spirit had a great resurgence in the early 1990s with "Grunge" music and the success of the Seattle sensation, Nirvana. Grunge is to be (slightly) distinguished from Punk in that Grunge bands sometimes employ quiet acoustic passages interspersed with loud, Punk-style sections in their songs, often in a formulaic manner (nicely parodied by the Austin Lounge Lizards in their "Grunge Song"). Punk music thrives today through popular bands such as Green Day and Blink 182. A later Punk trend to emerge from the underground is "Garage," exemplified by The Hives, The Vines, The Strokes, and The White Stripes. Punk continues in the 21st century, represented by Good Charlotte, My Chemical Romance, Jimmy Eat World, Bad Religion, NOFX, Fall Out Boy, Rise Against, and Alkaline Trio.

Musically, Punk is a relatively simple style featuring stripped-down instrumentation—generally bass, drums, one or two overdriven electric guitars, and a lead singer (almost always with no back-up vocals)—and rhythmically and harmonically simple songs which are generally played fast and at ear-splitting volume. (The dynamic range in Punk songs varies normally, if it varies at all, from very loud to unbearably loud.)

The distinguishing features of Punk drumming are that it's based on simple grooves and is almost always very loud. However, in spite of its simplicity, Punk music can be very challenging due to its loud and fast tempos, grooves and fills, all necessitating a high level of endurance for the drummer and other musicians. Frequently, Punk drummers use a small, trashy sounding drum set. There are many grooves available depending on tempo and song style. Below are the most common types of Punk beats. **Punk has a large tempo range of quarter note = 120–270 bpm, but tends to lean toward the faster tempos.**

EXAMPLE (CD 2, Track 29)

This is the Standard Rock Beat with a half-open hi-hat. Many bass drum variations are usable provided that they create a repeated pattern (see Standard Rock bass drum variations in Rock n' Roll chapter).

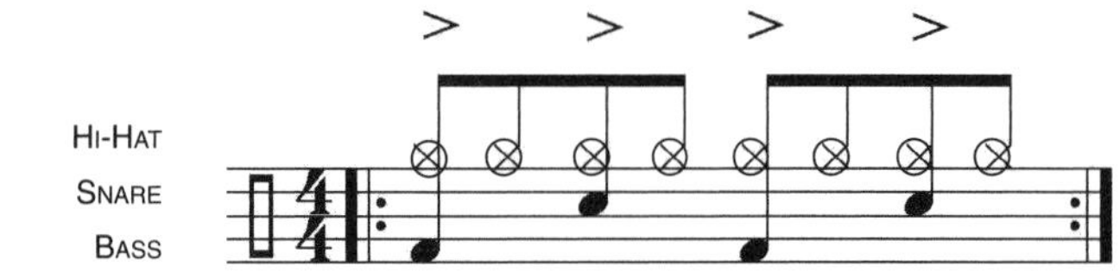

(Circled hi-hat notes are played half-open)

VARIATION 1 (CD 2, Track 77)

This is a common variation in Punk—the floor tom is played by the ride hand in place of a cymbal.

VARIATION 2

This has a double-time Rock feel. Though similar to a Polka or Two-Step, this Punk groove is played loudly, aggressively, and very fast.

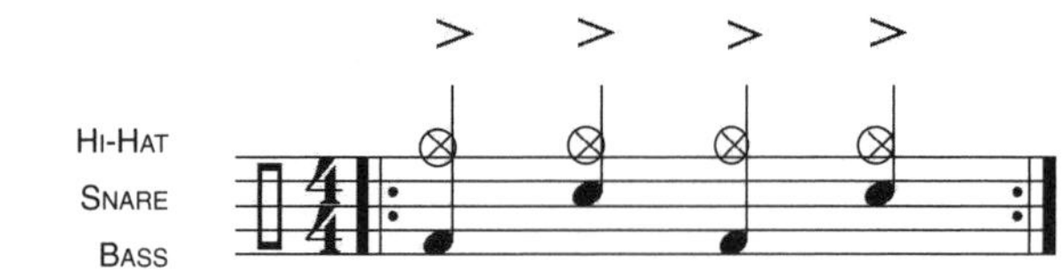

(Circled hi-hat notes are played half-open)

VARIATION 3

This is the Mersey Beat found in both Early Rock n' Roll and Surf.

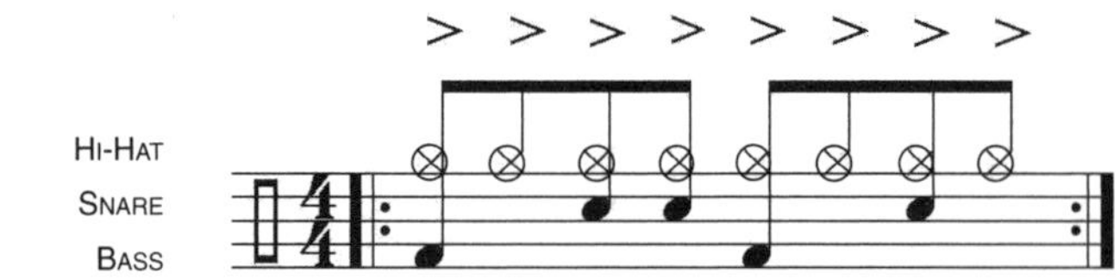

(Circled hi-hat notes are played half-open)

NOTE: The above example and variations can be played with the ride hand on a cymbal. However, in Punk Rock, the most common cymbal to ride is a large crash cymbal rather than a standard ride. In addition, hi-hat foot accompaniment on beats 2 & 4 is optional—it's not always used due to excessive sound from the other limbs.

24 Rock

Rock music in all its variations is arguably the most popular, identifiable, and universal style of music throughout the world. Due to the enormous number of Rock n' Roll composers, musicians, and bands, it is impossible to cite every major influence in this genre within the confines of this book. The ones mentioned in this introduction and the following sections are merely among the most prominent.

The names of many 20th century popular music styles were originally slang terms with sexual connotations (e.g., Swing, Jazz, Bop). Rock n' Roll is no exception. In the early 1950s, as Jazz became more of a listening music played by small ensembles, audiences sought music which provided an unwavering and obvious pulse for dancing. This factor, as well as the appeal of a lead singer emphasizing lyrics and the advancing development and use of electric instruments (guitar, bass, etc.) played with high energy, and with a heavy drumming backbeat, all contributed to the beginnings of Rock n' Roll. Though Alan Freed, an early 1950s disc jockey from Cleveland, Ohio, is often credited with coining the term "Rock n' Roll," it can be traced back much further, at least as far back as the song written by Richard Whiting in 1934 entitled "Rock and Roll."

The style really didn't come into its own, however, until the 1950s. A series of early hits, including "Sixty Minute Man," by the Dominoes, and several by Bill Haley and the Comets (notably "Rock Around the Clock"), grabbed the attention of American youth. As the new music gained popularity, musicians such as Antoine "Fats" Domino, Little Richard (Richard Penniman), and Chuck Berry emerged as its stars. In addition, with Elvis Presley's phenomenal rise, Rock n' Roll produced its first superstar. The music continued to gain popularity throughout the remainder of the decade with such artists as Sam Cooke, Buddy Holly, Richie Valens and many Rockabilly musicians, such as Carl Perkins, rising to prominence.

By the early 1960s, Surf music (see Surf chapter) had become very popular, and by the mid-1960s, Soul Music, and more especially "The Motown Sound," were also very popular. These driving forces of early/mid 1960s pop music firmly established Rock music's signature "straight" feel as opposed to the "swung" feel of the Jazz bands of the 1930s and 1940s and West Coast and Jump Blues, made popular in the 1940s and early 1950s by artists such as T-Bone Walker.

By the 1960s, Rock n' Roll had also found a large audience in Britain, inspiring the formation of many British bands and the "British Invasion" of the U.S. music scene. "Beatlemania" and the Beatles' continuing success were perhaps the best indications of Rock n' Roll's universal appeal and lasting popularity. "The British Invasion" also coincided with an emphasis on bands rather than individual musicians. But, paradoxically, some of the more famous names in drumming history came to prominence in this period: Ringo Starr (The Beatles), Charlie Watts (The Rolling Stones), Mick Avory (The Kinks), and Keith Moon (The Who). The mid to late 1960s saw a proliferation of Rock bands with prominent drummers, including Cream (Ginger Baker), The Doors (John Densmore), Jimi Hendrix (Mitch Mitchell and later Buddy Miles), and The Grateful Dead (Mickey Hart and Bill Kreutzmann). By this time, Rock drumming began to deviate from a simple and recognizable beat to include more challenging rhythms and fills requiring greater technical skill, with the "concert drum solo" becoming a common feature of Rock performances.

By the beginning of the 1970s, several bands had become well established—Led Zeppelin (with prominent drummer John Bonham), Deep Purple, and Black Sabbath—that are considered founders of the Metal style (see Metal chapter). Another category that had attained wide popularity by the early 1970s was Progressive Rock (see Odd Time chapter), a style of music and drumming characterized by lengthier compositions, odd time signatures, and a higher level of musicianship. Frank Zappa and the Mothers of Invention, Emerson, Lake & Palmer, Genesis, King Crimson (with drummers Michael Giles and Bill Bruford), Kansas, Yes, Jethro Tull, and Rush (with still-prominent drummer Neil Peart) all contributed to the development of this style that has influenced countless drummers for the past 30 years.

The success of Progressive Rock mixed with the instrumental improvisation of Jazz produced the Fusion style, initially pioneered by Miles Davis and very soon after further developed by the Mahavishnu Orchestra, Herbie Hancock and the Headhunters, and Weather Report. Billy Cobham, Tony Williams, Alphonze Mouzon, Lenny White and, later, Simon Phillips were (and for the most part still are) some of the most notable drummers in this style that mixes a Rock feel with Jazz improvisation, linear drum grooves, and odd time signatures, all requiring a high level of musicianship.

Other prominent Rock bands/musicians of the early to mid '70s included The Allman Brothers, Lynyrd Skynyrd, Chicago, Steely Dan, Aerosmith, The Eagles, Kiss, Styx, and David Bowie. They all helped create the genre now called Classic Rock, in which drumming returned to a driving beat in standard time signatures. In addition, session drummers such as Jim Keltner, Russ Kunkel, and Steve Gadd became firmly established at this time, appearing on numerous famous recordings. By the end of the decade, Punk music (see Punk chapter) was leading Rock music in still another direction—a loud, aggressive sound with loud, aggressive drumming.

With the debut of Music Television (MTV) in August 1981, Rock music rose to even higher levels of popularity. Music videos allowed audiences to not only hear but see popular rock artists/bands such as Prince, Michael Jackson, The Cars, Talking Heads, The Police (with Stewart Copeland), Toto (with the late Jeff Porcaro), Go Go's (drummer Gina Schock), and Bruce Springsteen and the E Street Band (with longtime drummer, Max Weinberg). Further, Hard Rock/Metal had begun to gain wide popularity through groups such as Motley Crue, Def Leppard, Judas Priest, AC/DC, and Van Halen. The drumming in this genre retained the force and musicianship of early Metal (Led Zeppelin, et al.), yet was focused on supporting song structure.

By the late 1980s, the division between Hard Rock and Metal became more apparent, as the louder, faster, and more aggressive style of Metal music and drumming found tremendous cult followings through bands like Metallica, Anthrax, Pantera, Iron Maiden, Megadeth, and Slayer. Dominating the mainstream sound were the Hard Rock bands Whitesnake, Skid Row, Dokken, Poison, and Guns n' Roses, many of which set a fashion trend of long hair, makeup, and costume-like clothing. Whereas Hard Rock continued to emphasize short songs with "hooks" and a recognizable drumming beat, Heavy Metal now firmly established its signature characteristics of rapid-fire double bass drumming, growling and/or high pitched vocals, and fast tempos.

Early in the 1990s, the Pacific Northwest and especially the city of Seattle gave birth to the "Grunge" or Alternative Rock movement, through bands like Nirvana, Pearl Jam, Soundgarden, and Alice In Chains, all featuring a raw, stripped-down sound and aggressive drumming. Bands following the Alternative trend through the middle of the 1990s include The Red Hot Chili Peppers and The Smashing Pumpkins, along with the lighter Counting Crows, Lennie Kravitz, and The Dave Matthews Band. The latter part of the decade saw a resurgence of the Punk style through bands like Green Day and Blink 182. As the decade closed, Metal returned fused with the vocal stylings of Hip Hop in a new "Rap Rock" style performed by Limp Bizkit, Korn, P.O.D., and Incubus.

The 21st century, not surprisingly, has seen an even greater number of bands in this genre. Though there are far too many to list, some of the more prominent recent bands include Linken Park, Death Cab for Cutie, Papa Roach, The Killers, Radiohead, Coldplay, Creed, Nickelback, 3 Doors Down, The Mars Volta, and The Foo Fighters (drummer Dave Grohl, originally with Nirvana, and co-drummer Taylor Hawkins).

Early Rock

Early forms of Rock n' Roll are typically dance music. Though the drumming patterns in the Blues and Surf chapters are an accurate representation of Early Rock 'n Roll drumming, the grooves found below are the most practical to use when playing Early Rock 'n Roll. For a more extensive list of patterns and variations, refer to the aforementioned chapters. A drummer's main role is to lay down a solid feel to support the music. **Standard tempos range from quarter note = 60 bpm (for slow ballads) up to 200 bpm.**

EXAMPLE 1 (Standard Rock Beat—CD2, Track 80)

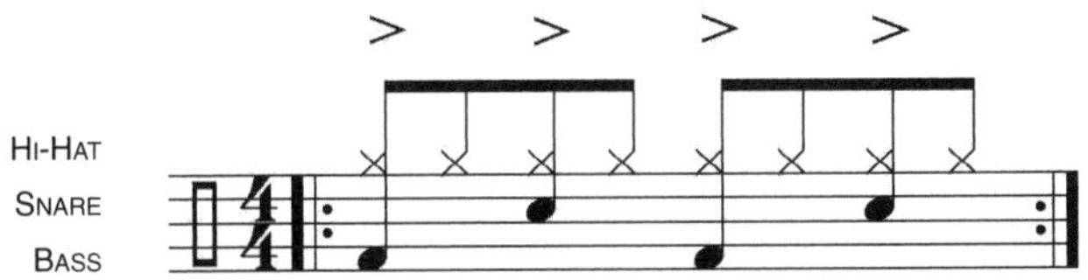

EXAMPLE 2 (Blues Shuffle—CD 1, Track 51)

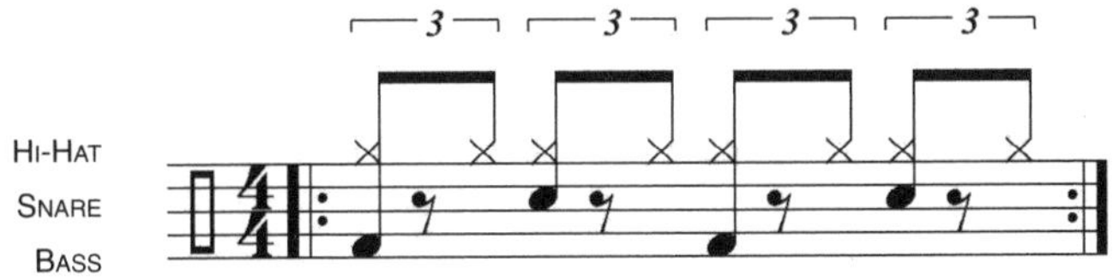

EXAMPLE 3 (Rockabilly—CD 2, Track 78)

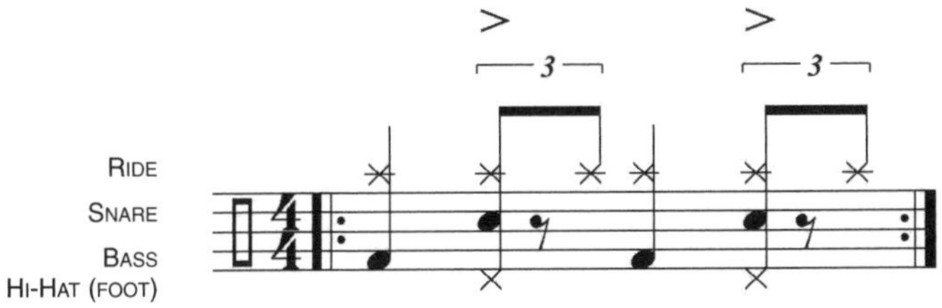

EXAMPLE 4 (12/8 Slow Blues—CD 1, Track 57)

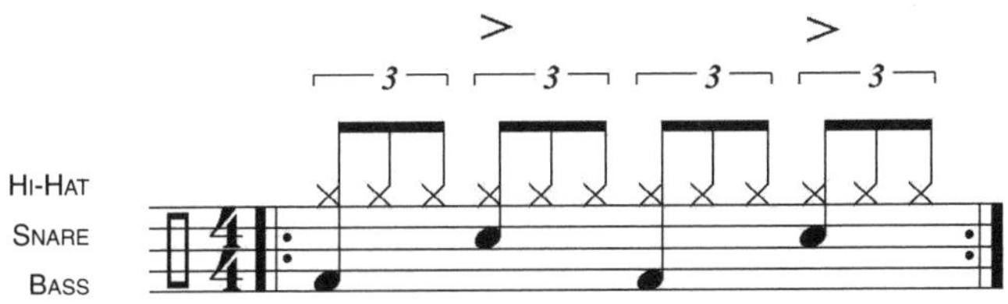

EXAMPLE 5 (Mersey Beat—CD 2, Track 85)

Originally developed in Liverpool, England and made popular by Cliff Richard and the Shadows, the Mersey Beat has been a staple of American Surf bands for decades (see Surf chapter).

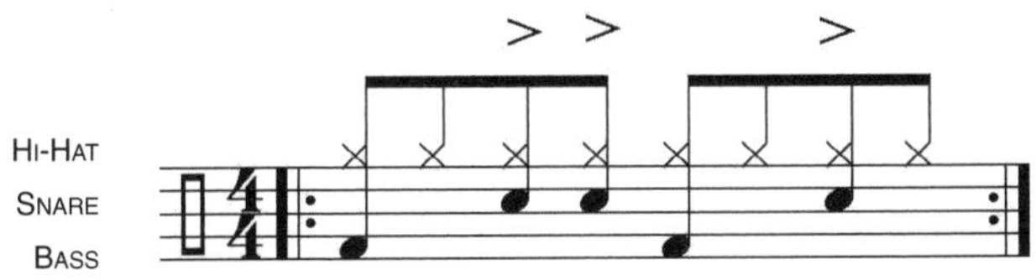

NOTE: Each of the above patterns can be played with the hi-hat pattern moved over to the ride cymbal with various accompanying hi-hat foot patterns, with beats 2 & 4 being the most practical. Another choice, found exclusively in Early Rock n' Roll drumming, is moving the ride pattern (straight or shuffled) to the snare drum.

Variation

This simple standard pattern allows the band, rather than the drummer, to dictate whether the song is played straight or swung. **The minimum tempo for this groove is 80 bpm.**

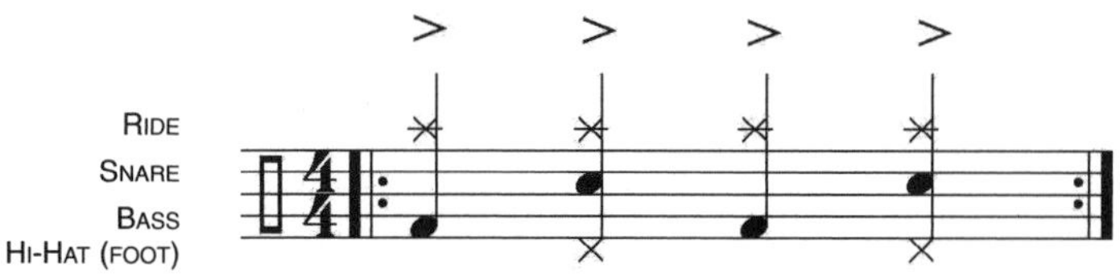

NOTE: All of the above grooves are best kept simple for Early Rock n' Roll. Variations from their corresponding chapters may be applied to more advanced forms of Rock n' Roll.

Rockabilly

One of the first forms of Rock n' Roll, Rockabilly emphasized a strong guitar and piano sound with a heavy backbeat on the snare drum, similar to that of Jump Blues. Prominent creators of the Rockabilly sound were Bill Haley and the Comets, Carl Perkins, Jerry Lee Lewis, and Elvis Presley. Its popularity diminished by the early 1960s, but has since found a resurgence through Dave Edmunds, The Stray Cats in the 1980s and, more recently, Brian Setzer (former Stray Cats guitarist) and the Reverend Horton Heat. **Rockabilly has a swung feel and has a large tempo range of quarter note = 120–240 bpm.**

Example (CD 2, Track 78)

This features the Jazz swing pattern on the ride cymbal.

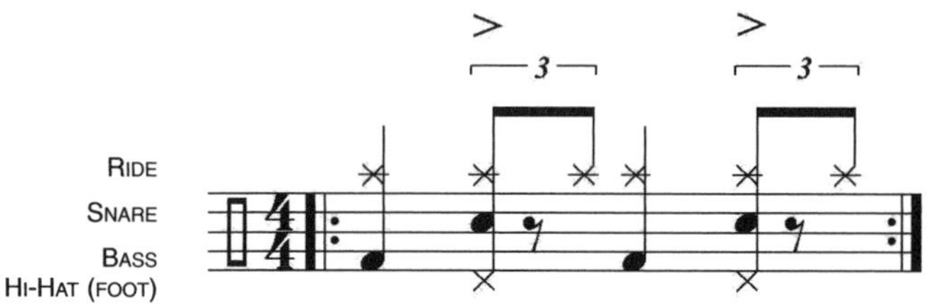

Variation (CD 2, Track 79)

When played in Rockabilly, the Train Beat is often shuffled. For more variations see Bluegrass Train Beat in the Country chapter and shuffle the 16th notes when appropriate.

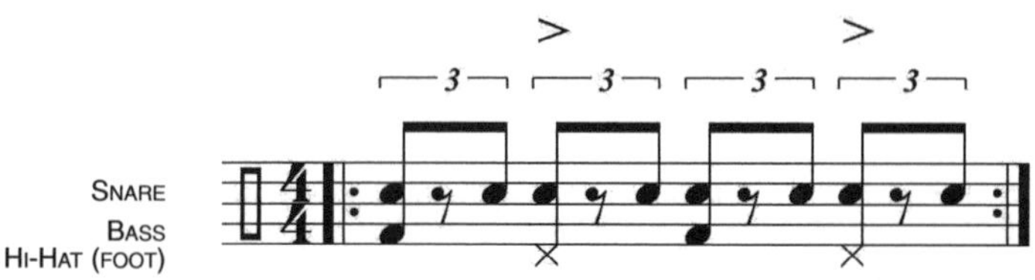

Standard Rock

The basis of Standard Rock n' Roll drumming is simple. Though most Standard Rock patterns and variations are relatively straightforward, Rock grooves may become quite complex depending on the requirements of a specific song. The Standard Rock grooves below can be applied to numerous styles within the Rock genre. These include Classic Rock, Pop Rock, New Wave, Top 40, Easy Listening/Soft Rock, Hard Rock, Alternative, Grunge, Latin Rock, Punk, and even Progressive Rock. **Standard Rock tempos range from quarter note = 60 bpm (for slow ballads) up to 200 bpm. However, most Standard Rock songs have tempos of quarter note = 110–120 bpm.**

Example (CD 2, Track 80)

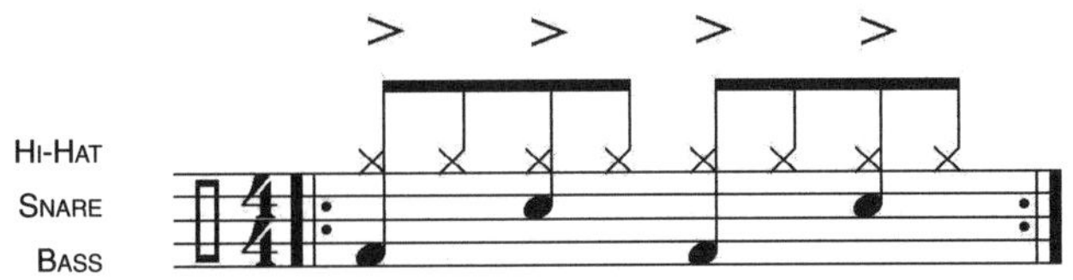

Bass Drum Variations

Variation 1 (CD 2, Track 81)

This is the "Phil Spector Beat," named after the famous producer. It was used in songs such as "Be My Baby."

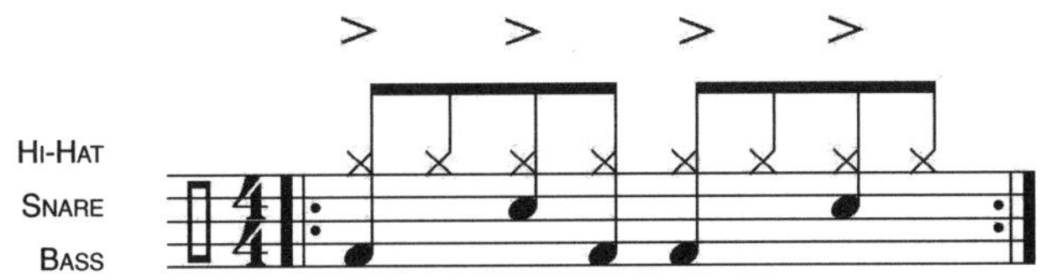

Variation 2

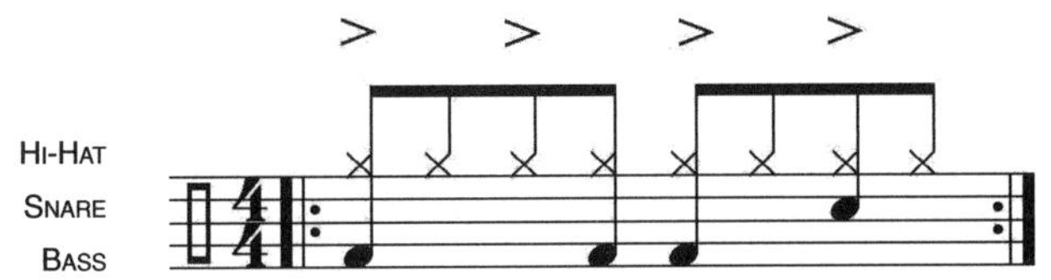

Variation 3

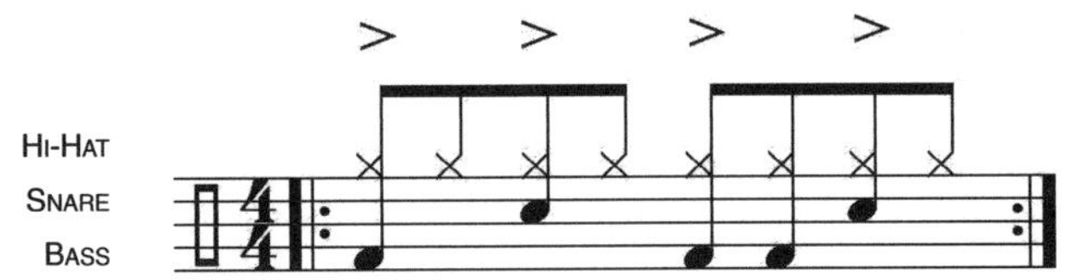

Variation 4

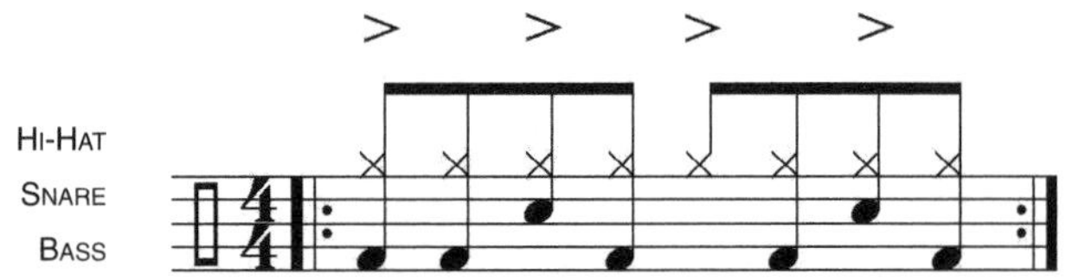

Variation 5

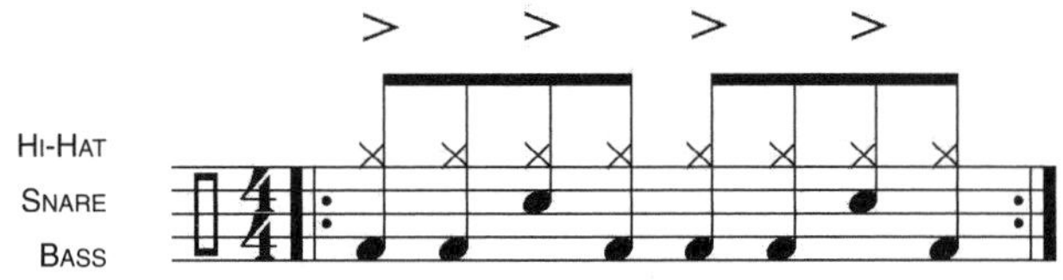

Variation 6

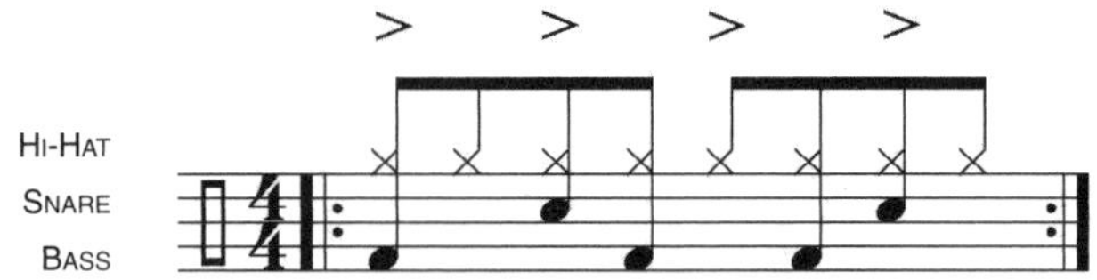

Snare Drum Variations

Variation 1 (CD 2, Track 82)

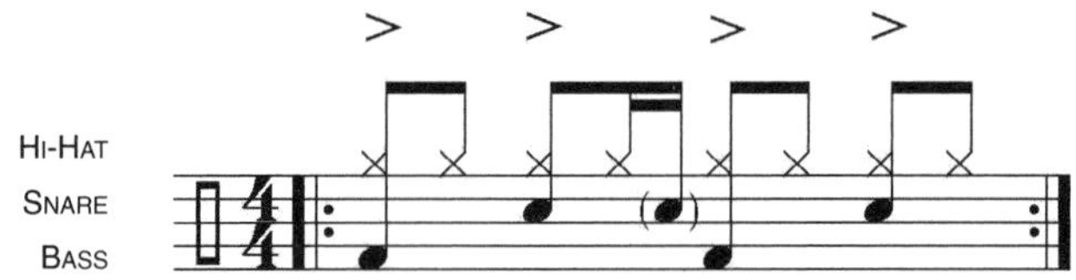

Variation 2

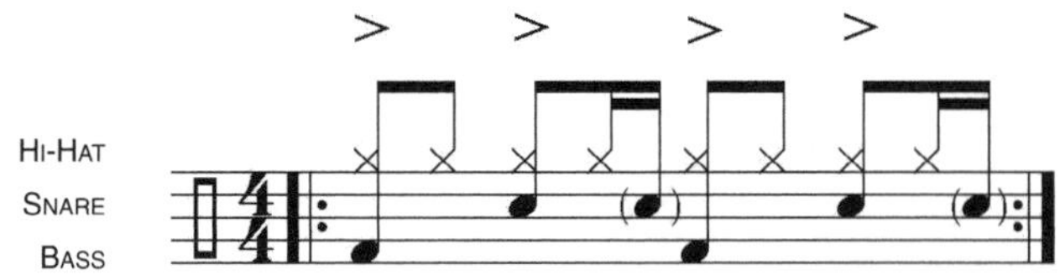

Variation 3

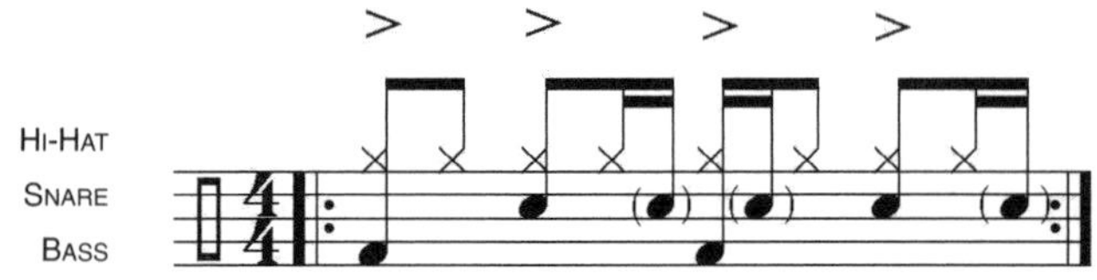

NOTES: 1) Rock drumming variations are virtually endless. A good rule is to maintain a strong 2 & 4 backbeat while adding snare drum and/or bass drum variations around it. Though beats 2 & 4 on the snare are by far the most common, snare displacement to other beats in is possible. Additional 8th-note bass variations are also possible (see Funk chapter). 2) The above snare drum and bass drum variations can be combined to create additional patterns. 3) The above grooves can be played with the hi-hat pattern moved to the ride cymbal with various accompanying hi-hat foot patterns, with beats 2 & 4 being the most practical. 4) Any snare notes other than the standard backbeats on 2 & 4 are normally played as ghost notes.

Riding the Snare

Example

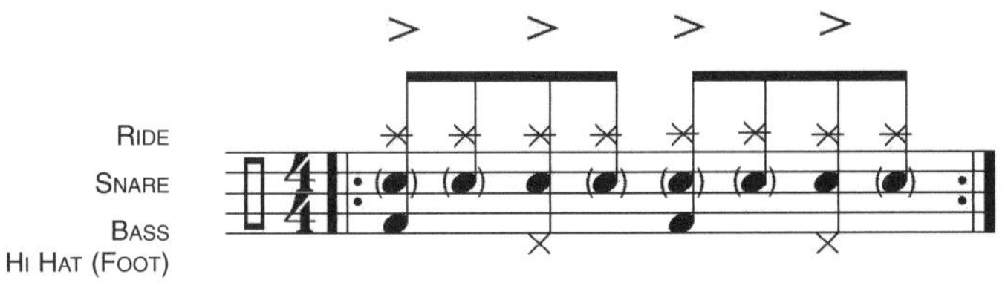

Variation

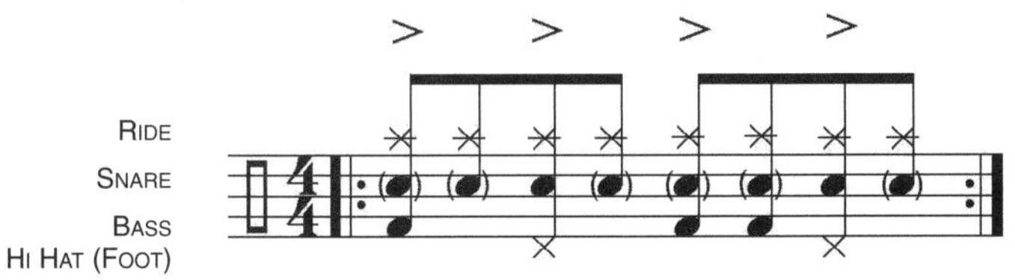

NOTE: Bass drum variations can create many more grooves. As these snare-riding grooves are already very full, bass drum patterns should be limited to 8th notes and quarter notes. Any combination of bass drum notes will work as long as beat 1 is played and beats 2 & 4 avoided.

Polka Beat / Rock Stomp

Example (Polka)

Both the Polka (Example) and its inversion (Variation—the Rock Stomp) are common in Rock. For examples of Polka see "Yakety Yak," by The Coasters, and (swung Polka) "At the Hop," by Danny and the Juniors. For an example of the Rock Stomp, see Ringo's break on "Birthday," by the Beatles.

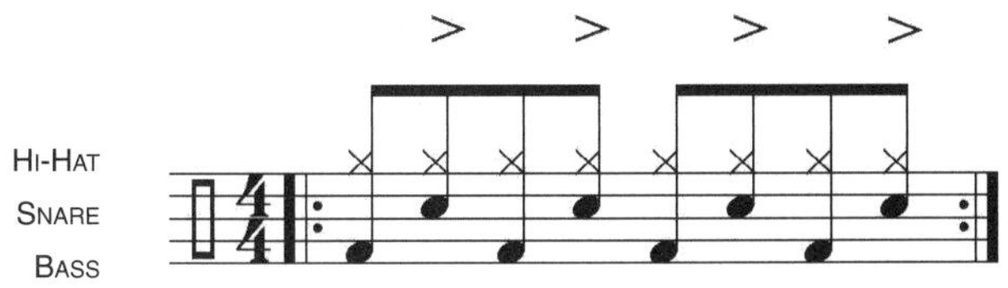

Variation (Rock Stomp)

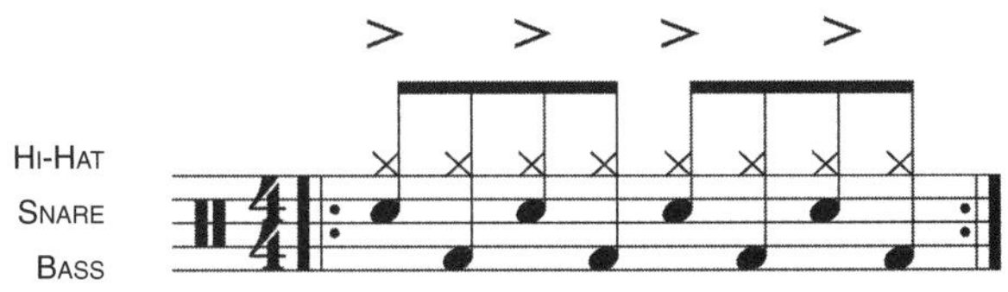

Half-Time Standard Rock Feel

Not so much a style as a feel, the purpose of Half-Time Standard Rock is to fill up the groove in slower Rock tempos. The addition of 16th notes from the ride hand creates the active feel in this groove, making it practical only for songs in slower tempos. **The tempo range is narrower than that of the Standard Rock range, with quarter note = 60–96 bpm.**

Example (CD 2, Track 83)

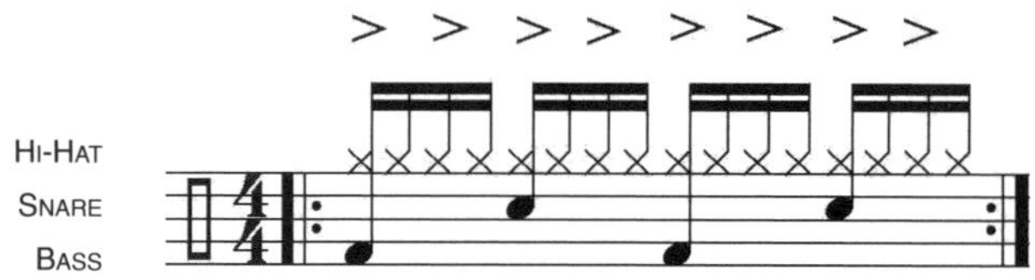

Variation

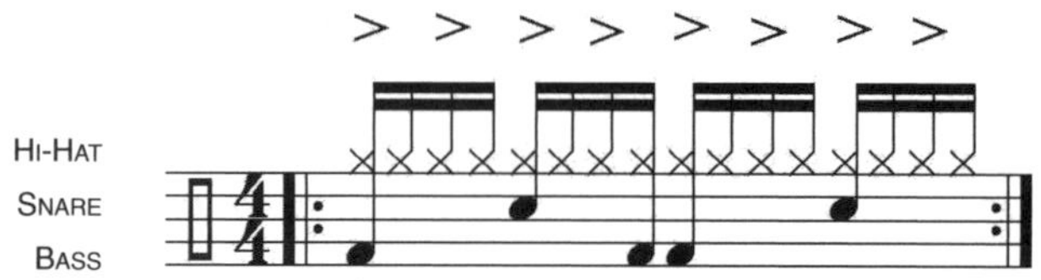

NOTE: Each of the above patterns can be played with the ride pattern moved to the ride cymbal and various accompanying hi-hat foot patterns, with beats 2 & 4 being the most practical for the hi-hat foot.

Fusion

The term "Fusion" refers to the fusing of many different styles into a distinctive sound. Predominately an instrumental form of music, Fusion is a mixture of Rock, Jazz, Funk, and Progressive Rock, and involves advanced musicianship and, oftentimes, "off" meters. In addition to the bands and musicians mentioned in the Rock n' Roll introduction, important fusion drummers include Alphonse Mouzon, Rod Morgenstein of the Dixie Dregs, Billy Cobham for his work with the Mahavishnu Orchestra and his milestone album, "Spectrum," and several drummers who have played with Chick Corea, including Steve Gadd, Lenny White, and Dave Weckl. Contemporary drummers such as Steve Smith, Will Kennedy (Yellowjackets), Paul Wertico (Pat Metheny), Omar Hakim, Dennis Chambers, Simon Phillips, Vinny Colaiuta, Terri Lyne Carrington, Cindy Blackman, Kim Plainfield, Aaron Spears, Ronald Bruner Jr., and Tony Royster Jr. are all outstanding Fusion players. Important Fusion groups/musicians include Miles Davis (who could be credited as the style's originator, with his "In a Silent Way" [1969] and "Bitches Brew" [1970] albums), Tony Williams Lifetime, Herbie Hancock and the Headhunters, the Mahavishnu Orchestra, and Weather Report. All Standard Rock examples and variations, as well as those from the Jazz, Odd Time, and Funk chapters, can be used when playing Fusion. Tempos vary widely in Fusion, but tend toward moderately fast.

Example 1 (CD 2, Track 84)

The following ghost note groove is but one of very many possibilities. The number of possible Fusion patterns is so large (due to the numerous styles that Fusion draws on) that we could not hope to present a comprehensive assortment of Fusion grooves. Look to the styles that Fusion draws on (see Standard Rock, Funk, Odd Time, and Polyrhythm) for additional possibilities. **Quarter note = 136–172 bpm.**

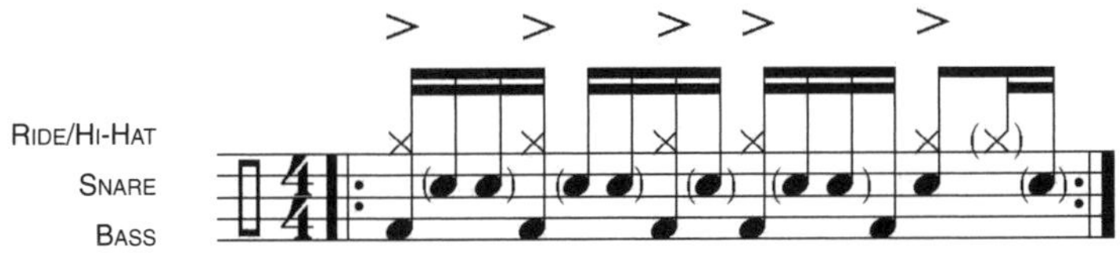

Variation 1

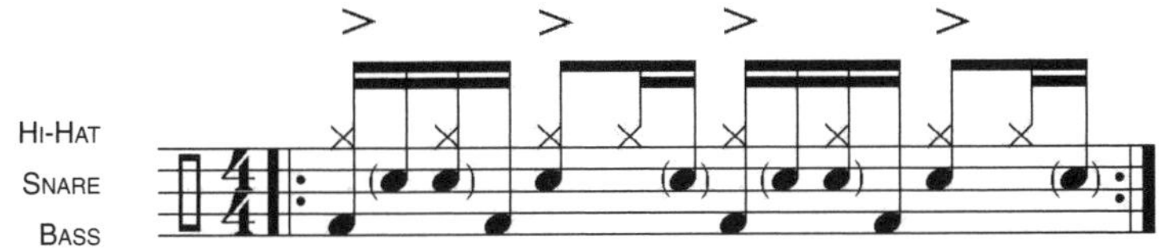

Variation 2

The following variation utilizes the same basic ghost note ideas as the previous example and variation, but is in 7/8, a very common meter in Fusion. **Eighth note = 272–344 bpm.**

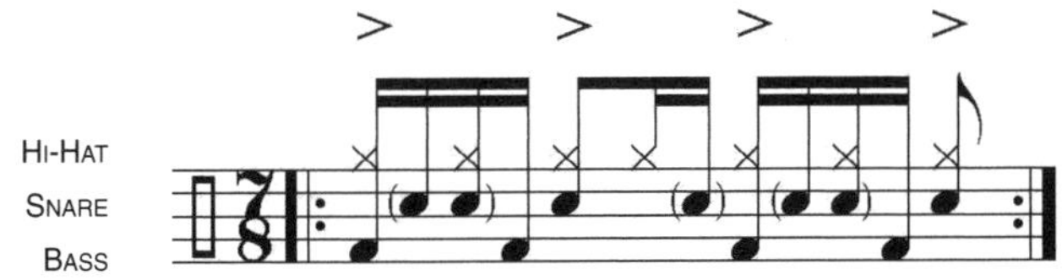

Example 2 (CD 2, Track 23)

This is the primary Linear Funk example. In Fusion it would be played considerably faster than in Funk. Notice the extensive use of ghost notes, which are a signature characteristic of Fusion drumming. **The tempo remains at quarter note = 136–172 bpm.**

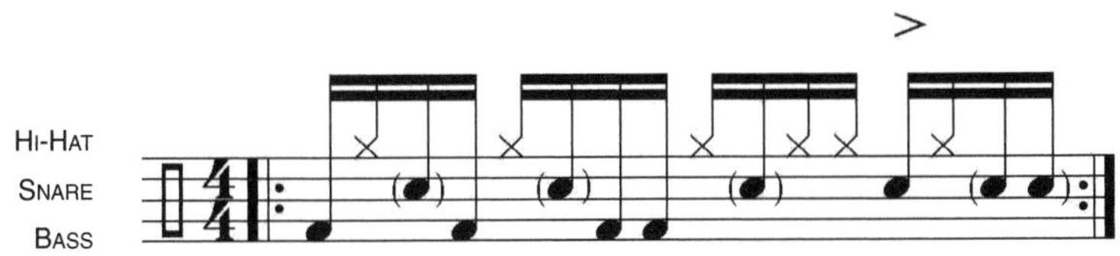

NOTE: It's common to play 16th-note combinations between the ride hand and snare drum, with the snare playing ghost notes. Variations of Fusion drumming using this technique are virtually endless. (See Ghost Note Funk and Linear Funk in the Funk chapter.)

25 Surf

Inspired by 1950s Rock n' Roll, Surf music was created in the early 1960s, initially as an instrumental genre, by artists such as The Surfaris, the Ventures, and guitarist Dick Dale. Purists consider the most authentic form of Surf music to be instrumental, emphasizing the drums and guitar (typically very trebly, somewhat overdriven, and with heavy reverb) to mimic the experience of surfing. When groups like Jan and Dean and The Beach Boys introduced lyrics (of a teen-jock-oriented type, usually sung in a high tenor—or outright falsetto—voice, with often extensive vocal harmonies), the style achieved mainstream popularity. Perhaps the most influential surfing drum song is the classic, tom tom-driven "Wipeout," recorded by the Surfaris (with drummer Ron Wilson) and further popularized by the The Ventures, while the most influential guitar-driven Surf song is probably "Walk Don't Run," by the Ventures. Vocal Surf classics include The Beach Boys' "Surfin' Safari" and "Surfin' USA."

In the mid to late 1960s, Surf was eclipsed by British Rock (The Rolling Stones, The Beatles, The Who, et al.) and the Psychedelic Sound (The Doors, Cream, Jimi Hendrix, Pink Floyd, et al.). However, the early 1990s reissue of Dick Dale's early song "Miserlou" on the "Pulp Fiction" soundtrack stimulated renewed interest in Surf music. The style is currently represented by newer bands such as The Mermen, The Red Elvises, The Aqua Velvets, and—still!—The Ventures, who are enormously popular in Japan.

The drumming pattern in a typical Surf song is characterized by an alternate (to that in standard Rock) backbeat pattern on the snare drum. In addition, many Surf songs include active and repetitive 16th notes on the toms, sometimes throughout an entire song. However, this technique tends to be used more in instrumental numbers than in songs with vocals. **The tempo is brisk at quarter note = 138–184 bpm.**

Example (CD 2, Track 85)

This is the Mersey Beat (from Liverpool, England—see Early Rock in the Rock n' Roll chapter). The Mersey Beat pervades Surf music.

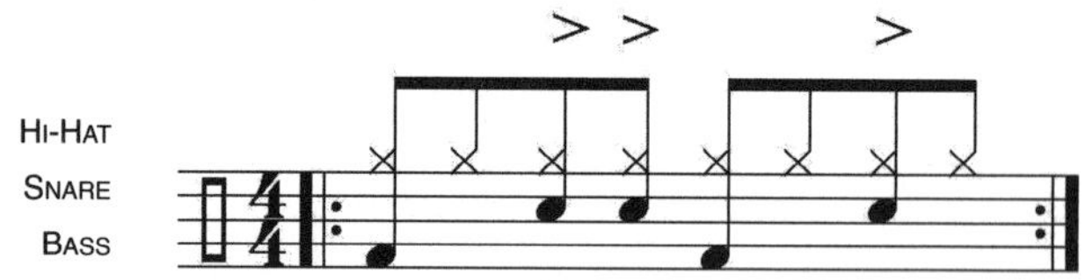

Variation 1

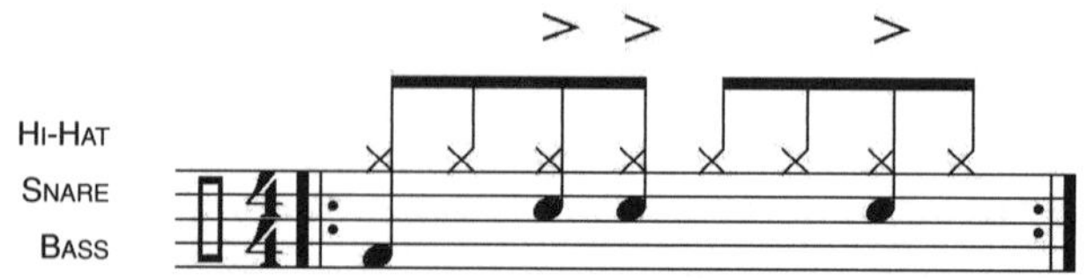

VARIATION 2

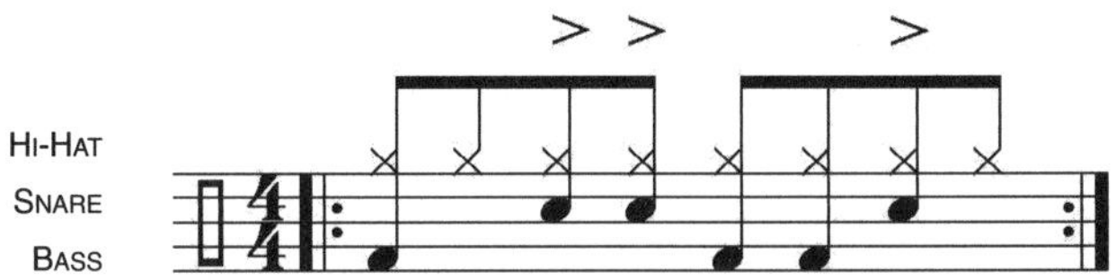

VARIATION 3

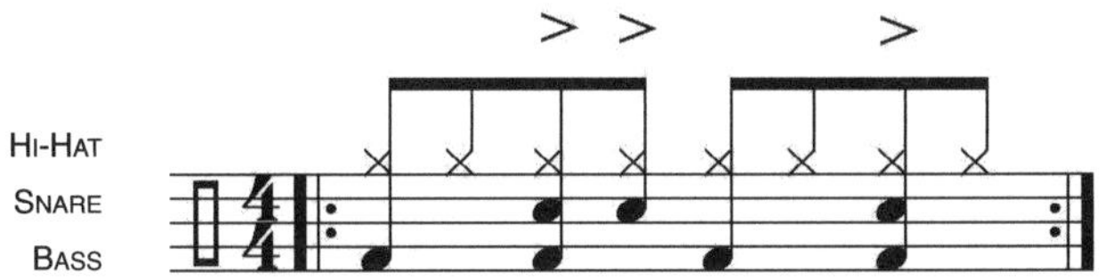

VARIATION 4 (CD 2, Track 80)

This is the Standard Rock pattern from the Rock n' Roll chapter. Other bass and snare variations are possible but should be kept simple.

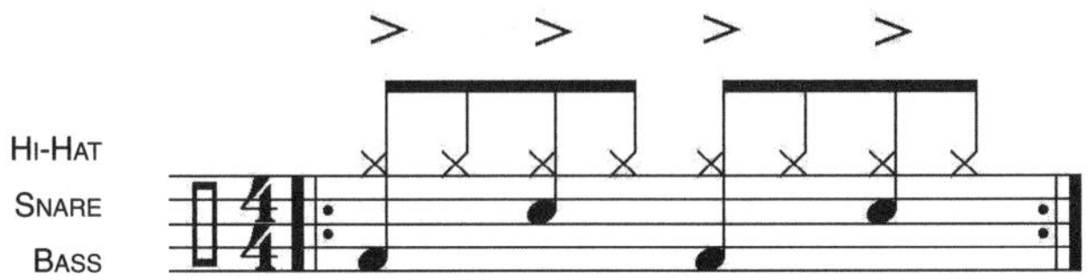

NOTE: The above example and variations may be played with the ride hand playing a ride cymbal and the hi-hat foot accompanying the snare drum on beats 2 & 4. The eighth note on the + of beat 2 on the snare drum can be left out of all of the above grooves to simplify the patterns.

SURF BALLAD

EXAMPLE (CD 1, Track 42)

This is the main example from the Bolero portion of the Afro-Cuban chapter. It may be applied to many Surf Ballads. This groove also works well with Hawaiian ballads such as Queen Lili'uokalani's familiar "Aloha Oe."
Quarter note = 74–120 bpm.

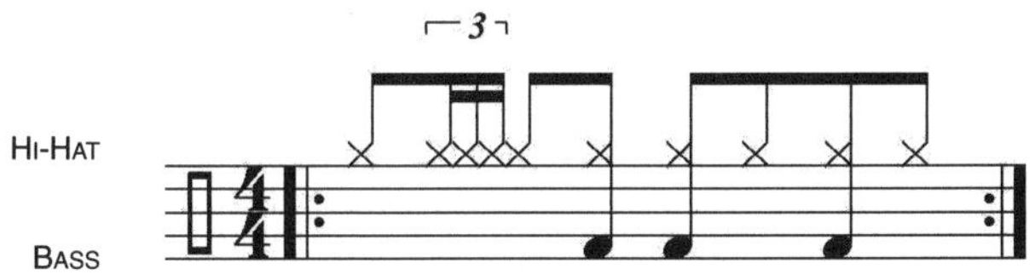

Surf Tom Pattern

Example

This two-measure pattern for the toms, displaying consistent 16th notes with accents, is taken from the Surf classic, "Wipeout." Frequently used in other instrumental surfing songs, such as "Pipeline," it is occasionally found in songs with lyrics as well. Beats 2 & 4 or all downbeats can be played with hi-hat foot accompaniment. In addition, the bass drum may accompany the groove with a "four on the floor" pattern. **Tempo on "Wipeout" is quarter note = 160 bpm.**

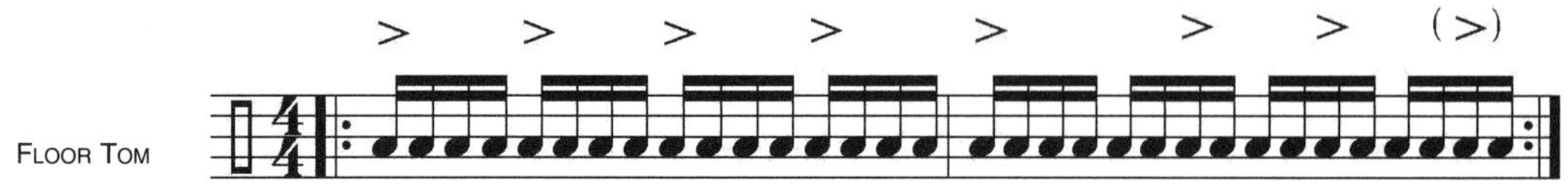

NOTE: The final accent is in parentheses in the above example because it isn't played in every repetition in the original recording of "Wipeout."

26 Techno

The invention of electronic instruments such as the Theramin and the Ondes Martenot in the 1920s and 1930s introduced a new method of creating music. This new approach remained largely confined to classical composers (e.g., Stockhausen and Messiaen) until the late 1960s and early 1970s when ensembles such as Beaver & Krause and Kraftwerk began to replace acoustic and electric instruments (guitar, bass, piano, etc.) with electronic instruments (synthesizers) producing "electronic music." By the 1980s, electronic music's influence had reached popular culture with artists such as Devo, The Buggles, Human League, Yaz, and Erasure, as electronically produced sounds became mixed with melodic pop songs. The term "Techno" emerged in the late 1980s, but the style only achieved popularity in the early 1990s (primarily in the UK) when harder, more powerful beats were merged with dance tracks to produce music which was heavily "dance driven."

In addition to Techno compositions, another term and style associated with this genre is "Remix," which means adding new tracks to a popular song, subtracting original tracks, especially drums, and then "remixing the result." This usually results in a faster feel and a heavy, repetitive drum beat. Currently, Techno has a large variety of sub-styles. House (with a non-deviating "four on the floor" rhythm), Ambient Wave, Trance, Trip Hop, Tribal, and Breakbeat (which led to the emergence of the "Jungle" style) are all modern branches of electronic, dance-driven music.

Though Techno is not usually performed with a live drum set player, incorporation of Techno sounds into other dance styles and the popularity of the Jungle and Drum n' Bass genres may at times require a drummer to replicate the sound of Techno. A useful set up for Techno is small, high-pitched drums with small, "trashy" cymbals. Also, the employment of an electronic drum kit or a triggered set up (drums that are wired to "trigger" electronic sounds) could prove useful in reproducing the sound of Techno. In contrast to those of Drum n' Bass/Jungle, Techno patterns are generally less intricate, require more consistency, and usually have a heavy, "four on the floor" bass drum pattern (though it may deviate). Techno's tempos are slightly slower than those of Drum n' Bass/Jungle. **The tempo range is quarter note = 110–184 bpm.**

Example (CD 2, Track 86)

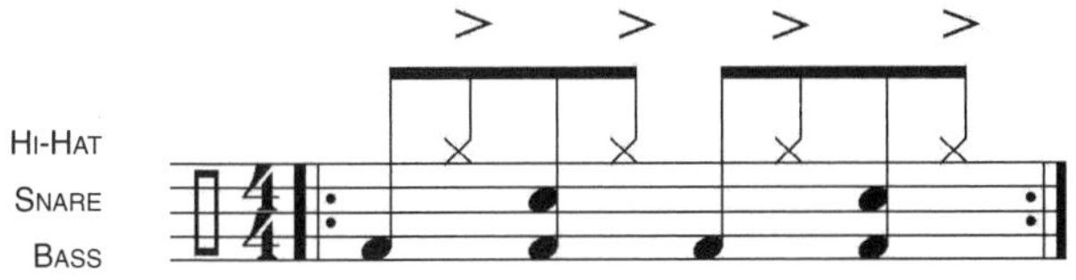

Variation 1

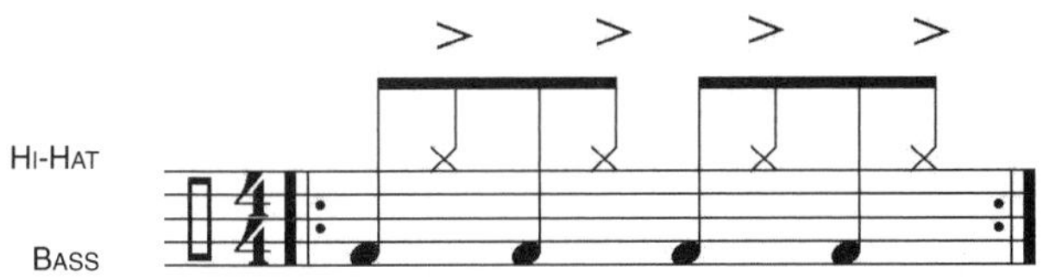

VARIATION 2

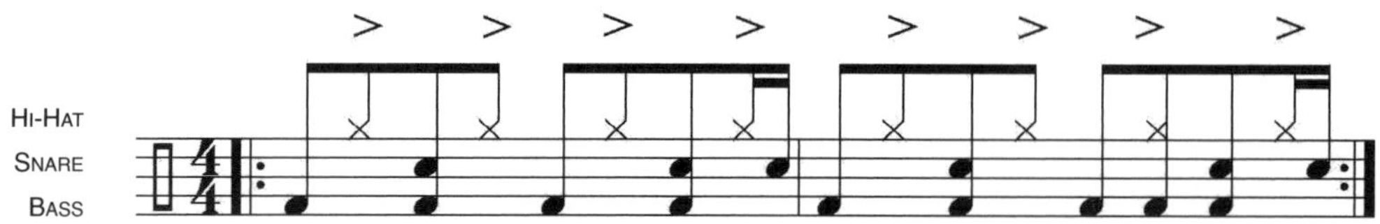

VARIATION 3 (CD 2, Track 11)

This is identical to the main Example from the Disco chapter, and is particularly suitable for the House style.

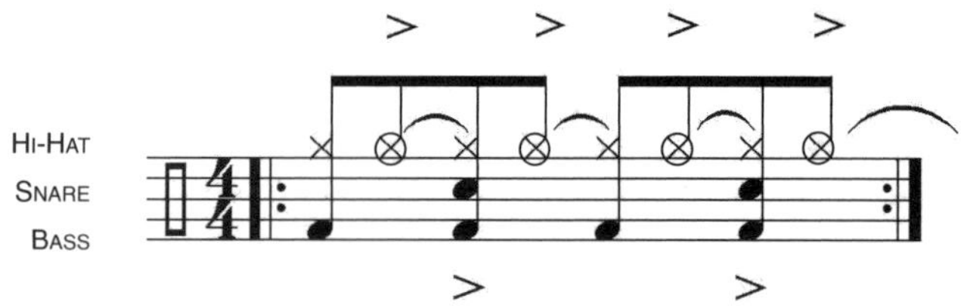

(Circled hi-hat notes are played open)

27 WEDDING DANCES

A knowledge of common wedding dances is a necessity for the working drummer. The following dance grooves are those most often played.

TARANTELLA

The Tarantella is a dance from southern Italy (Taranto). It's basically a march which often increases in tempo throughout the song. **Dotted quarter note = 135 bpm.**

EXAMPLE (CD 2, Track 87)

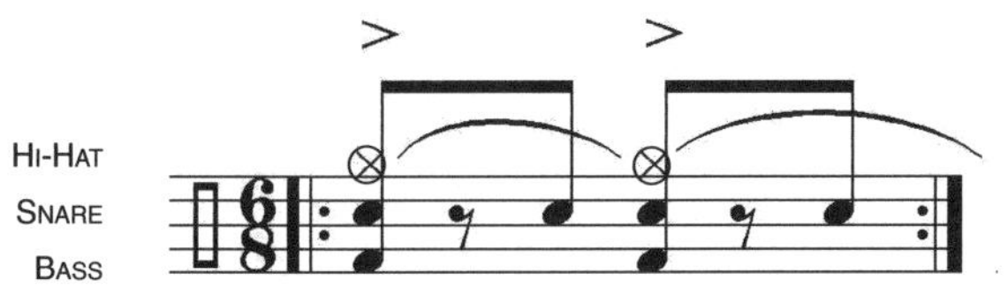

(Circled hi-hat notes are played open)

HAVA NAGILA

Hava Nagila is also commonly played at wedding receptions. A Jewish song and dance created in Jerusalem about 100 years ago, it means "Come, Let Us Be Joyful." Similar to the Tarantella, this dance often speeds up and is characterized by celebrants clapping, singing, and dancing in a large circle (a dance often referred to as the "Hora"—not to be confused with the Hora from the Klezmer chapter). **Quarter note = 144 bpm.**

EXAMPLE (CD 2, Track 88)

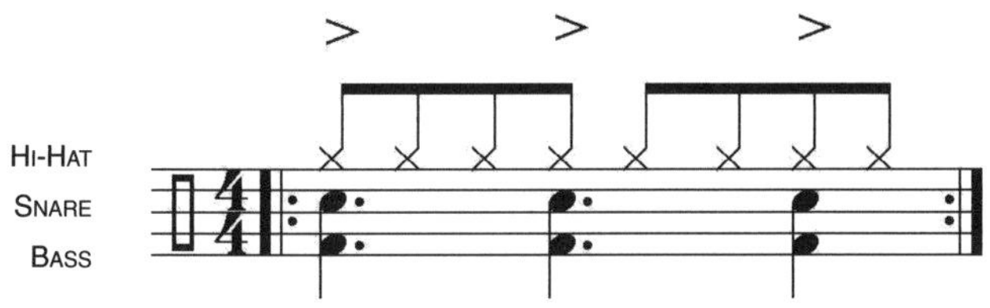

NOTE: The bridge section of Hava Nagila usually segues into a double time feel. The most appropriate groove in this second section is a standard Polka or Klezmer (Bulgar) pattern (see Polka and Klezmer chapters).

Rumba

Example (CD 1, Track 64)

The Rumba, which originated in Cuba, is another popular wedding dance. Dancers familiar with the Rumba style accentuate the staccato rhythms of the percussion section with vigorous, energetic moves. Rumba rhythms are also frequently used in contemporary pop songs. This pattern is the same as the Blues Rumba. **Quarter note = 144 bpm.**

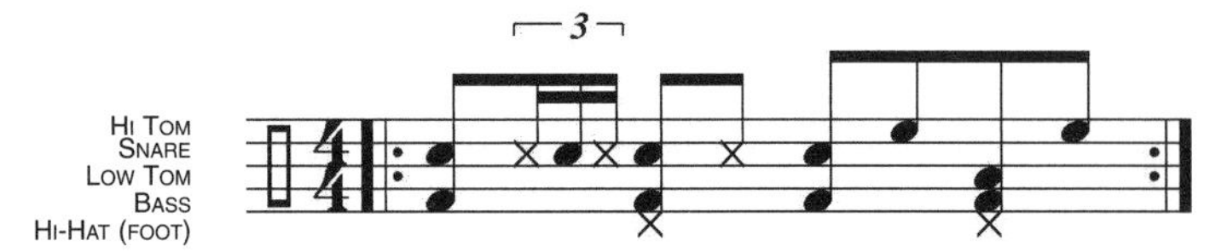

NOTE: Try playing this with the snares off, though the pattern is effective either way.

Tango

Example (CD 2, Track 89)

The Tango is a dance which developed in the brothels and bars of Buenos Aires during the late 1880s. The snare drum rhythm is derived from a common pattern originally performed by a castanet player. **Quarter note = 126 bpm.**

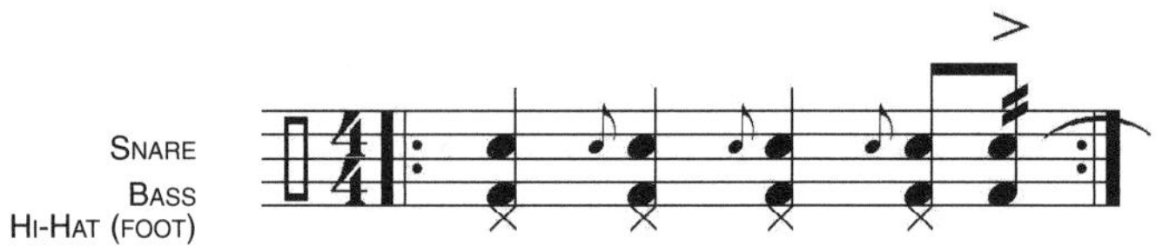

NOTE: Flams may be omitted from the Tango to produce a softer sound.

Viennese Waltz

Example (CD 2, Track 90)

From its development in Europe in the 1800s (attributed to Johann Strauss Sr. and Jr.), the Viennese Waltz remained the most popular European ballroom dance until World War I. **It is slightly more syncopated than other Waltzes and often played at brighter tempos with quarter note = 152–208 bpm.**

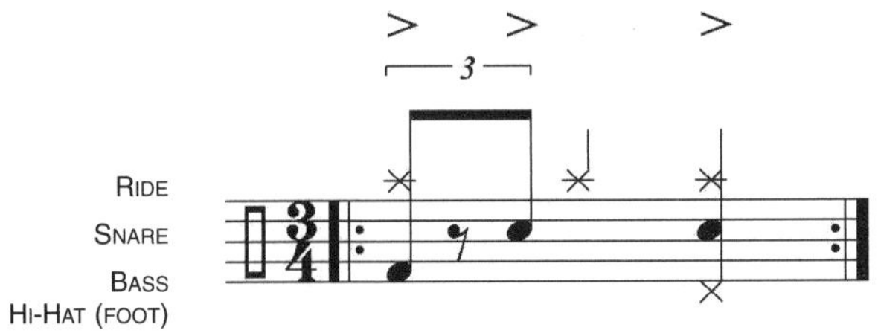

American Waltz

Example (CD 2, Track 91)

Somewhat slower than the Viennese Waltz and with less syncopation, the American Waltz (aka "The Boston," stemming from its development in Boston, Massachusetts) emphasizes beats 2 & 3 clearly. **The tempo range is quarter note = 132–176 bpm.**

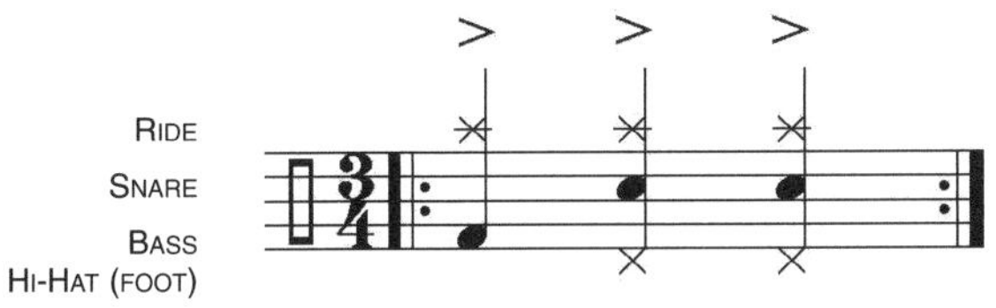

Fox Trot

Example (CD 2, Track 92)

The Fox Trot was created in 1914 by Vaudevillian Harry Fox "trotting" to Ragtime music. The Fox Trot has become one of the most important dances in ballroom dancing. **It requires simple 4/4 drumming grooves with a medium to slow tempo marking of quarter note = 120 bpm.**

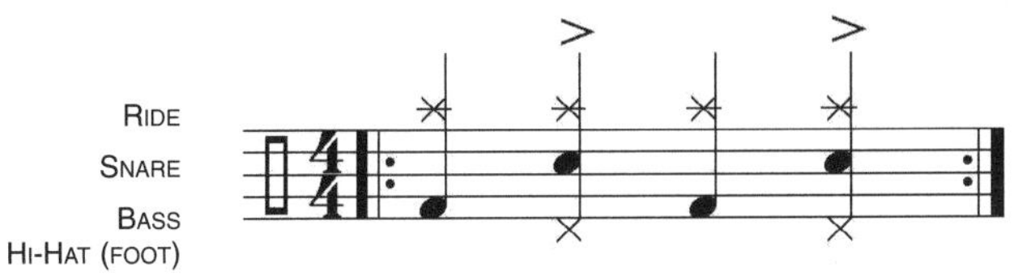

NOTE: It's a good idea to use brushes when playing Fox Trot grooves to match the soft nature of the music.

28 Misc. Grooves

While some of these "miscellaneous" patterns could be included in other chapters (Afro-Cuban, Funk, and Caribbean), we've placed them here for three closely related reasons: 1) In the preceding chapters, all primary examples are recorded as CD tracks; 2) The number of tracks per CD is very limited; and 3) These styles are so seldom encountered that they do not merit inclusion on the already tightly packed CDs.

Arara

Arara is a 6/8 Cuban rhythm with origins from the Dahomey region of Africa (now called Benin, bordering Nigeria). Though not an official drum set groove, a good pattern has been devised by David Garibaldi from his book *Timba Funk*. Notice the snare drum rim click. **Quarter note = 108 bpm.**

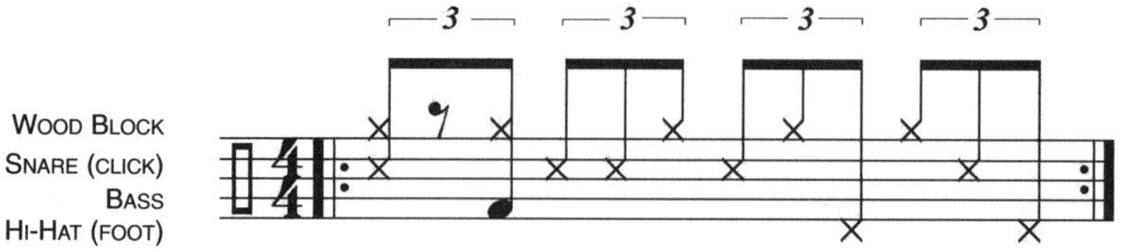

Boogaloo

Boogaloo, a style combining Salsa with Rhythm and Blues, was developed in the early to mid-1960s in New York City. Boogaloo patterns are often interpreted as syncopated early Funk or R & B patterns (see Displaced Funk in Funk Chapter). **The tempo range is quarter note = 88–120 bpm.**

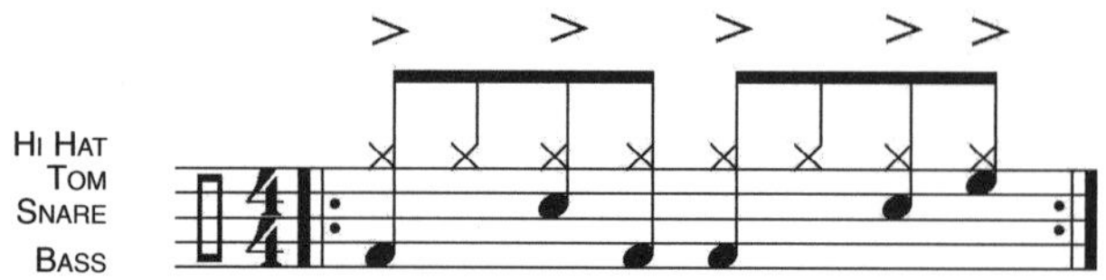

Guajira

This is a rural Cuban style dating from the 1600s; a very famous example is "Guantanamera." The bell pattern can be played on either the ride cymbal bell or a cowbell. **The Guajira tempo is slower and the feel more delicate than that in a Cha Cha, starting around quarter note = 92 bpm.**

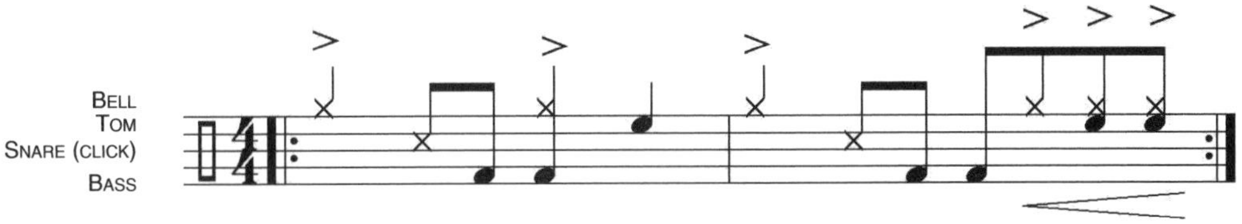

Habanera

A derivation of the contradanza, the Habanera started in Cuba in the 1800s and made its way to Argentina as the precursor to the Tango. **The tempo is most commonly played at quarter note = 108 bpm.**

Israeli Dance Pattern

The groove below proves practical in most modern Israeli dance music and is played quickly. **Quarter note = 272 bpm.**

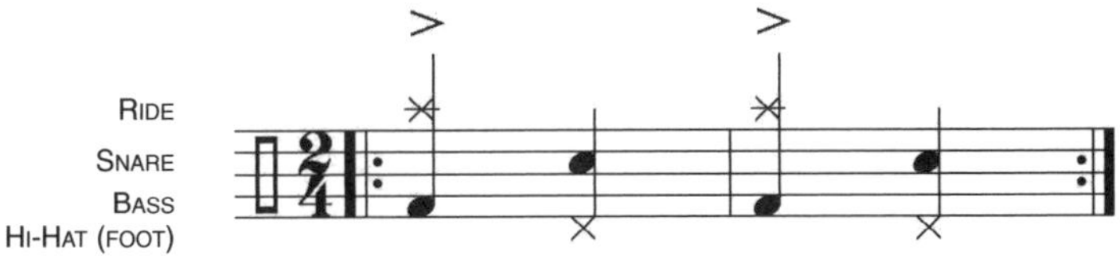

Jig

A festive dance originating in the Elizabethan era, the Jig is felt and written in 6/8. **It is commonly played at dotted quarter note = 138 bpm.**

JOROPO

The Joropo is a musical style and dance that is considered the national folkloric dance of Venezuela. Both African and European influenced, Joropos and their variations are typically felt in a meter of "3" and often have alternating meters or feels of 3/4 and 6/8. **The tempo is typically quarter note = 160bpm.**

EXAMPLE 1

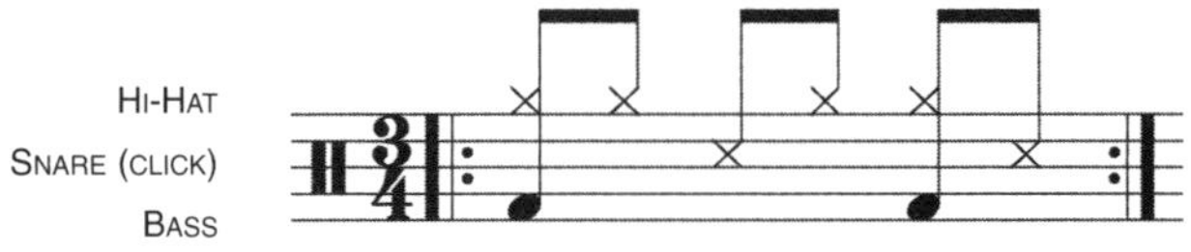

EXAMPLE 2

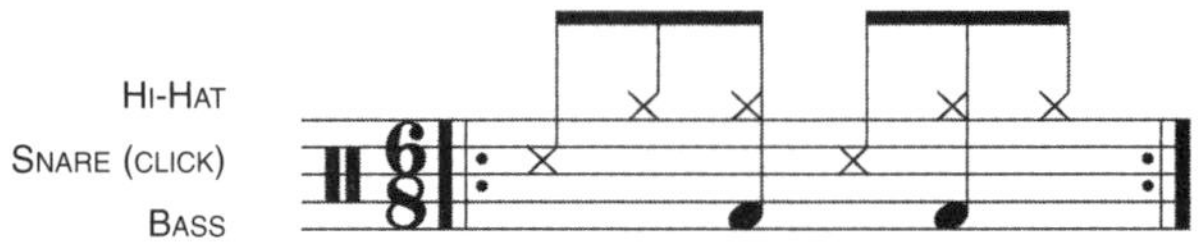

NANIGO

Nanigo is a 6/8 Cuban rhythm/dance, with African roots, similar in function to the Abakwa (see Afro-Cuban 6/8 in the Afro-Cuban chapter). The bell pattern can be played either on the ride cymbal bell or on a cowbell. **The tempo is most commonly played at quarter note = 108 bpm.**

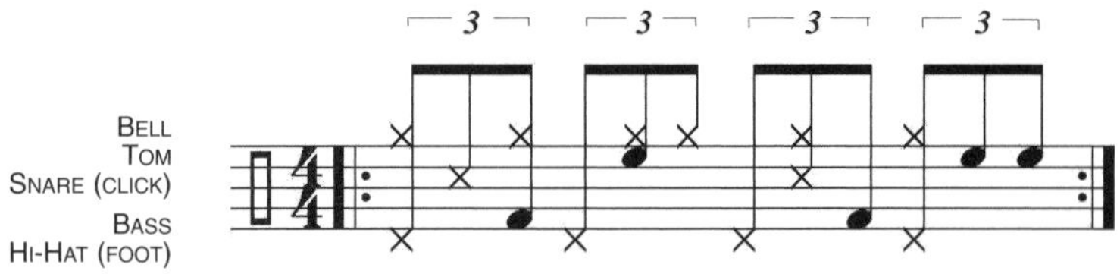

NORTEÑA

Norteña is a northern Mexican style closely related to the Ranchera style. They differ in that Norteñas use a Polka beat and variations on it, and Norteñas feature the accordion prominently, whereas Rancheras normally do not use accordion and do not use the Polka beat. **The tempo is around quarter note = 200 bpm.**

Example (CD 1, Track 2)

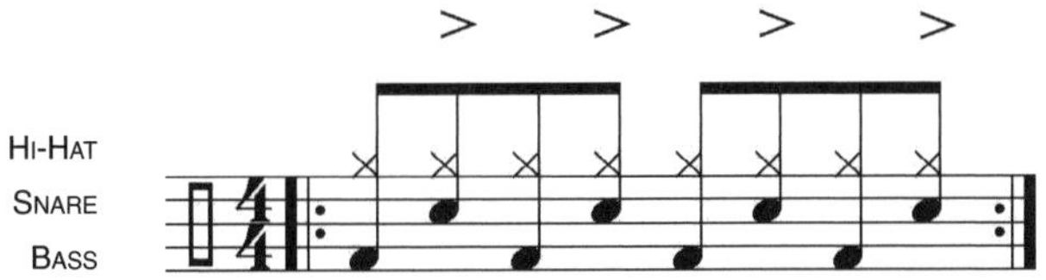

Variation 1

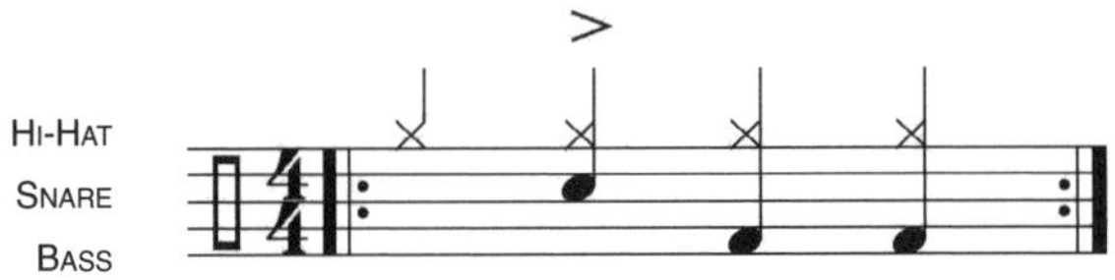

Variation 2

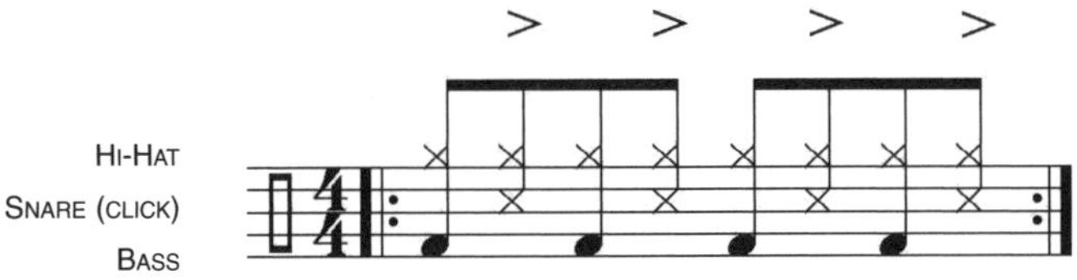

Pachanga

Devised in Cuba in the mid-1950s, Pachanga rhythms are a blend of Merengue and the Cuban Conga (see Afro-Cuban chapter). **The brisk tempo is quarter note = 224 bpm.**

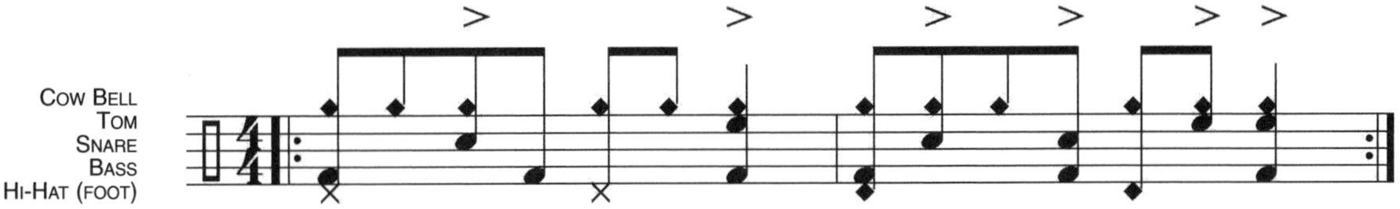

Paso Doble ("Two Step")

This simple Spanish style is similar to the Polka, though it is primarily played on the snare drum. The pattern is usually written and felt in 2/4 time. **The tempo is quarter note = 240 bpm.**

La Raspa ("The File")

La Raspa originated in Vera Cruz, Mexico, and the most famous example of it is the "Mexican Hat Dance." The drum set rhythm corresponds to the melody. **The tempo is commonly played at quarter note = 120 bpm.**

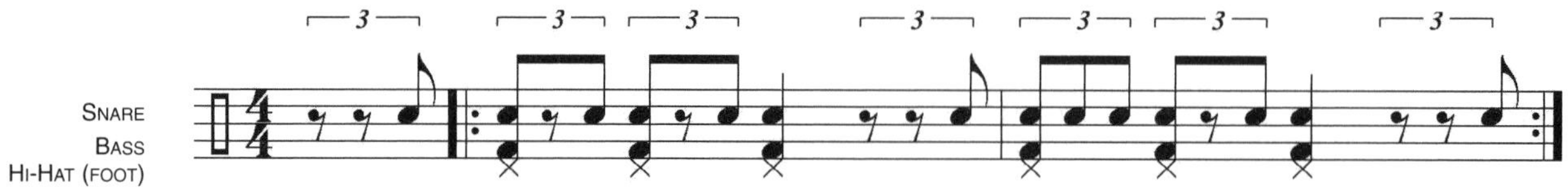

Tex-Mex

Tex Mex music combines the sounds of Mexican folk music and European folk music with the Country Western music of Texas. It developed primarily in the early 20th century when Tejanos (Mexicans born in Texas) began to blend the music of German immigrants in Texas (waltzes, polkas) with Mexican music. Some of the more prominent Tex-Mex artists include Flaco Jiminez, Freddy Fender, and The Texas Tornados. **There are two primary grooves for the style: Standard Rock Beat (quarter note = 120 bpm) and a Tex Mex Polka-style beat (quarter note = 240 bpm) which differs from the standard Polka beat in that all notes are accented.**

Example

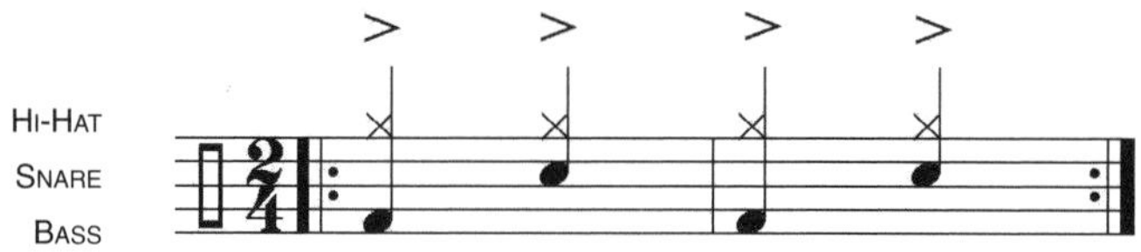

Variation

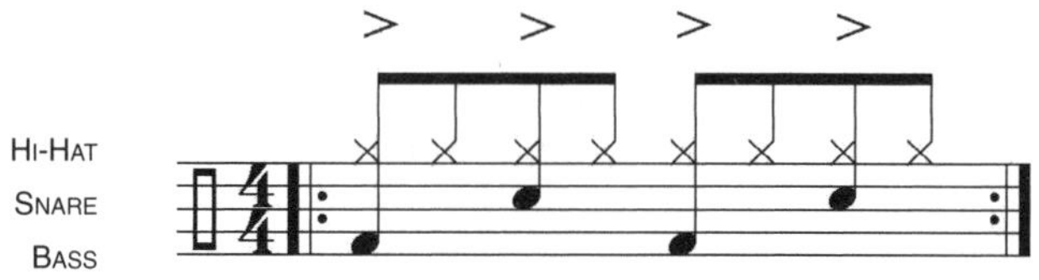

Zouk

Zouk is a primarily Haitian style that utilizes live and/or electric percussion. Combining other Caribbean styles, such as Mergengue, Guaguanco, Beguine and African styles like Soukous, the grooves generally have a strong "four on the floor" feel and usually feature a repetitive snare drum rim click rhythm. **The tempo range is quarter note = 92–126 bpm.**

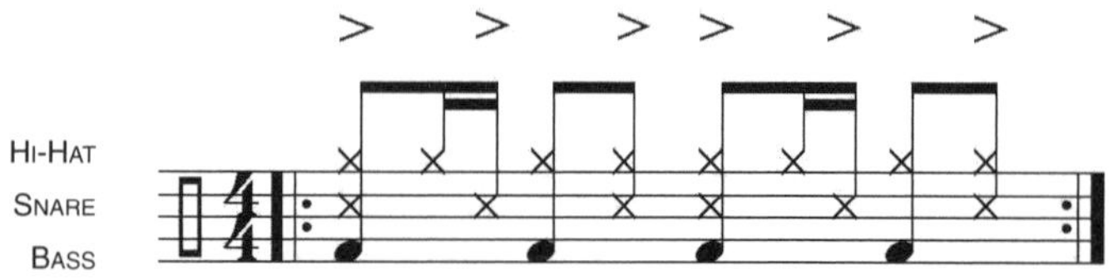

29 Fills

In addition to grooves, the other common element in drum set playing is fills. But however much fills may add to a song, they are never as essential as the groove itself, which serves as the indispensable backbone for the entire ensemble. Nonetheless, the integration between the two should be seamless, and fills should be played as solidly as grooves. When used in a song, fills usually serve as transitional figures connecting phrases and/or sections of a song (e.g., leading from the last measure of a verse to the chorus).

Keep in mind that the fills presented here are not definitive, but instead are suggestions on which one can develop endless variations.

Unlike grooves, which define a style through established (that is, standard) patterns, there are few standard fills. However, types of fills vary from style to style, and the ones presented below are common and practical choices. (A list of grooves appears at the end of this appendix specifying which fills are most suitable for each drumming style, and typical ways to begin and end fills in a particular style.) Of course, if a fill sounds good that isn't listed in or runs contrary to the suggestions in this chapter, the authors encourage you to use it.

Unless otherwise specified, the sticking for each fill is alternate, (i.e., R L R L or L R L R). For the sake of simplicity, each fill initially appears written for the snare drum. Choices and suggestions for orchestration are included in the final variation(s) of each fill. All of the fill examples have been written in 4/4 time. To transfer them into another time signature, simply retain the note value and adjust the number of notes per measure accordingly. The fill choices and variations have been organized by 1) Note Value; 2) Accents; 3) Syncopation; 4) Orchestration. If you want more rhythmic possibilities, refer to *Modern Reading Text in 4/4*, by Louis Bellson with Gil Breins, and/or *Syncopation for the Modern Drummer*, by Ted Reed. Suggested listening examples follow every particular type of fill, and the names of the drummers who played them are included.

Regarding orchestration, any of the following fills can sound good when played on different surfaces. Some drum orders will sound better than others, so experiment. Generally nothing will sound "bad" as long as the time is steady and the fill ends smoothly.

The fills in this chapter are arranged in sequential order from dotted quarters down to 16th notes in lengths of one or two measures. Though there are larger (whole notes, half notes) and smaller (32nds, 64ths, etc.) note values, the ones offered in this chapter are the most common and practical. Finally, to further an understanding of creating fills using rolls, see the Rudiments appendix.

Dotted Quarter Note

Example

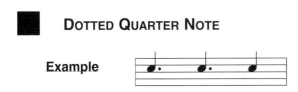

NOTES: Any surfaces work when using the dotted quarter note as a fill, though lower toms often work quite well. Variation 3 shows the two measure example orchestrated between the high, mid, and low toms. As the dotted quarter note is a long note value, it is possible to "fill up" a dotted quarter note fill with the ride and foot patterns of the groove being played. Because dotted quarters are "long notes," no accents are suggested in these fills.

Variation 1

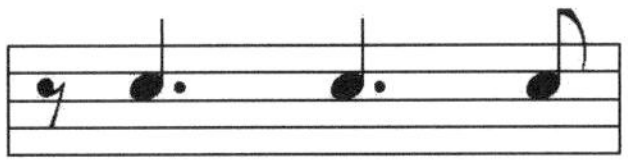

Variation 2

Variation 3

Tom 1
Snare
Floor Tom

Suggested Listening Example: “Cheers” theme song, fill in the 4th and 8th bars of each chorus.

Quarter Note

Example

Variation 1

Variation 2

This fill features a polyrhythm played over two measures (see Polyrhythm chapter).

Variation 3

Snare
Floor Tom

NOTE: As with the dotted quarter note fill, it is possible to “fill up” a quarter note fill with the ride and foot patterns of the groove being played.

Suggested Listening Example: "(I Can’t Get No) Satisfaction" by the Rolling Stones, fill in middle of each chorus (Charlie Watts); “Lucy in the Sky with Diamonds” by the Beatles, fill in measure before each chorus (Ringo Starr); “China Grove” by the Doobie Brothers, fill in measure before the second chorus (Mike Hossack/Keith Knudsen).

Quarter Note Triplets

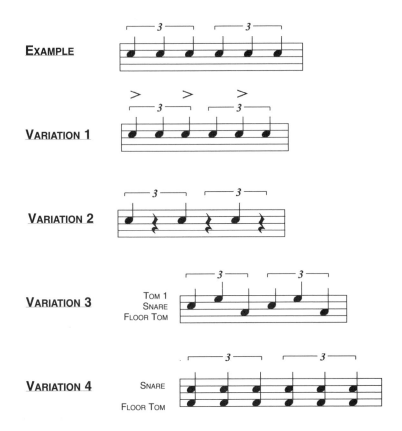

Example

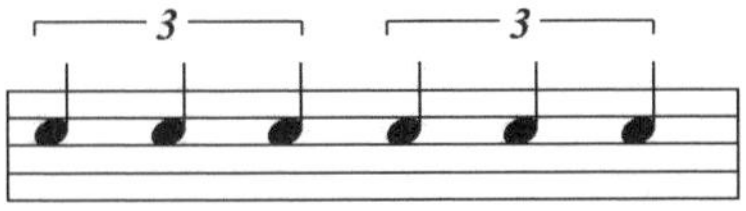

Variation 1

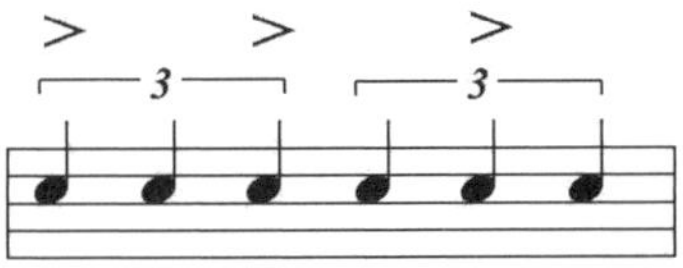

Variation 2

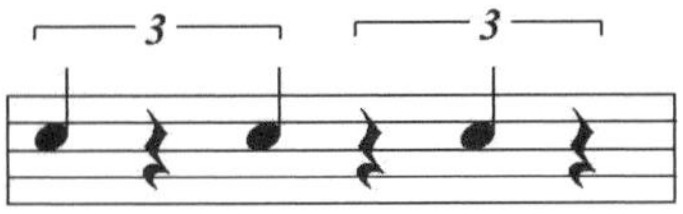

Variation 3

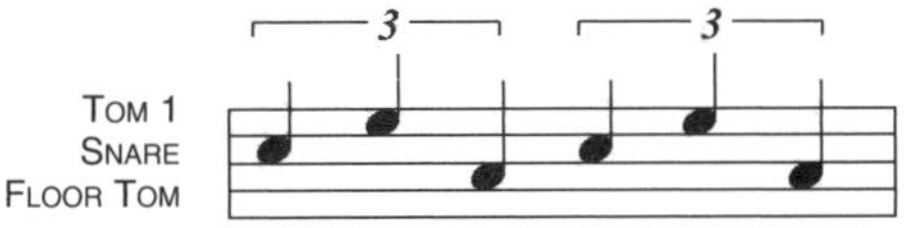

Variation 4

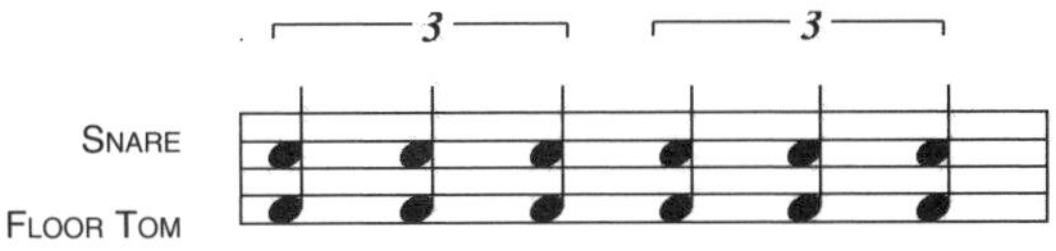

Suggested Listening Example: "Oye Como Va" performed by Santana, band hits at end of crescendo in interlude (Michael Shrieve); "Radar Love" by Golden Earring, band hits 1 measure before drum solo and drum fill eighth measure of last chorus (Cesar Zuiderwijk); "Whole Lotta Love" by Led Zeppelin, fill in last two 2 beats of measure before guitar solo (John Bonham).

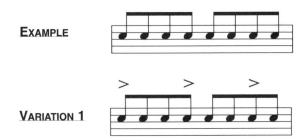

Eighth Notes

Example

Variation 1

Variation 2

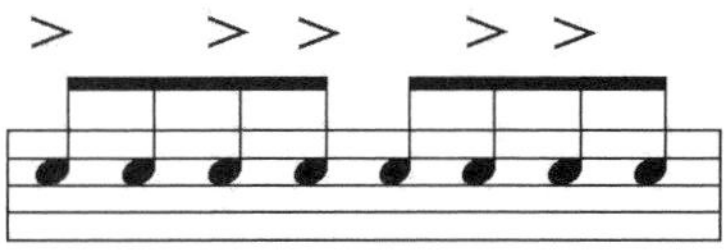

Variation 3

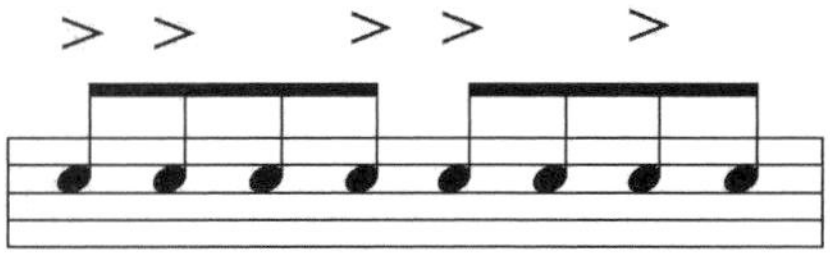

Variation 4

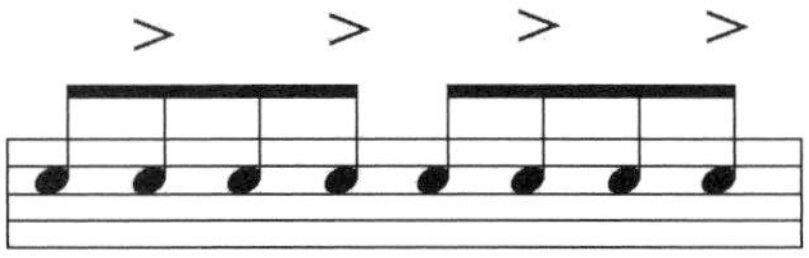

Variation 5

Variation 6

Variation 7

Variation 8

Variation 9

Variation 10

Variation 11

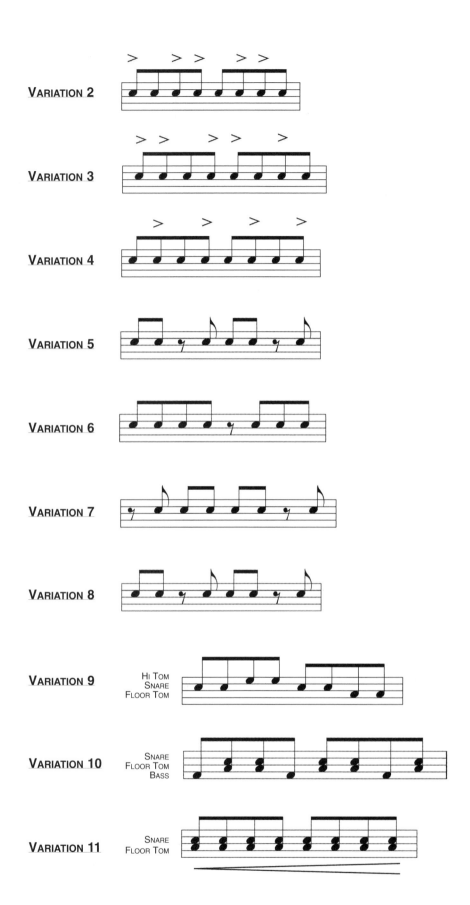

NOTE: Variations 1 through 4 feature different placement of accents. The notes in between the accents can be omitted to produce more syncopated rhythms. In variations 5 through 8, unaccented notes can be played in the place of the rests to create more variations.

Suggested Listening Examples: "Back In the USSR" by The Beatles, fill in measure before 2nd verse and bridge, and at end of bridge (Ringo Starr); "One Way or Another" by Blondie, build up in measures 5 through 8 of intro (Clem Burke); "Heartbreaker" by Pat Benetar, build up during 1-1/2 measure crescendo before the 1st & 2nd chorus and 2 measure crescendo before a cappella interlude & chorus (Myron Grombacher); "China Grove" by the Doobie Brothers, fill in measure before the second chorus (Mike Hossack/Keith Knudsen).

Eighth Notes Off The Beat

The example and variations listed in this section generally avoid strikes on the downbeats of each measure. This in effect "hides" the beat.

Example

Variation 1

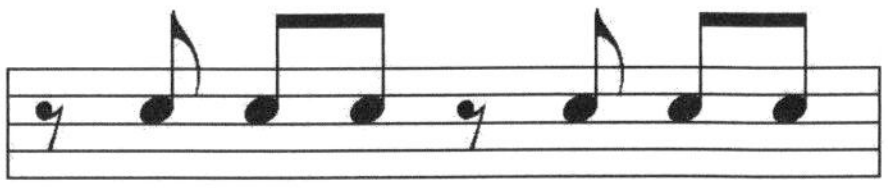

Variation 2

Variation 3

Variation 4

Suggested Listening Examples: "Love is a Battlefield" by Pat Benetar, fill before 3rd chorus (Myron Grombacher); "Love Her Madly" by The Doors, opening fill (John Densmore); "King of the Hill" theme song, band hits in the 9th and 10th measures of song (Ralph Humphrey); "China Grove" by the Doobie Brothers, fill in the 2nd to last measure of intro (Mike Hossack/Keith Knudsen).

Swung Eighth Notes

Example

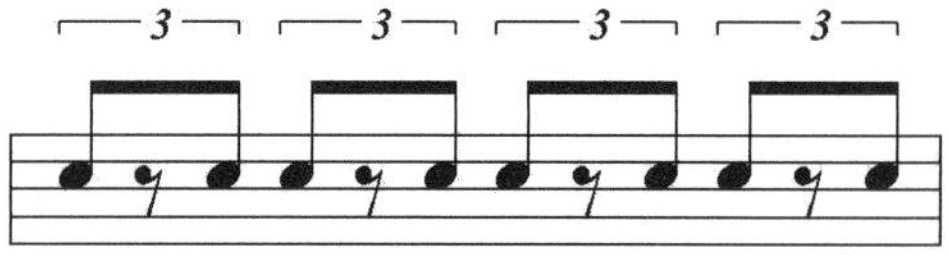

Variation 1

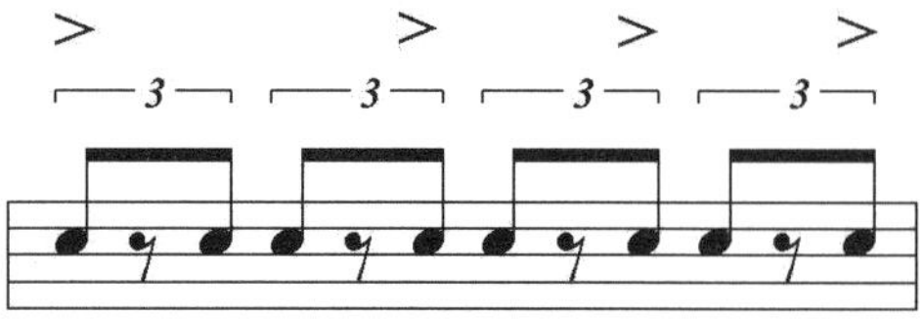

Variation 2

This variation breaks up the swing pattern over two measures to create a "3 versus 4" polyrhythm (see Polyrhythm chapter).

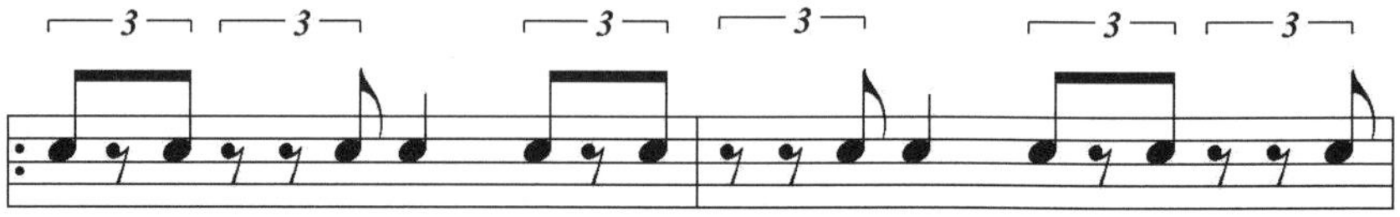

Variation 3

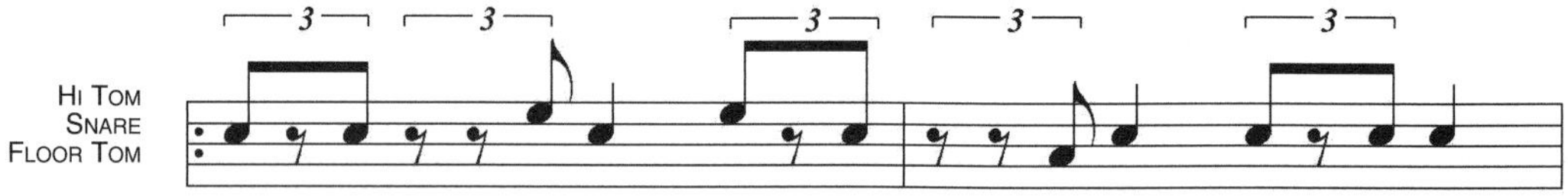

Suggested Listening Examples: "Bad, Bad Leroy Brown" by Jim Croce, fill in measure before each verse and chorus (Gary Chester); "Thing Called Love" performed by Bonnie Raitt, fill in last measure before each verse and chorus.

Swung Eighth Notes, Off The Beat (written as triplets)

Example

Variation 1

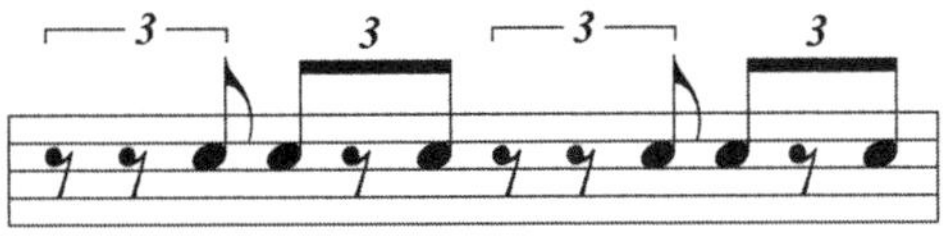

Variation 2

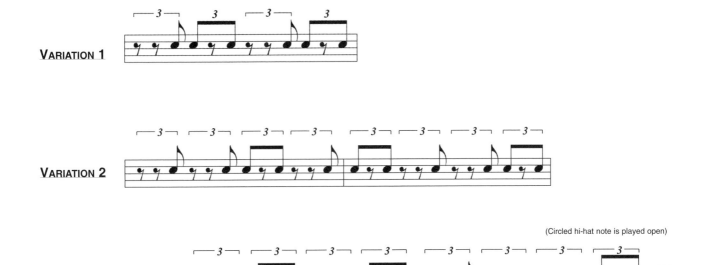

(Circled hi-hat note is played open)

Variation 3

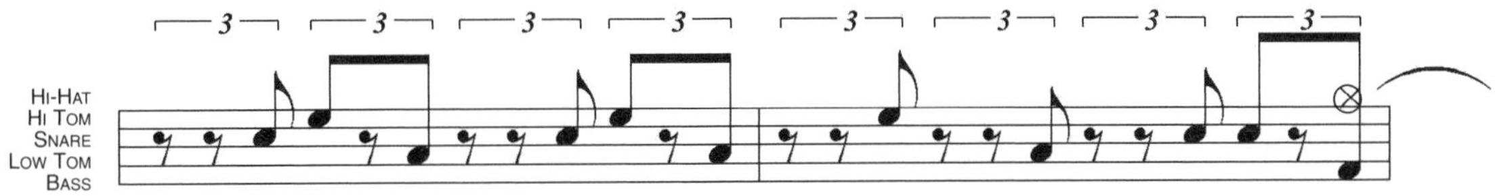

Suggested Listening Examples: "I Know A Little" by Lynyrd Skynyrd, band hits in intro of song and after each chorus (Artimus Pyle); "This Cat's on a Hot Tin Roof" by the Brian Setzer Orchestra, band hits in last two measures at end of song before final hold.

Eighth Note Triplets

Example

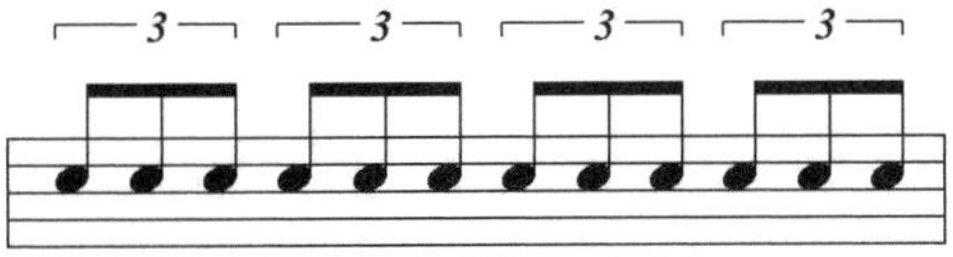

Variation 1

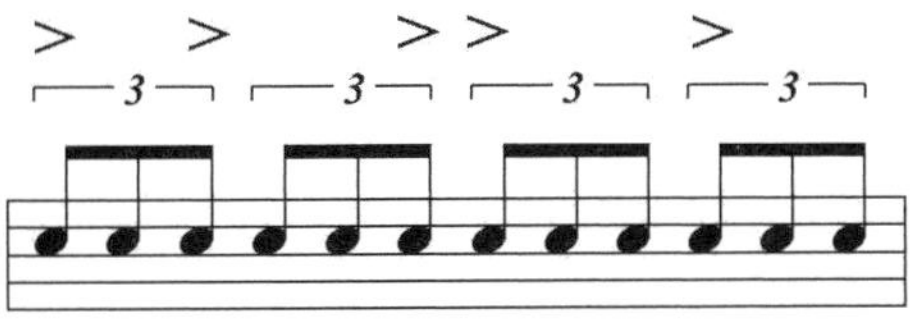

Variation 2

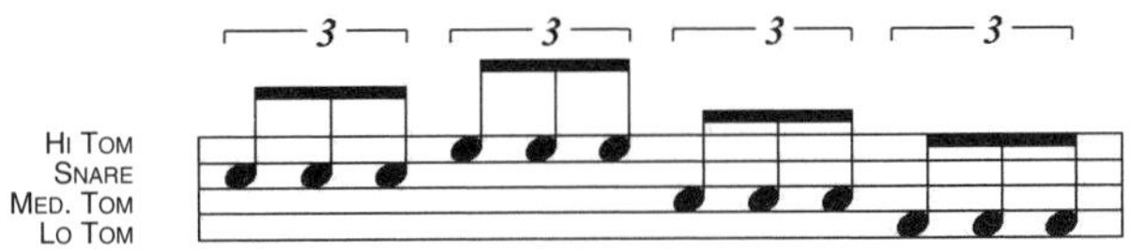

Variation 3

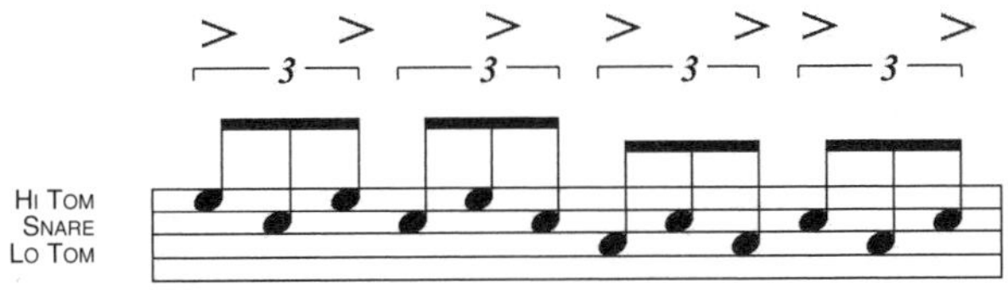

Suggested Listening Examples: "Detroit Rock City" by Kiss, fill in last 2 measures of short drum solo in the middle of the song (Peter Chris); "We're Not Gonna Take It" by The Who, fill at end of song before last chorus (Keith Moon); "It's Still Rock n' Roll to Me" by Billy Joel, fill 1 measure before 2nd verse (Liberty DeVitto).

Eighth Note Triplets Off The Beat

Example

Variation 1

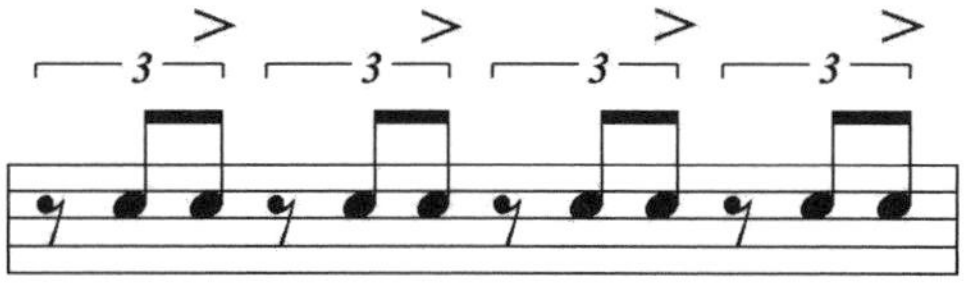

Variation 2

Variation 3

Suggested Listening Examples: "Smackwater Jack" by Carol King, fills throughout each chorus (Joel O'Brien); "La Grange" by ZZ Top, fill at end of intro and interlude before full guitar and bass join in (Frank Beard).

Sixteenth Notes

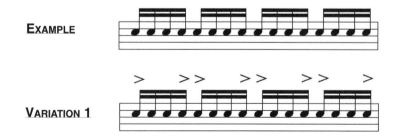

Example

Variation 1

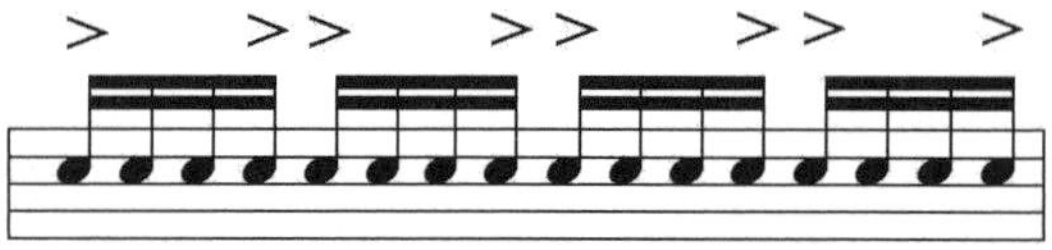

Variation 2

Variation 3

Suggested Listening Examples: "Born to Run" by Bruce Springsteen, fill in first 2 measures and last 2 measures of intro, right before sax solo and throughout song (Earnest "Boom" Carter); "I Love Rock n' Roll," performed by Joan Jett, fill in opening of intro (Lee Crystal); "Sweet Emotion" by Aerosmith, fill before musical "outro" of song (Joey Kramer); "Whole Lotta Love" by Led Zeppelin, fill in pick up measure out of last vocal fermata (hold) of song (John Bonham).

Sixteenth Notes Off The Beat

Example

Variation 1

Variation 2

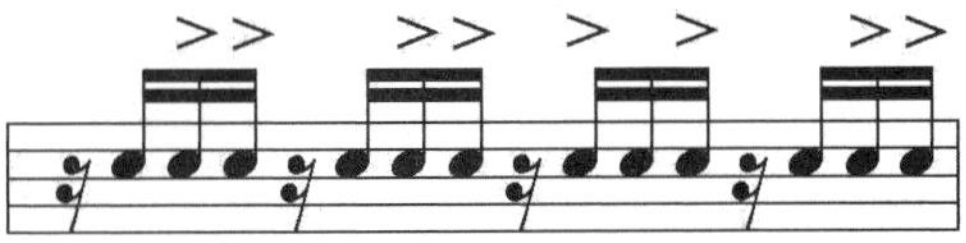

Variation 3

Variation 4

Suggested Listening Examples: "Burning Down the House" by Talking Heads, beats 2 and 3 of fill in last measure of intro (Chris Frantz); "Tommy the Cat" by Primus, fill in first measure of intro (Tim "Herb" Alexander).

Sixteenth Note Triplets and Sextuplets

Example

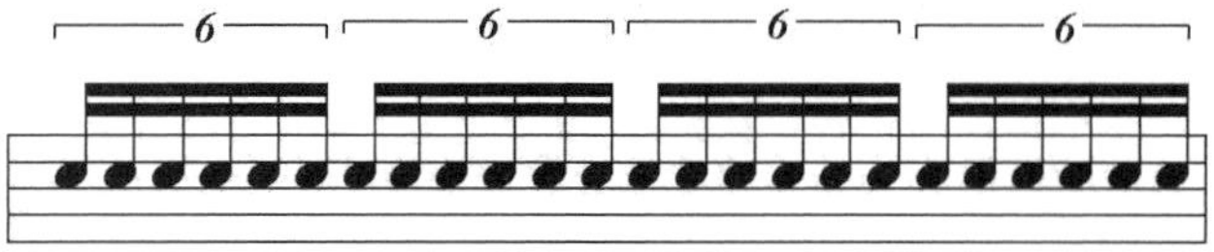

Variation 1

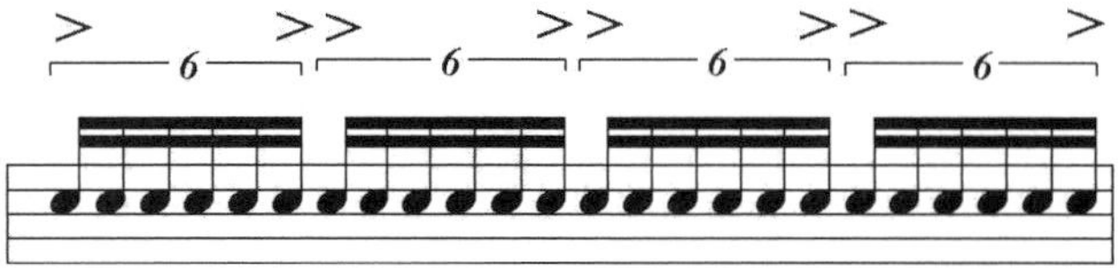

Variation 2

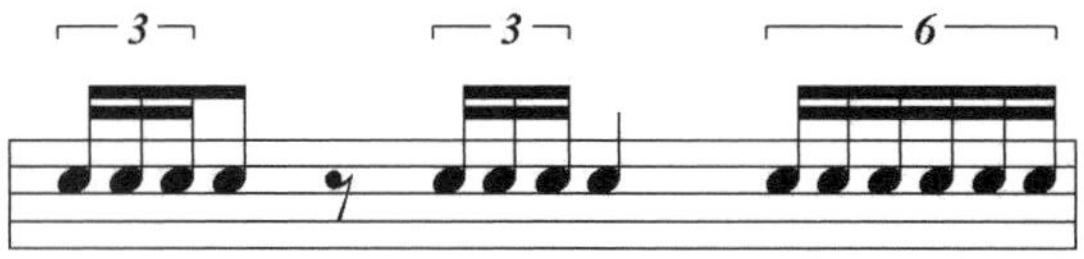

Variation 3

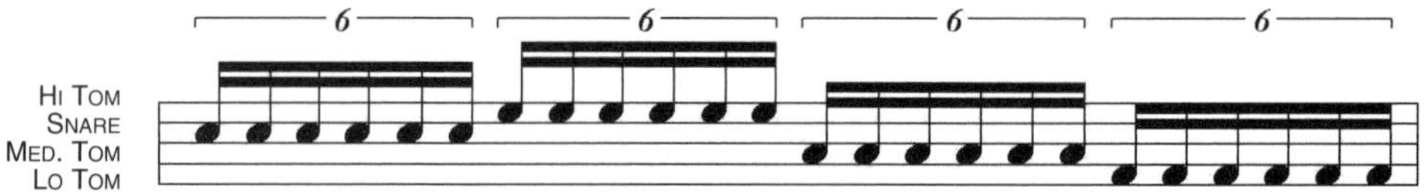

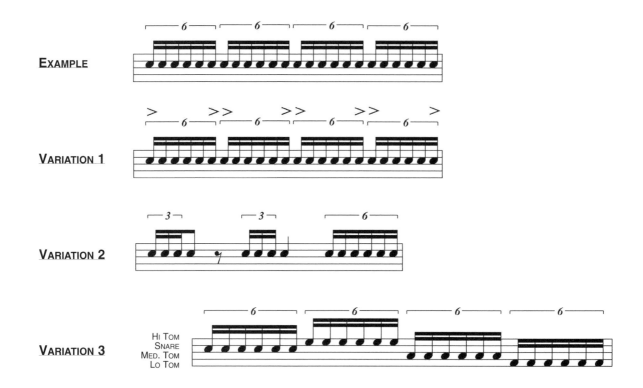

Suggested Listening Examples: "Whole Lotta Love" by Led Zeppelin, fill in first two 2 beats of measure before guitar solo (John Bonham); "Soul Sacrifice" by Santana, first drum fill in song and first and last fill of drum solo (Michael Shrive).

The Use of Fills

Though most fills can be used in all styles of music, there are stylistic considerations specific to genres. The guide below specifies which types of fills are most practical in particular styles.

Beginning and Ending Fills

Most styles use fills which end on beat 1 of the following measure. The consistent exceptions to this are 4/4 Afro-Cuban grooves (with fills commonly ending on beat 4 of the fill measure, referred to as the "Ponche," with the groove resuming on beat 2 of the following measure) and Jazz (with fills commonly ending on the + of beat 4 of the fill measure, with the groove resuming on beat 2 of the following measure).

1. Acid Jazz

Hip Hop: All fills, depending on whether the fill is swung or straight.

Standard Rock Beat: All fills

Jazz/Swing Pattern: All fills ("straight" fills are less common)

Bossa Nova: Dotted quarters, 8th notes, 8th notes "off the beat," 16th notes

Mambo: Quarter note triplets, 8th notes, 8th notes "off the beat," 8th-note triplets, 8th notes triplets "off the beat"

Displaced Funk: All fills (though triplet groupings are less common in a straight feel)

2. African

World Beat: Dotted quarters, 8th notes, 8th notes "off the beat," 16th notes

Soukous: Dotted quarters, 8th notes, 8th notes "off the beat," 16th notes

Bikutsi: Quarter note triplets, Shuffle/Swing 8th notes, Shuffle/Swing 8th notes "off the beat," 8th note triplets, 8th note triplets "off the beat"

3. AfroCuban

Afro-Cuban 6/8 Patterns for drum set: Quarter note triplets, Shuffle/Swing 8th notes, Shuffle/Swing 8th notes "off the beat," 8th note triplets, 8th note triplets "off the beat" (triplets written as standard 8th notes in 6/8)
Bomba: Quarter note triplets, 8th notes, 8th notes "off the beat," 8th note triplets, 8th notes triplets "off the beat"
Cascara for drum set: Quarter note triplets, 8th notes, 8th notes "off the beat," 8th note triplets, 8th notes triplets "off the beat"
Cha Cha: All fills; Abenico
Guaguanco: Quarter note triplets, 8th notes, 8th notes "off the beat," 8th note triplets, 8th notes triplets "off the beat"
Mambo: Quarter note triplets, 8th notes, 8th notes "off the beat, 8th note triplets, 8th notes triplets "off the beat"
Merengue: Dotted quarter notes, quarter notes, quarter note triplets, 8th notes, 8th notes "off the beat"
Mozambique: Quarter note triplets, 8th notes, 8th notes "off the beat," 8th note triplets, 8th notes triplets "off the beat"
Songo: Quarter note triplets, 8th notes, 8th notes "off the beat," 8th note triplets, 8th notes triplets "off the beat"
Beguine: 8th notes, 8th notes "off the beat," 16th notes, 16th notes "off the beat" (depending on the tempo)
Bolero: Dotted quarter notes, quarter notes, quarter note triplets, 8th notes, 8th notes "off the beat," 16th notes
Conga: Quarter note triplets, 8th notes, 8th notes "off the beat," 8th note triplets, 8th notes triplets "off the beat"
Cumbia: Quarter note triplets, 8th notes, 8th notes "off the beat," 8th note triplets, 8th notes triplets "off the beat"
Danzon: 8th notes, 8th notes "off the beat," 16th notes, 16th notes "off the beat" (use sparingly)
Palito: Quarter note triplets, 8th notes, 8th notes "off the beat," 8th note triplets, 8th notes triplets "off the beat"
Pilon: Quarter note triplets, 8th notes, 8th notes "off the beat," 8th note triplets, 8th notes triplets "off the beat"
Plena: Quarter note triplets, 8th notes, 8th notes "off the beat," 8th note triplets, 8th notes triplets "off the beat"

4. Blues

Shuffles (all): Quarter note triplets, Shuffle/Swing 8ths, 8th note triplets, 8th note triplets "off the beat"
12/8 Pattern: Shuffle/Swing 8ths, 8th note triplets, 8th note triplets "off the beat" (triplets are written as 8th notes in 12/8)
Straight Blues Rock: All fills (though triplet groupings are less common in a straight feel)
Blues Rumba: Dotted quarters, 8th notes, 8th notes "off the beat," 16th notes

5. Brazilian

Samba: Dotted quarters, quarter note triplets, 8th notes, 8th notes "off the beat," 8th note triplets
Batukada: Dotted quarters, quarter note triplets, 8th notes, 8th notes "off the beat," 8th note triplets
Baiao: Dotted quarters, quarter note triplets, 8th notes, 8th notes "off the beat," 8th note triplets
Bossa Nova: Dotted quarters, 8th notes, 8th notes "off the beat," 16th notes
Afoxe: Dotted quarters, quarter note triplets, 8th notes, 8th notes off the beat, 8th note triplets

6. Cajun/Zydeco

Two-Step: 8th notes, 8th notes "off the beat"
Waltz: Shuffle/Swing 8ths or straight 8th notes (depending on whether the feel is swung or straight)
Zydeco Shuffle: Shuffle/Swing 8ths, 8th note triplets
Zydeco Train: 8th notes, 8th notes "off the beat"
Cajun/Zydeco: 8th notes, 8th notes "off the beat"

7. Caribbean

Calypso: Dotted quarters, 8th notes, 8th notes "off the beat," 16th notes
Soca: Dotted quarters, 8th notes, 8th notes "off the beat,"" 16th notes
Ska: All fills (16th note triplets not as common)
Reggae: Shuffle/Swing 8ths, 8th note triplets, 8th note triplets "off the beat"

8. Country

Bluegrass: All fills (though triplet groupings are less common in a straight feel)
Western Swing: Shuffle/Swing 8ths, 8th note triplets, 8th note triplets "off the beat"
Country Two-Step: 8th notes, 8th notes "off the beat," 16th notes

Country Shuffle: Shuffle/Swing 8ths, 8th note triplets, 8th note triplets "off the beat"
Western: Shuffle/Swing 8ths, 8th note triplets (fills are rare)
Train: All fills (though triplet groupings are less common in a straight feel)
Country Rock/Modern Day Country: All fills (though triplet groupings are less common in a straight feel)
Country Waltz: Shuffle/Swing 8ths or 8th notes (depending on whether the feel is swung or straight)
Country Ballad: All fills (use sparingly, depending on whether the feel is swung or straight)

9. Disco

All fills

10. Drum 'n Bass

8th notes, 8th notes "off the beat," 16ths, 16th notes "off the beat"

11. Flamenco

Dotted quarters, 8th notes, 8th notes "off the beat," 16th notes

12. Funk

New Orleans Funk: 8ths, 8th notes "off the beat" (played "in the crack")
Displaced Funk: All fills (though triplet groupings are less common in a straight feel)
Linear Funk: All fills
Ghost Note Funk: All fills (though triplet groupings are less common in a straight feel)
Funk Rock: All fills (though triplet groupings are less common in a straight feel)
Cascara Funk: Quarter note triplets, 8th notes, 8th notes off the beat, 8th note triplets, 8th note triplets off the beat, 16th notes, 16th note triplets

13. Gospel

Fast Gospel (Polka groove): 8ths notes, 8th notes "off the beat"
Rock: All fills (though triplet groupings are less common in a straight feel)
12/8: Shuffle/Swing 8ths, 8th note triplets, 8th note triplets "off the beat" (triplets are written as 8th notes in 12/8)
Waltz: Shuffle/Swing 8ths or 8th notes (depending on whether the feel is swung or straight)

14. Hip Hop/Rap

All fills (swung or straight depending on feel)

15. Jazz

New Orleans Second Line: 8ths, 8th notes "off the beat," rolls (played "in the crack")
Dixieland: Dotted quarters, Shuffle/Swing 8ths, 8th note triplets, 8th note triplets "off the beat"
Big Band: All fills (straight fills are less common)
Small Band (Be Bop, Cool Jazz, Avante Garde): All fills (straight fills are less common)
Jazz Waltz: Shuffle/Swing 8ths, Shuffle/Swing 8ths "off the beat," 8th note triplets, 8th note triplets "off the beat"
Jazz Ballad: All fills (use sparingly, and adjust depending on whether it is a swung or straight feel)

16. Klezmer

Bulgar: 8th notes, 8th notes "off the beat," rolls (use sparingly)
Freylakhs: 8th notes, 8th notes "off the beat," rolls (use sparingly)
Hora: 8th notes, 16th notes, rolls
Khosidil: 8th notes, 8th notes "off the beat," rolls (use sparingly)
Terkisher: 8th notes, 8th notes "off the beat," rolls (use sparingly)

17. Latin Rock

Standard Rock: All fills
Baiao: Dotted quarters, quarter note qriplets, 8th notes, 8th notes "off the beat," 8th note triplets
Mambo: Quarter note triplets, 8th notes, 8th notes "off the beat," 8th note triplets, 8th notes triplets "off the beat"
Rumba: 8th notes, 8th notes "off the beat," 16th notes, 16th notes "off the beat"

18. March

Standard Marches: All fills (depending on whether the feel is swung or straight)
New Orleans Second Line: 8ths, 8th notes "off the beat," rolls (played "in the crack")
Cuban Comparsa: Quarter note triplets, 8th notes, 8th notes "off the beat," 8th note triplets, 8th notes triplets "off the beat"
Brazilian Baiao: Dotted quarters, quarter note triplets, 8th notes, 8th notes "off the beat," 8th note triplets

19. Metal

Standard Rock: All fills
Fast Metal (Polka groove): 8th notes, 8th notes "off the beat," 8th note triplets, 8th note triplets "off the beat"
Double Bass Grooves: All fills
Blast Beat: 8th notes, 16th notes

20. Middle Eastern Contemporary

Dotted quarters, 8th notes, 8th notes "off the beat," 16th notes
Traditional Rai/Maghreb (Example): Quarter note triplets, Shuffle/Swing 8th notes, Shuffle/Swing 8th notes "off the beat," 8th note triplets, 8th note triplets "off the beat"
Traditional Rai/Maghreb (Variation): Dotted Quarters, 8th notes, 8th notes "off the beat," 16th notes
Contemporary Rai: (see grooves' respective chapters)

21. Odd Time

All fills (to play fills in an odd time signature, retain the note value and adjust the number of notes per measure accordingly)

22. Polka

8ths notes, 8th notes "off the beat"

23. Punk Rock

All fills
Fast Punk (Polka groove): 8th notes, 8th notes "off the beat"

24. Rock n' Roll

Early Rock n' Roll: All fills (depending on whether the feel is swung or straight)
Rockabilly: Shuffle/Swing 8ths, 8th note triplets, 8th note triplets "off the beat"
Standard Rock: All fills
Half-Time Rock: All fills
Fusion: All fills

25. Surf

Standard Surf: 8th notes, 16th notes
Surf Ballad: Dotted quarter notes, quarter notes, quarter note triplets, 8th notes, 8th notes "off the beat," 16th notes
Surf Tom pattern: 8ths, 16ths

26. Techno

8th notes, 16th notes, 16th note triplets

27. Wedding Dances

Tarantella: Shuffle/Swing 8ths, 8th note triplets
Hava Nagila: 8th notes, 8th notes "off the beat" (use sparingly)
Rumba: 8th notes, 8th notes "off the beat," 16th notes, 16th notes "off the beat"
Tango: Quarter notes, 8th notes, 16th notes
Waltzes: 8th notes
Fox Trot: 8th notes

28. Miscellaneous Grooves

Arara: Quarter note triplets, Shuffle/Swing 8th notes, Shuffle/Swing 8th notes "off the beat," 8th note triplets, 8th note triplets "off the beat" (triplets written as standard 8th notes in 6/8)
Boogaloo: All fills
Guajira: 8th notes, 8th notes "off the beat," 16th notes, 16th notes "off the beat" (use sparingly)
Habanera: Quarter notes, 8th notes, 16th notes
Israeli Dance Pattern: 8ths notes, 8th notes "off the beat"
Jig: 8th note triplets (triplets written as 8th note in 6/8)
Joropo: 8th notes, 8th notes off the beat, 16th notes, 16th notes off the beat
Nanigo: Quarter note triplets, Shuffle/Swing 8th notes, Shuffle/Swing 8th notes "off the beat," 8th note triplets, 8th note triplets "off the beat" (triplets written as standard 8th notes in 6/8)
Norteno: Quarter note triplets, 8th notes, 8th notes "off the beat, 8th note triplets, 8th notes triplets "off the beat"
Pachanga: Quarter note triplets, 8th notes, 8th notes "off the beat," 8th note triplets, 8th notes triplets "off the beat"
Pasa Doble: 8ths notes, 8th notes "off the beat"
La Raspa: 8th Note Triplets
Tex Mex (example 1): All Fills
Tex Mex (example 2): 8ths notes, 8th notes "off the beat"
Zouk: Dotted quarters, 8th notes, 8th notes "off the beat," 16th notes

30 POLYRHYTHMS

POLYRHYTHMS ARE A USEFUL WAY to create interesting rhythmic variations. They consist of the combination of two contrasting (that is, you *cannot* subdivide one into the other) rhythmic pulses simultaneously, with the contrasting but simultaneous rhythms normally played on different instruments. (This includes different drums in the drum set.)

There are two main types of polyrhythms: rhythms that carry "over the bar" and rhythms that exist "within the bar."

"Over the bar" rhythms are those in which the standard pulse does not change, yet displaced accents, syncopation, and/or note groupings create the illusion of a different pulse or an alternate time signature coexisting with the primary pulse/time signature. As an example, if a drummer was playing a straight 4/4 pattern and a bassist was playing a pattern consisting of *five* quarter notes, a 5-versus-4 "over the bar" polyrhythm would result.

Polyrhythms "within the bar" use nonstandard groupings of notes that are played against the standard groupings in any given meter. Again, this means that the notes in one group *cannot* subdivide into the notes in the other; the simplest example of this is eighth note triplets ("swung" eighth notes) played simultaneously with eighth note duplets ("straight" eighth notes).

Examples of the two types of polyrhythms follow. Although polyrhythmic patterns are often useful as fills, they can also create interesting grooves. They're also very useful in fostering the development of limb independence.

As with fill choices, the possibilities for polyrhythms are far too extensive to enumerate, and those listed below are intended merely as a starting point. For the sake of simplicity and unity, the grooves and fills are representative of the Rock genre, while polyrhythms themselves can be used in virtually all styles.

"OVER THE BAR" POLYRHYTHMS

To produce "over the bar" polyrhythmic patterns, a good method is to begin with a simple groove such as the Standard Rock beat in 4/4 and simultaneously play a rhythm that contrasts to the main 4/4 pulse (for example, accenting every second or fourth eighth note would not offset the 4/4 pulse, whereas accenting every third or fifth eighth note would). The examples below all feature polyrhythms produced through displaced accents.

"3" Polyrhythm Grooves

Example (CD 2, Track 93)

The main example is a Standard Rock Beat with the ride hand playing polyrhythmic groupings of "3." (That is, every third eighth note is accented.) Since the polyrhythm imposes a "3 over 2" feel, it takes three bars for the accent to return to beat 1.

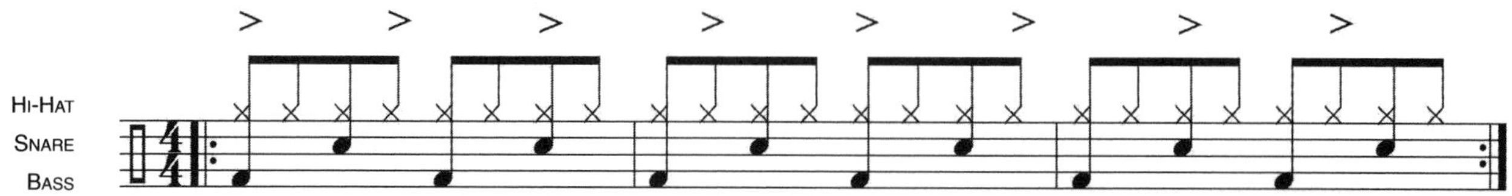

Variation

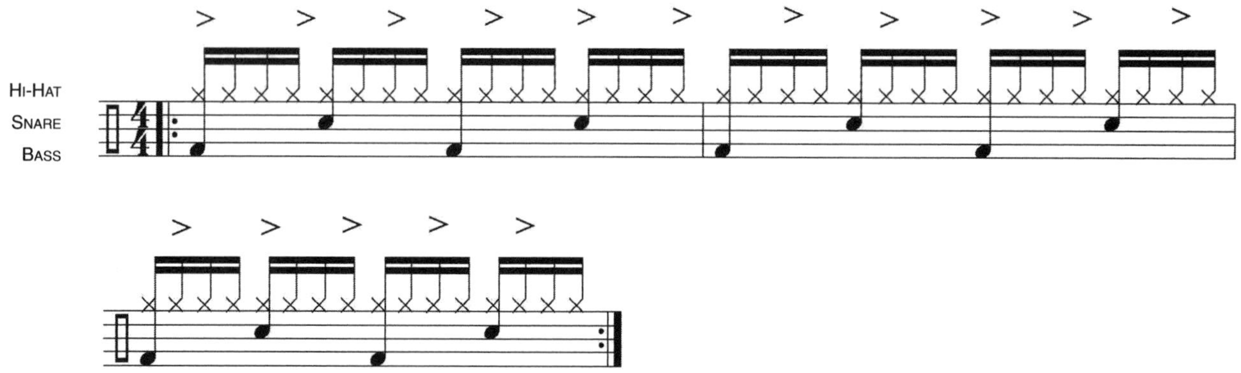

"3" Polyrhythm Fills

Example (CD 2, Track 94)

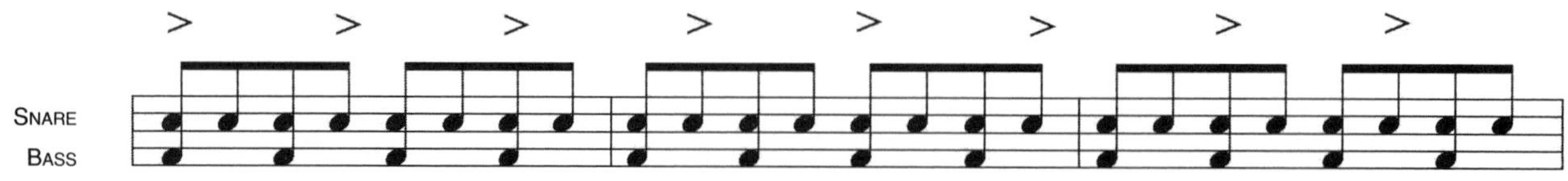

Variation

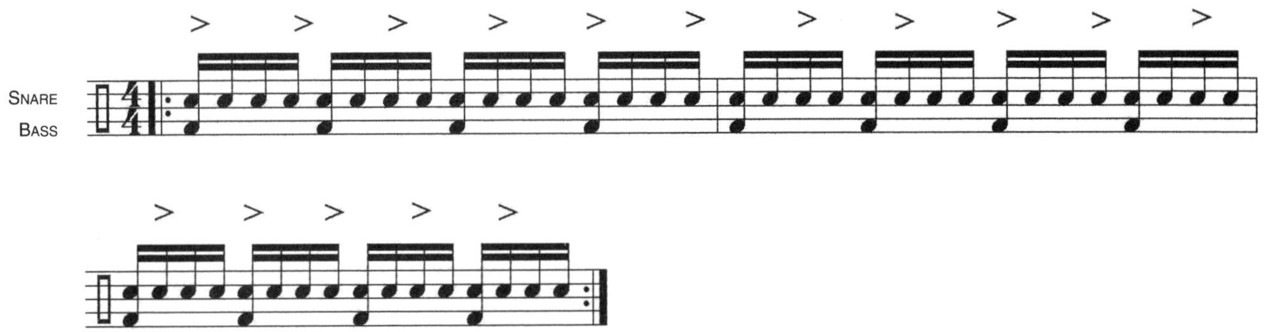

NOTE: It is usually impractical to play a fill for more than two measures. The length of the above fills simply displays the full extent of the polyrhythm. When used in fills, polyrhythms can begin or end on any beat or note of the measure. In addition, leaving out the unaccented notes changes the accented polyrhythms above into syncopated polyrhythms.

"5" Polyrhythm Grooves

Example (CD 2, Track 95)

This is a Standard Rock Beat with the accents of the ride hand shifted into polyrhythmic groupings of "5" (2 + 3). Since the polyrhythm imposes a "5 over 2" feel, it takes five bars of the groove for the accent to return to beat 1.

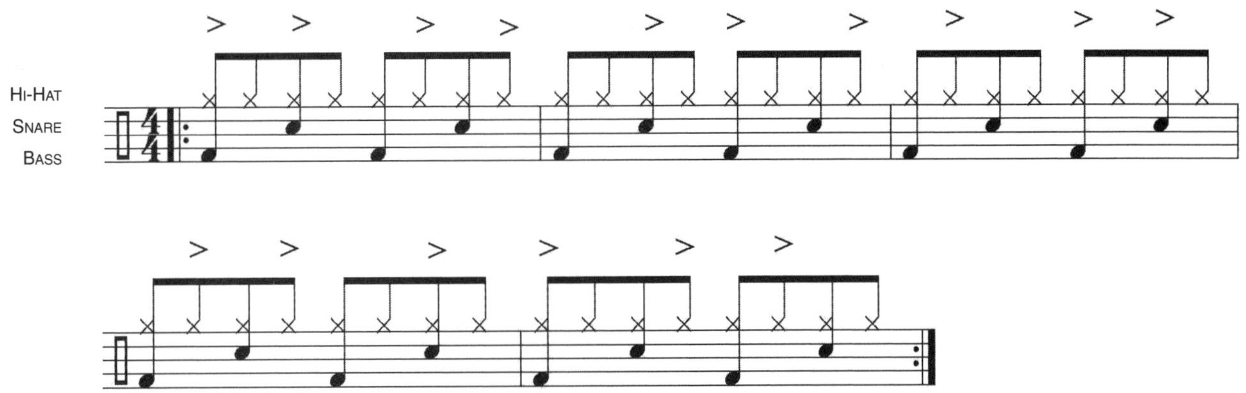

Variation

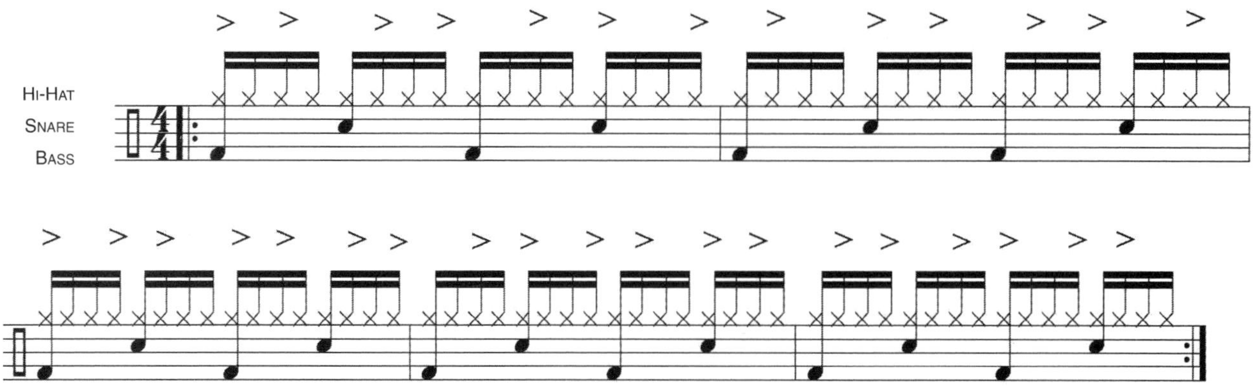

"5" Polyrhythm Fills

Example (CD 2, Track 96)

Variation

NOTE: "3" and "5" note groupings are included above as a practical starting point. To create your own polyrhythmic patterns, take any familiar drum pattern and overlay any contrasting rhythm.

"Within the Bar" Polyrhythms

To produce "within the bar" polyrhythmic patterns, it's good to begin with a simple groove such as the Standard Rock Beat in 4/4 and superimpose odd-numbered groupings within the measure (for example, "5s," "7s," etc.) so that the pattern repeats itself on either each beat or the start of each measure. All of the following are "5" patterns, featuring sixteenth note, eight note, or quarter note quintuplets.

Example 1 (Groove) (CD 2, Track 97)

Please note that the following example and variation are ***not*** polyrhythms. Rather, they simply subdivide the beat into quintuplets. However, when other players are present, these patterns will *produce* polyrhythms when combined with the normal subdivisions of the beat (into duplets or triplets) played by the other performers.

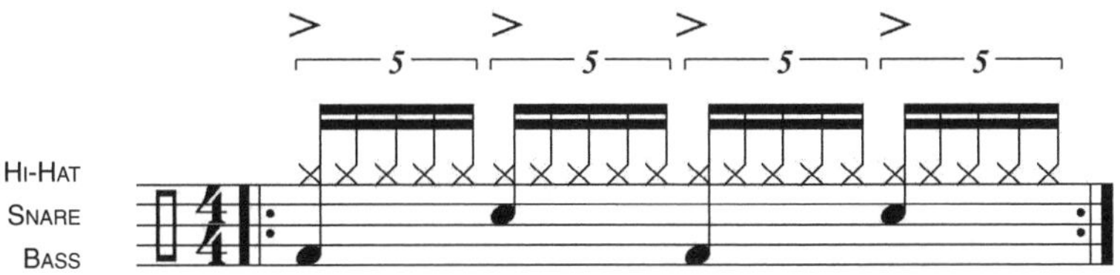

Variation (Fill) (CD 2, Track 98)

Alternate sticking is a good idea for this fill.

Example 2 (Groove) (CD 2, Track 99)

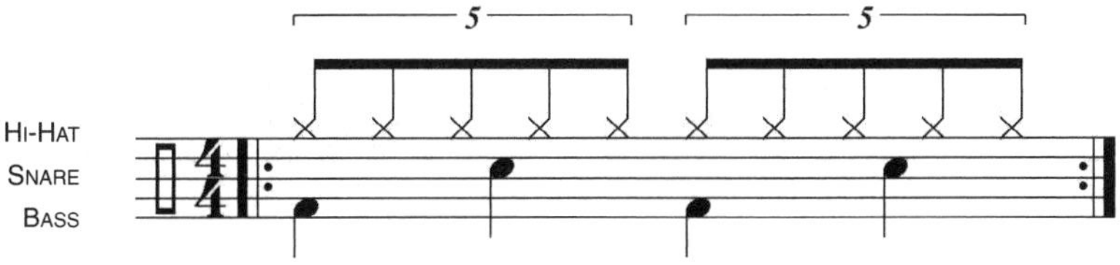

Variation (Fill)

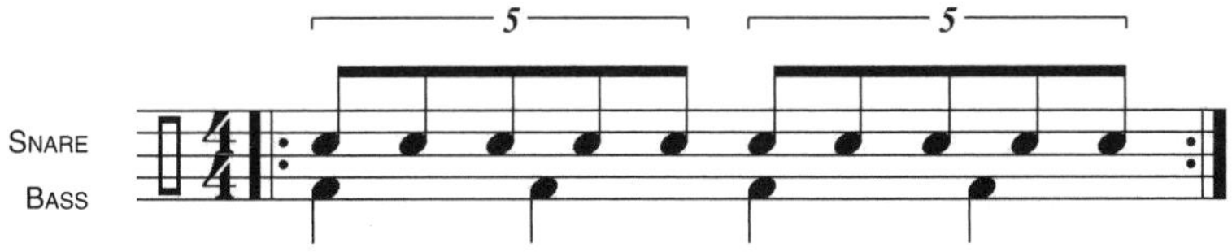

Example 3 (Groove)

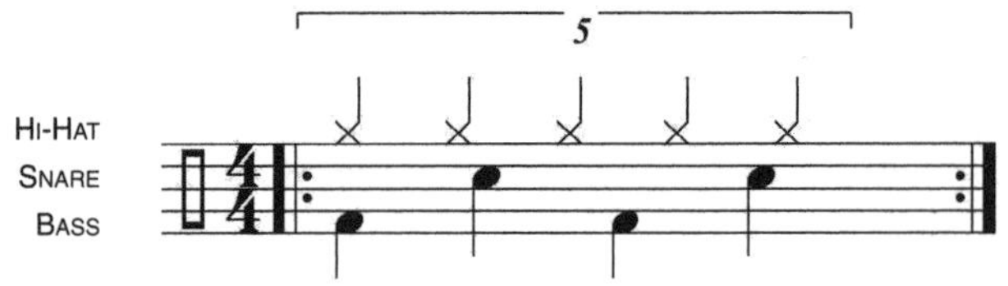

Variation (Fill)

NOTES: All of the above examples and variations (both "within the bar" and "over the bar") employ "3" and "5" polyrhythms. It's easy to create more complicated ("7"s, etc.) polyrhythms, but "3"s and "5"s are the most common types and serve well to illustrate how to create polyrhythms.

Another way to create "across the bar" polyrhythms in an ensemble is to have the rhythm section play in one time signature and the other instruments (horns, etc.) play in another. The simplest example of this would be to have the rhythm section play a simple duple meter (2/4 or 4/4) and for the other instruments to play in 3/4. (Of course, to avoid utter chaos in such a situation, all instruments must play at the same tempo.)

A TUNING

THE SOUNDS OF THE DRUM SET are not only determined by the pitch of the drums, but also by the various percussive instruments within the "trap set" such as cymbals, cowbells, woodblocks, etc. This appendix focuses on the sounds of the drums and cymbals, as choices for the other instruments are largely discretionary. Below is a list of each style covered in this book and its most appropriate tuning/cymbal choices. As no tuning sounds are definitive, the authors offer the choices below as reliable, accurate, and practical suggestions.

The abbreviations and descriptions below cover the possible choices for tuning combinations:

Bass Drum (BD)—high or low, (muffled or open)
Snare Drum (SD)—high, medium, low, (muffled or open)
Toms—high or low (i.e. all toms at a higher pitch or all toms at a lower pitch)
Cymbals (Cym)—dark, bright or trashy

When more than one choice for drum tuning or cymbal selection is appropriate, we have included all of the most practical options. As most of the tuning/cymbal combinations repeat themselves throughout different styles, the most common ones are labeled with the following names:

Early 20th Century Tuning
BD low (open); SD medium or low (open); Toms high or low; Cym dark or trashy

Traditional Jazz Tuning
BD high (open); SD medium (open); Toms high; Cym dark

Traditional Rock Tuning
BD low (muffled); SD high or medium (open or muffled); Toms low; Cym bright

Hip Hop/Drum & Bass Tuning
BD high (open or muffled); SD high (open or muffled); Toms high; Cym trashy or bright

In addition to tuning your drums higher or lower, it is possible to alter the pitch of your set by using smaller or larger drums.

The tuning for all of the styles below is identified by one of the above terms. If the tuning suggestion deviates from these four possibilities, the authors have named the closest tuning/cymbal combination and the specific differences from the standard tunings.

Styles & Appropriate Tunings

1. Acid Jazz—See the individual styles in their appropriate chapters: Hip Hop, Rock, Jazz, Brazilian (Bossa Nova), Afro-Cuban (Mambo), Funk

2. African—Traditional Rock Tuning

3. Afro-Cuban—Afro-Cuban styles generally require tuning similar to Traditional Rock Tuning except for the "open" (no muffle) snare drum, higher pitched toms, and perhaps brighter cymbals.
BD low (muffled); SD high or medium (open); Toms high; Cym dark or bright

4. Blues—Traditional Rock Tuning

5. Brazilian—Brazilian styles generally require tuning similar to "Traditional Rock Tuning" except for the "open" (no muffle) snare drum, higher pitched toms, and perhaps brighter cymbals.
BD low (muffled); SD high or medium (open); Toms high; Cym dark or bright

6. Cajun/Zydeco—Traditional Rock Tuning

7. Caribbean—Caribbean styles generally require tuning similar to Traditional Rock Tuning, except for a higher pitched snare drum and perhaps higher pitched toms.
BD Low (muffled); SD high (open or muffled); Toms high or low; Cym bright

8. Country—Use either Traditional Jazz Tuning for older styles or Traditional Rock Tuning for more recent styles.

9. Disco—Similar to Traditional Rock tuning except for perhaps higher pitched toms.
BD low (muffled); SD high or medium (open); Toms high or low; Cym bright

10. Drum & Bass / Jungle—Hip Hop/Drum & Bass Tuning

11. Flamenco—Similar to Traditional Rock Tuning except for a higher pitched snare drum and perhaps higher pitched toms.
BD Low (muffled); SD high (open or muffled); Toms high or low; Cym bright

12. Funk—Different Funk styles may require different tunings. The best determining factor is the time period in which the music was originally created.

Older New Orleans Funk: Traditional Jazz Tuning

All other Funk styles: Traditional Rock Tuning

13. Gospel—Traditional Rock Tuning

14. Hip Hop/Rap—Hip Hop/ Drum & Bass Tuning

15. Jazz—Jazz is a combination of many different styles. As it is usually not practical to retune the drums during the course of an evening, the best tuning/cymbal choice will depend on the styles being played.

New Orleans Second Line/Dixieland: Early 20th Century Tuning

Big Band/Small Band/Jazz Waltz/Jazz Ballad: Traditional Jazz Tuning

16. Klezmer—Early 20th Century Tuning

17. Latin Rock—Traditional Rock Tuning

18. March—Tuning will vary depending on style:

Standard Marches: Early 20th Century Tuning

New Orleans Second Line: Early 20th Century Tuning

Cuban Comparsa: Traditional Rock Tuning

Brazilian Baiao: Traditional Rock Tuning

19. Metal—Traditional Rock Tuning

20. Middle Eastern—Contemporary Middle Eastern styles generally require tuning which is similar to Hip Hop/Drum & Bass Tuning except for no muffle on the bass drum and lower toms.
BD high (open); SD high (open or muffled); Toms Low; Cym trashy or bright

21. Odd Time—As Odd Time is generally used in Progressive Rock, Fusion, or Jazz, the tuning would correspond to the particular style.

Progressive Rock & Fusion: Traditional Rock Tuning

Jazz: Traditional Jazz Tuning

22. Polka—Early 20th Century Tuning

23. Punk—Similar to Traditional Rock Tuning except for the use of trashy cymbals.
BD low (open); SD medium or low (open or muffled); Toms low; Cym bright or trashy

24. Rock—Rock n' Roll may require different tunings. The best determining factor is the time period in which the music was originally created.

Early Rock: Traditional Jazz Tuning

Modern Rock: Traditional Rock Tuning

Fusion: Traditional Rock Tuning

25. Surf—Though classified within the genre of Rock, Surf Music emerged in Rock n' Roll's early years and thus requires a drumming sound similar to Traditional Jazz Tuning.

26. Techno—Hip Hop/Drum & Bass Tuning

27. Wedding Dances—All of the different wedding dances can be played in either Traditional Jazz Tuning or Traditional Rock Tuning.

B Rudiments

Rudiments are fundamental to drumming and can be quite useful in developing drumming facility. They are as important to drummers as scales are to players of pitched instruments. We've reproduced the 40 standard rudiments here thanks to the kind permission of the Percussive Arts Society. We encourage you to practice these rudiments on the snare drum alone and to experiment with playing them on different surfaces.

Roll Rudiments

1. Single Stroke Roll

R L R L R L R L

2. Single Stroke Four

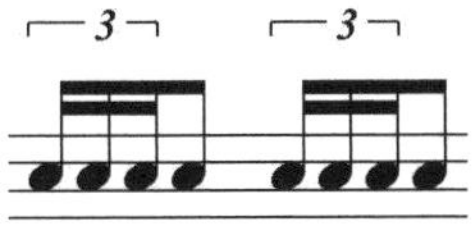

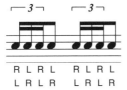

R L R L R L R L
L R L R L R L R

3. Single Stroke Seven

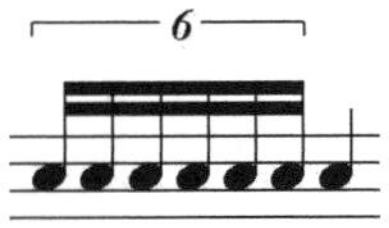

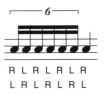

R L R L R L R
L R L R L R L

4. Multiple Bounce Roll

5. Triple Stroke Roll

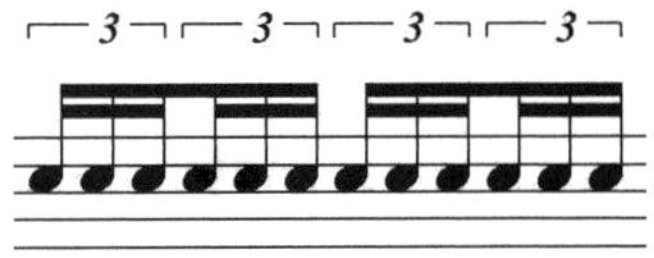

R R R L L L R R R L L L

6. Double Stroke Open Roll

R R L L R R L L

7. Five Stroke Roll

R R L L

8. Six Stroke Roll

R L R L
L R L R

9. Seven Stroke Roll

R L R L
L R L R

10. Nine Stroke Roll

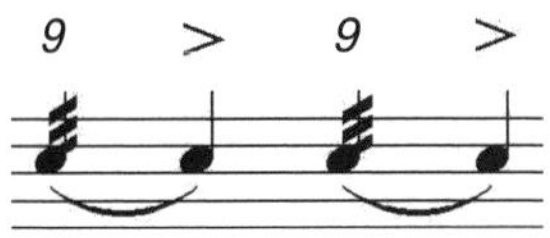

R R L L

11. Ten Stroke Roll

R R L R R L
L L R L L R

12. 11 Stroke Roll

R R L R R L
L L R L L R

13. 13 Stroke Roll

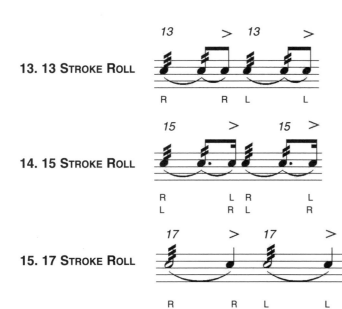

R R L L

14. 15 Stroke Roll

R L R L
L R L R

15. 17 Stroke Roll

R R L L

Diddle Rudiments

16. Single Paradiddle

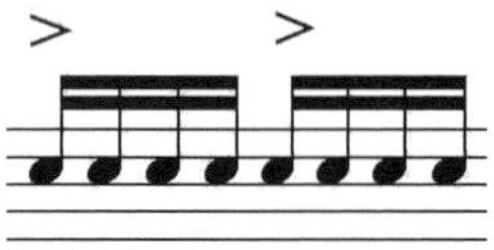

R L R R L R L L

17. Double Paradiddle

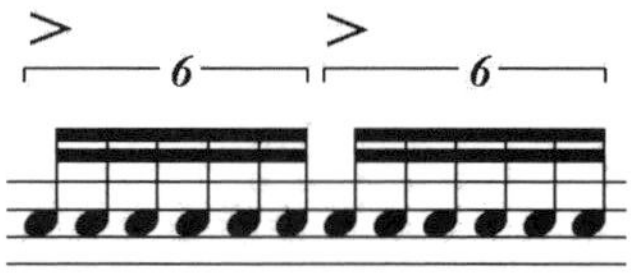

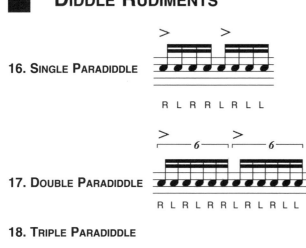

R L R L R R L R L R L L

18. Triple Paradiddle

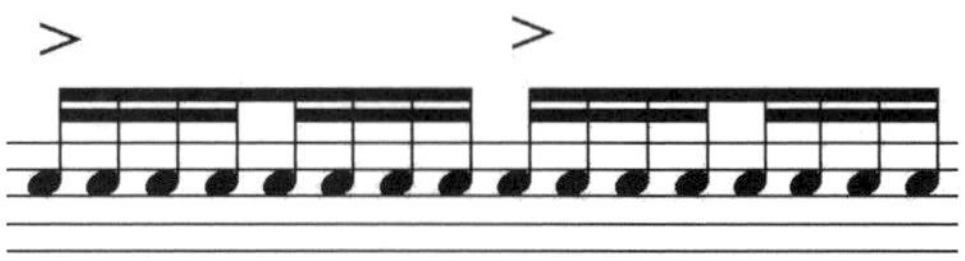

R L R L R L R R L R L R L R L L

19. Single Paradiddle-Diddle

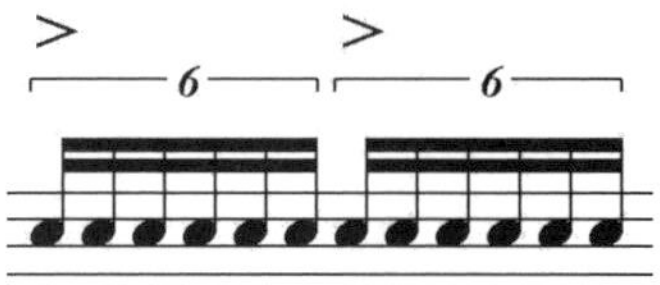

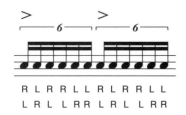

R L R R L L R L R R L L
L R L L R R L R L L R R

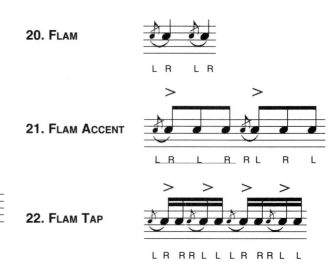

Flam Rudiments

20. Flam

L R L R

21. Flam Accent

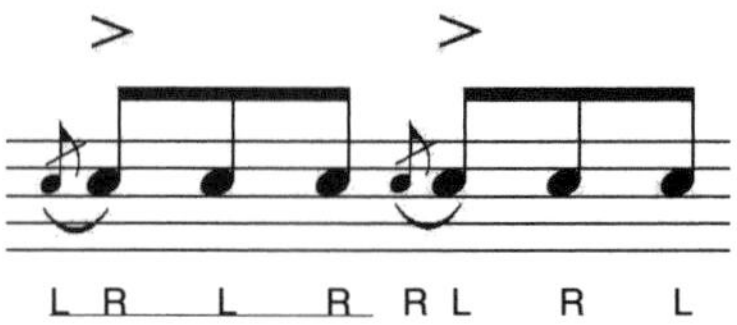

L R L R R L R L

22. Flam Tap

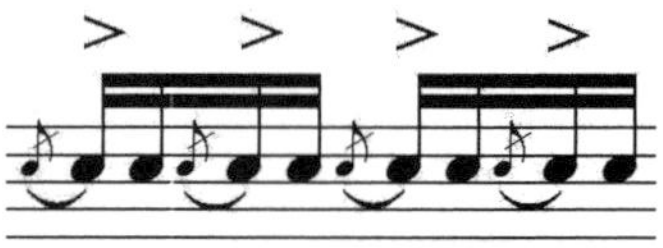

L R R R L L L R R R L L

23. Flamacue

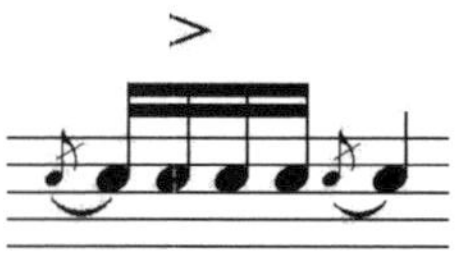

L R L R L L R
R L R L R R L

24. Flam Paradiddle

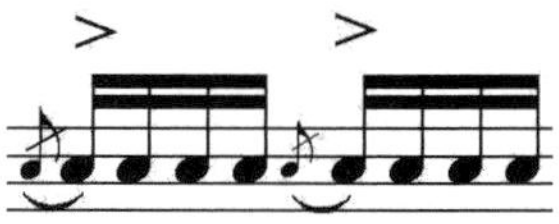

L R L R R R L R L L

25. Single Flammed Mill

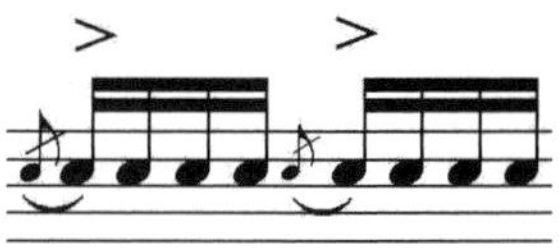

L R R L R R L L R L

26. Flam Paradiddle-Diddle

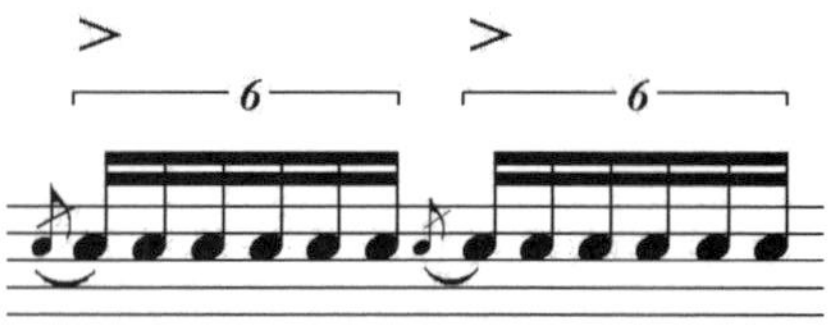

L R L R R L L R L R L L R R

27. Pataflafla

L R L R R L L R L R R L

28. Swiss Army Triplet

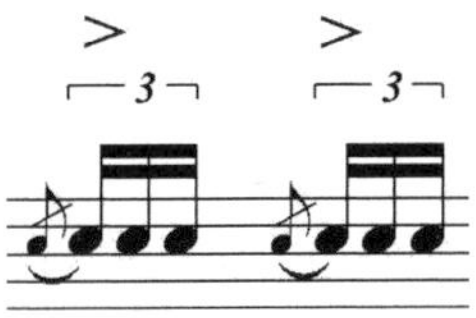

L R R L L R R L
R L L R R L L R

29. Inverted Flam Tap

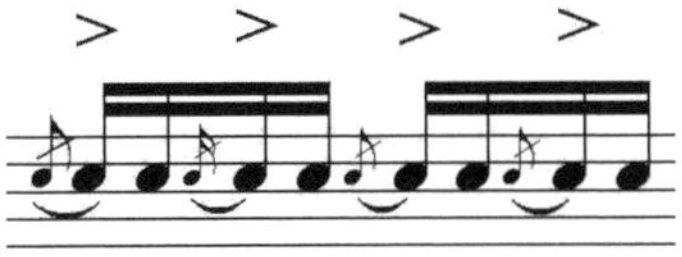

L R L R L R L R L R L R

30. Flam Drag

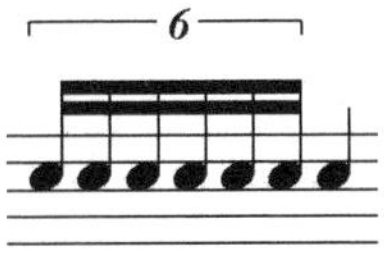

L R L L R R L R R L

Drag Rudiments

31. Drag

LL R RR L

32. Single Drag Tap

LL R L RR L R

33. Double Drag Tap

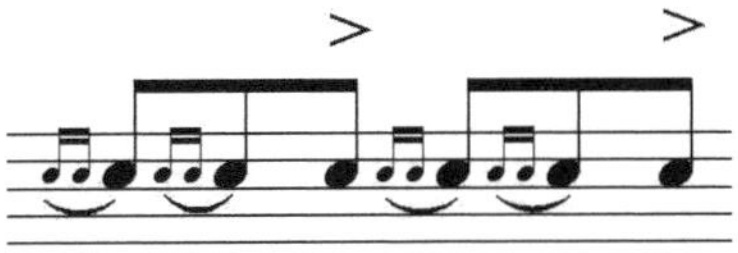

LL R LL R L RR L RR L R

34. Lesson 25

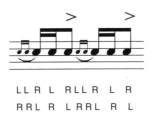

LL R L R LL R L R
RR L R L RR L R L

35. Single Dragadiddle

RR L R R LL R L L

36. Drag Paradiddle #1

R LL R L R R L RR L R L L

37. Drag Paradiddle #2

R LL R LL R L R R L RR L RR L R L L

38. Single Ratamacue

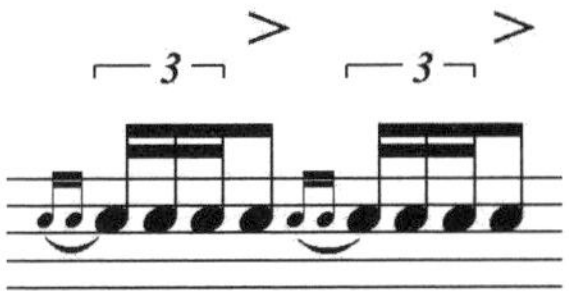

LL R L R L RR L R L R

39. Double Ratamacue

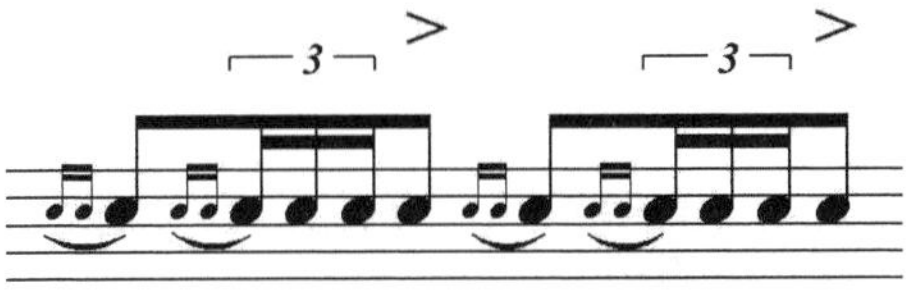

LL R LL R L R L RR L RR L R L R

40. Triple Ratamacue

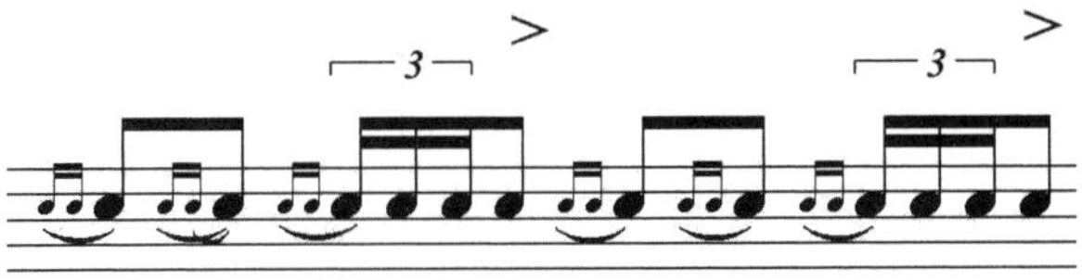

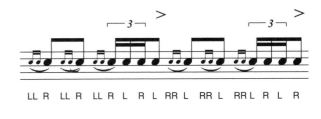

LL R LL R LL R L R L RR L RR L RR L R L R

C Most Commonly Played Grooves

As you go through this book, you'll notice a number of things; one of them is that a handful of grooves appear over and over again. This is no accident: Styles bear resemblances to one another, and so do some of the grooves used in them.

If you're learning new grooves and want them to be as useful as possible, the grooves in this appendix would be a good place to start. Learn these eight-grooves, and you'll have a command of grooves (either exactly as written here or in slightly modified form) that can be used in 20 styles. Please see the chapters covering the individual styles for modifications to particular grooves.

Standard Rock Beat (CD 2, Track 80)

This is probably the most common groove in pop music (at least North American pop music). There are many variations on it, and the tempo will vary depending on the style. It's used in Rock, Blues, Country, Metal, Surf, Acid Jazz, Reggae (Rockers), and Zydeco. **The most common tempo range is quarter note = 110–120 bpm.**

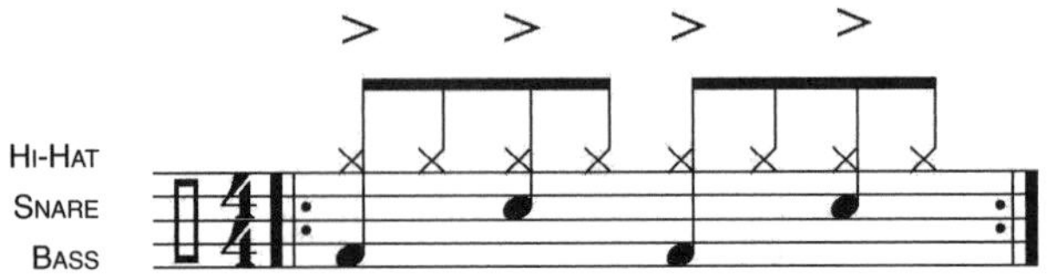

Standard Blues Shuffle (CD 1, Track 51)

This is also a very common groove in American popular music. It's used in Blues, Rock, Country, Western, Gospel, and Zydeco. **The tempo range is quarter note = 80–160 bpm.**

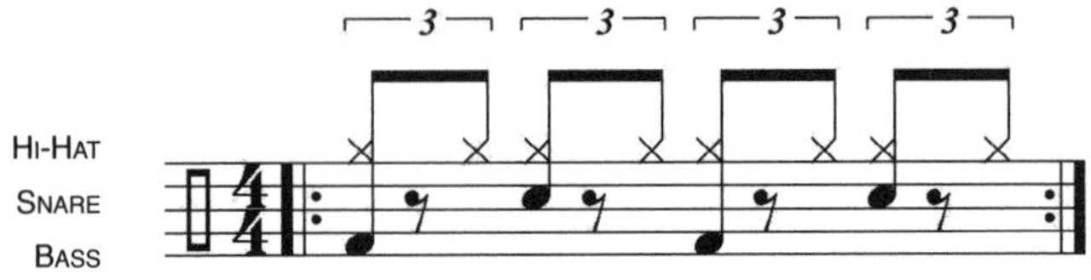

POLKA (CD 2, Track 76)

This Polka Beat is surprisingly versatile. Although felt and written in 2/4 in Polka, it's used in many styles written in and thought of as 4/4 styles (though it's still felt in "two"). In addition to Polka, it's used in Rock, Punk, Gospel, Tex-Mex, and Norteña. The tempo range will vary depending on style, with Tex-Mex and Norteña being on the slower end and Punk being on the brighter end. **The tempo range is quarter note = 184–260 bpm.**

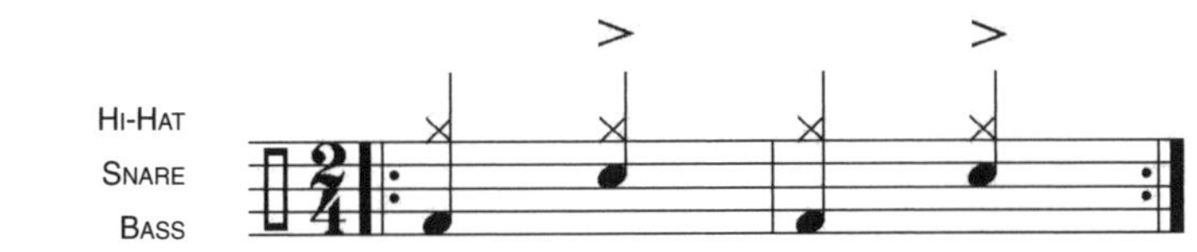

MAMBO (CD 1, Track 25)

The Mambo is probably the most common Latin groove. It's used in Afro-Cuban (Salsa), Blues, Latin Rock, and Acid Jazz. This is the primary example in the Afro-Cuban chapter. The pattern will vary slightly from this when used in Latin Rock, Blues, and Acid Jazz. **The tempo is quarter note = 180–220 bpm.**

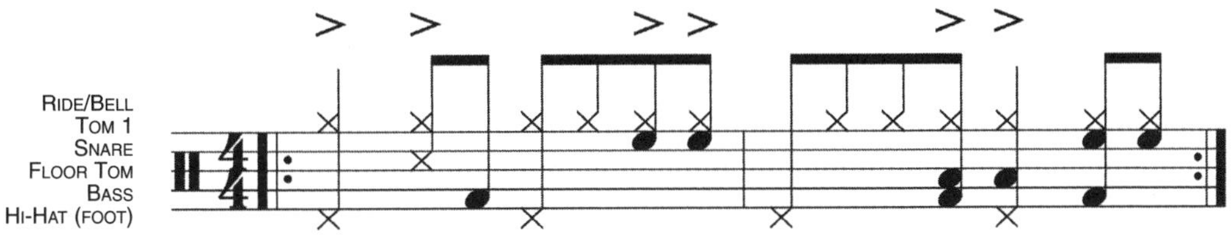

WALTZ (CD 1, Tracks 80 & 83; CD 2, Tracks 90 & 91)

The Waltz is the most common 3/4 groove, and can be played either swung (e.g., European Waltz), straight (e.g., Zydeco Waltz), or simply played on the beats (allowing the other players to determine if it's swung or straight). Accented beats vary depending on Waltz style. It's used in Cajun, Zydeco, Jazz, and Country, and also as a wedding dance. **Quarter note = 126–208 bpm.**

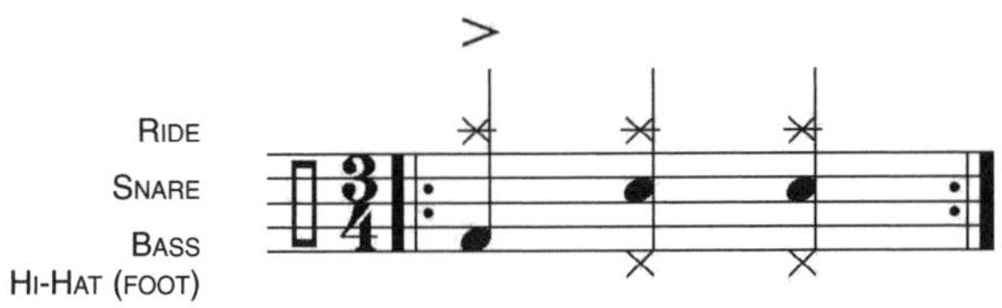

Jazz Ride Pattern / Rockabilly Beat (CD 2, Track 78)

This very common groove features the Jazz Swing pattern on the ride cymbal. It's used in Blues, Jazz, Country, Western Swing, Acid Jazz, and Rockabilly. The unembellished Jazz Swing pattern (just the hi-hat and hi-hat foot—CD2, Track 42) is also useful. **Tempos vary greatly with this pattern depending on style, from a low of about 80 bpm for Country ballads up to about 260 bpm for bop and other very fast jazz tunes.**

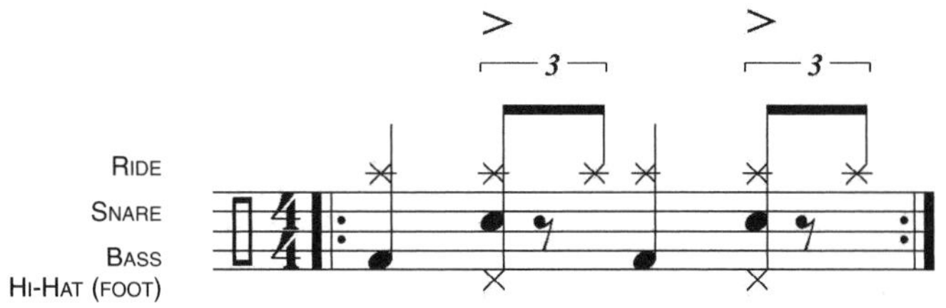

Train Beat (CD 2, Track 1)

This driving groove is commonly used in Bluegrass, Country, Rock, Rockabilly (played either swung or straight), and Zydeco (played straight, swung, or "in the crack"). Tempos will vary a bit depending on the style. **Quarter note = 80–160 bpm.**

Soca (CD 1, Track 87)

This groove can be used in a surprising variety of styles. In addition to Soca, it can be used in Flamenco, Rai, and Latin Rock. **Quarter note = 108–132 bpm.**

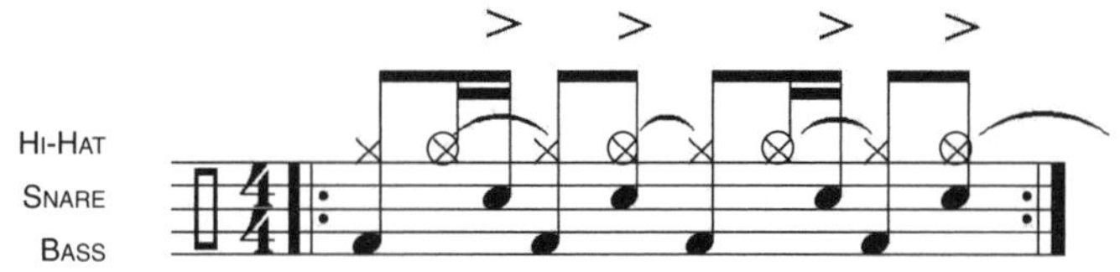

D LISTENING

THE LISTENING EXAMPLES in this appendix were chosen because they are good representatives of their styles. We've listed them in chronological order because this will help the listener to appreciate how they've developed.

ACID JAZZ

Emergency on Planet Earth, by Jamiroquai; Sony Soho2 (1993)
Reachin' (A New Refutation of Time and Space), by Digable Planets; Elektra/Cooltempo (1993)
Brother Sister, by Brand New Heavies; Delicious Vinyl (1994)
Groove Collective, by Groove Collective; Warner Music (1994)
Layin' Low in the Cut, by Alphabet Soup; Mammoth Records (1995)
Crazy Horse Mongoose, by Galactic; Volcano (1998)
Best of Acid Jazz, by various artists; Metro Music (2001)
Fueled for the Future, by United Future Organization; Compost (2006)
Acid Jazz Complete Anthology1968-2010, by various artists; Music Brokers (2010)

AFRICAN

World Beat

Rex Lawson's Greatest Hits, by Rex Lawson; Flame Tree (1997)
Red Hot + Riot: The Music and Spirit of Fela Kuti; MCA (2002)
Electric Highlife, by various artists; Naxos (2002)
Best of the Classic Years, by King Sunny Ade; Shanachie (2003)
Bokoor Beats: Vintage Afro-Beat, by Afro-Rick & Electric Highlife; Otrabanda (2007)

Soukous

Africa Worldwide: 35th Anniversary Album, by Tabu Ley Rochereau; Rounder Select (1996)
Avis De Recherche, by Zaiko Langa Langa; Stern's (1997)
The Rough Guide to Congolese Soukous, by Various Artists; World Music Network (2000)
Gozando, by Lokassa and Soukous Stars; Sterns Music (2008)
Super Soukous, by Diblo with Loketo; Shanachie Ent. (2006)

Bikutsi

Bikutsi Rock, by Les Tetes Bruless; Shanachie (1992)
Bikutsi Pop: Songs of So' Forest, by So' Forest; Naxos (2002)
Le Testament du Bikutsi Vol. 2, by various artists; TJR Prod. (2011)
Le Testament du Bikutsi Vol. 3, by various artists; TJR Prod. (2011)

AFRO-CUBAN

Many Afro-Cuban styles are often represented on one recording. The following are considered classic recordings which include various styles.

Dance Mania, by Tito Puente; RCA International (1958)
Con Un Poco de Songo, by Batacumbele; Tierrazo Records (1981)
Master Sessions, Vol. 1, by Cachao; Sony (1994)
Ritmo, Sonido, y Estilo, by Libre Conjunto; Montuno Records (1994)

The following are representative of individual styles:

Guaguanco

La Reina del Guaguanco, by Celeste Mendoza; ATX (1993)
Guaguanco, by Los Papines; Big World/Continental (1995)
Noche de la Rumba, by Celeste Medoza & Changuito; Tumi (2001)
Guaganco con Carlos "Patato" Valdez, by Orlando Contreras; Teca Music (2005)

Mambo

Mambo King 100th LP, by Tito Puente; RMM Records (1996)
Mambo Mucho Mambo, by Machito and His Afro-Cuban Orchestra; Sony Records (2002)
50 Years of Mambo, by Mambo Maniacs (2003)
The Best of Perez Prado: The Original Mambo No. 5; RCA (2010)

Cha Cha

Cubarama: Let's Cha Cha, by Tito Puente; RCA International (1994)
Danzon Cha Cha Cha, Vol. 1 & 2, by Enrique Jorrin; RCA International (1995)
Cha Cha Cha, by various artists; Andy Fortuna Productions (2003)
Pure Ballroom—Cha Cha Cha Vol. 1, by various artists; Andy Fortuna Productions (2009)

Mozambique

Mambo con Conga es Mozambique, by Eddie Palmieri; Tico (1966)
One Trick Pony ("Late In The Evening"), by Paul Simon; Warner Brothers (1980)

Songo

Suntan, by Michel Camilo; Evidence (1986)
Songo, by Los Van Van; Mango (1988)
Master Plan, by Dave Weckl; GRP Records (1990)
Palmas, by Eddie Palmieri; Nonesuch Records (1994)
History of Songo, by Changuito; Warner Bros. (2000)
Con un poce de Songo y Batacumbele; Disco Hit (2008)

Bomba

Somos Boricuas: Bomba y Plena en Nueva York, by Los Pleneros De La 21; Henry Street (1996)
Merengue Bomba, by various artists; Sony International (1999)
Bomba 2000, by Los Hermanso Rosario; Karen (1999)
Saoco: Bomba & Plena Explosion, by various artists; Sony (2011)

Merengue

Wilfrido Vargas, by Wilfrido Vargas; T.H. Rodven (1991)
Merengues, by Luis Kalaff & Los Alegres Dominicanos; International Music Dist. (1999)
Merengue Best Hits, by Meta Difosa (2008)
Los Mejores del Merengue 2011, by various artists; Sony (2011)

Beguine

Begin the Beguine, Artie Shaw; ASV Living Era (1938)
Golden Age of Beguine, by Various Artists; Universal/Demon (1996)
Begin the Beguine, by New York Trio; Venus Records (2009)

Bolero

Bolero Jazz: Tenderly, by Various Artists; Sony International (1994)
Senor Bolero, by Jose Feliciano; T.H. Rodven (1998)
Boleros for Lovers, by various artists; Yoyo Music (2005)
Los 100 Mejores Boleros de la Historia V, by various artists; Music Brokers (2005)

Conga

Congas Y Comparsas, Vol. 2, by Various Artists; T.H. Rodven (1993)
Rumbas & Congas: Gold Collection, by various artists; Fine Tune (1998)
Carnaval Habanero, by Various Artists; ANS Records (1999)
Congas and Rumbas from the Unforgettable Band, by Lecuona Cuban Boys; Yoyo Music (2005)

Cumbia

Greatest Cumbia Classics, Vol. 1 & 2, by Various Artists; Discos Fuentes (1999)
The Rough Guide to Cumbia, by Various Artists; World Music Network (2000)
Grand Classics de la Cumbia; Disco Fuentes (2006)
Original Sound of Cumbia, by various artists; Soundway (2011)

Danzon

El Centenario del Danzon, Vol. 1 & 2, by various artists; Orfeon (1996)
Mejor del Danzon: Coleccion RCA 100 Anos, by Various Artists; RCA International (2003)
Cuban Danzon: Its Ancestors & Descendants, by various artists; Smithsonian Folkways (2010)
Danzon y Salsa, by El Quinteto del Danzon; Open Records (2011)

Pilon

Ibraim Ferrer con Los Bocucos, by Ibraim Ferrer y Los Bocucos; Caravelas (2002)

Plena

Puerto Rico Tropical—Quinteto Criollo, by Los Pleneros de la 21; Latitudes (1997)
Plena Libre, by Plena Libre; Ryko Latino (1998)
Puerto Rican Plenas, by various artists; Disco Hit (2011)
Saoco: Bomba & Plena Explosion, by various artists; Sony (2011)

Blues

King of the Blues Guitar, by Albert King; Atlantic (1969)
Midnight Son, by Son Seals; Alligator (1976)
Texas Flood, by Stevie Ray Vaughan; Sony (1983)
Bad Influence, by Robert Cray; Hightone Records (1983)
Chess Box, by Willie Dixon; MCA (1988)
In Step, by Stevie Ray Vaughan; Sony (1989)
The Complete Recordings, by Robert Johnson; Sony (1990)
The Last Real Texas Blues Band, by Doug Sahm; Antone's (1994)
The Very Best of John Lee Hooker, by John Lee Hooker; Rhino (1995)
Everlastin' Tears, by Willie Edwards; JSP (1996)
Cruisin' for a Bluesin', by Bad News Blues Band; Trope (1996)
B.B. King's Greatest Hits, by B.B. King; MCA (1998)
Stormy Monday Blues: Essential Collection, by T-Bone Walker; Spectrum (2001)
The Best of Susan Tedeschi; Artemis (2005)
Continuum, by John Mayer; Columbia (2006)
Blues Blast, by Debbie Davies; Telarc (2007)
Queen Bee: The Antone's Collection, by Sue Foley; 101 Dist. (2009)
The Essential Coco Montoya; Blind Pig (2009)
Sugar Thieves Live, by Sugar Thieves (2010)

Brazilian

Samba

Brazil–Roots–Samba, by Wilson Moreira, Nelson Sargento; Rounder/PGD (1989)
Vol. 2, O Samba, by Various Artists; Luaka Bop (2000)
Cafe, by Trio da Paz; Malandro Records (2002)
Let's Dance Samba, by various artists; X5 Music Group (2009)
The Samba Night Club, by various artists; Lola's World (2010)

Baiao

O Rei Volta Pra Casa, by Luis Gonzaga; BMG (1998)
O Doutor do Baiao, by Humberto Teixeira; Biscoto Pino (2003)

Bossa Nova

The Legendary Joao Gilberto, by Joao Gilberto; Blue Note Records (1958)
Getz, Gilberto, Jobim, by Stan Getz, Joao Gilberto, and Antonio Carlos Jobim; Atlantic (1963)
Wave, by Antonio Carlos Jobim; A & M Records (1967)
Bossa Nova: Verbe Jazz Masters 53, by Stan Getz; Polygram (1996)
Bossa Nova Around the World, by various artists; Puntamayo (2011)

Cajun/Zydeco

100% Fortified Zydeco, by Buckwheat Zydeco; Black Top Records (1983)
La Musique Chez Mulate's, by various artists; Swallow Records (1986)
Silver Jubilee: Best Of Zachary, by Zachary Richard; Rhino (1999)
Zydeco Blowout—Clifton Chenier and His Red Hot Louisiana Band; Blues Factory (1999)
Absolutely the Best of Cajun & Zydeco, Vol. 1 & 2, by various artists; Varese Records (2001)
Encore Encore the Best of Beausoleil 1991–2001; Rhino Records (2003)
Best of Steve Riley and the Mamou Playboys; Rounder (2008)
Let the Good Times Roll, by Zydeco A-Go-Go; CDBY (2008)
Up in Flames, by Dwayne Dopsie and The Zydeco Hellraisers; Sound of New Orleans (2009)
Zydeco Junkie, by Chubby Carrier; Swampedelic Records (2010)

Caribbean

Caribbean Party Music: Jamaican, Calypso, Steel Drums and Other Music of the Caribbean, by various artists; Autumn Hill (2010)

Calypso

Calypso, by Harry Belafonte; RCA (1956)
Sing de Chorus: Calypso from Trinidad and Tobago, by various artists; Delos Records (1992)
Calypso: Vintage Songs from the Caribbean, by various artists; Putumayo World Music (2002)
Calypso Carnival, by various artists; Rounder (2010)

Soca

Soca Addict, by Ronnie McIntosh; Rituals Records (2001)
Soca Compilation, Vol. 2, by Iwer George, Various Artists; Import (2001)
Soca Gold, by various artists; VP Records (2011)
I Am Soca, by various artists; Bungalo Records (2012)

Ska

One Step Beyond, by Madness; EMI International (1979)
No Doubt, by No Doubt; Interscope (1992)
Devil's Night Out, by The Mighty Mighty BossTones; Taang (1992)
Foundation Ska, by Skatalites; Heartbeat/PGD (1996)
Ball of Fire, by the Skatalites; Universal (1998)
Ska Box Anthology, by various artists; Big Eye Music (2001)
Original Ska, by various artists; Hudson Van Dam (2006)
Ska Madness, by various artists; Uma (2010)

Reggae

The Harder They Come, by various artists; Universal (1972)
The Best of Toots and the Maytals; Trojan (1979)
Legend, by Bob Marley; Universal (1984)
Ultimate Collection, by Jimmy Cliff; Universal (1999)
Reggae Pulse: The Heartbeat of Jamaica, by various artists; Sanctuary Records (2002)
Best of Reggae, by various artists; Sonoma (2011)

Country

In addition to the individual styles within this chapter, many drumming grooves appear in the following classic country recordings:

Traditional Country

The Buck Owens Collection; Rhino Records (1992)
Hank Williams, Sr.—24 Greatest Hits; Polygram (1993)
The Essential Johnny Cash; Sony (2002)

Bluegrass

Country Boy, by Ricky Skaggs; Sony (1984)
16 Gems, Bill Monroe; Sony (1996)
Appalachian Stomp: Bluegrass Classics, by various artists; Rhino (1995)
20th Century Masters—The Millennium Collection: The Best of Flatt & Scruggs; Universal (2001)
Best Loved Bluegrass: 20 All-Time Favorites, by various artists; Rebel Records (2008)

Western Swing

A Tribute to the Best Damn Fiddle Player in the World, by Merle Haggard; Koch Records (1970)
Last Train to Hicksville, by Dan Hicks; MCA (1973)
The Essential Bob Wills & His Texas Playboys; Sony (1992)
Ride With Bob, by Asleep at the Wheel; Dreamworks (1999)
Western Swing: 40 Bootstompers from the Gold Age, by various artists; Primo (2007)
Doughboys, Playboys & Cowbosy: The Golden Years of Western Swing, by various artists; Proper (2010)

Western

Songs of the Old West, by Roy Rogers & Dale Evans; MCA Special Products (1998)
The Ultimate Collection, by Gene Autry; Prism Records (1998)
The Greatest Cowboy Songs Ever, by various Artist; Warner (2003)

Country Rock

Penitentiary Blues, David Allan Coe; SSS International (1968)
Wanted! The Outlaws, by Waylon Jennings, Willie Nelson; RCA (1976)
Eagles—Their Greatest Hits 1971-1975; Elektra/Asylum (1976)
Man of Steel, by Hank Williams, Jr.; Curb Records (1983)
Hank Williams, Jr.'s Greatest Hits, Vol.1; Curb Records (1993)
Country & West Coast: The Birth of Country Rock, by various artists; Big Heat UK (2006)

Modern Day Country

Guitars Cadillacs Etc. Etc., by Dwight Yoakam; Reprise (1984)
No Fences, by Garth Brooks; Capitol (1990)
The Wheel, by Rosanne Cash; Sony (1993)
Ten Feet Tall & Bulletproof, by Travis Tritt; Warner Brothers (1994)
Losin' Hand, by Al Perry and the Cattle; Addled Records (1995)
Clint Black—Greatest Hits, Vol.1 & 2; RCA (1996, 2001)
Greatest Hits, by Melissa Ehteridge; Island (2005)
Is and Then Some, by Brooks and Dunn; Arista (2009)
The Essential Dixie Chicks; Sony (2010)
Lady & Gentlemen, by LeAnn Rimes; Curb (2011)
This is Country Music, by Brad Paisleyñ Sony (2011)
Welcome to the Fishbowl, by Kenny Chesney; Sony (2012)

Disco

Saturday Night Fever: The Original Movie Sound Track, by Various Artists; Polygram Records (1977)
Best of K.C. and the Sunshine Band; EMI Gold (2002)
Pure Disco, Vol. 1–3, by Various Artists; Polygram (1996-1998)
Disco Gold, by various artists; Hip-O (2005)
100 Disco Hits of the '70s and '80s, by various artists; Goldenland Records (2010)

Drum & Bass / Jungle

Logical Progression Vol. 1, by LTJ Bukem, Various Artists; FFRR/Good Looking (1996)
Hell's Kitchen, by Ming & FS; OM (1999)
Urban Jungle, by Aphrodite, Various Artists; EMD/Priority (1999)
In The Mode, by Roni Size, Reprazent; Talkin' Loud (2000)
System Upgrade, by Dieselboy; Moonshine (2000)
True Colors, by High Contrast; Hospital (2002)

Flamenco

Flamenco Rumba Gitana, by various artists; ARC (1994)
Live—Gipsy Kings; Columbia (1997)
Gypsy Rumba Flamenco, by Manuel El Chachi; ARC (2001)
Barcelona Nights: The Best of Ottmar Liebert; Higher Octave (2001)
Flamenco Virtuoso, by Paco de Lucia; Emarcy Eur/Zoom (2009)
Area 52, by Rodrigo y Gabriela; ATO Records (2012)

Funk

New Orleans Funk:

Fess: The Professor Longhair Anthology; Rhino Records (1993)
Wild Tchoupitoulas, by Wild Tchoupitoulas; Mango Records (1976)
The Very Best of the Meters; Rhino Records (1999)
The Very Best of Dr. John; Rhino Records (1995)
The Very Best of the Neville Brothers; Rhino Records (1997)
Voodoo Soul: Deep and Dirty New Orleans Funk, by Various Artists; Metro Music (2001)
New Orleans Nightcrawlers; Rounder (2009)
Everybody Want Sum, by Dumpsta Funk; Controlled Substance (2011)
Carnivale Electricos, by Galactic; Anti/Epitaph (2012)

Displaced/Linear/Ghost Notes:

Live at the Apollo, by James Brown; Polygram (1962, 1990)
Thrust, by Herbie Hancock; Sony (1974)
Pickin' Up the Pieces: The Best of Average White Band (1974-1980); Rhino Records (1992)
Mothership Connection, Parliament; Universal (1975)
James Brown—20 All-Time Greatest Hits!; Polygram (1991)
What is Hip—Anthology, by Tower of Power; Rhino Records (1999)
Cold Heat: Heavy Funk Rarities 1: 1968-1974, by various artists; Now Again (2005)

Funk Rock

Sly & the Family Stone—Greatest Hits; Epic/Sony (1970)
Fire, by Ohio Players; Digital Sound (1974)
Songs in the Key of Life, Stevie Wonder; Motown/PGD (1976)
One Nation Under a Groove, by Funkadelic; Piority Records (1978, 2002)
The Best of Earth, Wind & Fire, Vol. 1; Sony (1978)
Gravity, by James Brown; Polygram (1986)
Mother's Milk, Red Hot Chili Peppers; Capitol (1989)
The Very Best of Kool & the Gang; Mercury (1993)
Under the Table & Dreaming, by Dave Matthews Band; RCA (1994)
The Ultimate Collection; Motown/PGD (1997)
What It Is! Funky Soul and Rare Grooves (1967-1977), by various artists; Rhino (2006)
Funk Classics Vol. 1, by various artists; DPM Records (2008)

Gospel

Complete Recorded Works, Vol. 1, Sister Rosetta Tharpe; Document (1996)
James Cleveland and the Angelic Choir, Vol. 3: Peace Be Still; Savoy Records (1962)
Spirit of the Century, by The Blind Boys of Alabama; Real World (1974)
Taking Flight, by The Gospel Hummingbirds; Blind Pig (1995)
Very Best of the Blind Boys of Alabama; Collectables (1998)
Al Green, Greatest Gospel Hits; Capitol (2000)
Complete Recordings of Sam Cooke with the Soul Stirrrs; Specialty (2002)
Vickie Winans' Greatest Hits; Artemis Strategic (2005)
Hello Fear, by Kirk Franklin; Gospo Centric (2011)
The Legacy Project, by John P. Kee; Verity (2011)
Gospel's Best Worship, by various artists; EMI Gospel (2011)

Hip Hop / Rap

Rapper's Delight, by Sugarhill Gang; Castle UK (1980)
Raising Hell, by Run D.M.C; Arista (1986)
Please Hammer, Don't Hurt 'Em, by MC Hammer; Capitol (1990)
Mama Said Knock You Out, by L.L. Cool J; Def Jam (1990)
Fear of a Black Planet, by Public Enemy; Def Jam (1990)
Straight Outta Compton, by N.W.A.; Priority Records (1988)
The Chronic, by Dr. Dre; Death Row (1992)
Doggystyle, by Snoop Dogg; Death Row (1993)
No Way Out, by Puff Daddy; Bad Boy Records (1997)
The Slim Shady LP, Eminem; Interscope (1999)
The Black Album, by Jay-Z; Def-Jam (2003)
La Bella Mafia, by Lil Kim; Atlantic (2003)
The College Dropout, by Kanye West; Def Jam (2004)
Curtis, by 50 Cent; Interscope Records (2007)
I Am Not a Human Being, by Little Wayne, Cash Money (2010)

Jazz

New Orleans Second Line

Mardi Gras Party! New Orleans Second Line, by Various Artists; Mardi Gras Records (1995)
Best of New Orleans Jazz, by Olympia Brass Band; Mardi Gras Records (1995)
Best of New Orleans Jazz, Volume 2, by Olympia Brass Band; Mardi Gras Records (1995)
Ultimate Rebirth Brass Band; Mardi Gras Records (2004)
New Orleans Second Line, by New Birth Brass Bandñ Marti Gras Records (2008)
Twenty Dozen, by The Dirty Dozen Brass Band; Savoy Jazz (2012)

Dixieland

Louis Armstrong and King Oliver; Milestone (1923)
When the Saints: Best of Dixieland, by Various Artists; Delta (1990)
The Best of Sidney Bechet; Blue Note Records (1994)
King Oliver's Creole Jazz Band: The Complete Set; Challenge (1997)
Marching Down Bourbon Street, by Preservation Hall Jazz Band; Sony Special Project (2001)
Pete Fountain Presents the Best of Dixieland; Polygram (2001)

Big Band

Mercy, Mercy [Live], by Buddy Rich; Blue Note Records (1968)
Complete Decca Recordings—1937, by Count Basie; GRP (1992)
Glenn Miller, Greatest Hits; RCA (1996)
1929–39—Chick Webb; Best of Jazz (1996)
The Dirty Boogie, by Brian Setzer; Interscope (1998)
Father of the Big Band, 1925–1937, by Fletcher Henderson; EPM Musique (1999)
Masterpieces: 1926–1949, Duke Ellington; Proper Box (2001)
Drum Crazy, by Gene Krupa Orchestra, Benny Goodman Orchestra; ASV Living Era (2001)
The Brian Setzer Orchestra: It's Gonna Rock; Surf Dog (2010)
A Hot Night in Paris, by Phil Collins Big Band; Atlantic (2010)

Small Band

Small Groups 1945-1950: Night in Tunisia, by Dizzy Gillespie; Giants of Jazz (1998)
Giant Steps, by John Coltrane; Atlantic (1959)
The Shape of Jazz to Come, by Ornette Coleman; Atlantic (1959)
Mingus Ah Um, by Charles Mingus; Sony (1959)
Kind of Blue, by Miles Davis; Sony (1959)
A Love Supreme, by John Coltrane; Atlantic/GRP Records (1964)
Unit Structures, by Cecil Taylor; Blue Note Records (1966)
Best of the Blue Note Years—Thelonious Monk; Blue Note Records (1991)
Science Fiction, by Ornette Coleman; Sony (1971, 2000)
Boss Bird [Box Set], by Charlie Parker; Proper Box (2002)
Line by Line, by John Patitucci; PID (2007)
Standards and Ballads, by Wynton Marsalis; Sony (2008)
Four Mf's Playin' Tunes, by Branford Marsalis; Marsalis Music (2012)
Further Explorations, by Chick Corea; Concord (2012)

Klezmer

Future & Past, by Kapalye; Flying Fish Records (1983)
Klezmer Music, by Brave Old World; Flying Fish Records (1990)
Klezmer Music 1925–56—Dave Tarras; Yazoo (1992)
First Recordings (1976-1978)—Klezmorim; Arhoolie Records (1993)
Master of Klezmer Music: Russian Sher—Harry Kandel; Global Village (1995)
The King of the Klezmer Clarinet—Naftule Brandwein; Rounder (1997)
The Rough Guide to Klezmer, by Various Artists; World Music (2000)
Jews with Horns, by the Klezmatics; Rounder (2002)
The Klezmer King, by Abe Schwartz; Columbia (2011)

Latin Rock

Santana, by Carlos Santana; Sony (1969)
How Will the Wolf Survive?, by Los Lobos; Warner Brothers (1984)
Just Another Band from East L.A.: A Collection [Box Set], by Los Lobos; Warner Brothers (1993)
Primitive Love, by Miami Sound Machine; Sony (1986)
Ricky Martin; Sony (1999)
Marc Anthony; Sony (1999)
Supernatural, by Carlos Santana; BMG/Arista (1999)
Los Hermanos Na Fundicao Progresso, by Los Hermanos; Sony (2008)
Las De Ley, by La Ley; We International (2009)
Coliumo, by Los Tres; Sony (2011)
Shakira: EnVivo Desde Pari; Sony (2011)

March

Standard March
40 Famous Marches, by various ensembles; Polygram Records (2000)
Best of Military Bands, by earious ensembles; EMI Gold (2002)
Greatest Military Marches: The Very Best of John Philip Sousa, by United States Marine Band; (2009)

New Orleans Second Line
Mardi Gras Party! New Orleans Second Line, by various artists; Mardi Gras Records (1995)
Second Line Soul, by Hustlers Brass Band; Mardi Gras Records (2009)

Cuban Comparsa
Congas y Comparsas, Vol. 2, by Various Artists; T.H. Rodven (1993)
Congas y Comparsas del Carnaval Habanero, by Orquesta de Camara de La Habana; Mojito (2008)

Brazilian Baiao
O Rei Volta Pra Casa, by Luis Gonzaga; BMG (1998)
Baiao de Viramundo: Tribute to uiz Gonzaga, by various artists; Stern's (2000)

Misc.
Still Crazy After All These Years ("50 Ways to Leave Your Lover"), by Paul Simon; Warner Brothers (1975)

Metal

Paranoid, by Black Sabbath; Warner Brothers (1970)
Led Zeppelin Box Set; Atlantic (1990)
Machine Head, by Deep Purple; Warner Brothers (1972)
Number of the Beast, by Iron Maiden; Sony (1982)
Master of Puppets, by Metallica; Elektra/Asylum (1986)
Harmony Corruption, by Napalm Death; Earache Records (1994)
Destroy Erase Improve, by Meshuggah; Nuclear Blast America (1995)
Death Cult Armageddon, by Dimmu Borgir; Nuclear Blast Records (2003)
Demigod, by Behemoth; Century Media (2004)
The Empires of the Worlds, by Biomechanical; Earache (2005)
Entity, by Origin; Nuclear Blast (2011)
American Capitalist, by Five Finger Death Punch; Prospect Park (2011)
Midnight in the Labyrinth, by Cradle of Filth; Ais (2012)

Double Bass
State of Euphoria, by Anthrax; Polygram (1988)
And Justice For All, by Metallica; Elektra/Asylum (1988)
Painkiller, by Judas Priest; Sony (1990)
Images and Words, by Dream Theater; Atlantic (1992)
Covenant, by Morbid Angel; Warner Brothers (1993)
Far Beyond Driven, by Pantera; Atlantic (1994)
Universe, by Planet X; Inside Out USA (2000)
Train of Thought, by Dream Theater; Elektra (2003)
ObZen, by Meshuggah; Nuclear Blast (2008)
Resolution, by Lamb of God; Epic (2012)
Fire from the Sky, by Shadows Fall; Razor and Tie (2012)

Middle Eastern

The Best of Saiidi & Baladi, by Hossam Ramzy; Arc Music (1997)
Rhythms of the Nile, by Hossam Ramzy; Arc Music (1998)
Sabla Tolo, by Hossam Ramzy; Arc Music (2000)
Desert Roses and Arabian Rhythms, Vol.1, by various artists; Ark 21 (2001)
Ayeshteni, by Natasha Atlas; Beggars Banquet (2001)
Arabic Groove, by Various Artists; Putumayo World Music (2001)
Moroccan Spirit, by Moroccan Spirit; Higher Octave (2002)
Greatest Hits, by Nancy Ajram; EMI (2008)
Latisideh, Lawa'ah, by Kadim al-Sahir; Rotana (2011)
Ya Tair, by Hatem Al-Iraqi; Qanawat (2012)

Rai
Kutche, by Cheb Khaled and Safy Boutella; Capitol (1989)
Let Me Rai, by Cheb Mami; Tote Records (1990)
C'est Pas Ma Faute: The Father of Rai Music, by Bellemou Messaoud; Wergo (1999)
Rough Guide to Rai, by Various Artists; World Music Network (2002)
Rai Revolution, by MC Rai; Embarka Records (2005)
Rai Superstars, by various artists; Mondo Melodia (2009)

Odd Time

Rock
In a Word: Yes Box Set; Elektra/Rhino Records (2002)
Tarkus, by Emerson Lake and Palmer; Rhino Records (1971)
The Concise King Crimson; Caroline (1993)
Thick as a Brick, by Jethro Tull; Capitol (1972)
The Lamb Lies Down on Broadway, by Genesis; Atlantic (1974)
Kansas Box Set; Sony (1994)
Hemispheres, by Rush; Polygram Records (1978)
Joe's Garage: Acts 1-3, by Frank Zappa; Rykodisc (1979)
Misplaced Childhood, by Marillion; EMI (1985)
Perfect Symmetry, by Fates Warning; Capitol (1989)
Images and Words, by Dream Theater; Atlantic (1992)
The Light, by Spock's Beard; Metal Blade (1994)
Superunknown, by Soundgarden; A&M Records (1994)
Lateralus, by Tool; Volcano Entertainment Records (2001)
De-Loused in the Comatorium, by The Mars Volta; Universal (2003)
Ghost Reveries, by Opeth; Roadrunner (2005)

Fear of a Blank Planet, by Porcupine Tree; Atlantic (2007)
A Dramatic Turn of Events, by Dream Theater; Roadrunner (2011)
Iconoclast, by Symphony X; Nuclear Blast (2011)
Clockwork Angles, by Rush; Roadrunner (2012)

Jazz/Fusion

Time Out, by Dave Brubeck Quartet; Columbia (1959)
Live In 3 2/3/4 Time, by Don Ellis Orchestra; Pacific Jazz (1967)
Turn It Over, by Tony Williams Lifetime; Polygram (1970)
The Inner Mounting Flame, by Mahavishnu Orchestra; Sony (1971)
Birds of Fire, by Mahavishnu Orchestra; Sony (1972)
Spectrum, by Billy Cobham; Atlantic (1973)
Special Edition, by Jack DeJohnette; ECM Records (1979)
A Part & Yet Apart, by Bill Bruford's Earthworks; Discipline (1999)
On the Virg: Serious Young Insects, by Virgil Donati; Vorticity (1999)
Actual Proof, by Mike Clarkñ Pgi Platform (2000)
Planet Earth, by Dennis Chambers; BHM (2005)
Where I Come From, by Sveti; (2007)
Forever, by Chick Corea; Concord (2011)
Live: One Great Night, by Steve Smith and Vital Information; BFM Jazz (2012)

Polka

25 Million Seller Polka Hits, Vol. 1,2 & 3 , by Various Artists; Dyno Polkas Records (1994)
Polka Polka Polka, by various artists; Madacy Records (1994)
24 Polkas Greatest Hits, by Myron Floren; Polka City (1995)
Songs of the Polka King, Vol. 1 & 2, by Frankie Yankovic; Cleveland International (1996/1997)
Hardcore 2/4, by Polkacide; Dog Patch Records (2000)
Six Fat Dutchmen: Greatest Hits 2; Polka City (2006)
The Greatest Hits of Polka, by Jimmy Sturr; Rounder (2009)

Punk

The Velvet Underground & Nico; Polygram (1967)
White Light/White Heat, by Velvet Underground; Polygram (1967)
Kick Out the Jams, by MC5; Elektra/Asylum (1969)
Fun House, by Iggy & The Stooges; Elektra/Asylum (1970)
Never Mind the Bollocks Here's the Sex Pistols; Warner Brothers (1977)
The Clash; Sony (1977)
London Calling, by The Clash; Sony (1979)
Wild in the Streets, by The Circle Jerks; Epitaph (1982)
Repo Man Soundtrack, by Various Artists; MCA (1984)
Give Me Convenience or Give Me Death, by The Dead Kennedys; Manifesto Records (1987)
Nevermind, by Nirvana; Geffen (1991)
Dookie, by Green Day; Warner Brothers (1994)
Hey! Ho! Let's Go: The Anthology, by The Ramones; Rhino (1999)
White Blood Cells, by The White Stripes; BMG (2002)
The Black Parade, by My Chemical Romance; Warner Bros. (2006)
Fever, by Bullet for My Valentine; Zomba (2010)
Cardiology, by Good Charlotte; Capitol (2010)
Damnesia, by Alkaline Trio; Epitaph (2011)

Rock

Early Rock n' Roll

The Essential Little Richard; Specialty (1985)
Buddy Holly's Greatest Hits; MCA (1996)
20th Century Masters: The Best of Bill Haley & His Comets; MCA (1999)
The Anthology, by Chuck Berry; MCA (2000)
Fats Domino Jukebox: 20 Greatest Hits; Capitol (2002)
Elvis 30 #1 Hits, by Elvis Presley; RCA (2002)
The Best of Eddie Copchran; EMI (2005)
Greatest Hits: Walking to New Orleans, by Fats Domino; Capitol (2007)

Rockabilly

Jerry Lee Lewis—18 Original Sun Greatest Hits; Rhino Records (1984)
Carl Perkins—Original Sun Greatest Hits; Rhino Records (1987)
Built for Speed, by The Stray Cats; DCC Compact Classics (1982)
Holy Roller, by Reverend Horton Heat; Sub Pop (1999)

Standard Rock

1962–1966 and 1967–1970—The Beatles; Capitol (1973)
Are You Experienced?, by The Jimi Hendrix Experience; MCA (1967)
Disraeli Gears, by Cream; Polygram (1967)
Wheels of Fire, by Cream; Polygram (1968)
Derek & The Dominos (Eric Clapton, Duane Allman); Polydor (1970)
Let It Bleed, by The Rolling Stones (1969)
Sticky Fingers, by The Rolling Stones; Virgin Records (1971)
L.A. Woman, by The Doors (1971)
Who's Next, by The Who; Decca (1971)
Led Zeppelin IV; Atlantic (1971)
The Allman Brothers Live at Fillmore East; Polygram (1971)
Exile on Main Street, by The Rolling Stones (1972)
Dark Side of the Moon, by Pink Floyd; Capitol (1973)
Toys in the Attic, by Aerosmith; Sony (1975)
Give Me Some Neck, by Ron Wood; Columbia (1978)
1984, by Van Halen; Warner Brothers (1984)
Appetite for Destruction, by Guns N' Roses; Geffen (1987)
Nevermind, by Nirvana; Geffen (1991)
Ten, by Pearl Jam; Sony (1991)
Superunknown, by Soundgarden; A&M Records (1994)
The Color and the Shape, by The Foo Fighters; Capitol (1997)
A Rush of Blood to the Head, by Coldplay; Capitol (2002)
Meteora, by Linkin Park; Warner (2003)
Plans, by Death Cab for Cutie; Atlantic (2005)
Only by the Night, by Kings of Leonñ RCA (2008)
Isn't Anything, by My Bloody Valentine; Sony (2011)
Here and Now, by Nickelback; Roadrunner (2011)
The King of Limbs, by Radiohead; TBD Records (2011)

Fusion

In A Silent Way, by Miles Davis; Columbia (1968)
Bitches Brew, by Miles Davis; Columbia (1969)
Emergency!, by Tony Williams Lifetime; Poloydor (1969)
A Tribute to Jack Johnson, by Miles Davis; Columbia (1970)
Turn It Over, by Tony Williams Lifetime; Polygram (1970)
The Inner Mounting Flame, by Mahavishnu Orchestra; Sony (1971)
Birds of Fire, by Mahavishnu Orchestra; Sony (1972)
Spectrum, by Billy Cobham; Atlantic (1973)
Headhunters, by Herbie Hancock; Columbia/Legacy (1973)
Hymn of the Seventh Galaxy, by Return to Forever, Chick Corea; Polygram (1973)
Mind Transplant, by Alphonse Mouzon; Blue Note (1974)
Black Market, by Weather Report; Columba/CBS (1976)
What If, by The Dixie Dregs; Capricorn/PGD (1978)
Special Edition, by Jack DeJohnette; ECM Records (1979)
Vital Information, by Vital Information; Columbia (1983)
Inside Out, by Chick Corea; GRP (1990)
Palmystery, by Victor Wooten; Heads Up (2008)
Emotion and Commotion, by Jeff Beck; Rhino (2010)
Pursuit of Radical Rhapsody, by Al Dimeola; Telarc (2011)
Human Element, by Scott Kinsey (2011)
Fusion III, by Michael Urbaniak; Wounded Bird Records (2012)
Sound Travels, by Jack DeJohnette; Entertainment One (2012)
Howle 61, by Wayne Krantz; Abstract Logic (2012)

Surf

Walk Don't' Run: The Best of the Ventures; Capitol (1990)
Wipe Out! The Best of the Surfaris; Varese Records (1994)
King of the Surf Guitar: The Best of Dick Dale & His Del-Tones; Rhino Records (1989)
Beach Boys Greatest Hits Vol.1; Capitol (1999)
Krill Slippin', by The Mermen; M.B. Burnside (1989)
Aqua Velvets; Heydey (1992)
Greatest Surf Guitar Classics, by Various Artists; Big Eye Music (2001)
Rare West Coast Surf Instrumentals, by various artists; Ace (2001)
Lost Legends of Surf Guitar, by various artists; Sundazed (2007)
The Birth of Surf, by various artists; Ace (2010)

Techno

Dew Drops in the Garden, by Deee-Lite; Elektra (1994)
Delusions of Grandeur, by Hardkiss; Universal International (1995)
Northern Exposure I-III, by Sasha and Digweed; Ultra/Unknown (1997–1999)
Movement in Still Life, by BT; Head Space (1999)
Global Underground Series (Nu Breed), by Satoshi Tomiie, Various Artists; Nu Breed (2000)
Global, by Paul Van Dyk; Mute (2003)
Perfect Playlist Techno; Robbin Ent. (2007)
50 Techno Dance Hits, by various artists; Believe Electro (2009)
Secret Weapon Techno Mix Vol. 1, by The Attorney General; Secret Weapon Records (2010)

Wedding Dances

Tarantella
25 Favorite Italian Love Songs, by Various Artists; Madacy Records (2000)

Hava Nagila
Hava Nagila & Other Jewish Memories, by Benedict Silverman; Sounds of the World (1996)

Rumba
The Fabulous Ballroom Collection, by Arthur Murray Orchestra; RCA (1998)

Tango
The Best Tango Album in the World Ever, by Various Artists; Capitol (2003)

Viennese Waltz
Strictly Viennese Waltz, by Various Artists; Madacy Duplicate Numbers (2000)

American Waltz
22 All Time Favorite Waltzes, by Lawrence Welk; Ranwood (1987)

Foxtrot:
Let's Dance the Foxtrot & Quickstep, by Graham Dalby & The Grahamophones; Let's Dance (1996)

E Bibliography

Web Sites

All Brazilian Music http://www.allbrazilianmusic.com/en/home/home.asp
The history of Brazilian music.

Blues.org
http://www.thebluehighway.com
An international home of Blues music.

The Flamenco Forms
http://users.aol.com/BuleriaChk/private/compas/compasa3.html#Tangos
A thorough treatment of Flamenco music.

The History of Gospel Music
http://afgen.com/gospel1.html
Gospel history and a wide range of other information.

The History of Rock 'n' Roll
http://www.history-of-rock.com/
A very thorough website on the history of Rock n' Roll

Jazzitude
http://www.jazzitude.com/
A history of Jazz and Jazz culture.

Middle Eastern Rhythms FAQ
http://www.khafif.com/rhy
Detailed information on Middle Eastern rhythms, dances, and musical groups.

Zydeco.org
www.zydeco.org
For all things Zydeco.

Percussive Arts Society
http://www.pas.org/publications/rudiments.html
The list of 40 drum rudiments.

ReggaeFusionJamaica
http://www.reggaefusion.com
Covers Reggae, past and present.

Drummers World
http://www.drummerworld.com
A web site for all things drum related

Drumming.com
http://www.drumming.com
A web site for all things drum related

Afrocubana Allstars
http://www.afrocubanallstarsonline.com
Covers contemporary Afro-Cuban bands today

Metal Archives
http://www.metal-archives.com
Information on over Metal 6000 bands

Gospel City
http://www.gospelcity.com
A wide range of information on Gospel Music, from Hip Hop Gospel to Reggae Gospel to Jazz Gospel

Middle Eastern Music Sites
http://www.dorak.info/music/linkmid.html
Links to Middle Eastern music sites

Soul Funk Music
http://www.soulfunkmusic.com
Info on '70s and '80s Funk

Hip Hop Music.com
http://www.hiphopmusic.com
The latest on Hip Hop recordings.

Klezmer Shack
http://www.klezmershack.com
All things Klezmer. Blogs, bands, history.

Bassist's Bible
The web site of Tim Boomer, author of *The Bassist's Bible.* Videos showing how bass lines interlock with (some of the) grooves from this book.

Drummer's Bible
www.drummersbible.com
The web site of the authors of this book. Many extras.

Books

Modern Reading Text, by Louis Bellson & Gil Breines. Miami: Warner Brothers, 1985.

Percussion Instruments and Their History, by James Blades. London: Faber & Faber, 1992.

Brazilian Rhythms for Drum Set, by Duduka da Fonseca & Bob Weiner. Miami: Manhattan Music, 1991.

Contemporary Country Styles for the Drummer and Bassist, by Brian Fullen with Roy Vogt. Van Nuys, CA: Alfred Publishing, 1994.

The Funky Beat, by David Garibaldi. Miami: Warner Brothers, 1996.

Afro-Cuban Grooves for Bass and Drums/Funkifying the Clave, by Lincoln Goines & Robby Ameen. Miami: Manhattan Music, 1990.

Afro-Cuban Rhythms for Drum Set, by Frank Malabe & Bob Weiner. Miami: Manhattan Music, 1990.

Salsa Guidebook for Piano and Ensemble, by Rebeca Mauleon. Petaluma, CA: Sher Music, 1993.

Contemporary African Drum Set Styles, Book One: Soukous, by Chris Miller. Carmel Valley, CA: Chris Miller, 1995.

Jungle/Drum n' Bass (for the Acoustic Drum Set), Johnny Rabb. Miami: Warner Brothers, 2001.

Progressive Steps to Syncopation for the Modern Drummer, by Ted Reed. Clearwater, FL: Ted Reed, 1958.

Garland Encyclopedia of World Music. New York: Garland Publishing, 1998.

Stick Control: for the Snare Drummer, by George Lawrence Stone. Alfred Publishing Company, Inc., 1935.

Advanced Techniques for the Modern Drummer, by Jim Chapin. Warner Bros. Publications, 1948.

Bass Drum Control, by Colin Bailey. Hal Leonard Corporation, 1964.

Realistic Rock, by Carmine Appice, Alfred Publishing Company, Inc., 1972.

Time Patterns, by Gary Chaffe, Warner Bros. Publications, 1980.

Master Studies, by Joe Morello, Modern Drummer Publications, Inc., 1983.

Double Bass Drumming, by Joe Franco. CPP/Belwin, Inc., 1983.

Advanced Funk Studies, by Rick Latham. Alfred Publishing Company, Inc., 1984.

The New Breed, by Gary Chester, Modern Drummer Publications, Inc., 1985.

Advanced Concepts, by Kim Plainfield. Alfred Publishing Company, Inc., 1993.

Polyrhythms – The Musician's Guide, by Peter Magadini. Hal Leonard Corporation, 1993.

The Art of Bop Drumming, by John Riley. Alfred Publishing Company, Inc., 1994.

New Orleans Jazz and Second Line Drumming, by Herlin Riley & Johnny Vidacovitch , Alfred Publishing Company, Inc., 1996.

The Commandments of R&B Drumming: A Comprehensive Guide to Soul, Funk & Hip Hop, by Zoro. Warner Bros. Publications, 1998.

Timba Funk, by Jesus Diaz, David Garibaldi, Michael Spiro, Miami, Warner Bros. Publications, 1999.

It's Your Move, by Dom Famularo & Joe Bergamini. Alfred Publishing Company, Inc., 2000.

Afro-Caribbean & Brazilian Rhythms for the Drumset, by Memo Acevedo, Kim Plainfied, Maciek Schejbal, Adriano Santos, Frank Katz and Chris Lacinak. Carl Fischer, Inc, 2002.

Conversations in Clave: The Ultimate Technical Study of Four-Way Independence in Afro-Cuban Rhythms, by Horacio "El Negro" Hernandez, Warner Bros. Publications, 2003.

Extreme Interdependence: Drumming Beyond Independence, by Marco Minnemann. Warner Brothers Music, 2001.

The Unreel Drum Book, by Marc Atkinson. Warner Bros. Publications, 2003.

Take it to the Streets, by Stanton Moore. Carl Fischer, Inc., 2005.

Funk Drumming: Innovative Grooves and Advanced Concepts, by Mike Clark. Hal Leonard Corp. 2005 .

Ultimate Play Along Drum Trax, by Virgil Donati. Alfred Publishing Company, Inc., 2005.

The Conga Drummer's Guidebook, by Michael Spiro with Josh Ryan. Sher Music Co., 2006

Creative Control, by Thomas Lang. Hudson Music, 2007

Hands, Grooves & Fills, by Pat Petrillo. by Visual Music Media, 2007.

Off the Record/ Inside the Playing of Today's Top Drummers, by Ed Breckenfeld. Modern Drummer Publications, New Jersey 2008

Groove Alchemy, by Stanton Moore. Hudson Music, 2010

The Evolution of Blast Beats, by Derek Roddy. Hal Leonard Corporation, 2010.

The Breakbeat Bible, by Mike Adamo. Hudson Limited, Inc., 2010.